The Aryan Jesus

The Aryan Jesus

CHRISTIAN THEOLOGIANS AND
THE BIBLE IN NAZI GERMANY

Susannah Heschel

PRINCETON UNIVERSITY PRESS
PRINCETON AND OXFORD

Third printing, and first paperback printing, 2010
Paperback ISBN: 978-0-691-14805-2

The Library of Congress has cataloged the cloth edition of this book as follows

Heschel, Susannah.
The Aryan Jesus : Christian theologians and the Bible in Nazi Germany / Susannah Heschel.
p.   cm.
Includes bibliographical references (p.TK) and index.
ISBN 978-0-691-12531-2 (hardcover : alk. paper)
1. Institut zur Erforschung und Beseitigung des Jüdischen Einflusses auf das Deutsche
Kirchliche Leben.   2. German-Christian movement.   3. National socialism and religion.
4. Church and state—Germany—History—1933–1945.   5. Protestant churches—Germany—
History—20th century.   6. Judaism (Christian theology)—History of doctrines—
20th century.   7. Holocaust, Jewish (1939–1945)—Causes.   I. Title.

BR856.H476 2008

274.3'0823—dc22   2008012566

British Library Cataloging-in-Publication Data is available

This book has been composed in Berkeley Old Style
Printed on acid-free paper. ∞

Printed in the United States of America

3   4   5   6   7   8   9   10

For my two daughters:

   Gittel Esther Devorah Heschel-Aronson

   Avigael Natania Mira Heschel-Aronson

1 Chronicles 29:19

Contents

List of Illustrations

A Note on Archival Sources

MY DISCOVERY of the existence of an "Institute for the Study and Eradication of Jewish Influence on German Church Life" began when I found several of its publications in the library of the Center for the Study of Antisemitism, at the Technical University in Berlin. I next searched for documents pertaining to its establishment and funding in the Central Archives of the German Protestant Church, also located in Berlin, and delivered my first lecture about the Institute at a 1990 conference on the German theological faculties during the Third Reich convened by Leonore Siegele-Wenschkewitz, a church historian with a strong interest in issues of Christianity and antisemitism.[1] That summer of 1991, I began my search for the archives of the Institute, long assumed to have been lost, with the first of many trips to the church archives of Thuringia, located in the city of Eisenach, where the Institute had been headquartered. Thuringia, in the geographic center of today's Germany, had become part of East Germany after World War II, and access to its archives by Westerners was highly restricted until the Berlin Wall fell. I was the first American, the first Jew, and the first person with a laptop, I was told, to appear at the Eisenach archive. In the early 1990s documents pertaining to the Institute were only beginning to be organized by the remarkable and highly knowledgeable archivist, Pastor Heinz Koch, who had studied theology in the postwar years with some of the theologians discussed in this book.

As more and more documents of the Institute archives surfaced during my annual trips to Eisenach, I began publishing my discoveries in a series of articles that appeared in the United States and in Germany.[2] A few members of the Institute were still alive in the 1990s and I was able to conduct useful interviews with them. Since three of the most active academic leaders of the Institute had also been professors of theology at the University of Jena, and many Institute members had been students of theology at Jena, I spent time working in that university's archives, which were highly accessible and rich with documentation. Searching for evidence of the Institute's influence, I traveled to church, state, federal, and university archives throughout Germany—Kiel,

[1] Susannah Heschel, "Walter Grundmanns Sicht des Judentums," International Symposium on German Theological Faculties under National Socialism, Frankfurt, October, 1990. Subsequently published as "Theologen für Hitler," 125–70.

[2] Heschel, "Nazifying Christian Theology," 587–605; "Theologen für Hitler," 125–70; "When Jesus Was an Aryan," 68–89; "Deutsche Theologen für Hitler," 147–67; "The Quest for the Aryan Jesus," 65–84.

Oldenburg, Heidelberg, Bonn, Weimar, Giessen, Tübingen—as well as Sweden and Austria, and at each archive I uncovered important evidence of Institute activities and impact. In only a few places was I frustrated by archives that had been damaged or destroyed during the war, or by archivists who were uncooperative, or by files that were suspiciously "purged" of material from the Nazi years, most likely to hide embarrassing evidence of Nazi activity by theologians and pastors.

Every chapter of this book draws heavily from archival materials. When I first consulted the archives of the Thuringian church, located in Eisenach, Germany, in the early 1990s, I examined material that had not been officially accessioned, organized, and given a catalogue number. During my subsequent visits to the archive, increasing numbers of documents had been filed with an inventory number. However, some of the materials that I examined during my earliest visits to the archive are cited in this book without a specific inventory number, as they were not yet catalogued at the time I consulted them. I regret any confusion that may result.

Many of the published materials of the 1920s, '30s, and '40s to which I refer are rare and only available at a few specialized collections. I was able to gain access to many of the printed versions during several summers that I spent at the Wiener Library at Tel Aviv University, while others I read on microfilm at the Leo Baeck Institute in New York City and at the Burke Library of Union Theological Seminary in New York City. Some were only available at libraries or archives in Germany, while a few of those written by prominent theologians could be obtained through interlibrary loan in the United States.

Acknowledgments

IT GIVES ME GREAT pleasure to express my gratitude to those who helped me shape this book. Two pioneer historians, Robert Ericksen and Doris Bergen, have forged new scholarly paths with their studies of the churches during the Third Reich and of Protestant theologians who supported Hitler. Both have been wonderfully generous with their time and advice in their many readings of this book.

My work has been enriched by discussions with colleagues in several fields. I would like to thank Anson Rabinbach for his excellent symposium at Princeton on "The Humanities in Nazi Germany"; Michael Ermarth for his insights into Nazism, antisemitism, and German anti-Americanism; Jeffrey Herf for his analysis of Nazi antisemitic propaganda; David Balch for his wise readings of early Christian texts; John Connolly for helping me assess the University of Jena in the postwar years; Suzanne Marchand and Peter Machinist for their insights regarding the rise of Oriental Studies; James McNutt for his analyses of Adolf Schlatter; Kevin Spicer for his important work on the German Catholic Church during the Third Reich; Donald Niewyk for his work on German antisemitism and his masterful historical mind; Kevin Madigan for conversations about Johannes Hempel and the churches more generally; Michael A. Meyer for his important work on German-Jewish history; Michael Brenner and Robert Schine for reading the manuscript and offering valuable suggestions; Bruce Duncan, Klaus Milich, Sibylle Quack, and Margaret Robinson for their translations of difficult idiomatic German; Richard M. Gottlieb for our exchanges about Christian dejudaization; and Lev Loseff for his help with Grigol Robakidse. Special thanks to Henry F. Smith for many stimulating discussions of race, religion, forgiveness, and Shakespeare, and to the late Sterrett Mayson for his insights into antisemitism. Above all, to Robert Jay Lifton for demonstrating the nobility of a scholar with a political conscience, and to the members of the Wellfleet Seminar that he leads.

Numerous lectures and discussions at Dartmouth concerning race and critical race theory have been very important to me. I would like to thank members of the Faculty Seminar on Race and, in particular, Patricia McKee for her insights concerning constructions of "whiteness."

I owe a great debt to colleagues in the field of New Testament and Christian origins, including Joseph B. Tyson, Eldon Epp, Denise Buell, Larry Hurtado, Jennifer Knust, and, for so many years, the late W. D. Davies; in particular, to my teacher and friend Krister Stendahl; Elaine Pagels for discussions about interpretations of the Gospel of John; Elisabeth Schüssler-Fiorenza and Laura Nasrallah for their conference on New Testament scholarship and race at Harvard Divinity School; and E. P. Sanders, whose work is the beacon of what New Testament studies ought to be, for his encouragement over the years.

I am also grateful to my colleagues who work on the churches in the Nazi period: Manfred Gailus, Hans Prolingheuer, Klaus Hödl, Horst Junginger, Gerhard Lindemann, Victoria Barnett, and, especially, the pioneer, Wolfgang Gerlach. Special thanks to Gerhard Besier for providing me with a copy of Walter Grundmann's Stasi file. I also owe thanks to my colleagues working on the Thuringian church during the Third Reich: Thomas Seidel, Birgit Gregor, Oliver Arnhold, and Tobias Schufer. This book would not have been the same without the groundbreaking scholarship on German antisemitism of Christina von Braun, Dirk Rupnow, Alan Steinweis, and Christian Wiese, and the sharp insights of Viola Roggenkamp.

I am fortunate to have extraordinary friends within the Lutheran church today—Rainer Graupner, Renate Jost, Tom Krüger-Day, Constance Parvey, and Siegfried Virgils—and to have had superb students and colleagues in the Protestant theological faculty at the University of Frankfurt when I taught there in 1992–93 as the Martin Buber visiting professor of Jewish religious philosophy. I would also like to remember the interest taken in this project at its earliest stage by colleagues at Frankfurt who are now deceased: Dieter Georgi, Leonore Siegele-Wenschkewitz, Christoph Raisig, and Willy Schottroff.

For grants that I have received, I extend my appreciation to the National Humanities Center for the yearlong Rockefeller fellowship that gave me a sabbatical to begin my research; to the Case Western Reserve University for the Jones grant that paid for several trips to Germany for archival research; and to Dartmouth College for a Senior Faculty grant that provided a sabbatical to finish writing the book.

Everything I write owes a debt of gratitude to the extraordinary reference librarian at Dartmouth College, William Fontaine, whose encyclopedic knowledge is exceeded only by his generosity of time and attentiveness. Of the many archivists whose help was essential to this project, I thank Margit Hartleb, University of Jena, for her generous help over many years; Eva-Marie Felschow, University of Giessen; the late Herr Renger, University of Heidelberg; Freifrau von Böselager, of the Auswärtiges Amt; Frau Graupner, of the Thuringian state archive in Weimar; David Marwell, former director of the Berlin Document Center; Frau Lampe, for her hospitality and many cups of coffee at the church archive in Eisenach, and Pastor Heinz Koch, for many years director of the Thuringian church archive, for conveying his extraordinary knowledge of the Nazi and postwar years, for providing me with an abundance of archival materials, even before they had all been catalogued, and for the many intense and sometimes difficult (but always rewarding) discussions we have had over the course of many years.

I am grateful for the assistance of the librarians at the Wiener Library, Tel Aviv University, at the Leo Baeck Institute in New York City, and at the Burke Library of Union Theological Seminary. My gratitude as well to Peter Black, Paul Shapiro, and Anne Millen at the Research Center of the United States Holocaust Memorial Museum, for responding quickly and helpfully to all of my queries. For photographs, I would like to thank Hans-Georg Vorndran, Marten Marquardt, Steven Martin, Wolfgang Gleiser, Judith Cohen, and Caroline Waddell. For very helpful private interviews and personal correspondence, I thank Herbert von Hintzenstern, H. J. Thilo, Mrs. Annelise Grundmann, and Max-Adolf Wagenführer.

My student assistants over the years have been wonderful: Timothy Baker, Laura Perovich, Jared Westheim, Sandeep Ramesh, Regina Feldman, Mikahil Akulov, Ian Storey, Kelly Sheridan, Catja Carrell, Billy Mann, and Cortina Krause; so have my administrative assistants: Meredyth Morley, Cheryl Singleton, and Margaret Brannen.

My thanks to all the babysitters and housecleaners who gave me time to read, write, and think, especially Angela Libby, Danra Kazenski, Dory Lyon, Kate Olsen, and Donna Taylor. Most of all, to Delia Fernandez, who cared for my mother during the last three years of her life with extraordinary devotion.

It has been a joy and an honor to work at Princeton University Press with Fred Appel, who combines intellectual vitality, inspiration, and remarkable editing talents; Debbie Tegarden, who went out of her way to shepherd the book carefully through production; Heath Renfroe, who handled the photographs with great skill; Carolyn Sherayko, who prepared a magnificient index; and the amazing Jodi Beder, who meticulously edited and polished the manuscript with insight and finesse.

For my colleagues at Dartmouth and for my friends Bernard Avishai, Jessica Benjamin, Alison Bernstein, David and Rachel Biale, Kathleen Biddick, Constance Buchanan, James Carroll, Richard Cogley, Sidra Ezrahi, Louise Fishman, James Forbes, Nancy Frankenberry, Gene Garthwaite, Barbara Geller, Sander Gilman, Shalom Goldman, Vincent Harding, Christopher Holland, Julius Lester, Sonya Michel, Annette Miller, Marilyn Reizbaum, Tova Rosen, Margrit Rustow, Naomi Seidman, Eli Zaretsky, and Froma Zeitlin, and my cousins Judie Bernstein, Thena Heshel, Pearl Heschel Twersky, and Karen Wolff, my thanks for your rich conversations, passions, and exuberance. Special thanks to my former Berlin roommate and dear friend Beatrix Jessberger, who traveled with me to Sweden, Eisenach, Jena, Weimar, and Warsaw.

My childhood home was filled with German-Jewish refugee scholars who vividly illuminated for me the intellectual world that was destroyed. I want to thank my father for conveying to me a taste of the Germany he experienced in the 1920s and '30s, and for constantly reminding me, Never despair! And always, to you, Jacob Aronson, for your delight at the sheer wonder of being alive. This book is dedicated to our two daughters.

List of Abbreviations

AA	Auswärtiges Amt (German Foreign Office), Bonn
BDC	Berlin Document Center (now part of the Bundesarchiv, Berlin)
BK Koblenz	Bundesarchiv Koblenz
BA Potsdam	Bundesarchiv Abteilung Potsdam
HSL	Archiv der Hansestadt Lübeck
KA	Kommunalarchiv, Minden
LAN	Landesarchiv Nürnberg
LBI	Leo Baeck Institute, New York
LKA Eisenach	Landeskirchen Archiv (Church archives of the regional Protestant church of Thuringia)
NEK	Nordelbisches Kirchenarchiv, Kiel
NSLB	Nationalsozialistische Lehrerbund, National Socialist Teacher's Organization
NSS	Niedersächsisches Staatsarchiv, Oldenburg
NSV	Nationalsozialistische Volkswohlfahrt, National Sociallist's People's Charity
SA	Sturmabteilung
SS	Schutzstaffel
ThHStA	Thüringisches Hauptstaatsarchiv, Weimar
UAG	Archives of the University of Giessen
UAH	Archives of the University of Heidelberg
UAJ	Archives of the University of Jena
UAL	Archives of the University of Lund
UAT	Archives of the University of Tübingen
UAV	Archives of the University of Vienna
YIVO	Institute for Jewish Research, New York City
ZAK	Zentral Archiv der Kirche (Central archives of the Protestant church), Berlin

The Aryan Jesus

Theology and Race

AT NOON ON SATURDAY, MAY 6, 1939, a group of Protestant theologians, pastors, and churchgoers gathered at the historic Wartburg Castle, resonant with Lutheran and nationalist significance, to celebrate the official opening of the Institute for the Study and Eradication of Jewish Influence on German Church Life (Institut zur Erforschung und Beseitigung des jüdischen Einflusses auf das deutsche kirchliche Leben). The Institute's goals were both political and theological. Seeking to create a dejudaized church for a Germany that was in the process of ridding Europe of all Jews, it developed new biblical interpretations and liturgical materials. In the six years of its existence, as the Nazi regime carried out its genocide of the Jews, the Institute redefined Christianity as a Germanic religion whose founder, Jesus, was no Jew but rather had fought valiantly to destroy Judaism, falling as victim to that struggle. Germans were now called upon to be the victors in Jesus's own struggle against the Jews, who were said to be seeking Germany's destruction.

On the theological level, the Institute achieved remarkable success, winning support for its radical agenda from a host of church officials and theology professors who welcomed the removal of Jewish elements from Christian scripture and liturgy and the redefinition of Christianity as a Germanic, Aryan religion. Members of the Institute worked devotedly, as did so many others in the Reich, to win the fight against the Jews. Their devotion took them to greater and greater extremes, abandoning traditional Christian doctrine in exchange for coalitions with neo-pagan leaders, and producing vituperative propaganda on behalf of the Reich's measures against the Jews. "Aryan," for them, meant not simply a physical or biological body type, but much more an inner spirit that was simultaneously of great power and also profoundly vulnerable and in need of protection from the degeneracy threatened by non-Aryans, particularly Jews. In Nazi Germany, racial hygiene was the field to learn how to protect the body housing the Aryan spirit; the Institute's theology attended directly to caring for that spirit.

Most members of the Institute, particularly its academic director, Walter Grundmann, professor of New Testament at the University of Jena, regarded their work as being in the theological avant-garde, addressing and resolving

1

a problem that had long plagued Christian theology: how to establish clear and distinct boundaries between earliest Christianity and Judaism and eliminate all traces of Jewish influence from contemporary Christian theology and religious practice. As a predominantly younger generation of scholars, trained by Germany's leading scholars of early Christianity—many members of the Institute were students of the distinguished Tübingen professor, Gerhard Kittel, himself a Nazi who produced antisemitic propaganda[1]—they saw themselves able to recover the historically genuine, non-Jewish Jesus and a Christian message compatible with contemporary German identity. Theirs was a goal of purification, authenticity, and theological revolution, all in the name of historical-critical methods and commitment to Germanness, to be achieved by eradicating the Jewish from the Christian. A Christian message tainted by Jewishness could not serve Germans, nor could a Jewish message be the accurate teaching of Jesus.

The Institute's goals were stated forthrightly at its opening by Grundmann, who delivered the keynote lecture on "The Dejudaization of the Religious Life as the Task of German Theology and Church." The present era, he declared, was similar to the Reformation: Protestants had to overcome Judaism just as Luther had overcome Catholicism. "The elimination of Jewish influence on German life is the urgent and fundamental question of the present German religious situation." Yes, Grundmann noted, people in Luther's day could not imagine Christianity without the Pope, just as today they could not imagine salvation without the Old Testament, but the goal could be realized. Modern New Testament scholarship had made apparent the "deformation of New Testament ideas into Old Testament preconceptions, so that now angry recognition of the Jewishness in the Old Testament and in parts of the New Testament has arisen, obstructing access to the Bible for innumerable German people."[2]

The Bible would have to be purified, Grundmann continued, restored to its pristine condition, to proclaim the truth about Jesus: that he sought the destruction of Judaism. Grundmann outlined the scholarly tasks that the Institute would undertake. This included clarifying the role of Judaism in early Christianity and its influence on modern philosophy. Any opposition to National Socialism from within the church, claimed Grundmann, arose from nefarious Jewish influence, such as the arguments of Jewish scholars that Jesus was a Jew. The Jews had destroyed Germans' "völkisch" (racial) thinking, Grundmann continued, and, with help from Bolshevism, they were now striving for world conquest, the "Weltherrschaft des Judentums" (world domination of Jewry).

---

[1] On Kittel, see Ericksen, *Theologians under Hitler*.
[2] Grundmann, *Die Entjudung des religiösen Lebens*, 9, 10.

The Jewish threat to Germany was grave: "For these reasons," Grundmann stated, echoing Nazi propaganda, "the struggle against the Jews has been irrevocably turned over to the German Volk."[3] The war against the Jews was not simply a military battle, but a spiritual battle: "Jewish influence on all areas of German life, including on religious-church life, must be exposed and broken,"[4] a phrase Grundmann frequently used in defining the Institute's purpose.

THE GERMAN CHRISTIAN MOVEMENT

The Institute was a well-funded, thriving achievement of the German Christian movement, the pro-Nazi faction within the German Protestant church that claimed a membership of 600,000 pastors, bishops, professors of theology, religion teachers, and laity. The movement's goal was to create a unified, national German church transcending Protestant and Catholic divisions that would exemplify the nazified Christianity it advocated. It began by trying to reshape the German Protestant (Lutheran) church. The movement was highly successful in gaining influence with many of the university theological faculties and regional churches, but most of all in developing an ideology disseminated through lectures, conferences, and numerous publications and that occasionally found common ground even among opponents within the Confessing Church, the Catholic Church, and the much smaller neo-pagan groups.[5]

The German Christian movement was a faction within the Protestant church of Germany, not a separate sect, and eventually attracted between a quarter and a third of Protestant church members. Enthusiastically pro-Nazi, the movement sought to demonstrate its support for Hitler by organizing itself after the model of the Nazi Party, placing a swastika on the altar next to the cross, giving the Nazi salute at its rallies, and celebrating Hitler as sent by God. It was ready and willing to alter fundamental Christian doctrine in order to bring the church into compliance with the Reich, and welcomed the April 1933 order of removing Jews from the civil service by demanding that the church do likewise and remove any non-Aryans, that is, baptized Jews, from positions within the church. That demand contravened the doctrine of

---

[3] Ibid., 9.

[4] Ibid., 17.

[5] The neo-pagan groups remained small; the German Faith Movement had about 40,000 members, and others, such as the Ludendorff Tannenberg League, were even smaller. The Roman Catholic Church had about 20 million German members, while the Protestant Church had the majority, 40 million Germans.

Figure I.1. Church altar, 1935.

baptism, according to which the sacrament transformed a Jew into a Christian, but the German Christian leaders insisted that the Nazi racial laws took precedence and that baptism could not erase race. Within a year, a group of disapproving Protestant theologians in Germany, including Karl Barth, one of the most distinguished theologians of his day, condemned the German Christian movement as heresy, issuing the now-famous Barmen Declaration in May 1934, which became the basis of a new movement within the German Protestant church that called itself the Confessing Church. The Confessing Church, which eventually attracted about twenty percent of Protestant pastors, remained a minority opposition group—not in opposition to Hitler or the Nazi Reich, but in opposition to the German Christian movement for its efforts to undermine Christian doctrine.[6]

Tensions between the two factions continued throughout the Third Reich, as the German Christians gained control of most of the regional Protestant

---

[6] Some members of the Confessing Church became notable opponents of Hitler, including Dietrich Bonhoeffer, who was killed in the last weeks of the war at a concentration camp, and Karl Barth, who had to emigrate to Switzerland. See Gerlach, *And the Witnesses Were Silent*.

churches in Germany, using the church's institutional structures and finances to promote their positions. In one area, however, the two factions were not at swords: while the Confessing Church supported Jews who had become baptized Christians, most of them agreed with the German Christians that Germany needed to be rid of its Jews and that Judaism was a degenerate moral and spiritual influence on Christians. Catholics were in a position similar to the Confessing Church: too theologically conservative to alter their doctrines or their liturgy to bring it in accord with Nazism, yet in basic agreement with their Protestant colleagues that Jews were a degenerate influence on German Christians. Munich's Cardinal Faulhaber, for example, delivered a series of Advent sermons in 1933 attacking the German Christian movement, but his argument, almost identical to what the Confessing Church leaders came to argue, was that the Old Testament need not be eliminated as a Jewish book, as some German Christians advocated; it was, rather, an anti-Jewish book, Faulhaber insisted, since the prophets were constantly condemning Israel for its sinful ways.[7] Faulhaber's objection, then, was not to the German Christians' antisemitism, but to their failure to realize that the Old Testament itself was on their side.[8]

The three ideological prongs of the German Christian movement within the Protestant church, as Doris Bergen has delineated, were its opposition to church doctrine, its antisemitism, and its effort to craft a "manly" church, all of which are reflected in the Institute's many publications.[9] Some of Germany's most prominent theologians became Nazi sympathizers and outspoken antisemites, as Robert Ericksen has demonstrated in his study of three of them, Gerhard Kittel, Paul Althaus, and Emanuel Hirsch.[10] Both the Institute and the German Christian movement from which it stemmed were influenced by the völkisch traditions and mood of cultural pessimism that George Mosse and Fritz Stern have shown were crucial in shaping Nazi ideology and that drew adherents across the political spectrum, from reactionaries to liberals.[11] The extent of the German Christian movement's influence, which was initially downplayed by historians, was reevaluated in a recent major study by Manfred Gailus. Examining 147 Protestant church parishes in Berlin, led by 565 pastors, he concluded that forty percent of the pastors were, at least for some time during the Third Reich, oriented toward the German Christian movement,

[7] Faulhaber, *Judaism, Christianity and Germany*.

[8] For a thorough and highly nuanced exploration of German Catholics during this period, including their reactions to the German Christian movement, see Spicer, *Resisting the Third Reich*.

[9] Bergen, *Twisted Cross*, 61–81.

[10] Ericksen, *Theologians under Hitler*.

[11] Mosse, *The Crisis of German Ideology*; Stern, *The Politics of Cultural Despair*.

compared to slightly more than one-third who were sympathetic to the Confessing Church. Of 131 church congregations, he found that one-quarter were dominated by German Christians, and half were split between Confessing Church and German Christians. While no comparable detailed social historical studies of the churches in other regions have been carried out, Gailus's findings would undoubtedly find parallels elsewhere in Germany, and perhaps an even greater proportion of German Christian sympathizers. The movement seems to have been stronger in urban than in rural areas, and to have infiltrated both university theological faculties and village parishes. Few Germans withdrew from the Protestant church on account of the new theology promoted by the German Christians, and German Christian rallies drew large crowds. Many pastors were sympathetic to the German Christian movement's theology, and their theological views were disseminated within the institutional structures of the Protestant church; there was no schismatic withdrawal and creation of alternative churches, nor is there evidence of large-scale objections to pastors preaching a German Christian message.[12] Efforts by the Nazi regime after 1937 to encourage Germans to withdraw from the church found only minimal response; the anti-Christian neo-pagan movements were not successful in drawing large memberships.

The Institute, too, was larger in its membership and influence than had been assumed before I began my study. Lacking the documentation from the archives, some church historians had told me when I began my study that it was a marginal phenomenon with little importance beyond its backwater location in Thuringia. The mountain of evidence I uncovered, only a portion of which can be discussed in this book, paints a different picture, one of Reich-wide influence, a substantial membership, an active program of publishing, and numerous conferences. The Institute was a model of success, no doubt due to its focus on the one issue central to the Nazi regime: antisemitism.

ANTISEMITISM AND CHRISTIANITY

Hitler did not achieve most of his political and military goals, but on the Jewish question he succeeded remarkably. If his antisemitic propaganda found resonance, its success can be credited in large measure to the unrelenting

[12] Gailus, *Protestantismus und Nationalsozialismus*. Note that an effort was made after 1937 by the regime to encourage Germans to withdraw from the church and yet declare themselves "Gottgläubige" (believers in God); only a small percentage did. The study by Gailus has been expanded: Manfred Gailus and Wolfgang Krogel, eds., *Von der babylonischen Gefangenschaft der Kirche*.

anti-Jewish Christian theological discourse that linked Nazi propaganda with the traditions and moral authority of the churches. That link was proclaimed with enthusiasm by Nazi Christians: "In the Nazi treatment of the Jews and its ideological stance, Luther's intentions, after centuries, are being fulfilled."[13] Antisemitism was the lingua franca of the Nazi era and was employed by church leaders to gain credibility with their own adherents—but also out of sincere antisemitic conviction. Antisemitism was also a tactic in the rhetorical battles among the different Christian factions, with each accusing its opponents of being "Jewish" while positioning itself as the true Nazi believer.[14]

Already in 1971 the historian Uriel Tal challenged the entrenched view that racist antisemitism is a new phenomenon that repudiates Christianity by arguing that it was actually utterly dependent on Christian anti-Judaism for its success: "it was not the economic crises that brought about this new political, racial and antireligious antisemitism, but completely the reverse, it was precisely the anti-Christian and antireligious ideology of racial antisemitism which hampered the first antisemitic parties in their efforts to utilize the economic crisis for their political development . . . [because] what still attracted the masses was the classical, traditional Christian anti-Judaism, however adapted it may have become to the new economic conditions."[15] Tal demonstrated that Germany's antisemitic, völkisch movements that arose in the nineteenth century had to abandon their initial anti-Christian stances in order to win supporters for whom Christian anti-Jewish arguments held profound political appeal.[16] Even within the so-called "church struggle" between German Christians and the Confessing Church for control of the Protestant church, antisemitism became the glue that united the otherwise warring factions. Similarly, however much Hitler made use of images of messianism, redemption,

---

[13] Meyer-Erlach, *Juden, Mönche und Luther*, 60.

[14] Such tactics of disidentification can be found in other political conflicts within racist societies: for example, in the racism that prevailed among the Afrikaner and the English in the struggle over South Africa during the Boer Wars.

[15] Tal, *Religious and Anti-Religious Roots of Modern Antisemitism*, reprinted in Tal, ed., *Religion, Politics and Ideology in the Third Reich*, 177.

[16] "In reality Nazism accomplished but few of its goals. But in one area, that of the Jewish question, political myth achieved its purpose to the full. Here the regime met the least opposition from those who in other matters were hardly in accord with Nazism—be it intellectuals, the churches or public opinion in the Reich or abroad. The Jew served as the focal point round which Nazism turned and on which the structural process of value-transformation and reversal of meanings took place. Among the values and meanings that were transformed, the symbol itself was turned into substance; consequently, the negation of Judaism had to be transformed into the annihilation of the Jew, this time not spiritually but rather physically, not symbolically but in substance." (Tal, *Religion, Politics and Ideology*, 111)

and other Christian motifs, the most useful and consistent aspect of Christianity for the Nazi movement was its anti-Judaism, just as the single most consistent and persistent feature of Nazism was its antisemitism.

Hitler was well aware of arguments that were central to the Institute: that Jesus was an Aryan, and that Paul, as a Jew, had falsified Jesus's message, themes he repeatedly mentioned in private conversations, together with rants against the church as a Jewish subversion of the Aryan spirit (though the reliability of his reported private conversations is uncertain). In a diatribe alleged to have occurred in October of 1941, the month Hitler made the decision to murder the Jews,[17] Hitler proclaimed that Jesus was not a Jew, but a fighter against Jewry whose message was falsified and exploited by Paul: "St. Paul transformed a local movement of Aryan opposition to Jewry into a super-temporal religion, which postulates the equality of all men . . . [causing] the death of the Roman Empire."[18] His views demonstrate that the German Christian diagnosis of Christianity as tainted by Jewish influence resonated at the highest levels of the Reich, but that its prescribed solution of dejudaization was met with skepticism if not sheer mockery. Was Christianity thoroughly impregnated with Judaism, or could it be dejudaized, as the Institute claimed?

Like the antisemitic parties of the nineteenth century, the Nazi Party could not reject Christianity—not only because it would offend the moral and social sensibilities of Germans, but because the antisemitism of Christianity formed the basis on which the party could appeal to Germans with its racial and nationalist ideology. Nazism's relationship to Christianity was not one of rejection, nor was it an effort to displace Christianity and become a form of "political religion." Nazism did not present racial antisemitism as antithetical to Christian theological anti-Judaism; rather, Nazi ideology was a form of supersessionism, a usurpation and colonization of Christian theology, especially its antisemitism, for its own purposes. The theology of the Institute was a similar effort at supersessionism in reverse, taking over elements of Nazi racial ideology to bolster and redefine the Christian message. The result was an uneasy competition between two sides seeking popular support and institutional control, though access to power was, of course, highly asymmetrical.

Thus, while seeking to undermine the political power and moral authority of the churches, Nazism simultaneously appropriated key elements of Christian theology into its own ideology both for purposes of winning adherents used to Christian arguments and also to give its own message a coherence and resonance with the age-old Christian teachings that had shaped European

---

[17] Browning, *Origins of the Final Solution*, 309–34, 352–73.

[18] Monologue of October 21, 1941, Bormann, ed., *Hitler's Secret Conversations*, 64.

culture. Conversely, German Christians appropriated Nazi rhetoric and symbols into the church to give its Christianity a contemporary resonance. Both the Nazis and the German Christians identified Hitler as Christ's second coming. That gave Hitler the status of a supernatural being and gave Christ renewed glory as a contemporary figure of enormous political significance. Both were suspicious of the institutional church. Factions within the Nazi Reich and the party saw the church as competition and a potential threat to be ultimately eliminated after the war.[19] The German Christians sought control and radical reform of the Protestant church, which they never fully achieved, leading them to bitter complaints and, in some cases, demands for its demolition. Meanwhile, Christianity was not to be banned nor the churches outlawed; rather, as the historian Ernst Piper writes, Nazi strategy was to control the churches and lead to "a steadily advancing process of delegitimization and disassociation, of undermining and repression" that would undercut the church's moral authority and position of respect.[20] In its own supersessionist theology, an amalgam of Nazism and Christianity, with a rejection of church authority and doctrine, an assertion of German supremacy and Jewish degeneracy, and absurd revisions of the Bible, the German Protestant church contributed substantially to the Nazi project of undermining Christianity.

The establishment of the Institute in 1939 and the proliferation of its projects during the war years demonstrates that the antisemitism of the German Christians was not simply rhetorical, but was intended to lend active support to Nazi policies against the Jews—or, at times, to push those policies in more radical directions. Indeed, certain Protestant theologians stood at the forefront in discussions of the so-called Jewish problem; Gerhard Kittel's notorious speech of May 1933, later published as a pamphlet, has been called the most antisemitic utterance of that year.[21] In considering ways to rid Germany of Jews, Kittel proposed not only expulsion and guest status, but extermination ("Ausrottung"), a method he rejected only because it was too difficult to implement. On February 24–25, 1936, a few months after the proclamation of the Nuremberg Laws, but long before Jews were being deported and murdered, a group of theologians, some of whom subsequently became leaders of the Institute, met in Dresden to discuss a merger of the German Christian

---

[19] Kroll, *Utopie als Ideologie*. See also Rissmann, *Hitlers Gott*.

[20] Piper, "Steigmann-Gall, the Holy Reich," 53.

[21] Kittel, *Die Judenfrage*; the evaluation comes from Horst Junginger, "Das Bild des Juden," 175. Along with Kittel's pamphlet as the worst antisemitic publication of 1933, Junginger includes an article by the Catholic theologian Karl Adam, "Deutsches Volkstum und katholisches Christentum," 40–63, in which Adam declares that the goals of Christianity are in agreement with the political antisemitism of Nazism. On Adam, see Spicer, *Resisting the Third Reich*, 172–78.

factions of the state churches of Thuringia and Saxony. During the course of the meeting, Siegfried Leffler, a German Christian leader, official in the Thuringian Ministry of Education, and, by 1939, figurehead of the Institute, stated:

> In a Christian life, the heart always has to be disposed toward the Jew, and that's how it has to be. As a Christian, I can, I must, and I ought always to have or to find a bridge to the Jew in my heart. But as a Christian, I also have to follow the laws of my nation [Volk], which are often presented in a very cruel way, so that again I am brought into the harshest of conflicts with the Jew. Even if I know "thou shalt not kill" is a commandment of God or "thou shalt love the Jew" because he too is a child of the eternal Father, I am able to know as well that I have to kill him, I have to shoot him, and I can only do that if I am permitted to say: Christ.[22]

What is striking is not only that Leffler spoke of killing Jews as early as February 1936, long before mass murder of the Jews became Nazi policy, but that there was no response to his comments from those attending, neither immediately nor later in the session; the discussion simply continued as if murder of Jews in the name of Christ was a customary topic.[23] The aryanization of Jesus into a manly, heroic, fighting spirit reflected among the theologians the "heroic realism" that prevailed in the 1930s within right-wing political thought. That "heroism" meant killing one's opponent without emotion but in accord with principles of natural law, in defense of one's own race and at the cost of personal sacrifice.[24] Paul Althaus, professor of theology at the University of Erlangen and a noted ethicist, was present at the meeting, but expressed nothing to indicate that he was appalled or disturbed by Leffler's remarks. The lack of outrage is evidence that ridding Germany of Jews had become an acceptable point of discussion among theologians, even when murder was proposed as a technique of achieving it. The Nuremberg Laws, while perceived by many German Jews as protection from far worse legislation, were viewed as an

---

[22] ThHStA A 1400, 293. The meeting was held February 24–25, 1936. Present: Paul Althaus, Martin Doerne, Erich Fascher, Wolf Meyer-Erlach, Dedo Müller, pastors, and senior ministers; Leffler, Leutheuser, Hugo Hahn (a church superintendent in Saxony who led the Confessing Church movement there); and Grundmann. It is striking that Anja Rinnen, in her biography of Siegfried Leffler, does not cite this document, and that Hahn does not describe the meeting in his detailed memoir of the period nor mention Leffler's comments. See Rinnen, *Kirchenmann und Nationalsozialist*. See also Hahn and Prater, *Kämpfer wider Willen*.

[23] Indeed, two historians mention the meeting but do not comment on Leffler's statement. Arnhold, "Dem Neuen Testament," 151–83; Meier, *Der evangelische Kirchenkampf*, 2:136.

[24] Herbert, "Ideological Legitimization," 103.

encouragement by the German Christian movement to take even more radical positions. Legal cases in German courts, brought in the wake of the Nuremberg Laws' criminalization of sexual relations and marriage between Jews and Aryans, and widely reported in the German press, implicated Jews as sexual predators of Aryans, further encouraging Christian theologians to insist on protecting Christian purity by eradicating Jewishness with even more radical measures.[25] The penetration of Christian bodies by Jewish sex reiterated a typical motif of racist rhetoric, the dangers of miscegenation, and reinforced fears that Aryanism was not immutable, but subject to destruction by Jews.[26] Antisemites had long insisted that German Aryan women were vulnerable to Jewish predation, and Jesus, whose gentleness and suffering was viewed as effeminate by German Christians, was depicted in one caricature as an Aryan woman on a cross with a lecherous Jewish man in the foreground: the crucifixion as the Jewish rape of Germany.

The use of laws and court procedures to control sexual relations within Germany and thereby create the Aryan racial nation was not in contradiction to Christian teachings; after all, as Jennifer Knust points out, the apostle Paul, Justin Martyr, and other early Christian writers asserted that those who reject Christ are by definition sexually repulsive, licentious, and "unnatural" in their sexual behavior.[27] Among the post-apostolic writers, the physical, and especially sexual, purity of Christians was the safeguard of moral and religious purity. Thus the Nuremberg Laws could easily be read as upholding classical Christian values and calling forth the sort of theological action that Leffler proposed just months after they were announced.

INSTITUTE ACTIVITIES

By the time the Institute was opened three years after the meeting in Dresden, the dejudaization of Germany was already in progress. Indeed, it was in the days following the Reich Kristallnacht pogrom on November 9–10, 1938, that a formal proposal to establish an institute that would dejudaize the church was circulated among church officials, linking the theological goals with the Nazis' actions. Theologically, the Institute was meant to signify a new Reformation, completing what Luther had begun. The date of the Institute's opening had been chosen deliberately to concretize that link. On May 4 in

[25] Szobar, "Telling Sexual Stories in the Nazi Courts of Law," 131–63.

[26] On the centrality of fear of miscegenation in the racist discourse of colonialism, see Stoler, "Racial Histories and Their Regimes of Truth," 183–206.

[27] Knust, *Abandoned to Lust*.

11

Figure I.2. Antisemitic cartoon, 1934.

1521, Martin Luther had fled his enemies and arrived shortly after at the Wartburg Castle, where he spent the next ten months translating the New Testament into German. Within a year of its opening on May 6, 1939, at the same Wartburg Castle, the Institute's own revised New Testament was published, purged of Jewish references and ready for the Nazi Reich.

From 1939 to 1945 the Institute functioned as a broad umbrella under which a range of anti-Jewish theological positions could be articulated by both scholars and pastors. Some, like Grundmann, called for the removal of the Old Testament from the Christian Bible on the grounds that the Old Testament was a Jewish book, while others, such as Johannes Hempel, professor of Old Testament at the University of Berlin, tried to retain the Old Testament for Christians, on the grounds that its core was a message about the Volk Israel (not the Jews) that was important for the German Volk to hear. Active members of the Institute included internationally renowned scholars of Jewish texts, such as Hugo Odeberg, but also theology students and demagogues, such as Hans-Joachim Thilo and Wolf Meyer-Erlach. By 1942, the year the greatest number of European Jews were murdered, the Institute had broadened its membership and its themes, inviting völkisch writers to lecture on Germany's Teutonic heritage and its compatibility with Christianity.

What united Institute members was a commitment to eradicating Jewishness as a means of purifying both Christianity and Germany. Known popularly as a dejudaization institute ("Entjudungsinstitut"), it was the Protestant church's instrument of antisemitic propaganda. Theological conclusions regarding Jesus's teachings and his interactions with the Jews of his day were shaped into a rhetoric that endorsed Nazi ideology, making Nazism appear to be realizing in the political sphere what Christians taught in the religious sphere. Institute conferences and publications were notable not for scholarly originality, but for developing biblical exegesis and religious history using racial methods. With members who were leading scholars of theology, professors or instructors at universities throughout the Reich, the Institute provided a scholarly and religious mantle for a politicized antisemitism that mirrored the Propaganda Ministry's rhetoric in describing the war as a defense against an alleged Jewish war on Germany. In offering proof that Jesus was not a Jew but an opponent of the Jews, Grundmann allied the Institute's work with the Nazi war effort.

The extent of the Institute's appeal was remarkable: the academics and students of Protestant theology who became Institute members represented a cross-section of disciplines, geographic location within the Reich, age, and level of scholarly accomplishment. In addition, some members were among the noted völkisch writers of the era, unaffiliated with a church. The popular appeal of the Institute among German theologians was paralleled by the broad appeal of the German Christian movement that spawned it, but also by the appeal of "dejudaization" among academics and intellectuals. Virtually all scholarly fields were compromised by efforts to synthesize their methods and topics of investigation with Nazi concerns, thereby offering an academic legitimation for National Socialist ideology. Nazi theologians drew easily from the work of their colleagues in fields as diverse as linguistics, archeology, anthropology, and so-called racial hygiene.

THE INSTITUTE'S SIGNIFICANCE

Institute statements regarding Jews and Judaism were mirrors, in Christianized language, of the official propaganda issued by the Reich during the course of the Holocaust: Jews were the aggressive enemies of Germans and Germany was fighting a defensive war against them.[28] Even as the Nazis carried out the extermination of the European Jews, their propaganda argued that it was Jews who were plotting the murder of Germans. In similar language, Institute members such as Grundmann argued that Jews were the mortal enemies of Jesus and all who followed him. Antisemitic propaganda was not incidental to the murder process, but formed, as Saul Friedländer has written, the "mobilizing myth of the regime."[29] Church leaders and theologians channeled Nazi propaganda into visual symbols, placing a swastika on the altar or on a banner hanging from the church ceiling until its use in churches was banned by the Nazi Party in 1936, and also into Christian language for the ninety-five percent of Germans who remained registered, tax-paying members of the Protestant and Catholic churches.[30] Members of other professional groups collaborated in similar ways, but, of course, an antisemitic message conveyed by clergy carried a unique moral weight.

That the theologians who ran the Institute were in any way responsible for the Holocaust was, of course, denied once the war came to an end. Indeed, it is precisely the closure of the Institute after the war by Thuringian church officials—on the grounds that funding was not available—that reinforced the disclaimer of responsibility. Since the postwar closure did not occur because

---

[28] Herf, *The Jewish Enemy*.

[29] Friedländer, *The Years of Extermination*, xix.

[30] Heschel, "Church Protests during the Third Reich."

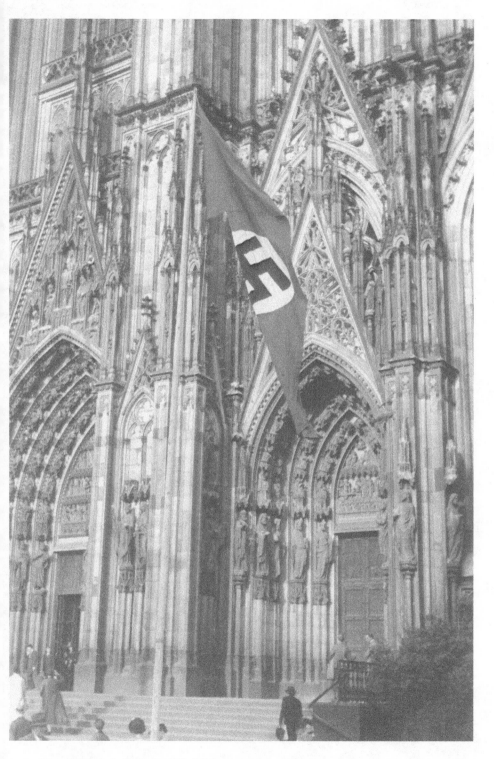

Figure I.3. Catholic Cathedral of Cologne, 1937.

the Institute was pro-Nazi or antisemitic, Institute members claimed that their work had been purely theological and scholarly. They hid their Nazi antisemitism beneath the cloak of traditional Christian theological anti-Judaism. Closing the Institute did not halt the spread and influence of its ideas, but allowed negations of Judaism to be presented as if they were Christian theological positions without any political implications.

What makes the Institute worthy of particular attention is its context: it carried out its program of eradicating the Jewish within Christianity precisely while the Jews of Europe were being deported and murdered. Theologians may have been far from the policy makers who set the agenda for the Nazi regime's domestic and foreign affairs, but they were part of a larger German apparatus of intellectuals who translated the often inchoate meaning of Nazism into a substantive discourse of Christian ritual and theology, giving Nazism religious and moral authority. As Wolfgang Bialas and Anson Rabinbach have argued, there was no single definition of National Socialism; it was less an ideology than an ethos, an indeterminate cultural outlook that could be defined in a host of ways.[31] In the writings of the Institute's theologians, Nazism became a symbol for Christianity, specifically for the pure and pristine original Christianity that they claimed they were recovering from the distortions of history. In that way, too, they argued that the racial theory of National Socialism provided the opportunity for the figure of Jesus to emerge in his original form and intention: as an Aryan fighting against Judaism. As part of a broader coalition of intellectuals and scholars who supported the regime, the theologians of the Institute provided an important religious legitimacy to the Nazis' "all-devouring manic obsession with the Jews"[32] and the "blend of hatred, self-righteous indignation, and paranoia [that] was at the core of the Nazi justification of genocide."[33]

Propagandists can be likened to desk murderers: they do not commit the murder, but give their written approval to the principle of the mission, and sometimes suggest the mission in the first place. Working at a safe distance from the machinery of murder, Nazi propagandists urged eradication of all expressions of Jewishness. Removing all positive Jewish references from Christian texts, denouncing Jews as enemies of Jesus's followers, and describing Judaism as a degenerate religion is not the same act as dropping Zyklon B into a sealed chamber filled with Jews. One cannot prove that the Institute's propaganda helped cause the Holocaust. However, the effort to dejudaize Christianity was

---

[31] Bialas and Rabinbach, *The Humanities in Nazi Germany*, xxxvi–xlii.
[32] Kershaw, *Hitler*, 151; cited by Herf, *The Jewish Enemy*, 3.
[33] Herf, *The Jewish Enemy*, 1.

also an attempt to erase moral objections to Nazi antisemitism. Institute-sponsored research, by describing Jesus's goal as the eradication of Judaism, effectively reframed Nazism as the very fulfillment of Christianity. Whether the Nazi killers of Jews were motivated by Institute propaganda cannot be proven, but some did express gratitude for Institute publications, apparently for alleviating a troubled conscience. Institute publications were not as widely disseminated as the propaganda issued by the Reich Minister of Propaganda, Joseph Goebbels, or the publications of Julius Streicher, who was hanged at Nuremberg for editing *Der Stürmer*, a weekly antisemitic propaganda rag. Yet the moral and societal location of clergy and theologians lends greater weight to the propaganda of the Institute; propaganda coming from the pulpit calls forth far deeper resonance than that spoken by a politician or journalist.

History of Investigations into the Institute

The existence of an antisemitic propaganda institute financed by the church first came to light with the publication of Max Weinreich's book, *Hitler's Professors*, in 1946.[34] Drawing on archives of the Ministry of Propaganda that had been confiscated by United States troops at the end of the war and deposited in the YIVO archives in New York City, Weinreich was able to outline much of the work of Grundmann and the Institute. Weinreich compared the theologians with other groups of scholars who put their academic training to work on behalf of the Nazi genocide. Yet Weinreich's study was largely ignored and did not influence the enormous number of studies of the churches during the Third Reich that were published during the first forty years after the war.

Indeed, for many years after the end of World War II, the very existence of the Institute was only vaguely acknowledged by historians of the church. Kurt Meier, professor of church history at the University of Leipzig, mentioned the Institute in his 1964 study of the German Christian movement, but did not explore its antisemitic dimensions, nor did he make use of the Institute's archives in Thuringia.[35] Both in 1964 and in a 1992 publication, Meier described the "apologetic" motivation of the Institute, defending Christianity against Alfred Rosenberg's charges that it was a Jewish religion. Grundmann, he wrote, attempted to counter the "defamatory propaganda that Christianity was Judaism for non-Jews";[36] again, Meier did not speak of the Institute's

---

[34] Weinreich, *Hitler's Professors*.

[35] Meier, *Die Deutschen Christen*.

[36] Meier, *Kreuz und Hakenkreuz*, 166.

antisemitism. More direct and critical were the publications of church historian Hans Prolingheuer, who, in a variety of semi-popular publications since the early 1980s, has continually exposed the antisemitism of the Nazi-era church, its persecution of Jews and non-Aryan Christians, and the nazified Christian teachings of that era.[37] Doris Bergen, in her 1996 book delineating the ideology of the German Christian movement, pointed clearly to the Institute's antisemitism and drew on a rich supply of archival sources from Berlin and Minden to delineate its activities.[38] By contrast, some historians, while acknowledging the virulence of the Institute's antisemitism, have minimized its significance within the Reich and within the history of Christian theology; an example is the recent book by Peter von der Osten-Sacken that presents the Institute as a "misuse of the Gospel." By describing the Institute as the creation of the German Christians of Thuringia, Osten-Sacken narrows its influence and its genealogy within Christian theology.[39] Nor does he place Institute arguments within the context of racist rhetoric, but limits its significance to a theological problem.

Most recently, Roland Deines has attempted to disconnect Grundmann from Nazi antisemitism on the grounds that "the Jew" in Grundmann's writings was never a concrete person, but an abstract, metaphysical "evil." Apparently unaware that racism always defines its target in such terms, Deines fails to recognize that for Nazi antisemites, combating the abstract danger of Jewishness inevitably demanded eradication of its concretized source, the Jewish people, as carriers of that danger. Even more striking, Deines criticizes Grundmann for his "literalistic pedantry," a euphemism for "Pharisaism" in traditional Christian anti-Jewish rhetoric, thus reiterating an image frequently invoked by Grundmann's own opponents during the Third Reich who mocked his dejudaization efforts as "Pharisaic" in order to tar him with the label of the despised Jew.[40]

THEOLOGY AND RACE

Why was it so easy to racialize Christianity? What made antisemitic ideas so appealing to Protestant theologians in Germany during the first half of the twentieth century? What are the affinities between theology and racism?

---

[37] Prolingheuer, *Wir sind in Die Irre gegangen.*

[38] Bergen, "One Reich, One People, One Church," 397–514, and Bergen, *Twisted Cross,* 148–54.

[39] Osten-Sacken, ed., *Das mißbrauchte Evangelium.*

[40] Deines, "Jesus der Galiläer," 129.

Numerous historians have traced the origins of racist thought to the period of the Enlightenment and blamed its emergence on the decline of religious belief. Colin Kidd, however, has argued not that race emerges as a consequence of the undermining of religion, but that race is implicated as a major factor in bringing about the "unraveling of Christian certainties."[41] Starting in the eighteenth century, race, according to Kidd, helped undermine the foundations of Christian belief: the universalism of its message, the uniqueness and historicity of its teachings, and the reliability and coherence of its scriptures. By the Nazi era, however, this book will argue, race was playing the opposite function: in its specific iteration as antisemitism, race was used by some theologians as a restorative force of coherence for Christian theology. Racism was viewed by many theologians not only as a political tool, but as an avant-garde method for understanding society and human nature.

By making use of racial arguments in their presentations of Christianity, Institute members thought they could bolster the appeal of Christianity to its Nazi despisers. Racism's argument that distinct and immutable orders exist in society lent support to a "theology of creation." One Institute member, Wilhelm Stapel, attempted to demonstrate that racism supported Christian claims to divine creation: just as God had created societal orders—marriage, family, Volk, profession, hierarchy, property, and so forth—God had given each Volk a task and place on earth.[42] Believers in racial hierarchy could see it as an extension of the biblical account of God's creation of hierarchical orders within nature, and social orders such as marriage, and Christians were told that racial hierarchies were an extension of the divine order.

Racism was also embraced as a tool to restore the uniqueness, historicity, and significance of Jesus and his teachings that had been undermined by historicism. Even if Jesus's teachings did not seem different from those of other Jews of his day, he was distinct in his race, as an Aryan and not a Jew. His racial identity was then used to read his teachings not as reflections of Judaism, but as repudiations of it. Institute publications argued that the Jews were violent people who sought the destruction of Jesus and continue to strive for world domination and the subjugation of all Gentiles. The Institute presented the war as a defensive life-and-death struggle against the Jews, and also as a Christian war in the name of the authentic non-Jewish Jesus, the Christianity he sought to bring into being, and the battle to destroy Judaism that he failed

---

[41] Kidd, *The Forging of Races*, 122.

[42] Stapel, who lectured at Institute conferences, was widely read and was one of the more sophisticated exponents of völkisch theology. Some of his publications are listed in the bibliography.

to win. Like the German military, the Institute presented its cause as a total eradication of the enemy, Judaism, and not simply its segregation or expulsion from the Reich.

The question of the dejudaization effort of the Institute has to be examined not only in terms of Third Reich politics, but as a Christian theological phenomenon that engaged a vast number of pastors, bishops, and academic theologians. Christianity came into being by resting on the theological foundations of Judaism; it is often said that Judaism and Christianity stand in mother-daughter relationship. Nearly every central theological concept of Christianity rests on a Jewish foundation, from messiah to divine election. Affirming what is central to Christian teaching usual entails an affirmation of a Jewish idea or a text from the Old Testament, so that attempting to eradicate the Jewish was a kind of "theological bulimia."[43]

Ridding Christianity of everything Jewish brought racism to the theological level. The appeal of racism to theologians remains a widespread problem not only in Germany and not only in the modern period. Theologians have long placed themselves at the service of racism, even as many have mustered religious arguments to combat it. The specific question raised by this study is how German Protestantism benefited from Nazi racism. Why were a sizable number of German Protestant theologians and pastors so drawn to racial theory that they created a form of racial theology? What theological benefit did they derive from racism?

The relationship between Christian theological anti-Judaism and secular, racist antisemitism has long been debated by historians and theologians. Despite the important research findings of Uriel Tal, a widespread consensus of historians, church leaders, and academic theologians is that Christian theological anti-Judaism is a phenomenon distinct from modern antisemitism, which is rooted in economic and racial thought, so that Christian teachings should not be held responsible for antisemitism.[44] That assumption is expressed, for example, in the 1998 statement by Pope John Paul II, "We Remember: A Reflection on the Shoah," that distinguishes between modern antisemitism and negative Christian teachings on Judaism, and also a Jewish-authored ad hoc statement on Christianity, *Dabru Emet*, issued in 2000. In part, the exculpation of Christianity for modern racism reflects a widely held assumption that Christianity is a universal religion open to all people, in contrast to Judaism, which links religion and ethnicity. Thus, Christianity, at

---

[43] I have developed that theme more extensively elsewhere; see Heschel, "Theology as a Vision for Colonialism," and "Theological Bulimia: Christianity and Its Dejudaization."

[44] See the discussion in Langmuir, *History, Religion, and Antisemitism*, 10.

the heart of its theology, is said to repudiate the exclusivity of racism. Recently the historian Denise Buell has challenged that assumption, arguing that the universality of Christianity is a modern construct, whereas in antiquity Christianity defined itself as a race.[45] The racialization of Christianity that came to the fore with the rise of German nationalism and Nazism can thus be seen as appealing to preexisting, early Christian currents as theologians, especially those linked to the völkisch movement, sought a Germanic Christianity. Eliminating the Jewish from Christianity constituted a renewed racialization, Christianity's reassertion of itself as a racial religion.

The affinities between German Protestantism and racial rhetoric lie still deeper than similarities in particular teachings regarding Jews, because race is ultimately concerned not with biology but rather with the human spirit. That was recognized by the racists themselves, who were concerned to define the spiritual natures of those they studied. Walter Wüst, professor of linguistics at the University of Munich and rector of that university from 1941 to 1945, became head of the Ahnenerbe, a research center established by SS chief Heinrich Himmler to study Indo-Germanic origins, made the link beween race and religion clear: "Today we know that religion is basically a spiritual-physical human activity and that it is thereby also racial."[46] Indeed, within the SS religion could survive only by being redefined as a racial phenomenon.

Long before the Nazi era, the concern of racists was not so much the inferiority of certain peoples' bodies—the shape of the nose or the cranium—as the degeneracy of their morality and spirituality and the alleged threat posed by such degeneracy to superior races. The body was presented as the physical representation of moral and spiritual qualities. Physiognomy was interpreted by philologists as signifying linguistic ability, language differences were taken as indicators of cultural levels, and "culture" was often used interchangeably with "race."

Indeed, scientific measurements of the body were rejected by leading race theorists, such as Houston Stewart Chamberlain. For Chamberlain, measurements were irrelevant because for Aryans, knowledge was intuitive, an argument revived by Grundmann in his claim that Jesus knew God's wishes intuitively, through his heart, in contrast to Jews, who only know God through reason and laws.[47] Even for those who measured skulls, such as the French

[45] Buell, *Why This New Race.*

[46] Wüst, *Indogermanisches Bekenntnis*, 68; cited by Arvidsson, *Aryan Idols*, 187. Examples of collaboration between theologians and Nazi race theorists deserve further exploration; see, for example, Fischer and Kittel, *Das antike Weltjudentum.*

[47] Chamberlain, *Foundations of the Nineteenth Century*; Grundmann, *Die Gotteskindschaft in der Geschichte Jesu.*

racial theorist Vacher de Lapouge, the results of the physical measurements pointed to moral conclusions: that Jews were dolichocephalic meant they were dangerous. But Chamberlain, who repudiated Lapouge's "scientific" approach, made that claim just as strongly.[48] Similarly, blood was also not a necessary determinant of racial identity. Hans F. K. Günther, a leading race theorist in the 1920s and '30s, argued that the British and Scandinavians had more Nordic blood than Germans, but Germans remained, for him, the superior race.[49] Thus, the distinction between Volk, a cultural and political grouping, and Rasse, race, a biological designation, was elided by the circular arguments of these theorists, who almost invariably made each the determinant of the other: culture indicated race, and race produced culture. What became key to racialist thinking was developing the proper hermeneutics: knowing how to "read" the body to learn what sort of moral and spiritual qualities are incarnate in it. The Jewish nose and hair, for example, are not dangerous by themselves, but to antisemites the Jewish body is the carrier of a degenerate Jewish morality. Training readers in the proper hermeneutics for interpreting the Jewish body and knowing its inherent danger was the goal of antisemitic texts.

Thus, if physiognomy was described at length as signaling racial difference, it never stood alone. Rather, modern race theorists saw the body as a carrier of the soul, of moral and spiritual potencies, making race theory a kind of theology. As Richard Dyer writes in his study of whiteness, "For all the emphasis on the body in Christianity, the point is the spirit that is 'in' the body. What has made Christianity compelling and fascinating is precisely the mystery that it posits, that somehow there is in the body something that is not of the body which may be variously termed spirit, mind, soul or God."[50] For racists, it is the moral and spiritual threat of lesser races—such as Jews—that racists worried about; the inferior bodies of those races are carriers of their corrupt spirits, not causes of the corruption.

The tired argument that racism is about biology fails to recognize that racism emphasizes the dangers posed by the body to the spirit. Flesh is crucial to racialist thinking because the body is not simply a symbol of the degenerate spirit; rather, moral degeneracy is incarnate within the body and the two cannot be separated. The fundamental relationship between body and soul characterizing modern racist discourse is a mirror of the body-soul dilemma at the heart of Christian metaphysics, and is precisely the stamp that Christianity has

[48] Hecht, "Vacher de Lapouge," 292–97.
[49] Field, "Nordic Racism," 525.
[50] Dyer, *White*, 16.

placed on Western philosophy.[51] Race additionally reinscribes the classical Christian distinction between the carnality of Judaism and the spirituality of Christianity.

Blood became central to racist discourse, as it is to most religions, because it links spirit and body, human and divine, metaphor and physical reality. In Christian theology spirit and body are linked by blood, in the nuances of transubstantiation as the actual or symbolic presence of the divine in matter. Racism similarly posits the presence of moral and spiritual qualities in the blood, nose, skin color, hair, and so forth, creating race through theological discursivity. It is therefore not surprising that National Socialism in its early years professed support of Christianity, with Hitler portraying himself as a religious man defending Christian faith against the enemies of the church—leftists and Jews. Hitler's use of Christianity was encouraged by the emergence of racial theology; for some Nazi propagandists, Christianity was a wonderful wellspring of antisemitism in creating what Richard Steigmann-Gall has called "The Holy Reich."[52] In this sense, too, the Institute's theology might be seen as treating Christianity as the body, National Socialism as the spirit—that is, making the church the bodily carrier of a Nazi soul, thus attempting to make Nazism incarnate in Christianity. At the same time, Nazism itself sought a supersessionist position in relation to Christianity, incorporating its key teachings into its own, more elevated political ideology, exploiting its language and ideational framework rather than trying to destroy it.

CONCLUSION

This book presents the history of the Institute: how it came into being and won approval and financing from church leaders; the nature of the dejudaized New Testament and hymnal that it published; the many conferences and lectures that it organized; who joined and became an active member, especially from the academic world of theology, and, in particular, the figure of its academic director, Walter Grundmann (1906–74). Grundmann's career as a scholar of New Testament spanned his student years during the Weimar Republic, his glory days in the Third Reich as professor at the University of Jena, and his lively postwar career within the Protestant church in the German Democratic Republic. For Grundmann and the other members, the Institute provided prestige and career advancement despite the Reich's contempt for

[51] Hodge, "Domination and the Will in Western Thought and Culture."
[52] Steigmann-Gall, The Holy Reich.

theology and notwithstanding the difficulties of the war years; the Institute helped its members solidify their academic reputations. Looking at their post-war successes, there is no doubt that the connections they formed through the Institute helped advance their careers within the field of theology after the Third Reich ended.

Further, this book situates the history of the Institute in the larger context of calls within Germany for dejudaizing Christianity, starting in the nineteenth century. The actual implementation of such efforts within the Third Reich, however, reveals the impact of Nazi antisemitism on the church, Christian in-volvement in the Nazi projects against the Jews, and the absence of significant Christian opposition to the Holocaust. The nature of Christian antisemitic propaganda might provide an added clue to understanding the social and cul-tural history of Germany during the Third Reich, and perhaps a reassessment of Hitler's relationship to the churches. The nazification of theological scholar-ship, as offered in the example of the University of Jena, also helps us under-stand the postwar career of antisemitic theologies within Germany; those theologies were transmitted from teachers to students in an intellectual environment that lacked the critical tools to challenge them.

The Institute was disbanded after the war, and its major achievements—removing the Old Testament from church liturgies, declaring Jesus an Aryan, dejudaizing the New Testament and hymnal—were discarded by the postwar Protestant church. Hitler was defeated and the Nazi Reich was deplored in postwar church declarations. Yet the significance of the Institute rests not solely on its ability to have influenced the politics of the twelve-year Third Reich, which certainly would have carried out its genocide of the Jews with-out the Institute's existence, but on its success in promoting antisemitic inter-pretations within the community of Christian theology.

The Institute's basic theological teachings were not systematically scruti-nized and repudiated after the war, leaving behind a troubling legacy of nega-tive teachings about Judaism that, in some cases, continued to be promulgated in Germany. The theologians who were active in the Institute were not investi-gated or censured for their antisemitism by the church, but continued to have active and often notable careers in the decades after the war, and, in some cases, were granted distinguished honors both by the church and the govern-ments of East and West Germany.

The vocation of a theologian, as defined by the German Protestants exam-ined in this book, was to determine with the greatest possible accuracy the historical origins of Christianity and the message of Jesus. That determination was to be conveyed to contemporary Christians in a manner that was both relevant and inspiring, profound and ethically rigorous. These were theologians who had been well trained in the most sophisticated methods and insights of their field, yet, like so many other professionals, academics, and intellectuals, their embrace of National Socialism leaves behind a troubling political legacy.

Draining Jesus of Jewishness

WHEN THE INSTITUTE for the Study and Eradication of Jewish Influence on German Church Life was established in 1939 in order to purge Christianity of all
Jewish accretions and restore it to its pristine Aryan origins, it drew on established theological arguments as well as antisemitic traditions rooted in German culture and politics. In the seventh year of the Nazi regime and its antisemitic propaganda, dejudaizing Christianity appealed as a sophisticated and
avant-garde modernization of theology in keeping with the new political and
cultural atmosphere of the Third Reich. The Institute built itself on the premise of institutionalizing within the church what had become a legitimate part
of theological discussion: that Jesus was not a Jew but an opponent of Judaism, and that the Old Testament was a Jewish book that had no place in the
Christian Bible. It was creating a Christianity appropriate for Nazis; as Grundmann declared, "Our Volk, which stands in a struggle above all else against the
satanic powers of world Jewry for the order and life of this world, dismisses
Jesus, because it cannot struggle against the Jews and open its heart to the
king of the Jews."[1] The conflict was clear; Jesus had to be drained of Jewishness if the German fight against the Jews was to be successful.

The Institute's foundation was not only Nazi politics. That Jesus was not a
Jew was "the ultimate Western fantasy," as the critic of modern racism, Robert
Young, writes.[2] It was also the secret hope of a strain of Christian theology
since the days of the second-century Christian theologian Marcion, who rejected the Old Testament and its God and was himself condemned as a heretic.
From Marcion to Grundmann, the dejudaization of Christianity was rooted in
the conundrum of Christian supersession: the appropriation by the New Testament and the early church of Judaism's central theological teachings, including messiah, eschatology, apocalypticism, election, and Israel, as well as its
scriptures, its prophets, and even its God, while denying the continued valid-
ity of those teachings and texts within Judaism as an independent path to salvation. The presence within Christianity of Jewish teachings, albeit transformed

[1] Grundmann, "Das Messiasproblem," 1:381.
[2] Young, *Colonial Desire*, 85.

from "old covenant" to "new covenant," and the Jewish identity of Jesus, Paul, and the apostles, formed the heart of the problem for Christian Nazis: to be a Christian inevitably meant affirming Jewish teachings—for example, that Jesus was the Christ (messiah) was based on the messiah described by the Old Testament prophets.

Supersessionism was structured as a kind of colonization of Judaism, metaphorically speaking, on the theological level. As a colonization, it did not seek the destruction of Judaism, but its arrogation and exploitation for Christian purposes. For Jesus to be affirmed as messiah, he had to be shown to be fulfilling the Old Testament promises of the messianic figure, thus placing Christian claims in a position of dependence on the religious truth of Jewish texts. Christianity's theological relationship to Judaism lent itself to a sense of ambivalent desire in conflict with a sense of repulsion. The conflict was exacerbated by a sense of shame over Christianity's origins and dependence on Judaism, encouraging theologians to invent alternative originary narratives within Buddhism, Zoroastrianism, or a vague "Aryanism." Within the Christian theological economy, the conflict reached a crisis with the emergence of modern racism and the dangers and desires of miscegenation that were racism's central trope. The promiscuity implied by the Jewish presence within Christianity impelled a desire for theological purity that the Institute promised to achieve through dejudaization.

The purging of Christianity put forward by Grundmann, with support from other members of the Institute, particularly the argument that Jesus was not a Jew but rather had sought the destruction of Judaism, based itself on several different political and scholarly arguments that were well established long before to the Institute's founding in 1939. These included racial theory, as it emerged in Europe during the nineteenth century, with theories about languages and religions as manifestations of race; historicist distinctions between Jesus's teachings and those of first-century Judaism, presented by New Testament scholars; claims that Jesus's religious teachings originated in Hellenism, Buddhism, Hinduism, or Iranian culture—anything but Judaism; and assertions about the Gentile population of the Galilee in the centuries leading up to Jesus's day, given academic credence by Assyriologists. Among scholars as well as populist writers, the bases of such arguments were weak if not nonexistent, sources were read tendentiously or taken out of context, and solid data was replaced by fantasy. Through the various methods, Jesus was transformed from a Jew prefigured by the Old Testament into an antisemite and proto-Nazi. As Thomas Howard has argued with reference to the nineteenth century, figural interpretation did not simply decline with the rise of historicism, but was transformed: "Instead of the Old Testament prefiguring Christ . . . , Christ

27

himself came to prefigure, or legitimize, various forms of Christian cultural awareness."[3] In the theology of the Institute, Jesus became a prefiguration for Nazi Germany's fight against the Jews.

Rejecting Jesus's Jewishness and defining him as Aryan was about not only redefining Christianity, but racializing Europe: reassuring Europeans that they were white. Images of Jesus were crucial to racism in establishing the primary criterion of whiteness: Christ himself. It is not the Caucasian male who was the model of the authentic white man, but rather an idealized "White Man," namely Christ. For the European male to define himself as a "white man" he had to fantasize himself as Christ, a Christ who had to be imaged not as Jew but as Aryan. Deleuze writes, "If the face is in fact Christ . . . then the first deviances, the first divergence-types, are racial: yellow man, black man, men in the second or third category. . . . They must be Christianized, in other words, facialized. European racism as the white man's claim has never operated by exclusion, or by the designation of someone as Other. . . . Racism operates by the determination of degrees of deviance in relation to the White-Man face. . . ."[4] Yet by converting to Christianity, blacks did not become white, any more than Jews became Aryans.

The ultimate impossibility of Christianizing nonwhites highlighted the problem of race at the heart of Christian theology. Missionary efforts recapitulated Christianity's fundamental supersessionist flaw: the effort to Christianize Judaism was a theological miscegenation. Artistic depictions by colonized groups of a black, yellow, female, or even Jewish Jesus were flawed efforts not so much to claim that Jesus was black, yellow, female, or Jewish, but to claim white maleness for the racially subjugated group via Christ. "Natural" gender distinctions between male and female lent further justification for racial distinctions.

PHILOLOGY, RELIGION, AND RACIAL THEORY

Modern racism, although dismissed for its philistinism, was actually the product of scholars working in a range of academic disciplines, to which theology was no exception.[5] The historian Colin Kidd has argued that the decline in the seventeenth century of the authority of Scripture "opened up an ideological

[3] Howard, *Religion and the Rise of Historicism*, 93. Howard is here arguing against Hans Frei, *The Eclipse of Biblical Narrative*.

[4] Deleuze, *A Thousand Plateaus*, 178.

[5] The simultaneous rise of distinct academic disciplines and racial theory, producing orderly divisions of knowledge and race, has been noted by Bernal, in *Black Athena*, 1:317–66.

space for the uninhibited articulation of racialist sentiments."[6] Race began its appearance with a theological challenge: monogenesis, the biblical idea that all humans were created by God, was thrown into question by the "discovery" of different races. The problem for Christian theologians, Kidd points out, was that if humanity was not united as a single creation, then original sin could not be universally transmitted to all people and Christ's death would not bring atonement to all human beings. Yet while the discovery of races initially seemed a threat to Christian doctrine, theological responses were formulated to defend against it or arrive at a compromise with it. Scriptures came to be used to justify racist but also antiracist claims, especially around slavery and monogenesis.[7] At another level, race threatened religion as omniscient hermeneutic, that is, as explaining the origins of humanity, culture, and religion; race was believed to be the key to history and destiny, the rise of civilizations and their degeneration.

Race was invented as a modulation of culture, and the term "race" was often used in place of "culture" in nineteenth-century tracts. Races, moreover, were not defined by their immutability, but were viewed as fragilely vulnerable to alteration and destruction, particularly through miscegenation.[8] Within Christian theology, supersessionism provided the model for Judaism's infiltration and the cultural dangers of religious "mixed breeding." Studies of race, particularly in the nineteenth century, did not always begin with biology, but with analyses of language that led to conclusions regarding religion, society, and morality. Racism had a linguistic and cultural genesis.

The search for an *Urheimat*, a primordial homeland of nation, culture, and Volk, characterized early German writings on race. The fascination with Indology characteristic of early nineteenth-century German romanticism offered an alternative to the biblical accounts of Eden, Babel, revelation, and divinely ordained diaspora. Not Mesopotamia or Palestine, but India became the geographic font of the West, as Sanskrit replaced Hebrew, in the work of Friedrich and Wilhelm Schlegel, Franz Bopp, and Friedrich Rückert, among others. Just as divine action occurred through speech, philologists viewed language as the vehicle for religion and, indeed, for salvation. Dominating philology in that era was the romanticist understanding of religion not as a set of propositions whose truth and falsity can be evaluated, but as an ineffable, prelinguistic experience expressed in language and symbol.[9] Languages such as Sanskrit and

[6]Kidd, *The Forging of Races*, 19.

[7]Ibid., 137.

[8]See, for example, the history of racism discussed by Todorov, *On Human Diversity*; Stoler, *Racial Histories*.

[9]Penner, "You Don't Read a Myth for Information."

cultic rituals of Zoroastrians or Buddhists were mined for the ineffable experience they encoded, windows into a putatively deeper level of religiosity, and readily interchangeable with Christian symbols and languages, since they considered the experience, not the symbol, as bearing truth and meaning.

The distinctions between Semitic and Aryan languages made by the pioneering philologist Friedrich Max Müller, a German scholar who became professor at Oxford University, were not only grammatical, but had cultural and religious implications.[10] Semitic languages, according to Max Müller, led to the monotheism of Judaism, Christianity, and Islam and kept them away from myth, which dominated Aryan religion—for him, Aryan meant South Asian. Though repudiating the racist uses of his work, Max Müller invoked a distinction between Semites as rootless wanderers and Aryans as rooted cultivators of nature that subsequently served to reinforce anti-Jewish stereotypes in insidious ways,[11] and his early writings, as Edwin Bryant has pointed out, slid easily from analysis of language to blood: "One has only to pick up any book on the subject from the period to see how effortlessly discourses of language slid into discourses of race from one sentence to the next."[12]

Crucial to Max Müller's analysis, however, was the linguistic determinism of religions. Here his classical liberalism became determinative: Religions varied, and all expressed an original, primitive religiosity common to all humanity, but the highest religious expression was European Protestantism. Christianity was one of the Semitic religions, and Jesus came, Max Müller wrote, to preach "the God of Abraham."[13] While Max Müller's argument attempted to be unifying, it left little room for genuine religious pluralism, and it opened wide the door to wild hypotheses regarding culture and religion often based on tendentious analyses of language structures.[14] Yet he was also sharply critical of the racial determinism set forth by Ernest Renan, a French Catholic scholar of linguistics and religion who wrote extensively on Semitic languages but also on Judaism, Islam, and early Christianity.[15] Renan's insistence that racial characteristics were instinctual, Max Müller wrote, failed to recognize the variety and

---

[10] The German word "Arier" was a translation of the term "Ary," used in the Rigveda, and also used in the Zend Avesta in reference to legendary migrants into Iran and northern India. In the 1830s the German Indologist Christian Lassen used "Aryan" instead of "Indo-Germanic" as having broader historical and geographic connotation. See Benes, "From Indo-Germans to Aryans."

[11] Arvidsson, Aryan Idols, 103.

[12] Bryant, Quest for the Origins of Vedic Culture, 33.

[13] Max Müller, "Semitic Monotheism."

[14] For an excellent study situating Max Müller in the history of philology, see Trautman, Aryans and British India.

[15] Renan, Histoire générale et système comparé des langues sémitiques.

complexity within each race.[16] Semites included more than Jews, and even many Jews rejected the monotheism Renan claimed was racially Semitic.

The search for the uniqueness of each Volk led both to efforts at recovering the ancient, original source of its existence and to distinguishing one Volk from another. Historicism was replaced by mythicization as the undercurrent of linguistic analyses, and the search for the originality of the Volk paralleled the quest for the historical Jesus to uncover the distinctiveness of his religious subjectivity once contextualization of the gospels had eliminated his uniqueness. Racial theory, however, raised a new problem. Responding to the quest for certainty by insisting that religiosity was instinctual, racial theorists asserted that Jesus's religiosity resulted naturally from his Semitic identity, undermining his differentiation from other Jews.

One avenue of response came from Max Müller's contemporary, the Swiss linguist Adolphe Pictet, who developed a field he called "linguistic paleontology," according to which analysis of language could reveal the substance of a culture and its religion.[17] Pictet refined Max Müller's argument: the original Aryans had possessed a unique kind of monotheism, mostly lost over time, but preserved in Zoroastrianism and revived by Christianity.[18] Thus, even if Jesus was a Semite, the Aryan race, Pictet argued, had talents the Hebrews lacked, so that the religion of Christ, infused with "Greek genius" and "Germanic energy," influenced the entire race of European Aryans, who in turn became the most important tools of God's plans for the fate of human beings.[19]

Linguistic studies reinforced proto-nationalist beliefs that a Volk was constituted not only by land and language, but by myth and ritual—that is, culture and religion. The most frequent antinomies were Aryan and Semitic, and the former was linked to Christianity, the latter to Judaism and Islam; as Bruce Lincoln writes, "Conceivably any number of 'others' could have been pressed into service by those who constituted themselves as 'Aryans.' Most often, however, "Semites" were the chosen people, with results that were rarely flattering."[20] Even though "Aryan" emerged as a South Asian linguistic category, it

---

[16] Max Müller, "Semitic Monotheism," 339.

[17] Pictet, Les Origines Indo-Européennes.

[18] The identification of Zoroastrianism with Judaism was argued in the nineteenth century by James Darmesteter, but quickly rejected by other scholars. Zoroastrian influence on Judaism, however, was more widely and persistently accepted. See Winston, "The Iranian Component in the Bible, Apocrypha, and Qumran," 183–216. For a description of Jewish scholarly responses to the argument of Zoroastrian primacy, see Simon-Nahum, La Cité investie.

[19] Pictet, Les Origines Indo-Européennes, 753f.

[20] Lincoln, Theorizing Myth, 74.

was quickly appropriated by groups of Europeans, particularly in Germany, Scandinavia, and central Europe, as a label for the origins and distinctiveness of Germanic culture and religion. Ernest Renan, Emile Burnouf, and Christian Bunsen, writing in the 1850s and '60s, advocated an objective, scientific study of religion untainted by theological commitments, yet described the physical but also cultural markers of the "Semitic race," and identified a transformative process within early Christianity that moved it away from Judaism. Jesus, claimed Renan, professor of Semitics at the Collège de France, may have been born into a Jewish milieu, but he managed to purify himself of Jewish influences and emerge an Aryan. Burnouf, professor at the University of Nancy and the cousin of Renan's teacher, Eugène Burnouf, offered a similar pattern, noting that the gospels gradually aryanized Jesus as the texts moved from Matthew to Luke to John; Christianity was an Aryan religion.[21] Bunsen, a German philologist serving in London as ambassador from Prussia, argued similarly that Christianity arose from Semitic foundations but transcended them to become the religion not of Semites but of Aryans, whom he identified, in contrast to Max Müller, not as South Asian but as Germanic.[22]

The transformation of nineteenth-century scholarly studies of philology into racist and even genocidal rants in the twentieth century also occurred within the theological literature known as the "quest for the historical Jesus." The story of Jesus, his origins within Judaism, and his emergence as the first Christian, served as a template for racializing religious and cultural analyses, especially since the "Semitic" was immediately available as a categorical "other" for the narrative. The drama of the plot, particularly the contrast between Jesus's life as a preacher and his death via crucifixion, also served as a palimpsest for nationalist motifs of suffering, redemption, and triumph. Most important for the racialization of the gospels was the interaction of spirit and body, culture and nature. If, as the racial theorists argued, religion was an expression of race, then Jesus's religious teachings, according to the theologians, were evidence for his racial heritage. If his religiosity was unique, he could be declared racially distinct from the Jews. Moreover, as Galilean came to be synonymous with Aryan, based on negligible evidence regarding the nature of the population of Galilee during the Second Temple period, calling Jesus a Galilean meant calling him an Aryan. As some German nationalists, antisemites, and völkisch thinkers in the early twentieth century increasingly identified their cultural

[21] Burnouf, *The Science of Religions*, trans. Julie Liebe (London: S. Sonnenschein, Lowrey, 1888), cited by Kidd, *The Forging of Races*, 180.

[22] Bunsen, *Outlines of the Philosophy of Universal History*, vol. 2. See also Lincoln, *Theorizing Myth*, 66–67, and Kidd, *The Forging of Races*, 181–82.

roots as Aryan, Jesus could be reclaimed and Christianity—properly purged of positive Jewish references—could be declared acceptable to Germany.

That Jesus was purified of Semitic dross, or that Christianity transcended its Semitic origins to become the religion of Aryans, left open the question of why European Aryans came "to venerate the Semitic Bible as their holy book"[23] rather than the Vedas or the Zoroastrian Avesta, which were considered Aryan in origin. Absence of historical evidence and explanations for Semitic infiltration of a supposed Aryan Europe plagued scholars, who argued through conjecture and probability, above all by dissociating Christian connections with Judaism. Christian theologians insistently divorced Jesus from Judaism on the basis of his religious teachings, which were consistently interpreted as a critique of Judaism rather than an expression of it. What Renan accomplished was to lend a determinist quality to Jesus's distinctiveness from Judaism: no longer simply the result of his considered critique of Judaism, it was predestined by his very being.

ERNEST RENAN AND THE RACIALIZATION OF CHRISTIAN ORIGINS

The vocabulary that proved indispensable to subsequent racializations of Jesus was provided primarily by the work of Renan.[24] His early, prize-winning studies of Semitic languages claimed that monotheism stemmed from a Semitic instinct, while Indo-Europeans were by nature polytheistic.[25] Semitic grammar, he argued, possessed a rigidity that was reflected by the alleged barrenness and monotony of Semitic culture, which, he claimed, lacked philosophy, science, and art. Its monotheism gave rise to absolutism and hindered the growth, creativity, and imagination characteristic of mythology, which he claimed was absent from Judaism and Islam.[26] Renan's distinction between the Semitic, which was identified by its negative qualities, and the Aryan, which he identified as the root of Christianity, grew stronger during the course of his career, from his 1857 *Studies in Religious History* to his five-volume *History of the People of Israel*, published 1888–96, in which language, race, culture, and religion

[23]Kidd, *The Forging of Races*, 174.

[24]On Renan's racism, see Cesaire, *Discourse on Colonialism*, 16, and Todorov, *On Human Diversity*, 106–14.

[25]Renan, *Histoire générale et système comparé des langues sémitiques*, originally written in 1847, when it won the prestigious Prix Volney. See a discussion of the critical responses in Masuzawa, *The Invention of World Religions*, 172 fns 30 and 31.

[26]His views of Islam are expressed beginning in his doctoral thesis, presented in 1852, *Averroes and Averroism*, and continuing in publications on Islam throughout his career.

became interchangeable, Semites (Jews and Arabs) were contrasted with Aryans, and Aryans were identified with Greeks, Indians, and Germans. By his later writings, "Aryan" was functioning as the inclusive term that superseded the "Greek" in the contrast between "Hellenism" and "Hebraism" that had long dominated European intellectual discourse.[27]

It is Renan's *Life of Jesus*, whose 1863 publication was proclaimed "one of the events of the century,"[28] that brought race to the heart of Christian theology and the figure of Jesus. The book created a sensation throughout a Christian Europe disturbed by debates over the legal emancipation of the Jews and increasingly anxious over the presence of Judaism at the heart of Christianity. Further, its republicanism and challenge to Catholic doctrine and religious authority caused Catholic clergy to issue condemnations of the book's blasphemy in depicting Jesus as entirely human and rejecting the miracles; the book was placed on the Church's Index Librorum Prohibitorum. In France Renan was called an atheist, and it was suggested that he was descended from Judas Iscariot and that his book had been subsidized by the Rothschild family.[29] Jews attacked Renan for his depiction of a rigid, stultifying Judaism and his insistence on the superiority of Jesus and Christianity.[30] Thanks to the outrage, the book immediately became a best seller, selling 60,000 copies within a few months, and was translated into thirteen foreign languages.[31] The book was highly romantic as well as blasphemous, a novel rather than a work of scholarship, over which fashionable ladies were said to swoon.[32]

Renan's love of God, Church, and Christianity had long been outstripped by his intimate, deeply emotional relationship with Jesus.[33] In his *Life of Jesus*, which draws primarily from the Gospel of John, long considered historically unreliable, Renan depicted Jesus as a Galilean who underwent a transformation from Jew to Christian, and described Christianity as emerging purified of any Jewishness. Jesus was not God, but was filled with the spirit of God's love and a unique religious consciousness. Renan's Jesus was a romantic, feminine

[27] The role of classical Greece in eighteenth- and nineteenth-century German cultural and scholarly life is described in the classic work by E. M. Butler, *The Tyranny of Greece over Germany*. One of Renan's Jewish critics, Ignaz Goldziher, wrote his book on Jewish mythology to counter those claims: *Der Mythos bei den Hebräern*.

[28] Reardon, *Liberalism and Tradition*, 296; see also Wright, "The Letter and the Spirit."

[29] Mott, *Ernest Renan*, 234.

[30] For two examples of contemporary Jewish critique of Renan, see Sulzbach, *Renan und der Judaismus*, and Levy, *La Synagogue et M. Renan*.

[31] Mott, *Ernest Renan*, 236.

[32] Bierer, "Renan and His Interpreters."

[33] These views, infused with reason and romanticism, are expressed in a group of nine diaries written from June 1845 to June 1846, and discussed by Mott, *Ernest Renan*, 41–64.

figure, similar to his late beloved sister Henriette as he had described her in a book the previous year.[34] For Renan, human nature corresponded to physical nature, so it was in lush, religiously pluralistic Galilee that Jesus flourished and in the dry desert of Jewish Judea that he was killed, in a kind of topographic determinism: "The North [Galilee] alone has made Christianity: Jerusalem, on the contrary, is the true home of that obstinate Judaism which founded by the Pharisees, and fixed by the Talmud, has traversed the Middle Ages and come down to us."[35] Although Renan, in his preface, cited the work of the Jewish historian Abraham Geiger with admiration, his descriptions of Judaism were diametrically opposed to those of Geiger, who identified Jesus as a Pharisee, standing in continuity with the religious traditions of ancient Judaism and offering no original teachings. Jesus's message was particularly appealing to Galilean Jews, Geiger argued, because they tended to have weaker religious educations and were susceptible to apocalyptic fantasies.[36]

For Renan, by contrast, the fact that Jesus was born into a Jewish milieu and practiced Judaism proved his greatness: his ability to overcome his Jewishness. After visiting Jerusalem, Jesus "appears no more as a Jewish reformer, but as a destroyer of Judaism. . . . Jesus was no longer a Jew."[37] Similarly, whereas Christianity originally was "Jewish to the core, over time [it] rid itself of nearly everything it took from the race."[38] Jesus transformed himself into a qualitatively higher being, both physically and spiritually, thereby overcoming his Semitic origins and launching his followers, spiritual Aryans, into the world. The racial component of Renan's analyses was already clear by 1855: "I am the first to recognize," he declared, "that the Semitic race compared to the Indo-European race represents in reality an inferior composition of human nature."[39] Renan did not condemn Judaism for being morally inferior, as did so many theologians in his day, but for being a religion of moral radicalism. That radicalism, he argued, stood at the heart of rabbinic Judaism, which exaggerated religious law into legalism, and impelled the prophets to extremes of condemnation and retribution. Judaism's fanaticism was evidenced by the Jews' hatred of Jesus, and the emergence of Christianity out of it at once

[34] Published privately; later published as *Ma Soeur Henriette* (1895).

[35] Renan, *The Life of Jesus*, 96. See the superb analysis of Renan's geographic determinism by Moxnes, "The Construction of Galilee as a Place for the Historical Jesus."

[36] For a more thorough review of Geiger's understanding of Jesus and his polemic against Renan, see Heschel, *Abraham Geiger and the Jewish Jesus*.

[37] Renan, *The Life of Jesus*, 206–7.

[38] Renan, *Oeuvres completes*, ed. Henriette Psichari (Paris, 1947–61), 5:1142, cited by Olender, *The Languages of Paradise*, 70.

[39] Renan, *Histoire*, 4.

marked both a nullification of Jewish teachings, and also, Renan wrote, the conquest by Judaism of the world via Christianity: "It is through Christianity that Judaism has really conquered the world. Christianity is the masterpiece of Judaism, its glory and the fullness of its evolution."[40] The inner conflict of faith that Renan himself experienced as a Catholic gave rise to contradictory claims; in the same paragraph, he writes that Judaism is "a withered trunk beside one fertile branch," Christianity, and that "Christianity is the masterpiece of Judaism."[41] Yet the degradation of Judaism was not intended to enhance Christianity; ultimately, Renan writes a few pages later, Judaism and Christianity "will both disappear."[42]

The murky future he envisioned for Christianity resulted, no doubt, from Renan's own religious turmoil as a one-time seminarian who was repudiated by the Roman Catholic Church for his writings and in doubt over his own faith. In that, he was similar to the many members of the Institute who also found the doctrines of their church untenable and searched for a new basis for their Christianity. Renan was a French Catholic, while they were German Protestants, but antisemitism was able to function as the common ground for Christians of different varieties and cultural contexts.

Renan established a framework in which early Christianity attempted a repudiation of degenerate Jewish religious influence but did not fully succeed, in part as a metaphor for his own struggle to overcome the Catholic Church and its hierarchy. However, it was not simply anticlericalism that motivated his work. He created a nondoctrinal image of Jesus as a person who freed himself of Jewish influence, and portrayed him with romantic coloration and little concern with textual evidence. Renan's theology, put to political uses never imagined by him, anticipated the Institute's theology: authentic Christianity at its moment of origin had rejected Judaism and now required the purging of Jewish accretions that had accumulated over the centuries to restore Jesus's original and authentic teachings.[43]

Given the rise of nationalist ideologies rooted in myths of blood rather than communities of culture, it mattered what kind of blood flowed in the veins of Jesus. Renan raised the question by denying he posed it: "It is therefore impossible to raise here any question of race, and to seek to ascertain what blood

---

[40] Renan, *Oeuvres complètes,* 5:356, cited by Masuzawa, *The Invention of World Religions,* 177.

[41] Renan, *Histoire,* 5:356.

[42] Renan, *Histoire,* 5:361.

[43] Both Stefan Arvidsson and Tzvetan Todorov argue that Renan was not motivated by antisemitism; I disagree, as did many of Renan's Jewish contemporaries, who wrote passionate denunciations of his presentation of Judaism. See Arvidsson, *Aryan Idols,* 107, and Todorov, *On Human Diversity,* 106–10. For the contrary argument, see Tal, *Christians and Jews in Germany,* 279–89.

flowed into the veins of him who has contributed most to efface the distinction of blood in humanity."[44] The German philologist Paul de Lagarde, by contrast, was more certain that Jesus was no Jew. In his critique of Christianity he argued that while Jesus was not a Jew, Paul, in his Jewish depravity, had judaized Christianity, which now required a liberation of Christianity from Jewish perversions.[45] The penetration of German Protestantism by völkisch ideology in the nineteenth century can be observed with conservative politicians' appeals to Lutheran teachings of throne and altar that substituted Volk for throne, and by a nationalist Protestant religiosity that spoke of a "German God" and "German religious message" identified with Jesus, while blaming Paul for the degeneration of his message.[46]

Was the transformation of Jesus from Jew to Aryan, as Renan describes, a racist argument? Debates over Renan's relationship to racism had already begun in the nineteenth century. He was frequently associated with the race writer Arthur de Gobineau, whose work he knew and cited; indeed, Gobineau complained that Renan had plagiarized from him, and the German race theorist Ludwig Schemann concluded that their work bore strong similarities.[47] Debates over Renan intensified during the years of the Dreyfus Affair; he was identified both as an antisemite and as a Dreyfusard, a monarchist and a republican. Whatever he intended in his use of "race" or his distinctions between Aryans and Semites, he was able to inspire and antagonize both sides equally.

More important, he provided a vocabulary and a logic, couched in the language of romantic pieties, to transform Jesus as a figure who was said to have criticized the Judaism of his day into one whose religiosity was determined by his Aryan identity, an identity he achieved by ridding himself of Jewish dross. Jesus's race emerged, for Renan, not at his birth but through a process of transformation. Renan's identification of the supposed religious and cultural characteristics of particular racial groups was not matched with an insistence on their immutability; Jesus was, after all, capable of transformation. It is commonly and incorrectly assumed that modern racism promotes a notion of immutable essence; biological immutability, it is argued, differentiates modern racism from earlier forms of prejudice.[48] Yet it is the instability of race, not its immutability, that lies at the heart of its invention; as Ann Stoler has concluded from her studies of race and colonialism, "the force of racial discourse

[44] Renan, *The Life of Jesus*, 66–67.
[45] See the discussion in Stern, *The Politics of Cultural Despair*, 40–43.
[46] Wolf, "Volk, Nation, Vaterland," 173.
[47] Schemann, *Gobineaus Rassenwerk*.
[48] Rodrigue, "Totems, Taboos, and Jews," 8.

is precisely in the double-vision it allows, in the fact that it combines notions of fixity and fluidity in ways that are basic to its dynamic."[49] Renan's contribution was an argument of racial purification through mutability: Jesus purged himself of Judaism, as did Christianity, and emerged transformed from Jew to Aryan. Renan's contribution was to convert discomfort over Jesus's Jewishness into a further indication of the Aryan genius, which knew how to transform an odious Hebrew monotheism into a glorious Christianity.[50] The cleverness of Renan's argument was that it made room for viewing monotheism as a divine gift and Christianity as the successful human activity of transforming and enriching it on behalf of the Aryan race. In his interpretation, history became a tool of race, and race was a matter of purification and protection against contamination. More specifically, Aryans were the race superior to Semites but were in danger of doom through a degeneracy contracted via pollution.

THE BUDDHIST JESUS

An alternative approach to viewing Jesus as a Jew who was somehow transformed into an Aryan was to place him entirely outside the context of Judaism. The identification of Aryans as having white skin, blond hair, and blue eyes reinforced Europe as the Aryan homeland.[51] During the 1880s, Eva-Maria Kaffanke has noted, German artistic representations of Jesus began to be criticized for being "too Jewish," so that artists made efforts to find "Oriental" models, at first Muslims and then Germans.[52] Deities from Teutonic myths were described as Jesus figures and their images were used to portray Jesus, and the attributes associated with Jesus were at times applied to figures such as Baldur, a deity in Norse and Teutonic mythology, but in literary sources Jesus was aligned with Buddha.

[49] Stoler, "Racial Histories and Their Regimes of Truth," 198.

[50] Renan, "Des religions de l'antiquité," 821–48. Renan's study of Semitic languages, *Histoire générale et système comparé des langues sémitiques,* argued that Semites lack mythology because they are instinctually monotheistic. Lacking mythology was no longer viewed as a triumph over paganism, but a deficit of religion, which reflected the Semites' intolerant and exclusivist nature, standing in utter opposition to Aryans in religion, language, and ways of thinking. George S. Williamson writes of Renan's views, "Compared to the Aryans, the Semites lacked scientific and artistic originality, had created no national epic or mythology, showed no ability to think abstractly, and could not organize large governments or military campaigns" (*The Longing for Myth in Germany,* 224).

[51] Arvidsson, *Aryan Idols,* 142. The anthropologist at the University of Halle, Theodor Pösche, in *Die Arier,* published in 1878, argued for Aryan racial origins on the border between Belarus and Ukraine, while others claimed Scandinavian origins. Poesche, *Die Arier.*

[52] Kaffanke, *Der deutsche Heiland,* 192. Discussions of Jesus's appearance occurred during the 1930s in scholarly and pseudo-scholarly forums. See Günther, "Wie sah Jesus aus?," 118–19.

As scholars in the nineteenth century came to identify religions that they designated as "Buddhism" and "Hinduism," they claimed to find affinities in those religions with the teachings of Jesus. In the 1880s, the historian of religion Rudolf Seydel, professor at the University of Leipzig, argued that the gospels were loosely based on collections of Buddha legends, evidenced by the numerous parallels in the myths of Jesus's and Buddha's childhoods. His work was frequently cited in efforts to "prove" the Indo-Germanic nature of Jesus.[53]

Connections between Jesus and Indian Buddhism were promoted by German and French romantics, whose fascination with "mother India" led them to see Christianity as derived from India's Aryan mythology.[54] Arthur Schopenhauer, for example, suggested parallels between Jesus and Buddha because both preached asceticism; the faith of Jesus was that of Indian religion and stood in sharp opposition to Judaism, the religion of optimism, not pessimism.[55] For Schopenhauer, the historical Jesus was of no consequence; he was simply a symbol for a negation of the world.[56] And under Schopenhauer's influence, the young Richard Wagner abandoned his play based on the gospels' account of the life of Jesus, written in late 1848, and instead sketched plans in 1856 to present a Buddhist Jesus in an opera entitled *Die Sieger*, based on a Buddhist legend published by the French Orientalist Eugène Burnouf. Wagner's views changed and instead he presented an Aryan redeemer in *Parsifal*, first performed in 1882 and recognized immediately in critical reviews as presenting a Germanic savior at the heart of Christianity in opposition to a Semitic one.[57] During its years of publication from 1878 to 1939, the *Bayreuth Blätter* contained various articles asserting that the God of Christianity was not the God of Judaism, and discussing the racial identity of Jesus; the Aryan Jesus was an idea widely promoted in Bayreuth circles.[58]

---

[53]See bibliography; see also Sysinga, *Indischen Einflüsse auf evangelische Erzählungen*.

[54]See, for example, Constantin-Francois Volney, *Les Ruines* (1791); Jacolliot, *La Bible dans l'Inde* (1876). Similar views were expressed by Johann Gottfried Herder and Frederich Schlegel.

[55]Schopenhauer, *Parerga and Paralipomena*, 2:246; cited by Arvidsson, *Aryan Idols*, 149–50.

[56]For further discussion of Schopenhauer, see Halbfass, *India and Europe*.

[57]See the reviews of Parsifal discussion in Kaffanke, *Der deutsche Heiland*, 161–64. In his 1848 essay on *Jesus of Nazareth*, Wagner argued that Jesus himself repudiated his Jewish lineage. Two years later, in his notorious antisemitic tract, *Das Judentum in der Musik* (*Judaism in Music*), Wagner described Jewishness as a degenerate condition that could easily inflict its damage on non-Jews by judaizing them. Wagner's own belief in Jewish degeneracy necessarily led to his conclusion that Jesus could not have been a Jew, but that Jewish elements had infiltrated Christianity and caused its degeneracy. On Wagner's influence, see Large and Weber, eds., *Wagnerism in European Culture and Politics*.

[58]Hein, *"Es ist viel Hitler in Wagner."*

Since religion was a product of race, and race was a matter of language, culture, and religion, in the nineteenth-century imagination, Jesus's racial identity could be determined by his religion and the language he spoke. Once Jesus was drained of his Jewish identity, his race could be extrapolated from his religious faith, which, under romanticist influence, was variously identified as Buddhist or Zoroastrian, both of which were viewed as Aryan—Indian or Persian. The Buddhist Jesus was received skeptically by scholars of Indian Buddhism,[59] but that did not prevent the link between Buddha and Jesus in the popular imagination. Speculation soon formed a chain of tradition.

Buddha had taked the place of Socrates as the idol of the educated elite, as Leopold von Schröder, professor of Indology at the University of Vienna and member of the Bayreuth circle, noted in 1905, and Jesus had been restyled in accord with the changing fashions.[60] Von Schröder viewed Aryan religion (which was never clearly defined) as a higher form of religiosity than Christianity, and his mild approval of it in 1893 became a more forceful endorsement by 1923, although he retained Judaism within the genealogy that led to both Jesus and Muhammad.[61] Scholars of early Christianity could only speculate about historical channels of influence between Indian religion and Christianity, but this was the heyday of the myth of the Aryan invasion of India, now extended to a myth of Europe's Aryan reclamation via Jesus. For Friedrich Nietzsche, Christianity, rooted in Judaism, undermined earthy, vigorous Aryan religion in its emphasis of values of compassion and submission, but Nietzsche's views were sufficiently slippery that he was not often cited by theologians advocating an Aryan Jesus, especially since he presented Christianity not as the opposition to Judaism but as an extreme form of Judaism.[62] As James Porter notes, while Nietzsche's work reproduces racial discourse, "the racial fantasy of Aryanism reveals itself to be faithfully represented by Nietzsche, in all its essential incoherence."[63] Nietzsche's Buddhist-inflected Jesus led to readings of his book, *Thus Spake Zarathustra*, as an "anti–Sermon on the Mount," in Karl Löwith's term, and some völkisch theologians in the early 1900s,

[59] Windisch, *Buddha's Geburt und die Lehre von der Seelenwanderung*.

[60] See Schröder, "Buddha und unsere Zeit," 216–17, cited by Marchand, "Nazism, 'Orientalism,' and Humanism," in Bialas and Rabinbach, eds., *The Humanities in Nazi Germany*, 267–305. See also Schröder, *Arische Religion*, and *Lebenserinnerungen*.

[61] Schröder, *Reden und Aufsätze*, 87; *Arische Religion*. Schröder, however, granted biblical monotheism a constructive role in infusing Aryan religion with ethics. Poliakov, *The Aryan Myth*, 313. See also Arvidsson, *Aryan Idols*, 162 fn 88. Houston Stewart Chamberlain dedicated his 1905 book, *Arische Weltanschauung*, to his friend von Schröder.

[62] Lincoln, *Theorizing Myth*.

[63] Porter, *Nietzsche and the Philology of the Future*, 283.

including Albert Kalthoff and Max Maurenbrecher, called on pastors to give Zarathustra equal theological presence with Jesus.[64]

The "Jesus of the East" was thus divorced from Judaism, and the appellation also lent a mysterious air to his origins. The East, however, was too remote and too effeminate for some nationalist Germans seeking their cultural roots. Protestantism, after all, was not simply a spiritual matter, but a national project, and a Jesus styled after an Indian Buddha met neither the nationalist nor the militaristic interests of Germany. Instead, starting in the 1890s, Jesus was the figure who combined the immanence of the Aryan of the East with the strength and racial purity of the German as exemplified in Teutonic myths. As the Protestant pastor and völkisch writer Arthur Bonus argued, Jesus marks the transition from God as transcendent to God as immanent within us, and such inner presence of God is proof of Jesus's Germanic identity.[65] Bonus's comment marks another transition: from concern with how God became incarnate in man to the divinization of the human, opening the door to identifying Hitler and also the German Volk as divine or even as personifications of Christ.

The Germanic Jesus

Houston Stewart Chamberlain, himself a Bayreuth enthusiast and son-in-law of Richard Wagner, gave the Aryan Jesus argument its broadest dissemination in his best-selling *Grundlagen des neunzehnten Jahrhunderts* (*Foundations of the Nineteenth Century*), published in 1899.[66] Although without formal training in theology, Chamberlain presented his case with reference to theological literature and in a tone not of insistent certainty but of suggestive probability. He defined Jesus as most likely racially Aryan but Jewish in certain teachings, while Paul was most likely racially Jewish and pagan in his religious thought.

[64]Löwith, "Nietzsche's antichristliche Bergpredigt," 39–50. See Kalthoff, *Zarathustra-Predigten*; Maurenbrecher, *Über Friedrich Nietzsche zum deutschen Evangelium*; see also Abresch, "Enfant terrible im Altar," 18–51.

[65]Bonus, *Von der Germanisierung der Religion*, cited by Lächele, "Germanisierung des Christentums,"165–83.

[66]Chamberlain's book was the "literary fad" of 1900. Field, *Evangelist of Race*, 225.There were three editions in the first year, and a cheap, popular edition printed in 1906 sold 10,000 copies in ten days. Kaiser Wilhelm II was so impressed with the book that he gave 10,000 RM to purchase copies for German libraries. See Tanner, *The Nazi Christ*. In the post–World War I years the book's popularity faded, but under the Nazis it became popular again. Translations followed into English, French, and Czech, and by 1938 there were 24 large printings in Germany.

Chamberlain's "proof" of Jesus's Aryan identity was based on claims that the Galilee's Jewish population had never recovered from the Assyrian invasion of the eighth century BCE, and that as late as the first century CE Galilean Jews were ignorant of Hebrew, were lax in their religious practice, and lived among a racially diverse non-Jewish population: "There is, accordingly, as we see, not the slightest foundation for the supposition that Christ's parents were of Jewish descent."[67]

Chamberlain's Jesus was "the God of the young, vigorous Indo-Europeans" who, he claimed, constituted the majority of Galilee's population at that time. "Was Christ a Jew? . . . In religion and education He was so undoubtedly; in race—in the narrower and real sense of the word 'Jew'—most probably not. . . . That Christ had not a drop of genuinely Jewish blood in his veins . . . is almost a certainty."[68] Jesus's teachings were not those of the Jews, whose goal, Chamberlain wrote, was subjugation of the world. Europe itself was shaped by the struggle between Semites and Indo-Europeans, and while the latter eventually attained military superiority, the Semitic danger continues to lie in its ability to infiltrate and cause degeneracy from within. An example of such infiltration, he writes, is Roman Catholicism; Protestantism, by contrast, represents a return to Indo-European genius. Though severely criticized in theological circles, the book secured a wide popular readership not for any perceived attack on theology, but rather for Chamberlain's effort to anchor German nationalism within a Christianity purified of Jewish dross; Kaiser Wilhelm II was particularly impressed by Chamberlain's efforts.[69]

Unlike Lagarde, who blamed Paul, "a Pharisee from head to toe,"[70] for judaizing and thereby falsifying the teachings of the Aryan Jesus, Chamberlain presented Paul as influenced by Hellenistic mystery religions. Those mystery religions were shaped by Oriental religions, particularly Buddhist and Persian. Finding India at the heart of the Pauline epistles was Chamberlain's way of permitting Christianity's inclusion in the cultural and spiritual revival of Europe through Indo-Aryan teachings. His argument was that Indian religion not only was free of all Semitic taint, but had preserved the original Aryan religious impulse of the German people. That impulse was of pure internal religious experience divorced from doctrine and ritual. Were religious purity to

[67] Chamberlain, *Foundations of the Nineteenth Century*, 1:206. Imitations of Chamberlain's argument flourished; examples include Müller, *Jesus ein Arier*; Hauptmann, *Jesus der Arier*; Steinmetzer, *Jesus und Wir Arier*.

[68] Chamberlain, *Foundations of the Nineteenth Century*, 1:202, 211.

[69] Their relationship is discussed in Field, *Evangelist of Race*, and is documented in their exchange of letters, Chamberlain, *Briefe*.

[70] Field, *Evangelist of Race*, 307.

be joined to racial purity, Chamberlain argued, it would lead the German people to an extraordinary revival as a nation. Recovering the history of Christianity at its inception as an Aryan religion was the key not only to Christian truth but to German national resurgence.

Chamberlain sought not to undermine Christianity but to strengthen faith by "purifying" its theology. The success of Chamberlain's book resulted from its remarkable ability to mediate several tensions. He was able to position Jesus as "not a Jew," to satisfy the antisemitic critics of Jewish-influenced Christianity, while retaining a theological Jesus embodying a supposedly Indo-European religiosity, to satisfy Germany's Christians. His denunciations of Catholics, while offensive to German Catholics, were nothing worse than the Protestant theological critiques of Catholicism in the 1890s and early years of the twentieth century.[71] And his rhetoric concentrated less on the dangers and degeneracy of Jews than on the need for a Germanic spiritual revival based on Germany's inherent cultural superiority. Chamberlain's book followed the contemporary mood, calling for radical, revolutionary spiritual upheaval, even while holding up an ideal of a premodern society. As Geoffrey Field concludes in his biography of Chamberlain, "Sometimes moderate, at others extreme, full of lavish hopes for the supremacy of German culture and brooding fears of subterranean social and moral decay, it fitted anti-Semitism into a more or less coherent nationalist Weltanschauung."[72]

Chamberlain's agenda provoked imitations. In 1905 the former pastor Gustav Frenssen published a wildly popular theological novel, *Hilligenlei*, that reconceptualized the gospels as an allegory of Germany and Jesus as a savior from Schleswig-Holstein, in northern Germany. Once Germany was able to recognize Jesus as German, it would be able to undergo a spiritual rebirth. The novel sold 250,000 copies in Germany between 1905 and 1944, and was translated into forty languages, provoking numerous discussions in theological periodicals.[73] In 1936 Frenssen published a polemical tract, *Der Glaube der Nordmark*, declaring Christian faith medieval and withered.[74] Advocating a rejection of Christianity in favor of paganism, he described God as an eternal power that heals, as the power within the "All," beyond understanding. Between

---

[71] Field notes that Catholic reviewers objected strongly to his attacks on Catholicism, while Protestants were largely silent, and neither objected to his antisemitism; the liberal Protestant journal, *Die christliche Welt*, praised the book, including its racism. See Field, *Evangelist of Race*, 225f, 240.

[72] Field, *Evangelist of Race*, 276.

[73] Frenssen became one of Germany's best-known authors of colonialist literature. See Lächele, "Germanisiertes Christentum," 107–9; and "'Germanisches' Christentum," 27–46.

[74] The 1938 edition notes that 70,000 copies had been sold.

the success of Chamberlain's tract and Frenssen's novel, it is unlikely that many literate Germans, on the eve of World War I, would have been unaware of the claim that Jesus was not a Jew.

Völkisch Movements and Their Jesus

Redefining Jesus was not a trend that stood in isolation from the practice of religion, but rather was integral to the widespread völkisch religious movements that arose between 1870 and 1945 in Germany, rooted in teachings of race and nationalism. Many of these movements came into being outside of the institutional churches, but völkisch ideology could be found within the Protestant church as well; each was marked by its questioning of the suitability of Christianity for Germany. Some popularized Teutonic and Norse myths as alternatives to Christianity, while others challenged the doctrinal formulations of the church, criticizing its clericalism and hierarchy as well as the alleged Jewishness of its theology. In 1913, the writer Adolf Bartels, a major ideologue of the völkisch movement who later became a member of the Institute, coined the slogan, "More Germanic Christianity, less Jewish Christianity."[75] The phrase was sufficiently ambiguous to allow a range of definitions of precisely what constituted the "Jewish" in the Christian.

The völkisch movement was brought into the church by individual pastors, calling for a "Germanized" Christianity that would excise the Old Testament and proclaim Jesus as an Aryan fighting against Jewish influence. One of the strongest ideological fathers of the effort was Friedrich Andersen, a pastor in Schleswig-Holstein.[76] Strongly influenced by Chamberlain,[77] Andersen called for a new, critical evaluation of the place of the Old Testament in Christianity in his 1907 tract, *Anticlericus*. The tract presents the history of Christianity as a conflict between clericalism (which he calls "Jewish") and "true" Christianity (the teachings of Jesus). His pamphlet was initially not well received by the church of Schleswig-Holstein, which took disciplinary steps against him, though not for the substance of his arguments but for presenting his theses in public without permission.[78] During World War I, Andersen's antisemitism rose dramatically, and he began blaming the Jews for the war and calling Judaism a world danger. Christianity had to be Germanized and Jesus aryanized as

[75] Puschner, "One People, One God, One Reich," 22.

[76] For a biographical introduction to Andersen, see Gisela Siems, "Pastor Friedrich Andersen," 13–34. Siems does not discuss Andersen's antisemitism.

[77] On Chamberlain's influence on Andersen, see Chatellier, "Wagnerismus in der Kaiserzeit," 887.

[78] Linck, "Vor zersetzendem jüdischen Einfluss bewahren," 135.

a defense against Judaism, he argued. The Old Testament could not possibly have been the heritage of Jesus; it had to be eliminated. "Why can a lovely flower not grow on a heap of dung?" he asked rhetorically.[79] In 1917 Andersen, in collaboration with three völkisch writers, published "Ninety-Five Theses for Reshaping the Church,"[80] which aroused not a word of protest from church officials.[81] Four years later, the four authors of this tract founded the Bund für deutsche Kirche (League for a German Church), the first formal organization within the church to promote a Germanic Christianity. The League brought the völkisch movement into the church, daring the church to respond to a growing cultural and political movement. The völkisch mood was both a rebellion against the church and its authorities and doctrines, and an excitement over being the newly emerging theological avant-garde.

In his best-known tract, *Der deutsche Heiland*, published in 1921, Andersen called for a German Christianity that would proclaim a pure teaching of salvation without "Jewish muddiness" ("jüdischer Trübung"). In 1923 he rejected the Old Testament altogether,[82] citing the authority of the most distinguished historian of early Christianity of the time, Adolf von Harnack, who himself had written that the elimination of the Old Testament from the Christian canon would complete Luther's Reformation.[83] Andersen was no mere kook; Otto Baumgarten, professor of theology at the University of Kiel, took him seriously enough to publish a pamphlet in 1926, *Kreuz und Hakenkreuz* (*Cross and Swastika*), in which he expressed, in calm, moderate tones, his differences with Andersen's views.[84]

THE LEAGUE FOR A GERMAN CHURCH IN THE WEIMAR ERA

Andersen's impact also extended to the world of politics. In 1924, he was elected as representative to the Flensburg city council under the "Völkisch-Soziale Block," a new political party that was a precursor to the Nazi Party (National-sozialistische Deutsche Arbeistpartei, NSDAP), and he used his political

---

[79]"Warum kann nicht eine schöne Blume gerade auf einem Misthaufen wachsen?" Friedrich Andersen, *Der deutsche Heiland* (1923), cited by Kraus, "Die evangelische Kirche," 254.

[80]Andersen, *Deutschchristentum auf rein-evangelischer Grundlage: 95 Leitsätze zum Reformationsfest*. Other signatories to the pamphlet included Adolf Bartels (Weimar), Ernst Katzer (Dresden), and Hans Paul Freiherr von Wolzogen (Bayreuth). Note that Bartels and von Wolzogen later became involved in the Institute.

[81]Linck, "Vor zersetzendem jüdischen Einfluss bewahren," 136.

[82]Andersen, *Das alte Testament—eine "Heilige Schrift"?*

[83]Harnack, *Marcion*, 217.

[84]Otto Baumgarten, *Kreuz und Hakenkreuz* (1926); cited by Linck, "Epilog," 51.

platform to attack the church for missionizing Jews, who, he insisted, should not be allowed in the church. In response to this political pressure, the synod of the Schleswig-Holstein church endorsed his efforts to combat the "degenerate Jewish influence" ("zersetzenden jüdischen Einfluss").[85] In 1925, Andersen took his political involvement one step further by joining the NSDAP. By 1928, at the age of 68, Andersen had become a propaganda orator at NSDAP rallies.

That calling Jesus an Aryan had political implications did not go unnoticed among Jewish observers. In 1928 a volume of Jewish responses to Christian anti-Jewish polemics was published in Hebrew that included this pungent observation:

> The antisemitic writers in Germany are trying to aryanize Jesus [la'asot et Yeshu le-ari]. Wishing to deprive the Jews of the Semitic affiliation of Jesus, they claim that his father was Panthera, a Roman soldier. . . . Were this their worse slander, we would happily forgive this insult; we are not at all proud of Jesus. On the contrary, we are enraged by his attempt to align himself with the Kingdom of David, and his wish to be our messiah. Indeed, there is now a sect in Germany, headed by General Ludendorff, which is trying to distance itself from Jesus, saying that it is improper for the great and worthy German nation to kneel down before a disgusting Jewish deity. To them we say: all the more power to you, just do not invoke another World War.[86]

The League's influence on the church expanded during the Weimar years, winning seats in the synods of Thuringia and the Old Prussian Union.[87] The presence within church synods of a theological movement that had earlier been on the fringe of respectable, mainstream church discourse decreased the sense of the strangeness of the League's ideas and encouraged efforts of accommodation.[88] While the League's theological challenges to the Old Testament and the

---

[85] Linck, "Vor zersetzendem jüdischen Einfluss bewahren," 137.

[86] Eisenstein, *Ozar Vikuhim*. Erich and Mathilde Ludendorff led a religious movement in Germany that combined Christian and Indian motifs. The gospel authors, the Ludendorffs argued, had stolen Indian legends, altered them with Jewish ideas, replacing Aryan princes and saviors, Krishna and Buddha, with Jesus, who was one of many revolutionaries in first-century Palestine. See Ludendorff, *Aus der Gotterkenntnis meiner Werke*, 29. The movement's popularity was enhanced by Erich Ludendorff's renown as a German general during World War I.

[87] In the church synod election of 1925, the League won twenty seats within the Old Prussian Union—though based on a very small voter turnout of 5–10 percent—and went on to sponsor racial measures in the synods of 1925 and 1927. In 1925 it formed an alliance with ten other Germanic Christian groups, and the following year it won three seats in the synod of the Thuringian Landeskirche.

[88] Borg, *The Old-Prussian Church*, 188.

Jewishness of Jesus continued to be seen as extreme, its nationalism could be affirmed unhesitatingly. The theological resistance to the League and to völkisch ideas was weak at best, as the conservative leadership of the church "tended to treat Germanic Christianity more as an excessive nationalism to be tolerated than as a heresy to be condemned."[89] In his heyday, League leader Friedrich Andersen attracted no stronger criticism from church officials than a statement by the church of Kiel, objecting to the "one-sidedness" of his teachings.[90]

Elsewhere in Germany, church synods faced similar efforts. At a 1932 synod in Brandenburg, Johannes Kunz, a pastor in Stollberg, called for the church to cease giving the Old Testament a central role in sermons, liturgy, and the hymnal, and proposed changing certain Hebrew terms to German—instead of Amen, "Das walte Gott" ("this God dispenses")—and eliminating references to cherubim, seraphim, zeva'ot, Zion, biblical Jerusalem, Israel, and the God of Jacob; the proposal was rejected by a vote of 180 to 6.[91]

The völkisch movement's emphasis on this world, rather than the afterlife, led to a focus on the body and on the practice of Christianity, reinforcing the affinity of völkisch religion for racial conceptions. Völkisch leaders criticized conventional Christianity for its otherworldly concerns and its global missionizing, insisting that the central religious concern for German Christians should be the creation of God's kingdom on earth.[92] The holiness of that kingdom could only be assured through a racial purification. Yet race, according to the völkisch Christians, was manifest not only in the body, but, just as importantly, in the soul. Character, personality, culture, and spirituality were all products of a racially impregnated soul, and it was through expressions of the soul that racial identity could be detected, as much as through the shape of the head or torso. Writing in 1933, Adolf Heger insisted that Aryan Germans were not only physically superior, but spiritually superior as well, as manifest in their sense of community as well as their religious beliefs. "Inwardness, earnestness, faithfulness [and] manly courage" were signs of Germanic essence.[93] By the early 1930s, books for children's Christian education were calling Jesus a "hero" and a "fighter" for Germany.[94]

---

[89] Ibid., 193.

[90] Thalmann, "Die Schwäche des Kulturprotestantismus," 159.

[91] Kunz, Die deutsche Schule und das Alte Testament, 11.

[92] Puschner, "One People, One God, One Reich," 21.

[93] Adolf Heger, Deutsches Wesen und Christentum: Schriften der Glaubensbewegung "Deutsche Christen" in Niedersachsen (Bordesholm in Holstein: Heliad Verlag, 1933), 2, cited by Kleine, "Religion im Dienste," 5.

[94] Erbt, "Ein nordisches Jesusbild," 308f; Spanuth, Das Leben Jesu; Cehak, ed., Jesus, der Künder und Kämpfer Gottes.

The New Ethics

On the political level, the Aryan Jesus was a symbol through which Germans could reimagine themselves and their cultural foundations. On the ethical level, the Aryan Jesus was used to create justifications for German atrocities, starting after World War I, creating a new kind of "conscience" even before Hitler came to power.[95] Although Germany emerged from World War I in good economic condition, compared to its neighbors to the east and west, myths immediately began to spread that it had been victimized by its antagonists. The Great War was interpreted as a Christian event, a horrific crucifixion of Germany; Hitler was later described as offering Germany its "resurrection." Although Germany was responsible for appalling atrocities during the war and also in its African colonies, some German theologians reversed that reality, instead describing German soldiers as the victims of Russian vengeance, in order to maintain the identification of Germany with Christ. That vengeance, in turn, was blamed on the God of the Old Testament, who, lacking compassion, viewed mass death with indifference. Old and New Testaments were thus kept as distinct and opposing religions.

Above all, the Aryan Jesus was emblematic of racial theology and legitimated the use of racism to reconstruct Christian origins and teachings as well as the use of Christianity to justify racist oppression and murder.[96] War atrocities against women, children, and prisoners of war were said to characterize Semitic behavior, exemplified by Old Testament passages such as Joshua 6:21. By the time of the Weimar Republic, the church had come to see its duty as representing the interests of the nation against the democratic politics of the state.[97] In a similar projection, members of the League described Jews as violent people just as violence against Jews was increasing during the Weimar era.[98] Kurd Niedlich, a Berlin high school teacher and cofounder of the League, wrote that Jesus had waged "a life and death struggle against the Jewish spirit."[99] Jesus should be recognized as Nordic "Führer" in contrast to the Jewish "Yahwe," and

[95] In arguing that the völkisch theologians anticipated the Nazis on the question of reformulating the conscience, I hope to adumbrate the important argument put forth by Koonz, *The Nazi Conscience* .

[96] Eifer, *Jehovah und seine Auserwählten*, 15; see also Eifer, *Die Rache Jehovahs*.

[97] Wolf, "Volk, Nation, Vaterland," 174.

[98] Hecht, *Deutsche Juden und Antisemitismus*.

[99] Joachim Kurd Niedlich (1884–1928), who had been a close friend of the notorious antisemite Theodor Fritsch, and wrote extensively on Germanic mythology. Sievers, "Völkische Märcheninterpretationen," 91–110; Sievers, "Völkischer Heimatschutz" (part I), 36. Niedlich's early death

Niedlich called for eliminating Semitic elements from Christianity, including the Old Testament, as foreign to Germans.[100] Germanic myths and folktales and Teutonic rituals were to be combined with Christian elements, and Niedlich saw the Germanic prefiguring and paralleling the Christian: Jesus's birth and the birth of the sun take place on the same day; both Jesus and German folktales warn of wolves in sheep's clothing.[101] Indeed, he argued, Germans possessed a special "racial soul" ("Volksseele") that allowed a singular "marriage of Christianity and Germanness."[102] Such parallels bore ethical consequences; Jesus was not the lamb of God, reassuring the meek that they would inherit. Reflecting the new political and religious ethos, Niedlich identified Grimm's gruesome fairy tale of the "Twelve Brothers" as a sister gospel that God had given to the Germans, one better suited to militarism and murder.

After complaints in the 1880s that Jesus looked too Jewish, artists turned to other models. Yet the transformation was not only of his physiognomy, but his political meaning for Germans. During and after World War I, veterans flocked to the famous Isenheim altar, brought temporarily from a church in Colmar to Munich in 1917, and its depiction of Christ's crucifixion was interpreted as an uncanny representation of the contemporary postwar agony, meaningful only to Germans who could understand the Nordic message of the artist, Matthias Grünewald.[103] Yet agony and crucifixion were unheroic and thus unsuitable to the Nazi movement. Later, at the 1937 Nazi exhibit of Degenerate Art, such depictions of Christ's anguish on the cross were displayed as examples of the unacceptable.[104] Instead, Christ had to become a heroic, aggressive, manly warrior whose life was the focus, not his death. Artistic representations of Jesus increasingly aryanized his appearance and portrayed him in heroic poses, and archeological finds were interpreted as demonstrating his purported "Nordic" appearance.[105] At the very least, his death had to be interpreted

---

precluded his involvement in Nazi-era German Christian activities, but his influence on the church was exerted through his writings, especially those on religious pedagogy; through his close relationships with German Christian leaders Kurt Freitag and Reinhold Krause; and through the League's work with the German Christian movement in the context of the church elections of 1932, as described by Olaf Kühl-Freudenstein (Kühl-Freudenstein, *Evangelische Religionspädagogik*).

[100] Niedlich, *Jahwe ode Jesus?*

[101] Niedlich, *Das Mythenbuch*. 29, cited by Sievers, "Völkische Märcheninterpretationen," 105.

[102] Sievers, "Völkische Märcheninterpretationen," 105–6.

[103] Stieglitz, "The Reproduction of Agony," 87–103.

[104] At the entry of the exhibit stood a wooden crucifix by Ludwig Gies, taken from the Lübeck cathedral; also displayed was Emil Nolde's *Life of Christ*, which shows a Christ in physical agony.

[105] Franz Wolter, *Wie sah Christus aus?* ((1930). See the discussion of the book by Günther, "Wie sah Christus aus?," 118–19. The term "Nordic" came into vogue in the 1920s and was used interchangeably with Aryan, greatly popularized by Günther, *Rassenkunde des deutschen Volkes*. See

as the immediate prelude to a grand resurrection, as in Grundmann's 1940 interpretation of the Isenheimer altar.[106] Jesus received his Nazi depiction in a church built in a Frankfurt am Main suburb in 1935, one of very few built during the Third Reich. A huge wall mural in the sanctuary, facing the congregation, depicts a blond, handsome, muscular Jesus, gazing upward, hanging on the cross. Jesus has a heroic expression, and is flanked on his left by a Roman soldier on a horse and on his right by a hideous Jew on a cross portrayed in the style of *Der Stürmer*: long black hair, a prominent nose, and an ugly face and body.[107] Other churches, too, decorated themselves with Nazi symbols, placing a swastika on the altar or, after 1936, when the Nazi Party forbade such uses of its symbols, painting a cross inside a wreath with the German Christian motto, "Germany is our Task, Christ is our Strength" ("Deutschland ist unsere Aufgabe, Christus ist unsere Kraft"). In one Thuringian church, the cross was moved to the side and pictures of Hitler and Luther were placed at the front of the sanctuary. Another church painted a young man wearing a Hitler Youth uniform on its ceiling.[108]

That Jesus's Aryan identity had not been previously recognized was a further staple in the arsenal of arguments: it was an additional sign of the Jews' depravity in suppressing Christian knowledge. As German theologians revised the New Testament to demonstrate that Jesus was not a Jew but an Aryan, they argued that they were recapturing the authentic gospel that had been falsified by the Jews. Writing in 1936, Martin Slotty, a pastor, blamed Paul for having transformed Christianity into a Jewish religion, and blamed all of the major theologians of the church, from Augustine to Luther, for failing to liberate Christianity from Judaism.[109] Once Judaism had entered Christianity's theological door, Jews had achieved world rule not through weapons, but through "the race- and species-negating, disempowering Pauline-Christian teachings of superstition," as Ernst Klein described it in 1939.[110] On the other hand, Paul was defended by Emanuel Hirsch, one of Germany's most prominent theologians, on the grounds that, properly understood, he was Judaism's greatest

---

Field, "Nordic Racism," 523–40. On some examples of the biases inherent in scholarly interpretation of sculpture of Jews, see Broshi, "How to Recognize a Jew," 81–84.

[106] Grundmann, "Der Isenheimer Altar," 129–35.

[107] The mural was painted by Hans Kohl (1897–1990) for the Lutherkirche of Offenbach-Bieber, one of the few churches built during the Third Reich; the church was dedicated on July 28, 1935. Today its pulpit is engraved with the Hebrew word, "shalom."

[108] The first church was in Untermassfeld, the second in Bad Frankenhausen. Personal communication, Pastor Heinz Koch, February 1993.

[109] Slotty, *Kann die deutsche Christenheit das Alte Testament preisgeben?*, 7.

[110] Klein, *Der Tor von Nazareth*, 96.

Figure 1.1. Wall mural, Luther Kirche in Offenbach-Biber.

Figure 1.2. Crucifixion (detail, wall mural).

opponent.[111] Even Paul knew that Jews displeased God and were repulsive to all people, wrote Otto Borchert, a pastor in Hanover, in 1934; anti-Judaism was itself Pauline. Jews, Borchert wrote, are godless and wish to destroy all religions.[112]

When Renan described Jesus emerging from Judaism to become an Aryan, he spoke in the language of German romanticism that allowed him to appropriate feminine images to signal Jesus's masculinity. The tenderness of Jesus was a mark of his lofty spiritual greatness. By the 1920s and '30s, however, the masculinity of Jesus was expressed in very different language, as a heroic fighter. The pastor Immanuel Berthold Schairer was one of many writers who denounced the emasculating nature of the traditional Jesus, and insisted that

[111]Hirsch, "Lebt Paulus?," *Kommende Kirche* 3 (January 21, 1940), cited by Heinonen, *Anpassung und Identität*, 225.

[112]Borchert, *Das Volk und der Christ*, 49.

Figure 1.3. Resurrection (detail, wall mural).

the genuine Jesus would harden the German people.[113] The Aryan Jesus was now the male figure who required rescuing from the effeminizations of Judaism. In 1936, for example, Reich Bishop Ludwig Müller published a revised, Germanized version of the "Sermon on the Mount" that transformed its gentle message into a militaristic, warrior-like tract. Matthew 5:4–5 became: "Happy is he who bears his sufferings like a man; he will find the strength never to despair without courage. Happy is he who is always a good comrade; he will make his way in the world."[114] The aryanization of Jesus also meant a shift in the theological understanding of masculinity, from the pure-hearted Jesus of Renan to a tough, hard-hearted Jesus.

[113] Schairer, *Volk, Blut, Gott*.
[114] Müller, *Deutsche Gottesworte*.

Figure 1.4. A Jew on cross (detail, wall mural).

If Jewishness had to be removed from Christianity, the presence of baptized Jews in the church was also problematic. Missionary activity directed to Jews was challenged by some church leaders, who saw in it a threat of miscegenation. By 1930, hostility toward missionizing had grown to the point that regional churches began reducing their financial subventions for it.[115] Complaints against converting Jews were filed with local churches throughout the

[115] Clark, *The Politics of Conversion*, 286.

1930s, coming both from Nazi officials and lay people: "just as a pig remains a pig, even if you put it in a horse's stall, so a Jew still remains a Jew, even if he is baptized," declared a 1933 article in the journal *Arische Rundschau*.[116] Jewish requests for baptism continued, and when the Reich did not outlaw the practice,[117] those regional churches controlled by the German Christians ultimately took their own action by firing non-Aryan church employees, forbidding non-Aryan Christians from attending church services, and denying pastoral care to baptized Jews.

Jews were not only pigs, they were defined as standing outside the moral constraints of Christianity, and their religion was said not to have its own moral compass. The laws and commands of Judaism, Grundmann argued, did not bear the moral weight of the religion of the heart, Christianity, and the essential difference of Jesus was his intimacy with God as father that created in him a morality of the heart.[118] According to several Institute publications, Judaism was a violent religion, and Jews were commanded to destroy Jesus and all who followed him. Grundmann, for example, argued that Jews had forcibly circumcised non-Jews in the Galilee during the Hasmonean era, a claim based on a tendentious reading of a verse in 1 Maccabees.[119] Such definitions of Jews as threatening to non-Jews are typical of the racism that permeates situations of genocide, massacre, and colonialism: by defining the target as immoral, the perpetrators permit themselves to violate their own moral norms (as had already been well-exercised in Germany's colonial exploits in Africa). That permission may be defined after the atrocities have already occurred, as Isabel Hull demonstrates, as an ex post facto justification for action.[120] Within the Institute's theology, antisemitism became the basis for a new ethics as well as a radically revised history and theology of Christianity.

ASSYRIOLOGY AND THE GALILEE

The search for the Aryan roots of Christianity was not limited to demagogues and pastors, but was part of the agenda of scholars as well. Even the rather abstruse, scholarly field of Assyriology became an arena for discussing the

---

[116] "Schluss mit den Judentaufen," *Arische Rundschau* (1933); EZA 1/C3/170 vol. 2, fol. 19; cited by Clark, *The Politics of Conversion*, 291.

[117] By 1936, the only remaining official mission to the Jews was in Berlin; it closed in 1941 by Gestapo action. See Clark, *The Politics of Conversion*, 301–2.

[118] Grundmann, *Die Gotteskindschaft in der Geschichte Jesu*.

[119] That point will be discussed further in chapter 3.

[120] Hull, *Absolute Destruction*.

Aryan Jesus by establishing the nature of the population of Galilee following the Assyrian conquest in the eighth century BCE. The fantasized differentiation between Gentile and Jewish populations of Galilee and Judea has long been used to signal a distinction between the teachings of Jesus as Galilean and Judaism. Such geographic theology received its greatest impetus from Renan and subsequent surveyors of Palestine who described a kind of "golden age" of Galilee during the lifetime of Jesus. Scholars, starting with Emil Schürer in the 1870s, speculated on the non-Jewish composition of Galilee's mixed population following the Assyrian conquests of the eighth century BCE.[121] Allusions in texts of antiquity to "Galil HaGoyim" ("Galilee of the nations," Isaiah 8:23), to Galilean laxity of religious observance and knowledge of Torah (Palestinian Talmud, Shabbat 16:8; 15d), and to an absence of prophets arising from Galilee (John 7:52) were used to substantiate the claim that in Jesus's own lifetime, Galilee was an essentially Gentile region, with Jews living there as a minority.[122] Galileans who were Jews were said by some modern scholars not to have been ethnically Jewish, but to have been forcibly converted under Aristobulus I (104–103 BCE), a point underscored by Schürer, though based on weak and uncorroborated evidence from 1 Maccabees and Josephus.[123] Central to the argument was the claim that the Galileans and the Judeans stood in opposition to each other on a host of issues, religious and political, and that the Galilean Jews did not feel themselves bound by the authority of the Jewish leaders who controlled the Jerusalem Temple and regulated the observance of Jewish law.

Support for the depiction of Galilee, particularly in Chamberlain's work, was taken from the survey of Jewish history by the nineteenth-century German-Jewish historian Heinrich Graetz, who presented the Galilean Jews as ignorant and less pious than the Jews of Judea.[124] His evidence, in turn, was based on some rabbinic comments disparaging the Galilean Jews as "ignoramuses" ("amei ha'aretz"), and Graetz used it as an excuse to blame their ignorance for their alleged gullibility regarding claims to miracles, apocalyptic fantasies, and false messiahs, including Jesus. Graetz, in turn, was heavily cited

---

[121] Emil Schürer, *The History of the Jewish People in the Age of Jesus Christ*, rev. and ed. Geza Vermes and Fergus Millar, 3 vols. (Edinburgh: T&T Clark, 1973–87), I:142, 216–18; II:7–10; cited by Chancey, *Myth of a Gentile Galilee*, 15.

[122] Schürer, *History*, I:142; cf. II:8; cited by Chancey, *Myth of a Gentile Galilee*, 37.

[123] Schürer, *History*, I:216–18; II:7–10; cited by Chancey, *Myth of a Gentile Galilee*, 42.

[124] In his chapter on "The Revelation of Christ," (*Foundations of the Nineteenth Century*, 1:174–250), Chamberlain cites extensively from Heinrich Graetz, *Volkstümliche Geschichte der Juden* (Leipzig: Oskar Leiner, 1888–89). Graetz's depiction of Galilee is more fully drawn in a chapter first included in the second edition of his eleven-volume *History of the Jews*; see Graetz, *Geschichte der Juden*, vol. 3, chapter 11. For further discussion of this point, see Heschel, *Abraham Geiger and the Jewish Jesus*, 136.

by Chamberlain in his depiction of Galilee, though Graetz never claimed an Aryan identity to Galilee's population.

That the population of Galilee was at least partially Aryan—and that Jesus descended from one of those racially Aryan families—stemmed from an argument based on construal, not evidence. That "foreign populations" settled in Galilee following the Assyrian conquests was attested by primary sources, foremost Josephus, but in identifying those foreign colonizers as Aryan, even the most learned scholars turned to myth-making. At the Third International Congress for the History of Religions, in 1908, the distinguished Assyriologist Paul Haupt, Director of the Oriental Seminary of the Johns Hopkins University, who had been a student of Friedrich Delitzsch, professor at the University of Leipzig and Germany's leading Assyriologist, delivered a lecture on "The Aryan Ancestry of Jesus." Haupt argued that "Bethlehem" was derived from an old Assyrian name for the capital of Galilee, Nazareth, so that Jesus was a born Galilean. That Galilee was free of Jews after its conquest by the Assyrians was a claim well known to scholars, but Haupt asserts, without citing any evidence, that the Assyrians had "sent Assyrian colonists to Galilee."[125] "Many of the Assyrian colonists settled in Galilee were Aryans (Iranians)," according to Haupt, so that "it is by no means certain that Jesus of Nazareth and His first disciples were Jews by race; they may have been Aryans."[126] That support for the Aryan Jesus argument could come from a scholar of Haupt's rank indicates the extent to which scholars of high international standing could lend their prestige in support of fraudulent claims at an international scientific meeting without arousing protest.

What the primary sources indicate is the deportation of the Israelite population by the Assyrians, attested in cuneiform annals; they say nothing about an Assyrian effort to repopulate Galilee with Assyrian "Aryans." A colonization under Persian rule occurred, but there is no evidence of who was involved. The first book of the Maccabees (1 Maccabees 5:9–23) indicates that the small Jewish population was evacuated to Jerusalem by Simon Maccabee during the Seleucid rule, around 165 BCE, though recent interpretation suggests that those were Jews from the coastal areas of Galilee and that the transfer to Jerusalem may have been mythic, written to suggest the Maccabees' fulfillment of biblical promises of an ingathering.[127]

Other Assyriologists attempted to redefine Jesus as a Babylonian myth. Peter Jensen, professor at the University of Marburg, published a pamphlet in 1909

[125] Haupt, "The Aryan Ancestry of Jesus," 203.
[126] Haupt, "The Ethnology of Galilee."
[127] Chancey, *Myth of a Gentile Galilee*, 41.

asserting that Moses, Jesus, and Paul were three variants of Babylonian divinities.[128] A year later he published another pamphlet, questioning the reliability of sources for Jesus's life as related in the gospels, and suggesting it was contrived along the lines of hero myths such as the Gilgamesh epic.[129] Jensen wanted to "prove" that the Gilgamesh epic shaped world literature from the Old Testament to Islamic, Egyptian, Indian, Teutonic, and other mythic literatures.[130] The following year Heinrich Zimmern, director of the Semitics Institute at the University of Leipzig, published material from Babylonian sources in an attempt to prove that the "Jesus myth" was derived from the legends of the Babylonian god Bel-Merodach.[131]

JESUS AS GALILEAN SON OF MAN, NOT MESSIAH

The Galilean Jesus argument entered the work of university theologians in the 1920s and '30s who were rejecting supernatural miracles and established Christian dogma in favor of a historical approach to scriptures, and many were influenced by the methods of the History of Religions school. As historians, they rejected the binding nature of church doctrine and viewed texts as products of the cultural and religious beliefs of their era; the canonicity of texts was irrelevant to their weight as historical evidence for the circumstances of Christianity's origins. Given that all German clergy, Protestant and Catholic, were trained at university theological faculties, such arguments were not limited to a rarified ivory tower, but were translated through the pulpit to a mass audience.

William Wrede, professor of New Testament at the University of Breslau and one of the architects of the History of Religions school, insisted that messianic claims about Jesus were theological constructs of the gospel authors and not reliable evidence for Jesus's own beliefs.[132] That, in turn, reinforced the difference between the faith of Jesus and that of the gospel authors, and the possibility of sharp differences among them, or at least of alterations of Jesus's message in the gospels. Since some gospel authors were thought to have been Jews, or at least living in a Jewish cultural milieu, the History of Religions methods were useful to Grundmann, among others, in claiming that Jesus was

---

[128] Jensen, *Moses, Jesus, Paulus.*

[129] Jensen, *Hat der Jesus der Evangelien wirklich gelebt?*, especially 18–25.

[130] Jensen, *Das Gilgamesch-Epos in der Weltliteratur*, vols. 1 and 2.

[131] Zimmern, *Zum Streit um die "Christusmythe."*

[132] Wrede, *Das Messiasgeheimnis in den Evangelien.*

an Aryan whose views were distorted by the Jewish authors of the gospels. Theologians were confident of historicism's ability to identify with accuracy the strata of the gospels and the nature of Jesus's personality and message independent of the strictures of doctrine and church discipline. But theological scholarship was also shaped by contemporary politics, and the story of Jesus's struggle with the Jews became at times an allegory for Germany's so-called Jewish question.

Given the central role of eschatology in Jesus's teachings, a crucial first question was whether he understood himself to be the promised messiah of the Jews. That Jesus was not the messiah anticipated in Jewish scriptures was a prominent claim in the work of the History of Religions school. Gustav Dalman, for example, argued in 1898 that the "son of God" was not a conventional messianic title in pre-Christian Judaism, based on his analysis of Jewish biblical and rabbinic texts.[133] A few years later, Paul Fiebig had gathered rabbinic references to "man" in order to clarify the meaning of Jesus's use of "son of man," in contrast to "messiah."[134] Wilhelm Bousset, professor of New Testament at the University of Göttingen and one of the pioneers of the History of Religions school, lent his scholarly prestige to the argument that that phrase "son of man," though it first appears in the Old Testament, was not found or even anticipated as a formal title within Judaism. In *Die Religion des Judentums*, first published in 1903, Bousset argued that "son of man" stemmed from a syncretistic religious milieu within "Hellenism"—a category he employed to serve as a kind of witch's brew of religious notions from India, Persia, Greece—but not from Jews. That brew, which gave rise to early Christianity, was said to have gained an eschatological valence through contact with Judaism, but little more.

Other New Testament scholars were also drawn to an Orientalist brew of religions to explain major facets of early Christianity, but the one religion that was never part of that Orient was Judaism. In the hands of History of Religions scholars, the Orient interrupted the direct transmission of Judaism to Christianity and provided a genealogy for Germany and its putative Aryan origins. The originality of Jesus's faith was restored by removing it from the context of Judaism, its prophets and rabbis, and presenting him instead as "a heroic figure with a daring faith in God that led him to stand uncompromisingly against the false piety of his day."[135] Instead, Judaism was portrayed by

---

[133] Dalman, *Die Worte Jesu*, 1:223.

[134] Fiebig, *Der Menschensohn Jesu*.

[135] Bousset, *Kyrios Christos*, cited by King, *What Is Gnosticism?*, 93.

Bousset as diametrically opposed to Christianity: "Judaism and Jesus are at completely opposite poles to each other."[136]

The antagonism between Jesus and Judaism was further supported by the claim that Galilee and Judea were opposing cultural and religious centers, and that Jesus's own identity as a Galilean refuted his identity as a Jew. First popularized by Chamberlain, the argument received enormous prestige in the world of New Testament scholarship through the work of the distinguished scholar of early Christianity, Walter Bauer, professor of New Testament at the University of Göttingen. Bauer validated the distinctions between the political, cultural, and religious life of Galilee and Judea in a 1927 article, "Jesus der Galiläer," in which he placed the Pharisees in control of Judea, while identifying the Galilee as decidedly unJewish and outside the realm of the political influence of Jerusalem.[137] That, according to Bauer, explained the positive reception of Jesus in the Galilee, in contrast to Jerusalem and its Temple. Jesus's own teachings did not contain what one might expect of a Jew in his day: he did not uphold Levitical purity; he rejected fasting; he denigrated Sabbath observance;[138] and he made the scribes and Pharisees his enemies throughout his public life.[139] Jesus did not consider himself a messianic king, but a heavenly son of man, an identity he drew from the syncretism of the Hellenistic world.[140] Yet the Galilee was also not the ultimate site of Jesus's impact, Bauer notes, because its population of Hellenized Jews, recognizing Jesus as prophet and miracle worker, not as son of man, abandoned him after the crucifixion and did not participate in the Easter faith.[141] As a result, Jesus left no communities in the Galilee, and the early Paul, in persecuting Christians, went not to Galilee but to Damascus.[142] That was the situation as Jesus left it; as a Galilean, Bauer argued, Jesus was not bound to the law, but encouraged free thinking and acting, allowing even Jerusalem Jews, such as Peter and Jacob, to become his disciples.[143] Jesus and his disciples left the Jewish milieu in time: "Christian faith had overflowed the boundaries of Judaism long before the fossilization of Jewish Christianity into Judaism could paralyze its wings and could destroy its mobility."[144]

[136] Bousset, *Jesu Predigt in ihrem Gegensatz zum Judentum*, 69, cited by King, *What Is Gnosticism?*, 95.

[137] Bauer, "Jesus der Galiläer," 16–34; reprinted in Bauer, *Aufsätze und Kleine Schriften*, 100.

[138] Ibid., 103.

[139] Ibid., 105.

[140] Ibid., 105.

[141] Ibid., 105–6.

[142] Ibid., 106.

[143] Ibid., 108.

[144] Ibid., 108.

Certainly not all scholars agreed with the growing consensus of a Gentile Galilee. The studies by Albrecht Alt, professor of Old Testament at the University of Leipzig, attempted to inject a sobering scholarly tone. Based on excavations in Galilee and biblical texts, he traced the history of the region from the eighth to the first centuries BCE, distinguishing between the impacts of the two Assyrian invasions, in 734 and 722 BCE.[145] The first attack, against Galilee, left the general population unscathed, with only the ruling elite deported. The second attack, against Samaria, resulted in a general deportation of the population and resettlement by non-Israelites (Alt makes no mention of Aryans). Alt identified a Galilean population with a strong Israelite identity that welcomed the Hasmonean conquests of the second century BCE as a chance to reunite with their coreligionists, not with the Samarians, a non-Jewish population.[146] Alt's argument undermined claims of an Aryan Galilee, yet did not stop scholars, including Grundmann, who studied under Alt at the University of Leipzig, from continuing to identify the Galilee as Gentile and Aryan. Just as irresponsibly, Emanuel Hirsch, professor of systematic theology at the University of Göttingen, and a Nazi sympathizer, claimed, without evidence, that the numerical relation between Gentiles and Jews in Galilee in the first century was nine to one and that "Science has no reason to define Jesus's blood origin in any more definitive way than by 'non-Jewish.'"[147]

The opposition between Galilee and Judea also became a typology for two different kinds of eschatologies, Jewish and Christian, which were used to distinguish Jesus from Judaism. The prominent historian of religions, Rudolf Otto, in a 1933 study, *Reich Gottes und Menschensohn*, written after his retirement in 1929 from the University of Marburg, conceded that "Jesus was a Jew and was descended from the Jews," but then claimed that his message was not authentically Jewish because late Jewish apocalypticism was derived from Chaldean and Iranian traditions of a dualism of divine and evil forces, a notion that did not arise in Israel but originated in ancient Aryan sources and

---

[145] Alt, "Galiläische Probleme."

[146] For a contemporary reevaluation of Alt's argument, see Freyne, *Jesus, a Jewish Galilean*, 61–62; Horsley, *Galilee*, 25–29; and Younger, "The Deportation of the Israelites," 117. All three conclude that today's archeological evidence does not support Alt's contention of continued Israelite presence in the region, but rather points to a break in the settlement patterns in lower Galilee in the seventh–sixth centuries BCE, with signs of an upturn in the number of settlements appearing in the Persian period, continuing unabated until the Byzantine period, calling into question the biblical accounts of the Assyrian conquests, and also lending support for a mixed population within Galilee rather than an Israelite one. Freyne writes that the biblical narratives should be seen as post-exilic ideological constructions.

[147] Hirsch, *Das Wesen des Christentums* (Weimar: Verlag Deutsche Christen, 1939), appendix, "Die Abstammung Jesus," 158–65.

was expressed in texts such as the birth account in 1 Enoch 105.[148] Otto wrote, "As a Galilean, Jesus belonged to unofficial Judaism, which was certainly not typically Jewish."[149]

Most influentially, in 1936 the New Testament scholar Ernst Lohmeyer, professor of New Testament at the University of Breslau, where he was "disciplined" in 1935 for his support of Jewish colleagues, distinguished between two first-century eschatologies, originating in Galilee and Jerusalem and representing Gentile and Jewish viewpoints, respectively: a son of man eschatology in Galilee and a messiah eschatology in Judea.[150] Lohmeyer's starting point was John 7:41: "But some asked, 'Surely the Messiah does not come from Galilee, does he? Had not the Scripture said that the Messiah is descended from David and comes from Bethlehem, the village where David lived?'" The rhetoric of the verse, according to Lohmeyer, distinguishes the expectations of Jews in Judea for a messianic redeemer from the Galileans' understanding of Jesus, and suggests that some among the followers of Jesus denied that he could be the messiah because they "knew" that he was a Galilean and had not been born in Bethlehem.

Lohmeyer was not an antisemite, a Nazi, or a racist. Yet he, too, distinguished between the religiosity of Galilee and Judea, effectively separating the eschatological teachings of Jesus from a Jewish framework. A student of Adolf Deissmann, one of the major figures in the History of Religions school, Lohmeyer was an innovative scholar, often called the Ferdinand Christian Baur of his generation, after the great nineteenth-century New Testament pioneer who had made a distinction between Jewish and Gentile Christianity as the central driving forces within the emerging Christianity of the first two centuries. Lohmeyer transferred Baur's Jewish/Gentile theological distinction to a geographic dichotomy and argued for a two-site eschatology associated with two different early Christian communities of the first century. His argument became widely influential among New Testament scholars, but was also exploited during the 1930s and '40s in Germany as the political ramifications of a non-Jewish, Galilean Jesus became clear.[151] For example, in his 1937 guide to religious instruction, Johannes Leipoldt, professor at the University of Leipzig who later

[148] Rudolf Otto, *Reich Gottes und Menschensohn* (Munich 1934). See Rudolf Bultmann's extended discussion of the book in *Theologische Rundschau* new series 9 (1937), 1–35; Otto, *The Kingdom of God*, 14.

[149] Otto, *Kingdom of God*, 15.

[150] Lohmeyer, *Galiläa und Jerusalem*.

[151] Oepke, "Das Bevölkerungsproblem Galiläas"; see also Büchsel and Michaelis in *Deutsches Pfarrerblatt* 44 (1940), 122, 238ff, 250f, 365ff.

joined the Institute, presented a Jesus who opposed the messianism of the Jews.[152]

Lohmeyer, like Bauer, did not identify Galilee as "Aryan," simply as Gentile, based not on biologically rooted racial claims but on what he identified as its religious difference from Jewish Judea. Given the presumption in racist theory that religion reflects race, however, it was a short step for others to use his work to claim that the Gentile religious nature of Galilee reflected the unique racial identity of its population.

While scholars debated whether or not Jesus originated within Judaism, they were in greater agreement that the movement around him took root not within a Jewish milieu, but a Greek one; many more of his adherents were drawn from the Greco-Roman pagan world than the Jewish. Yet the lack of enthusiasm on the part of Jews could also be taken as evidence of Jesus's essentially un-Jewish teachings. Even the great historian of early Christianity, Adolf von Harnack, in his major study of early Christianity, insisted that Christianity is fundamentally Greek, even though it originated on Semitic soil: "There is hardly any fact as certain as the fact that the religion of Jesus could not fasten to any roots within Jewish and Semitic ground. There must have been something in this religion that is related to the free Greek spirit. In a certain sense, Christianity has remained Greek until the present day."[153]

CONCLUSION

Numerous trails led up the mountain that came to constitute the Aryan Jesus. By the time Grundmann and his fellow Institute members began to call for a dejudaization of the church, insisting that Jesus was not a Jew, that Galilee was populated by non-Jews, and that Judaism was a violent religion threatening all Christians, they could simply use the arguments already put forward by several preceding generations of theologians, philosophers, intellectuals, and demagogues. The dissociation of Jesus from Judaism functioned for some as an affirmation of German identity or simple contempt for Jews, while for others it was a genuine effort to uncover new intellectual genealogies of religion in an era of new enthusiasm for the "Orient." Christian theologians, who had long sought to clarify the difference between Jesus and other Jews of his day,

[152] Leipoldt, *Jesus der Künder und Kämpfer Gottes.*

[153] Adolf von Harnack, *The Mission and Expansion of Christianity in the First Three Centuries,* trans. James Moffatt (New York,: Harper, 1962), 64.

were gratified by ways to preserve Jesus's uniqueness despite the pressures of historicist contextualization.

Regardless of their training and the high standards of historical scholarship for which German universities were so respected, a remarkable number of academics in a range of fields came to stand behind claims that Jesus was a Buddhist or that Galilee was Gentile. To many, racial theory did not appear insidious, but rather a new and sophisticated social scientific method of analysis. For some, such as Renan, racial difference constituted a realm of order comparable to laws of nature, expressed in human groups, culture, religion, and even topography. Race was a reality that could be known through hermeneutical methods of intuition and subjective experience, highly inflected by romanticism. For others, scientific evidence could be amassed from texts and archeological excavations to demonstrate the historical development of racial groups whose characteristics, both physical and cultural, would then be evaluated and ranked.

Studies of Jesus made use of both kinds of methods. Seeking to understand the "religious consciousness" of Jesus through a selective reading of certain gospel passages led to claims that Jesus's intimacy with God established a morality that was utterly different from the legalism of Judaism, as Grundmann came to argue in a 1938 book, *Die Gotteskindschaft Jesu.* Another Institute member, Hugo Odeberg, professor at the University of Lund, Sweden, argued on linguistic grounds that Jesus could not have been a Jew: he claimed that the Aramaic spoken by Jesus was distinct from Hebrew and bore greater affinities, in its sophistication and worldliness, to German.[154]

Such ideas might have remained in the realm of demaguery or bad scholarship had it not been for the establishment of the Institute in 1939. With the enthusiasm of its directors and the support of its sympathizers within the church, the Institute transformed bad ideas into dangerous realities. As the Nazis began their crusade to eradicate Jews from Europe, the Institute launched its crusade to eradicate Jews from the church, Judaism from Germany, and any traces of "Jewishness," however loosely defined, from the heart of Christianity.

Malcolm Quinn has described the swastika as an "orientation" device, "an anchoring object for the wayward, anxious and subjective discourses of occultism and Aryanism on the margins of rationalist thought." The swastika "functioned as the mnemonic for a lost object," namely an original Germanic identity, and Nazism, Quinn continues, "supplied the answer to this questioning and yearning with its discourse of 'national salvation.'"[155]

[154] Odeberg, "Die Muttersprache Jesu."
[155] Quinn, *The Swastika*, 9.

Figure 1.5. German Christians at a rally in Berlin; date uncertain.

The Aryan Jesus functioned for Christian theology in analogous fashion. As Jesus, he was the anchor of the Christian identity of Germans, and as Aryan, of the Germanic identity of Christianity. Jesus was an anchor in a nazified society that was undertaking a radical overhaul of culture as well as institutions, and a Christian counterpoint to the presence of the swastika, symbolic of the pre-Christian Teutonic. Most important, in the context of Third Reich politics, Jesus was the figure through whom the fundamental race distinction between Jew and Aryan could be affirmed.

Völkisch groups had the swastika, and Christian racists wanted both the swastika and the cross. If, as Quinn argues, the swastika was tautological, feeding back to Germans what they had produced for their mythic imaginations, the Aryan Jesus functioned similarly, announcing German Christians' racism even as it functioned to instruct and affirm the new Germanic Christianity of the Nazi Reich. Both the swastika and the Aryan Jesus were self-referential symbols that "sold the German back to her/himself as an Aryan."[156] The Aryan

[156] Quinn, *Swastika*, 138–39. See the discussion of Quinn in Caplan, "Politics, Religion, and Ideology," 28–36.

Jesus was additionally a claim of Germany against Europe, for whom Jesus had long served as central symbol and signifier. The Jewish Jesus with the Christian message for all humanity was now to be replaced by a Germanic Jesus with a message in accord with Germany's military and racial goals of domination over Europe. A radical nationalism had combined with religion to produce race as its essential tool for uniting Germans. By manipulating the theological and moral teachings of Christianity, Institute theologians legitimated the Nazi conscience through Jesus.[157] Antisemitism was the glue that joined the various theological methods and impulses and also brought passion to religion. As the German Christian Friedrich Wieneke once remarked, "Not what we think, but rather what God wants, is decisive."[158] The problem was that they failed to distinguish between God and Hitler.

[157] On the construction of a Nazi "morality" via racism, see Hecht, "Vacher de Lapouge."

[158] Friedrich Wieneke, *Christentum und Nationalsozialismus: Aussprache-Schrift der Christlich-deutschen Bewegung*, 2nd ed. (Küstrin-Neustadt, 1931), 48; cited by Weiling, *Die "Christlich-deutsche Bewegung,"* 134.

The Institute for the Study and Eradication of Jewish Influence on German Church Life, 1939 to 1942

THE THIRD REICH ARRIVED as both a delight and a disappointment to leaders of the German Christian movement. The Nazi regime seemed at first to be promising the sort of overthrow of entrenched authorities and ideas that German Christians hoped to bring about in analogous fashion within the church and theology. Yet their expectation of playing an active leadership role in the Reich and the Nazi Party was soon disappointed. Bringing individual regional churches under the control of German Christian pastors and bishops and declaring Christian support for the Führer did not result in the hoped-for admiration from Hitler nor positions of authority within the regime for individual pastors and bishops. The Nazi disinterest in including the church as a full partner in the creation of the new Reich was exemplified in a 1936 Nazi Party edict that ordered the removal of the swastika from church buildings and publications. Many pastors protested, to no avail.[1] As a result of the edict, a journal sponsored by the German Christian movement and edited by Walter Grundmann, *Christenkreuz und Hakenkreuz* (*Cross and Swastika*), had to change its name to *Deutsche Frömmigkeit* (*German Piety*). Similarly, in 1937, the Kirchenbewegung Deutsche Christen (KDC), the Thuringian branch of the German Christian movement, had to rename itself the Nationalkirchliche Einung Deutsche Christen (National Church Union of German Christians), as it was now forbidden to all but official Nazi organizations to use the term "Bewegung" (movement). In sum, the promise of full partnership, to which many in the German Christian movement had hoped their active support of Hitler would lead, did not materialize, and church leaders of all stripes found themselves increasingly held at a distance by the party and regime.

Although annoyed and even embittered by the lack of enthusiasm from the regime, leaders of the German Christian movement by no means abandoned the object of their unrequited affection. Instead, they redoubled their devotion to Hitler by speaking, for example, of the "Führer Jesus" and describing Hitler as "God's agent [beauftragter] in our day."[2] To carve a place for themselves

---

[1] Heschel, "Church Protests during the Third Reich," 377–88.

[2] From "Bericht über die Arbeitstagung der 'Deutschen Christen' Gruppe Rheinland," 144–46, cited by Faulenbach, *Ein Weg durch die Kirche*, 161.

within the Nazi Reich, they emphasized that Germans required both physical and spiritual strength, and they would provide the latter. Christianity could not simply be abandoned; they insisted that the German people had a spiritual hunger and that loss of faith was as dangerous as poisoned blood: "The yearning for God in the German people is not a marginal attribute, but makes their blood healthy."[3] In later years, German Christians would describe the war as being fought on both physical and spiritual battlefields; the racial struggle was spiritual as well as physical.

Carrying out the racial battle on the spiritual plane was the goal of the Institute. The faith that the German people needed for the spiritual battlefield was not the old, "Jewish" Christianity, but a Christianity that was truly German—namely, purged of Jewishness. The goal was not only to radically revise the church and its teachings, eradicating all "Jewish" expressions, but to produce antisemitic propaganda in the service of the Reich's efforts to create a Germany purged of Jews. This would be accomplished by revising the hymnal, Bible, catechism, and other liturgical materials, and producing new versions incorporating Teutonic myths that were viewed as congruent with the teachings of Jesus—once the Jewish falsifications were removed from the New Testament and his true Aryan nature was restored. Justifications of those goals were presented for both popular and scholarly readerships through Institute publications, conferences, lectures, and publicity of its activities, and through promulgation of declarations that were signed by officials of most of the German regional churches.

The Institute was headquartered in Eisenach, in buildings owned by the church of Thuringia, but its impact was Reich-wide and even Europe-wide, with a branch in Romania and a cluster of support in Scandinavia. The physical location in Thuringia and the membership of so many Thuringian pastors does, however, call attention to the hospitality the Institute found within Thuringian state and church institutions and the enthusiastic support it enjoyed from Thuringian church leadership, which was dominated by German Christians. The state of Thuringia had been the first to experience Nazi governance when the Nazi Party entered into a ruling coalition in 1930.[4] The Thuringian church, considered among the most open in Germany during the 1920s and '30s to theological experimentation at both liberal and Nazi ends of the spectrum, attracted members of the German Christian movement who felt

---

[3] Report on the German Christian gathering in Jena, April 8, 1937 (LKA Eisenach, BK A 124).

[4] Hitler's February 1930 letter to Wilhelm Frick, who entered the Thuringian government, representing the NSDAP, advises that he first gain control of the ministries of the interior, particularly the police force, and education. See Dickmann, "Die Regierungsbildung in Thüringen," 454–64.

doctrinally constrained elsewhere.[5] The Institute's nominal director, Siegfried Leffler, was an official in the Thuringian Ministry of Education, and was also a pastor who had moved to the Werra Valley of Thuringia from the Bavarian church in 1927. He and his close friend, the pastor Julius Leutheuser, who came with him from Bavaria, simultaneously organized branches of the Nazi Party and the German Christian movement while pastoring congregations.[6] Leffler's government position and Leutheuser's position as an official in the Thuringian church's governing council helped to guarantee the power of pro-Nazi factions within the church. During the Third Reich, the Thuringian church was well under the control of the German Christians, especially after the appointment of its notorious bishop, Martin Sasse, in 1934, a staunch Nazi and virulent antisemite.[7] The Thuringian church eagerly implemented whatever anti-Jewish measures were possible, even ceasing to present couples celebrating their fiftieth wedding anniversary with a copy of the Old Testament; starting in the spring of 1939, the church instead gave couples a picture of the Wartburg, with its nationalist and antisemitic connotations.

The antisemitism promoted by the Institute grew out of a broad mixture of theology and nationalism, and functioned as a kind of glue linking church with state in what was said to be a "higher cause," the German Volk. As Germany became increasingly accepting of racial politics during the course of the 1930s, its Christians grew more accepting of racial theology. At the same time, the racism promoted by German Christians as a form of theology functioned as a moral sanction for the racism of the Nazis. For example, when in November 1933 Reinhold Krause, a German Christian leader, had called for eliminating the Old Testament as an expression of an inappropriate Jewish "morality" of "cattle traders and pimps," and denounced Paul as a Jewish theologian, he received thunderous applause from the 20,000 attending a rally in Berlin, but

---

[5] The church of Thuringia was unified even before the state of Thuringia came into being. Following the November 1918 revolution, the University of Jena theological faculty, which was the only church institution representing the entire region, initiated an effort to overcome regional theological differences and establish a unified church for the state. Divided into seven small, regional churches, the Thuringian evangelical church consolidated itself on December 5, 1919. Given the disparities in the region, the church constitution, formulated in 1924, mandated toleration: "It [the Thuringian evangelical church] is by origin and nature a Lutheran church. It wishes to be a home of evangelical freedom and toleration." Indeed, it is the very openness and liberality of the Thuringian church that has sometimes been blamed for allowing the German Christian movement to come to power.

[6] The pastor Paul Schwadtke was leader of the SA troops of the Werra Valley in the late 1920s when Leutheuser and Leffler arrived.

[7] Sasse joined the NSDAP on March 1, 1930, receiving membership number 204010 (BDC, Sasse materials).

he was roundly condemned by some respected theologians, a number of whom withdrew from the German Christian movement; indeed, that rally was one impetus for the ultimate emergence of the Confessing Church.[8] Within a few years, however, Krause's language no longer sounded outrageous, and the time seemed ripe to implement the call to rid Christianity of Jewish influences. And if the Old Testament could be removed from Christian scriptures on antisemitic grounds, and Paul, considered the founder of Christianity and its theology, could be rejected for being a Jew, there was little basis left for a Christian to affirm Jews or Judaism.

FIRST STEPS TOWARD THE INSTITUTE: ORGANIZATION FOR GERMANIC CHRISTIANITY

Proposals for a formal dejudaization of Christianity came to the forefront of German Christian discussions under the auspices of the Organization for Germanic Christianity (Bund für deutsches Christentum), an alliance of regional church leaders, members of the German Christian movement, that formed in November 1936. Groups such as the Bund, representing German Christian ideology, served as guarantors of National Socialism within the church.[9] Members of the Bund were bishops of regional churches, including the jurist Friedrich Werner, president of the governing church council of the Old Prussian Union (APU), the largest and most important component of the Protestant church, and a veteran of the Nazi Party (an "Alter Kämpfer").[10] Walter Grundmann was also a member of the Bund, as both an academic theologian and major ideologue of the German Christian movement. On November 10, 1936, leaders of German Christian–controlled regional churches, including Grundmann, considered one of the major theologians of the German Christian movement, met in the Wartburg Castle outside Eisenach, and formed the Bund.[11]

---

[8] Bergen, *Twisted Cross*, 17.

[9] Friedrich Wieneke, "Deutsche Christen," written Berlin, June 1942 (ZAK, Bestand A4/94).

[10] Werner joined the NSDAP on January 1, 1931, with the number 411184 (BDC, Werner materials).

[11] The Bund was initiated by Bishop Oberheid of Bad Godesberg. Wieneke, "Deutsche Christen" (fn 9 above) For a biography of Oberheid, see Faulenbach, *Ein Weg durch die Kirche*. On the Bund, see Meier, *Die Deutschen Christen*, 147f. See also Heinonen, *Anpassung und Identität*, 87f. The Bund was composed of leaders of the German Christian movement in Thuringia as well as leaders of the German Christian–controlled regional churches of Thuringia, Mecklenburg, Anhalt, Bremen, and Lübeck.

The Bund's pamphlets called for a national, "Jew-free" church that would bring "the National Socialist revolution" to the church through both the gospel and the Nuremberg Laws.[12] The Bund distinguished between those following the "Jewish Christianity" of Paul—the Confessing Church and the Catholics—and those following the anti-Jewish Christianity of Jesus—the German Christians.[13] The Bund praised Joseph Goebbels, the Nazi Minister of Propaganda, for recognizing that "Jesus was the first really distinguished adversary of the Jews. The Jews took the opportunity for the first time in history to nail eternal truth to the Cross."[14]

Jesus, in other words, was to be affirmed as a kind of proto-Nazi who fought against the Jews, making Christianity an antisemitic, not a Jewish, religion. The public reception of such declarations is difficult to determine, but a Bund-sponsored meeting in March 1937 at a church in Hanover attracted an audience of 1,200 people.[15] On July 14, 1937, the German Christians issued a new, nine-point platform proclaiming: "The National Church Movement German Christian stands for an overcoming and eradication of all Jewish and foreign völkisch spirit in church teaching and ways of life and confesses German Christianity to be the racially appropriate religion of the German Volk. Christ is not the scion and fulfiller of Judaism but rather its deadly enemy and conqueror."[16] The platform, entitled "Intention and Goal of the German Christians" ("Wille und Ziel der DC"), was printed in a Nazi-style typeface (the "S" looks like a swastika) and repeated the movement's slogans, "One Volk—One Faith" ("Ein Volk—Ein Glaube"), "Germany is our Task, Christ is our Strength" ("Deutschland ist unsere Aufgabe, Christus ist unsere Kraft"), and "Service to the Volk is Divine Service" ("Dienst am Volk ist Gottesdienst").

[12] "Unser Bekenntnis," Bund für deutsches Christentum, undated. (NEK, Kiel, Archives of the Confessing Church of Schleswig-Holstein, Signatur 41, Neue Nummer 241). Subsequent meetings were held in Berlin on December 2, 1936, and in Jena on December 7–8, 1936. On the Berlin meeting, see NEK, "Kirchenkampf Lübeck," no. 52: Bund für deutsches Christentum, Rundschreiben, 1937. On the Jena meeting, see LKA Eisenach, A776a, files of the Governing Council of the Protestant church of Thuringia concerning the Bund für deutsches Christentum, 1936–42.

[13] Typed pamphlet, unsigned, dated June 26, 1937 (NSS 134/57: Bund für deutsches Christentum).

[14] Pamphlet, *Das Ringen der Deutschen Christen um die Kirche* (Verlag Deutsche Christen, 1937), 7 (NSS 134/57).

[15] A report states that the church was "bursting full," and notes that two-thirds of the audience were women. Report on the gathering of the Bund für Deutsches Christentum in Hanover, March 17, 1937, in the Bethlehem Church in Hanover-Linden (NEK, Archive of the Confessing Church of Schleswig-Holstein, Signatur 41, Neue Nummer 241).

[16] Pamphlet, *Wille und Ziel der DC* (Nationalkirchliche Bewegung), dated July 14, 1937, signed by Leffler (LKA Eisenach).

Members of the Bund were church leaders who were passionate antisemites but also opportunists, seeking power within a Nazi regime that had little to offer pastors. Neither their ideological antisemitism nor their crass opportunism could be sacrificed or even modified; they were "working towards the Führer," in Ian Kershaw's phrase.[17] By 1938, with Germany in a mood of increasing militarization at all levels of society and antisemitic propaganda on the rise, the German Christian leadership's desire for official recognition from the regime led to its most dramatic step, attempting a thorough dejudaization of the church and its theology. Plans began in earnest in 1938, with early competing proposals sketched out for either a university-based research institute or a church-headquartered office to propose and carry out the necessary changes in theology, liturgy, catechism, and training of pastors. The goal was creating a judenrein Christianity for a judenrein Nazi Reich. Dejudaizing the church would have strategic political purposes as well. German Christian leaders believed that making antisemitism a central policy of the church, not just a rhetorical flourish of theology, would rekindle Hitler's sympathetic attention to the churches and demonstrate the potential usefulness of the German Christian movement to skeptical Nazi officials by rallying Christian support for Nazi policies.[18] Hitler, meanwhile, was concerned in 1938 with Gestapo reports of growing oppositionist trends within the Catholic and Protestant churches, as well as among political conservatives,[19] and was pressuring Hanns Kerrl, Reich Minister for Church Affairs, to unify and discipline the church. Kerrl, while sympathetic to the German Christians, was also mistrustful of them, sentiments they reciprocated.[20]

Although the German Christians were declaring their devotion to the Reich, not all regional churches, pastors, and laity were in agreement. Hitler's mandate to the Reich Ministry for Church Affairs was to create unified support of the churches. Kerrl found church leaders unyielding and the task seemingly impossible. However, political machinations within the ministry resulted in a shift of authority. Kerrl was overshadowed during the months of February through November, 1937, by a subordinate in his ministry, Hermann Muhs, a lawyer, politician, and early member of the Nazi Party (1929) and SS (1931).

[17] Kershaw took the phrase "working towards the Führer" from a speech delivered by Werner Willikens, State Secretary in the Prussian Agriculture Ministry, at a meeting of representatives from state agriculture ministries held in Berlin on February 21, 1934. Kershaw, *Hitler*, 529; see also McElligott and Kirk, eds., *Working towards the Führer*.

[18] Wagener, "Gott sprach," 38.

[19] Bankier, *The Germans and the Final Solution*, 61.

[20] On Kerrl, see Siegele-Wenschkewitz, "Politische Versuche einer Ordnung der Deutschen Evangelischen Kirche," 121–38.

Thanks to the ascendancy of Muhs's influence, the ministry increased its financial support of German Christian efforts, including a 20,000 Reichsmark (RM) subvention for its national meeting in Eisenach in October 1937, which drew 12,000 people, and at which Muhs himself was greeted with hearty applause.[21] During 1937, Hitler also initiated an effort to establish a legal separation of church and state, an effort that had to be carefully presented to the public as a law that would preserve "freedom of religious belief," so as not to arouse public suspicions of a Nazi prejudice against Christianity.[22]

OATH TO HITLER

In the course of their meetings in 1938, the Bund sought to define a Christian basis for Nazi racial principles. In the face of the ongoing insistence by both Christian theologians and völkisch propagandists that Christian and German (Aryan) identities were irreconcilable, they issued a statement affirming the Christian basis of German racial identity:

> The religious burden under which millions of German racial comrades [Volksgenossen] are suffering arises because German identity and Christian identity are viewed as mutually exclusive. This error, which is damaging to the Volk, is being instigated by Christian and also by völkisch-religious fanatics. In order to restrain their instigation, the undersigned church leaders have gathered today and decided to equip the church in the service of a positive Christianity for the Volk community [Volksgemeinschaft].[23]

These leaders sought "to create . . . a unified position on specific questions of church life and church order."[24]

---

[21] Kreutzer, *Das Reichskirchenministerium*, 302–3. Kreutzer argues that there were three eras in which Muhs dominated the Reich Ministry: February 12, 1937, to early November 1937; November 1937 to February 1938; and after Kerrl's death in December 1941. She labels these eras as the "triumph of the German Christians," 300.

[22] Ibid., 303.

[23] A meeting was held on January 26, 1938, at Berlin's Hotel Fürstenhof at Potsdamer Platz. Present were bishops, church presidents, and other official representatives of regional churches, including Hossenfelder, Hahn, Propp, and Werner (Berlin); Leffler, Tegetmeyer, Franz, Sasse, Hohlwein, and Grundmann (Thuringia); Balzer (Lübeck); Berthold, Kretzschmar, and Klotsche (Dresden); Wilkendorf (Dessau); Kipper (Darmstadt); Diehl (Speyer); Wahle (Bremen); Schultz and Schmidt zur Nedden (Schwerin). See letter from Propp to Grundmann dated February 5, 1938 (LKA Eisenach, Bestand DC, III, 2f, and report from Propp, dated February 5, 1938, ZAK 1/A4/168).

[24] ZAK 1/A4/168.

The Bund called for a nationwide pastors' oath of loyalty to Hitler: "I swear: I will be loyal and true to the Führer of the German Reich and Volk, Adolf Hitler, follow the laws and consciously fulfill the duties of my position, so may God help me."[25] By April 1938, the oath already had been implemented in Thuringia and Mecklenburg, with efforts to introduce it in the Old Prussian Union. In June, a church official in Anhalt reported that not one pastor in his region had refused to take the oath, not even those affiliated with the Confessing Church.[26] In July, the Ostmark (Austrian) church president similarly announced that all of his pastors had also supported the oath.[27] In Thuringia, most of the Confessing Church pastors took the oath as well.[28]

Yet after the oath had been implemented in the church, Reich officials repudiated it; Martin Bormann, head of the party chancellery and long-time antagonist of the churches, declared it voluntary and a matter of internal church concern.[29] No special recognition of the church by the Reich would be granted in exchange for the oath of loyalty. Moreover, the German Christians still had not achieved total control of all the regional churches, leaving the mood among leaders of the movement glum. In June 1938, the Leffler, one of the movement's major demagogues, wrote to Werner:

> We have had to struggle out of the position of pariah within the German Protestant church. But still today it is unacceptable, and for us unbearable, to be tolerated yet still shut out from any influence on really positive work in the National Socialist sense within the Protestant church. And this only because we as Christians in the church of our fathers approve the National Socialist world view![30]

The frustration with the hindrances German Christians encountered within the church and from Kerrl and other Nazi government officials left them seeking new tactics and more dramatic action to win power.

The escalating antisemitic propaganda and measures taken against the Jews in 1938 served as an inspiration. Just a week after Leffler's letter to Werner, on June 15, 1938, over a thousand "asocials," among them Jews, were brought to the Buchenwald concentration camp, which had been opened in July of 1937

[25] Conway, *Nazi Persecution of the Churches*, 211.
[26] Senior church councillor Wilkendorf of Anhalt (Dessau). See report dated June 27, 1938 (ZAK 1/A4/168).
[27] See report by Dr. Kauer of July 1, 1938 meeting (ZAK 1/A4/168).
[28] Lautenschläger, "Der Kirchenkampf in Thüringen," 477.
[29] Conway, *Nazi Persecution of the Churches*, 211; Boberach, *Berichte des SD und der Gestapo*, 317f.
[30] Letter from Leffler to Werner, dated June 8, 1938 (ZAK 1/A4/167).

on a hill visible from the town of Weimar, where Leffler's offices were located; as of July 1, 1938, nearly 1,300 Jews were imprisoned there.[31] Given the circumstances, focusing more intently on antisemitism made perfect sense, since the Nazis by now were paying more attention to the Jews than to the churches. At a May 1938 German Christian rally in Berlin, the keynote address was entitled, "Overcoming and eradicating all Jewish and racially foreign spirit in the teachings and structures of the churches."[32] The agenda was set; the task was to clarify the means to the goal.

Competing Proposals for the Institute

The means to the goal of dejudaizing the church came in a series of memoranda by Hugo Pich, a church superintendent from West Prussia who had recently retired and moved to Thuringia.[33] Pich proposed establishing a dejudaization institute that would achieve the "dejudaization of church and Christianity" ("Entjudung von Kirche und Christentum"), and sent successive drafts of his proposal in 1937 and 1938 to German Christian leaders and also to Reich Bishop Ludwig Müller, State Secretary at the Ministry for Church Affairs Hermann Muhs, and to Gerhard Hahn, one of the German Christians' top men in Berlin.[34] In the version sent to Hahn in October 1938, Pich called for the establishment of an "Office for the Dejudaization of the Church" ("Amt für Entjudung der Kirche"), explaining that "for the realization of the National Socialist, German fight against world Jewry, the quick and thorough execution of the dejudaization process in the Christian church [is] of utmost and

[31] Statistics about the camp population did not include Jews as a separate category until April 1942, but among the 7,723 prisoners at Buchenwald, 1,272 were Jewish. Stein, "Funktionswander des Konzentrationslager Buchenwald," 167–92.

[32] Speakers included Grundmann, who spoke on "Paul and Luther: A Contribution to the German Formation of Christianity," and Richard Hoffmann, professor of New Testament at the University of Vienna, who spoke on "The Concept of Faith in the New Testament" (ZAK A4/93: Deutsche Christen, November 1933–December 1938).

[33] Pich (1882–?) had recently left the West Prussian town of Schneidemühl (population 45,847, with 116 Jews) because of a medical condition and political conflicts and had moved to Eisenach (see letter from the president of the Protestant Church Governing Board, Berlin, December 13, 1939, LKA Eisenach). Pich came to be known as the "spiritual father" of the Institute (personal communication, Pastor Heinz Koch, director of the Thuringian church archives). He served as business manager of the Institute from June 15, 1940, after Erwin Brauer was called to military service (ZAK 7/4166).

[34] The first draft proposal, dated June 15, 1938, and sent to Muhs and Müller, has not been located in the archives, but Pich refers to it in a letter dated September 13, 1938, sent to Leffler, Leutheuser, Franz, Hahn, and Hohlwein (ThHStA 1522).

essential priority." Dejudaizing Christianity was required not only for the sake of the church, but also for the Nazi project: "Only when the dejudaization of the Christian church is accomplished can the German Volk, with its religious faith, internalize and support this struggle of the Führer and help him to fulfill God's covenant with the German Volk."[35]

On October 14, 1938, the German Christian leadership held a press conference in Weimar to call for a "thorough" and "clean treatment" of the Jewish question, and to warn against a dilettantish approach to this important matter.[36] A series of forthcoming publications warning of the Jewish danger was announced, with titles such as "The Jew in the Hymnal," "Not Jewish Knowledge, but Faith," "Judea in Germany," and "A Jew Makes Germanic Imperial Politics." But the German Christian leaders wanted to do more than echo the escalating propaganda of the Nazi regime, and so cast about for an ambitious project that would draw Nazi attention to their efforts to subsume the church to the regime, and to indicate support for Nazi Jewish policy. A few weeks later, on November 7–8, 1938, the German Christian leadership met in Weimar to hear a round of presentations by Grundmann, Leffler, Leutheuser, and Eugen Kühnemann, a professor of philosophy at the University of Breslau.[37] The speakers distinguished between Judaism and Christianity not only as two different religions but as two different kinds of religion.[38] The very next night brought the pogrom that destroyed most synagogues in Germany and brought an end to viable Jewish life in the Reich. In the days following the pogrom, 1,178 Jewish men from Thuringia were incarcerated at Buchenwald.[39]

On November 15, just days after the pogrom, the bishop of Thuringia, Martin Sasse, issued his response: a pamphlet entitled *Martin Luther on the Jews: Away with Them!* (*Martin Luther über die Juden: Weg mit Ihnen!*), in which he reprinted excerpts from Luther's notorious 1543 pamphlet, *Against the Jews and Their Lies*, urging the destruction of Jewish property. Realizing that the time was ripe to take action on matters of dejudaization, that same week Hahn circulated copies of Pich's proposal to the bishops of Thuringia, Schwerin, and Lübeck, knowing they would be sympathetic to its goals.[40] In his cover letter

---

[35] Huge Pich, *Denkschrift*, 13 (LKA Eisenach, A 921).

[36] Weitenhagen, *Evangelisch und Deutsch*, 474–75.

[37] ZAK Bestand A4/93.

[38] Landesbischof Walther Schultz, Schwerin (Mecklenburg) "Deutsches Christentum und Kirche" (NSS 134/57).

[39] Liesenberg, "Wir täuschen uns nicht."

[40] This was the second draft of Pich's proposal. The same day that Hahn circulated Pich's proposal, November 15, 1938, Bishop Sasse of Thuringia issued his pamphlet of Luther's antisemitic writings. Such responses to Kristallnacht were not isolated.

to Pich's proposal, Hahn made explicit the link to the pogrom, which had left 300 synagogues burned, hundreds of shops looted, and 25,000 Jews arrested: "I continue to be of the opinion that, in conjunction with the general cleansing of German racial life of everything Jewish, the time has arrived for action to be taken either by the German Christian movement, led by Leffler, or by the German Christian church leaders through similarly appropriate measures in this direction." Theoretical discussions of dejudaizing the church had already taken place, he wrote, but no practical solutions had yet been achieved. The German Christian movement must carry out the negative work required to "free the field for the positive work of shaping a true German Christianity."[41] Hahn concluded his letter by drawing attention to Pich's proposal for the creation of an office within the church that would carry out a dejudaization through baptism of Jews only by Jewish-Christian pastors; gathering Jewish Christians in separate communities; and removal of non-Aryan pastors from service in the church. Meanwhile, Grundmann and two of his colleagues from the University of Jena's theological faculty, Heinz Eisenhuth and Wolf Meyer-Erlach, lectured on the necessity for dejudaizing Christianity to groups of pastors.[42]

The plans themselves were mild compared to the more thorough theological dejudaization described by Grundmann in his proposal, dated November 21, 1938, entitled "Plan for the Creation and Work of a Central Office for the Dejudaization of Religious and Church Life" ("Planung für die Schaffung und Arbeit einer Zentralabteilung zur Entjudung des religiösen und kirchlichen Lebens").[43] He began by declaring, "The Jewish question has entered its most acute phase. In the churches the decision against Judaism has to be executed with complete clarity, and from this decision draw the consequences for all areas of church and religious life."[44] He then called for carrying out three

---

[41] Über die Entjudung der Kirche, letter from Hahn, dated November 15, 1938 (LKA Eisenach A921).

[42] On November 10, 1938, for example, the church of Anhalt declared a new training program for pastors. The first day of that training, January 17, 1939, in Dessau, made its orientation clear: Grundmann, Meyer-Erlach, and Eisenhuth were the invited speakers. In his lecture, "The Problem of Judaism in the History of Early Christianity," Grundmann addressed the current task of liberating the German Volk, including in the realm of Christianity, from the spirit of Judaism. Eisenhuth spoke on "Character and Piety," and how they affect one another. Meyer-Erlach, in "Contemporary Tasks of the Sermon," argued that a sermon should not be about theology and confession but must be instead a "Glaubenspredigt," a profession of faith that awakens the power of faith, duty, and obligation in the listeners. Report by Heinz Dungs, printed, source not clear, (LKA Eisenach A921).

[43] Grundmann, memorandum on Creation and Planning (LKA Eisenach Bestand DC, III).

[44] Ibid.

Figure 2.1. Grundmann and his colleagues at a pastors' conference in Dessau, January 17, 1939. *Left to right:* Meyer-Erlach; Church Councilor Rudolf Wilkendorf of Dessau; Heinz Eisenhuth; Walter Grundmann; Magdeburg pastor Körner.

projects: one, establishing a research institute at the University of Jena to investigate "the problem of Judaism," and publishing its results in a theological journal to be entitled *Theologie und Frömmigkeit* (Theology and Piety); two, establishing a Bible Society that would create a "Volksbibel" and hymnal "purified of all Jewishnesses," and that would produce "devotional books [created out of] valuable witnesses of German piety"; and three, creating a central office within the church to carry out the reeducation of pastors, teachers, and church representatives based on the new research, produce press material, and prepare educational meetings for the German public.

Grundmann had been teaching in the faculty of theology at the University of Jena since 1936, and he proposed that the research institute be established at that university. An academic affiliation, he insisted, would give the institute added prestige. In addition, its presence at a university would downplay the institute's origins as a political initiative of the German Christian movement and make it appear more independent in the eyes of both the church and the academic world. Grundmann proposed that the institute be run by university professors who were also members of the NSDAP, and suggested Pastor Karl-Erich Wilken of Magdeburg, one of his doctoral students at the University of Jena, as a good candidate for office manager. The institute's academic journal, he wrote, should appear under the joint editorship of Emanuel Hirsch, a distinguished systematic theologian at the University of Göttingen, Hans Wilhelm Schmidt, professor of Old Testament at the University of Halle, and Grundmann, with Heinz Dungs, head of the German Christian publishing house in Weimar, as the journal's editorial assistant.

While located at the university, the research institute as conceptualized by Grundmann would be linked to the Protestant church, which would appoint its director and secure funding for its projects. Grundmann also called for consultation with several branches of the Nazi government, including the Ministries of Propaganda, Education, and Church Affairs, as well as with Nazi Party leadership and, specifically, with Julius Streicher, the Nazi Party district leader of Franconia and editor of *Der Stürmer*.[45]

The three prongs of Grundmann's proposal were ultimately downgraded. Once established, the Institute held no formal university affiliation, established no central office within the church for dejudaization, and never won approval to publish a journal. However, funding for the Institute was sufficient to carry out a range of academically respectable tasks, primarily conferences and publications, that attempted to be ideologically persuasive. Grundmann's claim that the Institute would be an independent center for scholarly research was undercut, however, by his call for cooperation with government ministries, and, especially, with Streicher. Affiliation with the University of Jena was undermined by Jena's rector, Karl Astel, a professor of medicine and a racial theorist, who rejected the proposal and instead undertook a general downgrade of the status of the faculty of theology.

Indeed, in both his November 1938 proposal and, increasingly, in 1939, Grundmann's conception of the Institute was less of an independent forum for

---

[45] Ibid.

theological scholarship and more of a theological buttress for the National Socialist project. This was made especially clear in the following undated description of the work of the proposed institute, written by Grundmann in the early months of 1939:

> The dejudaization that is being executed in all segments of German life has to be extended to the religious and church realms of life. On the one hand, the influence of the Jews in Germany can only be entirely broken if it is broken in the religious realm. On the other hand, for many Germans the question of the relationship between Christian origins and Judaism is becoming increasingly urgent under the influence of the demand for dejudaization and the anti-Christian propaganda that is bound up with it. So the question of a possible Jewish influence on German religious life requires a fundamental clarification, and so also with regard to a direct influence—one can point to the traces that Spinoza left on German pantheism. Thus the task of the churches is, on the one hand, to account for any possible Jewish influence within its own history, and, on the other hand, because of their responsibility for German life, to remove any possible Jewish influence. The accomplishment of this task is simultaneously the starting point of the recognition and promotion of a German-inflected Christianity and a German piety as well as the realization of the gospels as the joy-inspiring message of God.[46]

In this same memorandum, Grundmann also expressed the expectation that the Institute would be welcomed at its opening by representatives of the party and state and concluded with a list of expectations to which he assumed all directors and members, and all affiliated academics and clergy, would agree:

1. Every candidate for membership has to prove that he has a thorough knowledge of racial theory and the laws of heredity.
2. The test can only be passed if it demonstrates that the candidate clearly recognizes the fundamental, unbridgeable antagonism between the Jewish religion and Christian faith and can substantiate that the recognition of this antagonism decisively influences his scholarly and practical work.[47]

Godesberg Declaration

The proposals by Pich and Grundmann won the full support of members of the German Christian leadership; the Institute was as good as established.

[46] ZAK 1/A4/168.
[47] Ibid.

The task was now to generate a national consensus of support, which they engineered through a church declaration, written by a group of German Christian leaders in March 1939 at a meeting in the Bonn suburb of Bad Godesberg, hosted by Bishop Heinrich Oberheid.[48] The Godesberg Declaration asserted that Christian churches could not be international; that National Socialism is an extension of Martin Luther's efforts; and that Christianity repudiates Judaism.[49] The centerpiece of the declaration was its question and answer: "Is Christianity derived from Judaism and is it its continuation and completion, or does Christianity stand in opposition to Judaism? We answer this question: Christianity is the unbridgeable religious opposition to Judaism."

Several different political agendas coincided to produce the declaration, which was supposed to unify the church around German Christian racial principles. Kerrl, under pressure from Hitler to create a unified Reich church, thought such a declaration would overcome theological differences and would also force church leaders to turn away from politics and focus on spiritual matters. Rivalries within the movement, especially between the German Christian leadership in Thuringia and Bishop Heinz Weidemann's German Christian group in Bremen, were to be smoothed over by a renewed commitment to racism. With the declaration, German Christian leaders sought to suppress leaders of the Confessing Church, whom they accused of instigating tensions between the Nazi Party and the church, causing Nazi Party discrimination against German Christian pastors; one German Christian pastor complained that he was denied Nazi Party permission to wear his SA uniform at the upcoming Nuremberg rally. Confessing Church pastors in some regions were keeping the donations they collected and not turning them over to church officials who were German Christians, and the German Christians complained that the Confessing Church was acting as a "competing regime."[50]

Publication of the declaration in the church's official Law Gazette (Gesetzblatt) on April 4, 1939 carried the added announcement that its principles

---

[48] For a biography of Oberheid and a description of his involvement in establishing the Institute, see Faulenbach, *Ein Weg durch die Kirche*, 180–81.

[49] Signatories were the German Christian leaders of eleven regional churches: APU, Saxony, Nassau-Hessen, Schleswig-Holstein, Thuringia, Mecklenburg, Pfalz (Palatinate), Anhalt, Oldenburg, Lübeck, and Ostmark (Austria), all of which were dominated by the German Christian movement. The Confessing Church denounced the declaration, as did the Reformed Confederation for Germany, and the World Council of Churches issued a statement opposing it.

[50] Three-page letter from Oberpfarrer G. Pachtner to Werner, dated May 16, 1939 (ZAK 1/A4/170, Document 45–46).

would be implemented by establishing an Institute for the Study and Eradication of Jewish Influence on the Church Life of the German Volk.[51]

The national press had a field day. Most hailed the document as a call for eliminating Jewish influence within the church. The headline of Frankfurt's *Generalanzeiger*, for instance, proclaimed: "Against Jewish Influence and Politics in Religion," while Kassel's *Kurhessische Landeszeitung* bluntly declared: "Jews Annihilate Christian Faith: Collective Work of Church Leadership against Jewish Influence in Religion." The Vienna *Neues Wiener Tagblatt* cheered, "Clear Front against Hypocrisy," while the *Württemberger Zeitung* of Stuttgart announced, "Faith in Christ Is Opposite of Judaism: Collective Principles of Protestant State Church Leaders." Newspapers in Frankfurt and in Hanover headlined their stories by proclaiming that the Protestant church had adopted the principles of the German Christians.[52]

While the declaration was intended to provide a national church consensus for German Christian principles, the public perception was that the German Christians had taken over the Protestant churches. Yet even some German Christian church leaders refused to sign the statement. Weidemann, for example, did not object to the content of the Godesberg Declaration, but he did not want to give added strength to an alliance between Leffler and Kerrl.[53]

Church opponents of the declaration claimed they were concerned about the exclusion of baptized non-Aryans from the church. That issue had already divided at least some members of the Confessing Church from the German Christians since 1933, when the German Christians sought unsuccessfully to implement the Nazi regime's laws banning non-Aryans from the civil service within the church. For the Confessing Church, baptism remained a sacrament, taking precedence over Nazi racial laws, whereas German Christians rejected Christian doctrine concerning baptism and viewed race as transcendent. For the Confessing Church, the formulators of the declaration, in excluding baptized non-Aryans from the church, were "enemies of the cross of Christ . . . (and) had divorced themselves from the holy Christian church." Some accused the German Christians of "Pharisaism": "Christ created a holy body and a Christian church out of Jews and pagans. The fence that Christ broke down has been erected again and the Christian church has been turned

[51] Other provisions of the addendum, including founding a central office in the church to fight against the misuse of religion for political goals, were not carried through.

[52] Newspaper clippings at LKA Eisenach.

[53] Heinonen, *Anpassung und Identität*, 256. Weidemann's German Christian group began to fall apart in in the fall of 1941, and many of his supporters had already left him by then to join the Thuringian division of the German Christian movement; some became active members of the Institute. Weidemann himself was arrested and imprisoned for perjury in the fall of 1944.

into a Pharisaic sect."[54] Some pastors saw the declaration as a forbidden intrusion of religion into political affairs that would lead to a "secularization of the Christian message."[55] Those who supported the declaration complained that the Confessing Church was causing conflicts between the party and the church.[56]

Critics of the declaration worried that its condemnation of Judaism might end up being misused as an attack against Christianity; nowhere was concern expressed about its potential antisemitic consequences. The three "neutral" bishops who held themselves aloof from both the German Christians and the Confessing Church objected to the unclarity of the term "Jewish" in the Godesberg Declaration because it might encourage attacks on Christianity. Bishop Hans Meiser of Bavaria asked if "Jewish" referred to the "Jewish-Talmudic religion" or to the apostle Paul's teachings concerning justification (by faith), which were intended as a sharp refutation of the "Jewish-Pharisaic spirit"; "or was the declaration directed not against the genuine opposition between Jewish religion and Jewish spirit but rather against the divine revelation of the Old and New Testament?"[57] Jewishness was getting dangerously close to the heart of Christianity.[58] Bishop Marahrens also objected, writing, "What is correct in this declaration is self-understood. Whatever in it is not self-understood is false."[59] He complained that the declaration did not differentiate Judaism from the Old Testament, which remains unquestionably part of the Christian Bible, just as Jews remained potential converts to Christianity, not racial outcasts to be excluded from the church.[60] Even some German Christians were dissatisfied with the declaration and felt it did not go far enough in separating Christianity from Judaism; Bishop Sasse of Thuringia, a hotheaded antisemite and an early and devout member of the German Christian movement and the Nazi Party, demanded that the language about the degeneracy of Judaism be strengthened: "There is for me no messianic line leading from the Old Testament to Christ." [61]

[54]Letter from the Council of the Protestant Church of the APU (signature indecipherable) to Werner, dated May 12, 1939 (ZAK 1/A4/170).

[55]Letter to Werner from the Pastors' Assembly of the Church of Gramzow, with 24 handwritten signatures, protesting the Bekanntmachung, dated May 10, 1939 (ZAK 1/A4/170).

[56]Letter to Werner from a senior pastor, G. Pachtner, dated May 16, 1939 (ZAK 1/A4/170).

[57]Letter from Bischof Meiser to Rat der Evangelischen Lutherischen Kirche Deutschlands, dated May 5, 1939 (NEK, Repertorium des Archivs der Bekennenden Kirche Schleswig-Holstein, Signatur 57, Neue Nummer 323).

[58]Lindemann, "Typisch Jüdisch," 263.

[59]Letter from Marahrens to Werner, dated April 19, 1939 (ZAK 1/A4/168).

[60]Ibid.

[61]Telegram from Sasse to Werner, date not clear; see also letter from Sasse to Werner, dated May 27, 1939 (ZAK 1/A4/170, Document 85–86).

Figure 2.2. Bishop Martin Sasse of Thuringia.

Hans von Soden, professor of New Testament at the University of Marburg and a member of the Confessing Church, wrote a strong critique of the Godesberg Declaration in which he argued that the sharp opposition between Christianity and Judaism was not due to a break between Old and New Testaments. Rather, von Soden argued, the split was the fault of the Jews, who rejected Jesus because theirs was a legalistic religion that claimed a racial-völkisch privilege in relation to God and regarded Jesus and his apostles as enemies of their Volk. Furthermore, he attacked those calling for a dejudaization of the church as in fact judaizing it by failing to distinguish between the religious heritage of Judaism (presumably the Old Testament) and the Hebrew words used in Christian texts. Using the occasion for a broader critique of the German Christians, von Soden stated that "it is a historical fact that Christianity arose out of Judaism. The assumption that Jesus was racially not a Jew," he continued, "cannot be excluded in light of the populations of his Galilean homeland, but remains utterly arbitrary and cannot be founded on scientific grounds."[62] Von Soden pointed out the Jewish identity of Paul and of many of the first Christians as reason to reject the declaration's claim that Christianity is the "unbridgeable religious opposition to Judaism," yet he continued by asserting that Judaism remained a threat to Christian faith. That threat, however, came not only from Jews but from anyone who misinterpreted the gospels in a "Jewish" fashion.[63] His critique of the Godesberg Declaration was thus a defense of the Old Testament as divine revelation and an opportunity to label the German Christian opponents of Judaism as themselves Jewish.

There was also political unease over the Godesberg Declaration. Bishop Marahrens of Hanover, head of one of the three "intact" regional churches in Germany that had not fallen under the control of the German Christians, refused to sign the Declaration. He expressed concern that by carrying the signatures of only one faction of regional church leaders, the declaration would discredit the others: "Judging by the nature of the declaration, your publication must give the impression that the group of church leaders involved intended to politically discredit all other church leaders. This is how the declaration continues to be perceived."[64] However, Marahrens did not foreclose signing a statement; at a meeting with Leffler on May 4, two days prior to the Institute's opening, Marahrens expressed a greater willingness to acknowledge the centrality of race as a point of conjuncture between Nazism and Christianity.[65] That, in turn, encouraged Kerrl to try again to summarize the Godesberg

[62] Soden, "Die Godesberger Erklärung," 7.
[63] Ibid., 9.
[64] Letter from Marahrens to Werner, dated April 13, 1939 (ZAK 1/A4/170).
[65] Lindemann, "Typisch Jüdisch," 264.

Declaration into a brief list of "Principles" that could be signed by all the heads of the regional churches. The resulting "Principles" ("Grundsätze"),[66] which carried far more signatures than the Godesberg Declaration, was signed on May 31, 1939, by bishops Hollweg, Drechsler, Meiser, Ewerbeck, Wurm, Happich, Henke, and Kühlewein. Apparently convinced that this was a last chance to achieve a settlement, Bishop Marahrens, Bishop Helmut Johnsen of Brunswick, and Pastor Friedrich Happich, representing Hessen-Waldeck, agreed to sign the statement, adding some minor explanatory commentary.

The language was also toughened in certain respects; the text of the Godesberg Declaration was reformulated into principles proclaiming the loyalty of Christians to National Socialism based on Luther's claim that politics and religion cannot be divided. Luther was invoked to build a bridge to Lutheran factions within the church; Werner Petersmann, a pastor in Breslau who was head of the "Luther Deutsche" faction within the Protestant church, responded by writing that the "Jewish question" required sharp theological responsibility and practical solutions; he later joined the Institute.[67] The invocation of Luther was intended to overcome conservative opposition, and then went on to state: "The National Socialist worldview fights with all relentlessness against the political and spiritual influence of the Jewish race on our völkisch life." The "Principles" then had to clarify that "Jewishness" did not imply Christianity: "In the realm of faith there is a sharp opposition between the message of Jesus Christ and his apostles and of the Jewish religion of legalism and political messianic hope that is also already being fought against in the Old Testament. In the realm of völkisch life an earnest and responsible racial politics is necessary for the preservation of the purity of our Volk." By distinguishing between the Old Testament and Judaism and by defining the Old Testament as anti-Jewish, a position followed by the theologically conservative Confessing Church and Catholics, the principles responded to the concerns of Marahrens and won support from the "neutral" bishops. Racial politics were affirmed, both Jesus and the Old Testament were placed in opposition to Judaism, and National Socialism was declared binding on Christians; such was the "moderate" position of those who rejected the Godesberg Declaration.

In fact, the establishment of the Institute, as proclaimed in the Gesetzblatt, raised no outcry. Marahrens's only doubts about the Institute, he wrote, were whether dejudaization had not already been the subject of extensive work, and whether the Old Testament would be considered to fall under the definition

---

[66] "Grundsätze für eine den Erfordernissen der Gegenwart entsprechende Ordnung der Deutschen Evangelischen Kirche."

[67] The comments appeared in the German Christian journal that Petersmann edited, *Aufbau im Positiven Christentum* (1939), 61.

of "Jewish": "Jewish influence and the importance of the Old Testament are of course different things."[68] Meiser wrote that he was not opposed to the creation of the Institute, but was concerned that its work not be too negative to be fruitful.[69]

Those criticisms and internal church conflicts were not resulting in the kind of internal church harmony that Kerrl was supposed to produce, and made him hesitate to finalize his financial support for the Institute through the summer and early fall of 1939. His failure to fulfill his mandate from Hitler, to achieve a unity within the church that would keep it from interfering with the regime, meant that his own status within the Reich was undermined; he never recovered his political prestige.

As a result of Kerrl's delays in supporting the Institute, monies for its work were not transferred prior to the Institute's official opening in May of 1939. Meanwhile, however, organization of the Institute proceeded apace. Werner was surprised to receive an invitation to the Institute's opening celebrations, not expecting it to open so quickly, particularly since the legal relationship of the Institute to the regional churches had not yet been finalized.[70] Another church leader was upset because the invitation to attend the formal opening arrived too late to make arrangements to attend.[71] At least one bishop, Volkers of Oldenburg, a German Christian, was surprised by the Institute's opening because he had signed the declaration as a matter of principle, not expecting an immediate demand for financial contributions.[72]

Just before the Institute opened, Heinz Hunger, a pastor from Friedebach, Thuringia, who served as the Institute's business manager, described its purpose in a newspaper article. The goal was to liberate Germany from the "Near East and return to what is one's own. . . . The most important task of the Institute is to terminate even the last hideout of Jewish cultural pollution, namely of church life, which is dishonorable for our great present-day situation."[73]

---

[68] Letter from Marahrens, no addressee (most likely Werner), dated April 12, 1939 (ZAK 1/A4/ 168).

[69] Letter from Bischof Meiser to the Rat der Evangelischen Lutherischen Kirche Deutschlands, dated May 5, 1939 (NEK, Repertorium des Archivs der Bekennenden Kirche Schleswig-Holstein, Signatur 57; Neue Nummer 323).

[70] Report by Pettelkau, dated August 18, 1939 (ZAK 7/4166).

[71] Letter from Schlesien (signature unreadable) to Werner, dated May 6, 1939, complaining that the invitation to attend the Institute's opening had just arrived that day (ZAK 7/4166).

[72] Letter from Volkers to Werner; dated May 3, 1939 (ZAK 7/4166).

[73] Newspaper clipping (unidentified source, undated, ZAK 7/4166, Document 8). After the war, Hunger became a noted psychologist in Germany, writing extensively on sexual issues. See

OPENING OF THE INSTITUTE

The Institute was formally inaugurated on Saturday, May 6, 1939, in the Wartburg Castle and the invitations, signed by Leffler, made its name official: Institute for the Study and Eradication of Jewish Influence on German Church Life.[74] Werner attended, which may have been unexpected, since his name does not appear in the printed program. He expressed his greetings and welcomed the Institute with the hope that it would distance itself from theological special-interest groups and bring honor to German theological scholarship: "I add to this my confidence that the result of your work must contribute to a new encounter between the Protestant church and the people, a new reception of the unadulterated gospel by the people of the Third Reich."[75] The assembled guests then listened to a string quartet playing an adagio by Mozart, sang a hymn, heard a speech by Leffler, and then another quartet, by Schubert. The opening set a pattern: most Institute conferences made extensive use of music, interspersing church hymns, Nazi songs, and classical chamber music, reflecting the broader effort during the Third Reich to affirm national identity by playing "Germanic" music.[76] Defining music as "Germanic" turned out to be as impossible as defining an "Aryan Christianity," since so many beloved hymns and songs had actually been composed by non-Germans; likewise, many aspects of Christianity turned out not to be acceptably "Aryan," ranging from Gospel teachings about meekness, to identification of Jesus as "lamb of God," and even to Paul himself, who was not only a Jew but a Pharisee.

But the mood at the Institute's opening was optimistic and enthusiastic. The assembled audience sang "Wir glauben das Neue" ("We Believe What Is New"), an anthem affirming the Institute's goal of creating a new Christianity, which, like the other hymns sung that day, contained no reference to God, Christianity, or Jesus. Grundmann then delivered the keynote address, "The Dejudaization of the Religious Life as the Task of German Theology and Church," setting forth his aspirations for the Institute: "The elimination of Jewish influence on German life is the urgent and fundamental question of the present German

---

Herzog, *Sex after Fascism*, 22, 277. Leffler was the titular head, while Grundmann served as academic director, with assistance from Rudolf Meyer and Ernst Bardey, the former as an alleged expert in Talmud, the latter as a proclaimed expert in Teutonic piety during the period that Germany was Christianized.

[74] ZAK 7/4166, document 9.

[75] ZAK 7/4166, document 24.

[76] Applegate and Potter, eds., *Music and German National Identity*; Potter, *Most German of the Arts*.

Figure 2.3. The Wartburg Castle.

religious situation."[77] His lecture repeated many of the themes of the memoranda and position papers by him, Pich, and others in the months before the Institute's opening. Grundmann rejected a biblical salvation history (Heilsgeschichte) leading from Abraham to Moses to the prophets and finally to Jesus. The Old Testament, he insisted, has no monopoly on salvation history; every race receives God's intervention. Church doctrine, he asserted, had arbitrarily omitted the religious insights of figures such as Zarathustra in creating a falsely exclusive salvation history linking the Old and New Testaments.

Members of the Institute would use racial theory, Grundmann stressed, to investigate the religious history of Palestine and of Jesus. Racial theory would clarify the role of Judaism in early Christianity and also expose its nefarious influence on modern philosophy. Such Institute projects would have political

[77]Grundmann's lecture was printed as a pamphlet and distributed through the German Christian publishing house in Weimar, run by Heinz Dungs, an Institute member. Six thousand copies were printed, at a cost of 2,070 RM, apparently paid for by Werner, who had promised Grundmann he would distribute the text to pastors within the APU. As announced in the first issue of the *Verbandsmitteilungen*, the Institute's newsletter, membership in the Institute was open to a circle of subscribers, who paid 1 RM and received the newsletter, as well as a discount on Institute publications (ZAK 7/4166, documents 37 and 38).

as well as ecclesiological and theological consequences; Grundmann blamed opposition to National Socialism within the church on theologians tainted by Jewish influence. Eradicating the Jewish from the Christian would undermine such opposition. Grundmann's rhetoric borrowed liberally from Nazi Party rallies: Jews had destroyed völkisch thinking and, with help from Bolshevism, they were now striving for world domination; For these reasons, the struggle against the Jews has been irrevocably turned over to the German Volk."[78] The war against the Jews was not simply a military battle, but a spiritual battle: "Jewish influence on all areas of German life, including on religious-church life, must be exposed and broken."[79] That sentence, in turn, became the defining slogan of the Institute, used whenever Grundmann had to explain its purpose.

The opening of the Institute was hailed in the May 14, 1939, issue of the German Christian journal, *Positives Christentum*, which was edited by Leffler. A huge banner headline, underlined in thick red ink, declared: "Dejudaization of Church Life: Institute for the Study and Eradication of Jewish Influence on German Church Life Founded." The entire front page was devoted to a description of the opening ceremonies.[80] A German newspaper in Hermannstadt (Sibiu), Romania, where there was to be a branch of the Institute, hailed its opening as an effort to carry forward Luther's Reformation.[81] Newspapers controlled by anti-Christian völkisch circles, such as *Nordland* and *Die Sigrune*, took a very different line, mocking the Institute by insisting that once Christianity was dejudaized, there would be nothing left to it. The journal *Der Weltkampf* concluded that the Institute's work could only reveal that Christianity was nothing more than a form of Judaism—a further indication that the German Christian movement's design to become a full, power-sharing partner in the Nazi regime was meeting with opposition.[82]

Grundmann responded to the Institute's Nazi critics in the pages of a German Christian weekly, *Deutsches Christentum*, in July 1939.[83] Claiming that critics exemplified "Jewish journalism," he asserted that Hitler himself understood the need to develop a sharper view of the Jewish problem in order to

---

[78]Grundmann, *Die Entjudung*, 9.

[79]*Ibid.*, 17.

[80]ZAK 7/4166, document 23.

[81]*Siebenbürgisch-Deutsches Tageblatt*, Hermannstadt, May 18, 1939, cited in a summary of press reports at ZAK 7/4177, document 30.

[82]*Der Weltkampf: Die Judenfrage in Geschichte und Gegenwart* was founded by Alfred Rosenberg and edited by Hans Hauptmann, author of *Jesus der Arier: Ein Heldenleben.*

[83]Another answer to the critique in *Die Sigrune* was published by Julius Leutheuser ("Der Weg zum Gottglauben der Deutsche," 300): for Jews, he wrote, faith is "the murder of the heart"

expose and eradicate Jewish influence in German life.[84] The very insistence that Christianity was a mere extension of Judaism was a falsehood perpetrated by Jews seeking political emancipation in the eighteenth and nineteenth centuries. Those who insisted on emphasizing the links between Christianity and Judaism would have to explain why the Jews "prepared the cross for Jesus of Nazareth. . . . And it must be further clarified why the Jews everywhere were the most fervent persecutors of Christ and Christians." Finally, he argued, viewing Christianity as an extension of Judaism would suggest that Germans through the centuries who had worshiped Jesus had fallen victim to Judaism, a defamation of German history.[85]

NAME AND PURPOSE

Was the Institute intended as a purely academic enterprise, as Grundmann was to argue after the war, or was its dejudaization goal stated from the outset? The question has been raised by scholars in connection to its name; the term "eradication" ("Beseitigung") does not always appear as part of the Institute's name in its publications, giving the impression that its function was solely to "study" Jewish influence. In his postwar statements of self-defense, Grundmann asserted that the Institute had been established as a neutral, academically objective "research" institute, and not as an antisemitic, pro-Nazi organization. He claimed that "eradication" was a term foisted on him by Reich Minister Kerrl and that he had opposed it. Yet Kerrl's support for the Institute came only months after it was established, at a time that "eradication" was part of its name and the Institute's goals were clear. Moreover, Grundmann's own

---

through "destructive and emotionless reason," whereas for Christ faith is "reverent and grateful revelation of the heart of God." This was, apparently, a task for men. In the section of the magazine devoted to women, no mention is made of antisemitism or the Institute. Instead, there are exhortations to wifely duties, accompanied by photographs of pious late medieval statues of mothers with draped heads holding infants. A remarkably simpleminded explanation of race was presented to women in *Christenkreuz und Hakenkreuz* 4, 7 (July 1936):14:

> Finally it is necessary to explain to German women, as mothers of children, what race is, so that it has a good resonance within marriage. Racially German people have pure, undiluted Teutonic blood, which they often inherited for centuries. . . . Racially pure men are often Siegfrieds, racially pure women are often Brunhilde figures in the struggle for existence. National Socialism does not want to fight Christianity, as it is often accused, but rather wants to deepen it.

[84] ZAK 7/4166, document 48.

[85] Grundmann, "Wir Fragen die Sigrune," *Deutsches Christentum* 4, 28 (July 9, 1939) (ZAK 7/416, document 48).

intentions of eradicating Jewishness are made clear not only in his opening address of May 6, 1939, but also in a letter he wrote to Kerrl on September 8, 1939, a week after the outbreak of the war:

> In a moment in which world Jewry in its hatred of the German people has struck a decisive blow and the German Volk has been placed in a struggle for its rights and its life, I turn to you as the director of the scholarly work of the dejudaization institute, which was created by a group of regional churches with your approval. . . . We approached the work of this Institute with the conviction that Jewish influence on all areas of German life has to be exposed and broken, indeed also in the religious-ecclesiastical realm.[86]

The Godesberg Declaration of March and the Bekanntmachung of April 1939, both of which give broad church support to the Institute, as well as the Institute's own by-laws,[87] include the term "eradication" in its name. Yet at a meeting of Institute leaders and in 1940 Grundmann requested that the word "eradication" be stricken from its charter. He said he did not want to appear to anticipate the results of the scholarly investigations undertaken by the Institute by suggesting that eradication was its starting point; he also argued that the actual eradication of Jewish influence on Christianity was a task to be implemented by the church, not by the Institute. Instead, he wanted the Institute to be an open and independent vehicle for German Protestant scholarship to examine Jewish influences on the church. The two examples he mentioned were determining the influence of a Jew, Friedrich Julius Stahl, in shaping the constitution of the Prussian church, and determining which elements in Paul's writings were Jewish, and which had entered his work from non-Jewish influences.[88] Presumably, Grundmann assumed by the time of this meeting in 1940 that Jesus's racial identity as an Aryan had been resolved so that the Institute could now turn to the problem of Paul, a Jew steeped in rabbinic religion, whose writings had constituted the theological foundation of the church. A full dejudaization of Christianity would require eliminating Paul's epistles from the New Testament, yet Paul's status was so important, especially for Martin Luther and all Lutherans, that only a cautious examination of his writings could be suggested in 1940; a more radical solution would have to wait.

[86]Letter from Grundmann to Kerrl, dated September 1939 (ZAK 7/4166). Grundmann used similar language in a letter to Werner two months later, November 13, 1939 (ZAK 7/4166).

[87]Osten-Sacken, "Die Grosse Lästerung, 316 fn 12.

[88]Transcript of a meeting between Grundmann and senior church councillor Buschtöns, April 24, 1940, in Jena (USHMM archive, RG-11.001M reel 80, microfilm of Osobyi Archive [Moscow] records, 1932–45; 1993.A.0085 UC).

The word "eradication" was dropped from the three anthologies of academic papers delivered at Institute-sponsored conferences that were published in 1940, 1941, and 1943, and also from a published collection of papers that had been delivered at a Wittenberg conference in March 1940. In July of 1940 the word was also dropped temporarily from the Institute's stationery, but it reappeared in March of 1942, disappearing again in June 1942.[89] Precisely that spring, the small Jewish community of Eisenach was deported. In a June 1940 Institute invitation to join its Förderkreis (supporting membership), the word "eradication" does not appear. Instead, there is a call for the "Dejudaization of Church and Christianity" ("Entjudung von Kirche und Christentum") as the unavoidable and decisive duty of present-day Christian life, essential to the future of Christianity.[90] In his 1943 farewell letter to the Institute's supporting members marking his retirement, Pich explained that the name had been shortened out of a wish for a "shorter name" for the Institute. The name expresses the "decisive point of departure of our work," Pich wrote, but could be shortened to "Entjudungsinstitut" ("Dejudaization Institute"), except on posted mail, which required the full name.[91]

Omitting "eradication" made the Institute sound like a "research" center, though its anti-Jewish motives never changed, and everyone was well aware of them.[92] The Institute was colloquially referred to as the "Entjudungsinstitut" throughout its existence, though Werner called it a "Judeninstitut" ("Jews' Institute").[93] Institute publications advertised its books for sale with the heading, "In the Struggle for the Dejudaization of Religious Life" ("Im Kampf für die Entjudung des religiösen Lebens"). Omission of "eradication" may have at times been a ironic; by late 1942 and 1943, Germany had eradicated its Jews.

That some historians omit "eradication" when discussing the Institute may stem from a desire to conceal its antisemitic intentions, or from a failure to fully grasp the aggressive antisemitism at the heart of the Institute's theological venture.[94] Kurt Meier, for example, consistently omits the word "eradication" and argues that the Institute's purpose was to defend the church and "counter

[89] See stationery of a letter from Brauer to the APU, dated March 22, 1942, and a letter from Grundmann to Werner, dated June 19, 1942 (ZAK 7/4166).

[90] June 1940 membership application (USHMM archive, RG-11.001M, reel 80, microfilm of Osobyi Archive [Moscow] records, 1932–45; 1993.A.0085 UC).

[91] Grundmann and Pich, "An die Förderer des Institutes," March 25, 1943 (LKA Eisenach III 2f).

[92] Letter from Grundmann to Werner, dated July 10, 1940 (ZAK 7/4166).

[93] Memorandum by Werner, February 7, 1940 (ZAK 7/4166).

[94] Examples of works that omit "Beseitigung" and fail to acknowledge the Institute's stated purpose include Meier, Kreuz und Hakenkreuz, 165–66; Faulenbach, Ein Weg durch die Kirche, 181; Erich Stegmann, Der Kirchenkampf in der Thüringer Evangelischen Kirche 1933–1945, 104.

Figure 2.4. Deportation of Eisenach Jews, May 9, 1942.

the defamatory propaganda that Christianity was Judaism for non-Jews."[95] Meier substantiates his claim by referring to an unpublished autobiography written by Grundmann in 1969, in which Grundmann claims that as a result of his protests, the word "eradication" was stricken from the name of the Institute because it implied a prior conclusion had been reached regarding Jewish influences.[96] By ignoring the eradication of Judaism that was the stated goal of the Institute, the antisemitism of the Institute is misrepresented and cannot be properly interpreted. Viewing the Institute solely in the context of the church and its politics, rather than the larger network of the many similar pseudo-research institutes that flourished during the Third Reich, ignores its function as a generator of antisemitic propaganda.

MANAGEMENT AND MEMBERSHIP

The process of negotiating the Institute's legal status lasted through the summer and fall of 1939 and was not finalized until January 1940. A charter setting

[95] Meier, *Kreuz und Hakenkreuz*, 166, 167.
[96] "Erkenntnis und Wahrheit: Aus meinem Leben," (typescript, LKA Eisenach), 45.

forth the Institute's governing organization was signed by the church leaders of Thuringia, Saxony, Nassau-Hessen, Lübeck, Anhalt, and Mecklenburg, only six of the eleven who had signed the Godesberg Declaration.[97] Efforts continued to win the support of the all-important Old Prussian Union (APU), which was under Werner's leadership.

Hesitations of both Kerrl and Werner made the financial status of the Institute uncertain for its first six months of operation. Werner's hesitance may have arisen as a result of reluctance by some members of the governing board of the APU to support the Institute's work.[98] Kerrl, writing to Werner on August 24, 1939, informed him that ventures such as the Institute could only be undertaken with the consent of those members.[99]

The governance of the Institute was overseen by an administrative board composed of representatives of the seven churches serving five-year terms. The director of the Institute, Leffler, served without pay for five years and was appointed by a board of directors, chaired by Johannes Sievers, a church official from Lübeck. In addition, a scholarly advisory board directed the projects to be undertaken; Grundmann served as director of that board. Finally, a treasurer, Erwin Brauer, a church governing councillor in Thuringia and a national German Christian leader, handled the finances, assisted by Hunger, the business manager, together with Hugo Pich. A committee to oversee financial matters included Sievers, Brauer, and Willy Kretzschmar, a church official from Saxony.

In December Grundmann prevailed upon his friend and Institute member, Johannes Hempel, professor of Old Testament at the University of Berlin and editor of the distinguished journal of Old Testament studies, *Zeitschrift für alttestamentliche Wissenschaft*, to intervene with Kerrl and Werner.[100] In a series

[97] Of the six who signed, four were clearly dominated by strong and radical German Christian leaders, while Nassau-Hessen and Saxony were not.

[98] Erwin Brauer, Schatzmeister of the Institute, appealed in November 1939 to Bishop Walther Schultz to intervene with Werner, explaining that without immediate financial subsidy, Pich's work at the Institute was threatened. Werner had supported the Institute at its inception, Brauer wrote, but was not hesitating to finance it. Letter from Erwin Brauer to Walther Schultz dated November 17, 1939 (ZAK 7/4166).

[99] Memorandum by Werner of meeting with Bischof Peter and Pfarrer Dungs, dated February 6, 1940 (EZA 7/4166).

[100] Grundmann wrote to Hempel on December 24, 1939, expressing his gratitude and indicating that he had told the Institute's business manager to prepare a contract on the basis of a board of directors whose initial members were Leffler, Hempel, Meyer-Erlach, Preisker, Opitz, Sasse, Schultz, Sievers, Wilkendorf, Seck, Hunger, and himself. He added, "I beg you to talk to Werner and find out what that fox wants." LKA Eisenach III 2f.

of letters to Grundmann, Hempel explained that Kerrl was reluctant to use church taxes to fund a Thuringian project, and wanted the Institute to be independent of the state church. Kerrl wanted to distance the Institute from the church and urged an affiliation with a university, though he was aware that the rector at Jena, Karl Astel, was antagonistic toward the field of theology.[101]

Accccording to Hempel, Werner's concerns were primarily legal and political, not theological—namely, how to support the Institute while maintaining the national political balance of the Protestant church. Werner, according to Hempel, approved the Institute's antisemitic agenda and expected a wave of antisemitism to arise as a consequence of the war.[102] The APU ultimately signed the charter, but Werner attempted to keep a low profile by refusing to serve as chair of the Institute's governing board. He provided financial support, on December 22, 1939, transferring 1,500 RM to the Institute;[103] he insisted, however, that the APU not be listed as one of the regional churches that helped establish the Institute.[104]

Ultimately, Kerrl withdrew his objections to the church's funding of the Institute, in a letter to Werner dated January 26, 1940. That same day, one of Kerrl's colleagues at the Ministry for Church Affairs wrote to Grundmann informing him that those churches wishing to give financial support to the Institute would be permitted to use funds from their church tax collections.[105] Once the APU was able to participate, financial contributions began to flow. Five thousand RM were sent to the Institute, on Werner's directive, in early February 1940.[106]

Institute expenses were met through donations from regional churches and the sale of its publications. Its offices were located rent-free in Eisenach in a large church-owned villa at Bornstrasse 11 that also housed the Thuringian Predigerseminar, where theologians, after their examinations, were trained in practical pastoral work. In 1940 Institute offices were moved to Fritz

---

[101] Letters from Hempel to Grundmann, dated December 2, 1939 (LKA Eisenach).

[102] Letter from Hempel to Grundmann, dated January 6, 1940 (LKA Eisenach).

[103] To bank account 298 in the Stadtsparkasse in Eisenach (ZAK 1/C3/174).

[104] Transcript of a meeting in Jena between Grundmann and OKR Buschtöns, April 24, 1940 (USHMM archive, RG-11.001M, reel 80, microfilm of Osobyi Archive [Moscow] records, 1932–45; 1993.A.0085 UC). See also the letter sent by (apparently) Werner to the Reich Security Main Office (RSHA), dated June 11, 1940, regarding the April 24 meeting.

[105] Letter from Stahn to Grundmann, dated January 26, 1940 (ZAK 7/4166).

[106] Memorandum by Werner of meeting with Bischof Peter and Pfarrer Dungs, dated February 6, 1940 (ZAK 7/4166); see also letter from Brauer to Werner dated February 22, 1940, thanking him for agreeing to pay 500 RM (ZAK 7/4166).

Figure 2.5. The church-owned villa in Eisenach that housed the Institute.

Reuterweg 2a, another building owned by the church, where the national offices of the German Christians were also located. Institute staff earned salaries
from their churches or universities,[107] leaving only expenses for telephone,
secretary, and heating, and conferences.[108] Holding a conference was a major
expense, and the Institute sponsored an extraordinary number of them. The
gatherings were held at conference centers, such as Weissenfels, or at hotels,
and involved receptions, hotel accommodations, travel costs for invited speakers, and, of course, publicity. Institute publications were sold and brought
earnings, and travel to conferences was sometimes underwritten for invited
speakers by the regional churches that had agreed to act as sponsors. Werner
remained financially generous to the Institute; whenever extra money was
needed for a project, it was quickly forthcoming from his office. After attend-

[107] The only employee paid directly by the Institute was the secretary, a Fräulein Peter, brought
to Eisenach from Berlin, whose talents were extolled at Institute board meetings.
[108] Budget: 44,000 RM; telephone 700 RM; heat 100 RM; secretarial 2,500 RM (ThHStA Weimar, Akte Thüringisches Volksbildungsministerium 1522, 1939/40).

ing a meeting of the Institute's governing board in Leipzig on February 7, 1940,[109] for example, Werner turned over an additional 5,000 RM.[110]

Although generally supportive of the German Christians, Werner retained concerns. In a letter to Grundmann dated June 28, 1940, Werner wrote that people were still objecting to the Institute, saying that it encouraged church politics. Furthermore, according to Werner, there was not enough money to support its projects, although he said he would continue his 5,000 RM donations. The Institute, in his view, should concentrate on fewer projects and have the character of a free research institute, independent of the churches.[111] Grundmann, who initially wanted a university-affiliated research institute, changed his mind, apparently realizing the financial boon of church affiliation: at a meeting of the governing board of the Institute on May 29, 1940, he said he wanted 35,000 RM to make the Institute "*the* research center of the German Protestant church."[112] At the meeting church councillor Sievers suggested that Werner increase his annual donation to 10,000 RM for three years. Brauer, the comptroller, reported that the Institute's finances in the fiscal year 1939/40 totaled 32,450.65 RM in income, and 30,476.78 RM in expenses, leaving a balance of 1,973.87 RM. In addition to the funding from Werner's office, the Thuringian regional church contributed over 42,000 RM over the five-year course of the Institute's operations. On another occasion, Werner donated 40 RM so that ten students from Berlin would be able to attend an Institute conference.[113]

The names of Institute members have been difficult to confirm with certainty. Not all of the people listed as members in the four issues of the Institute's newsletter (*Verbandsmitteilung*) lectured at its conferences or participated in its working groups. Some, such as Rudi Paret, professor of Islam at the University of Bonn, and Georg Beer, professor at the University of Heidelberg, seem to have been members in name only. Others who considered themselves members and attended meetings are not always listed, such as Georg Biundo, a German Christian pastor and church historian from the Palatinate, and Gerhard K. Schmidt, a German Christian pastor in Berlin who promoted church

---

[109]Transcript of a meeting of the governing board (ZAK 7/4166).

[110]Letter from Institute bursar Brauer to Werner, dated February 22, 1940, thanking him for the donation (ZAK 7/4166).

[111]Letter from Werner to Grundmann, dated June 28, 1940 (ZAK 7/4166).

[112]Report to Werner from church councillor Buschtöns on the governing board meeting in Eisenach, May 29, 1940 (ZAK 7/4166). According to Buschtöns, "As necessary as a research center for the German Protestant Church may be for the numerous scholarly projects of the church, the Jew Institute is in no way qualified, neither in scholarship nor church politics, for such a task."

[113]Letter from G. Spielmann to Buschtöns, dated February 12, 1941. (ZAK 7/4166).

use of the Institute's dejudaized New Testament.[114] By the end of 1939, the Institute claimed 80 members, and two years later that number reached 180. Most important is the number of professors, mostly of theology, who were members, and it is striking to note the range of the theologians: old and young, distinguished professors and junior instructors from universities throughout the Reich, representing a range of disciplines. In sheer number alone, they constituted a significant percentage of the field of theology in Germany. Other members were teachers, pastors, bishops, and church superintendents. There was also a category of "supporting membership," similar to the SS, presumably geared to laity who paid a nominal annual fee, but a list of those members is no longer extant.

The Institute addressed itself both to scholars and to laity, to the church and to the Nazi Party. Its scholarly publications were often accompanied by shorter, popularized versions. In November 1940 the Institute announced the publication of Grundmann's *Jesus der Galiläer*, followed by a popular rendition of his findings, *Wer ist Jesus von Nazareth?* The purpose, according to Institute publicity, was "to discredit Jesus as a Jew and resurrected messianic fantasy."[115] While *Jesus der Galiläer* pretended to present scholarly proof that Jesus was a Galilean non-Jew, *Wer ist Jesus?* was more direct in stating the political implications:

> The German Volk has waged a war against the Jew in order to liberate itself from the disintegration of its life and essence. The inciter behind the war that England inflicted upon the German Volk, as well as behind the world war, is the Jew. In opposition to Judaism the German Volk is conscious of its essence in all aspects of life. The question, whether at the center of the religious message there can stand a man who might be the messiah of the Jews, becomes bitterly earnest and difficult. Thus the question for inner German life becomes a burning one: What about Jesus Christ? [116]

WORKING GROUPS

The Institute's work had three prongs: working groups charged with scholarly tasks; conferences of scholars and clergy; and publications. Even before the

[114] Webster, "Dr. Georg Biundo," 92–111. On Schmidt, see Linck, "Gerhard K. Schmidt," in Göhres, Linck, and Liß-Walther, eds., *Als Jesus "arisch" wurde*, 74–75.

[115] Institute memorandum, signed by Pich, dated November 1940 (LKA Eisenach III 2b). *Wer ist Jesus von Nazareth?* was sold for only 60 cents.

[116] Grundmann, *Wer ist Jesus von Nazareth?*, 3.

Institute's formal opening in May 1939, Grundmann and his colleagues organized several working groups that included a mixture of professors and pastors and that varied in frequency of meetings and productivity.[117] Most important was the group assigned to investigate Christian origins from a racial perspective, chaired by Grundmann. Its first formal meeting was held in Leipzig the evening of July 15, 1939, and the participants included Georg Bertram, Gerhard Delling, Rudolf Meyer, Herbert Preisker, Carl Schneider, and Heinz Hunger.[118] Although the Egyptologist Siegfried Morenz, a lecturer at the University of Leipzig, was listed as a contributor to the planned publication of the working group, he was not present at the meeting. A second group, led by Johannes Hempel, professor of Old Testament at the University of Berlin, considered the racial composition of Israel in terms of its influence on ancient Israelite history. Its members included three professors—Hartmut Schmökel, Fritz Wilke, and Georg Beer—and an instructor, Karl Euler. The particular question addressed, Hempel reported, was ancient Israel's inability to build a state as a consequence of its racial mixing and religious history. The group was also to address Aryan influences on Israel's religious history.[119]

Hunger led a group of pastors studying the differences between Aryan and Semitic religiosity.[120] Faculty members from the University of Heidelberg led another group investigating attitudes toward Jews and Judaism from the Greco-Roman period to the sixteenth century.[121] A project spearheaded by Leffler in the spring of 1939, and drawing on German Christian and Institute members from Thuringia, published a dejudaized hymnal.[122] Additionally, the

[117] Although Grundmann initially had proposed fourteen working groups, only six were eventually created, and the war disrupted the possibility of regular meetings and publications.

[118] The stated purpose of the conference was an "Investigation of the origins of Christianity from the perspective of the new volkisch, racial points of view, with plans for a large history of Jesus and of Christian origins in a series of volumes."According to a report by Heinz Hunger, the investigators were divided into the following working groups: I. Palestine in the first pre- and post-Christian century (Meyer); II. The world of Hellenism (Schneider); III. Judaism in the Hellenistic world (Bertram); IV. The traditions about Jesus of Nazareth (Grundmann); V. Jesus; VI. The early communities of Palestine and Antioch (Grundmann); VII. Paul (Delling); VIII. The Johannine literature and theology (Preisker); IX. The spread of early Christianity in Asia Minor (Preisker), Egypt (Siegfried Morenz, Leipzig), Rome (Schneider) (ZAK 1/C3/174; see also LKA Eisenach A921).

[119] ZAK 1/C3/174.

[120] It first met in Berlin on June 9–10, 1939; its members included Johannes Hempel (LKA Eisenach A921).

[121] The group first met on June 8, 1939; it was led by Erwin Kiefer and included Josef Berenbach, an Arabist who served as librarian at the University of Heidelberg, and Rudi Paret, professor of Semitics and Islamic studies at the University of Heidelberg, after 1940 at Bonn.

[122] Kurt Thieme chaired the committee, Heinz Dungs handled the finances, and Erhard Mauersberger, music director of the Thuringian church, and Paul Schwadtke, a school director and SA

Institute encouraged the scholarly theological projects of students; it published several doctoral dissertations that had been written at the University of Jena,[123] as well as the racially inspired work of pastors advocating a dejudaization of Christianity.[124]

The first years of the Institute's work were its most productive. In addition to publishing the dejudaized New Testament, members worked jointly on a variety of ecclesial concerns, including a new catechism. By 1942, when the machinery for the mass murder of Jews was well underway, the Institute could celebrate its success: Germany was quickly becoming "judenrein," devoid of Jews—literally, pure of Jews—and scholars of distinction were participating in Institute conferences, leaders of the Institute were lecturing throughout the Reich and also for Wehrmacht troops, and research projects were proceeding well. Hostility toward Christianity, however, had not been eliminated but continued, based on links with Judaism. One German Christian leader, Friedrich Wieneke, overheard the dinner prayer of some German soldiers at a military rest center in 1941 in Zakopane, Poland: "Peace will only come when the last Jew hangs on the last bowel of the last parson."[125] The eradication of Jewish influence had to continue, but by 1942 the Institute had turned its attention to Teutonic traditions, working to create a synthesis of Christian and Germanic religion and presenting Christianity as the expression of Aryan culture.

INSTITUTE CONFERENCES

Institute conferences were a mixture of religion and scholarship, pageantry and passion. Music was always included, and the singing of both hymns and Nazi songs opened and closed the meetings, along with the Nazi salute. Evenings

---

officer, were in charge of the music. Paul Gimpel, a pastor and schoolteacher, revised the hymns (LKA Eisenach DC III/2f). See Baier, *Die Deutschen Christen Bayerns*, 22.

[123] These included Wagenführer, *Die Bedeutung Christi für Welt und Kirche*.

[124] Hans Pohlmann's book, for example, was announced by Pich as presenting the fundamental problem: "the necessity for the dejudaization of Christianity and the church" (Institute notice signed by Pich, dated November 1940, LKA Eisenach). Pohlmann, *Der Gottesgedanke Jesu als Gegensatz*. Rudolf Grabs published *Wegbereiter deutschen Christentums*, on the work of Paul de Lagarde and Houston Stuart Chamberlain and the necessity of dejudaizing Christianity (Verlag Deutsche Christen). The Institute newsletter also promoted a book, *Das Christentum im ersten Jahrhundert völkisch gesehen* (Weimar: Verlag Deutsche Christen, 1940), by Friedrich Schenke, who, like Grundmann, claimed that Jews had falsified the text of the New Testament.

[125] Report from Wieneke, "Attacks on Pastors," dated April 9, 1941 (BA Koblenz R 43 II/478a, Fiche l, document 19).

were devoted to Germanic culture—string quartets or readings of völkisch poetry. Attendance was usually open to the public, but papers were delivered by invitation. Discussion was encouraged, though the level was not always very sophisticated, as one observer, Wieneke, sarcastically noted.[126]

At times, the Institute's conferences and publications sounded like antisemitic war propaganda rather than scholarship. Wolf Meyer-Erlach, an avid Institute member and professor of practical theology at the University of Jena, told a conference in Rostock and a convention of pastors from Thuringia and Saxony that England had been judaized through its Reformation's emphasis on the Old Testament, in contrast to the Aryan quality of Nordic Christianity, the topic of a series of lectures he subsequently delivered to German troops.[127] Hempel, by now serving as a military chaplain, spoke on "The Religious Problem in the Present War."[128] At a meeting of Institute members in September 1941, Grundmann explained the war as a German "struggle to the death, a struggle against world Jewry and against all subversive and nihilistic powers."[129]

Despite its pretense of pursuing scholarly research, the commitment of the Institute was to Hitler and National Socialism, and its priority was a radical change of the church. Nazism, in the words of Meyer-Erlach, was liberating the church from its "ghetto." Dejudaization was not simply a matter of removing Hebrew terms or Old Testament concepts or redefining Jesus as Aryan; rather, the "Jewish" was used even more broadly, as Meyer-Erlach wrote in a 1941 letter:

With this work [of the Institute] we know we are bound to one thing as a foundation and guiding principle: to the work of the Führer. Just as the Führer liberates the peoples of the West through the Reich from the curse of suicidal petty states, so, too, the Reich liberates humanity from the ghetto of the churches. We are, as National Socialists, convinced, out of unconditionally

[126] Friedrich Wieneke, "Kirche und Weltanschauung 1933 bis 1945," typescript (ZAK 7/4166), 49–53.

[127] At the conference in Schneidemühl, January 13–14, 1941, Meyer-Erlach spoke on "Englischer Krieg und deutsche Kirche," while at a conference in Eisenach February 24–26, he spoke on "The Racial Character of Christianity in the Nordic Lands" (ZAK 7/4166). Meyer-Erlach, *Der Einfluss der Juden auf das englische Christentum.*; Meyer-Erlach, *Ist Gott Engländer?* The Jewishness of England was also proclaimed in a lead headline in *Deutsches Christentum*, a weekly newspaper edited by Siegfried Leffler and Heinz Dungs, on June 25, 1939: "World Politics with the Old Testament! England: Politics and Religion" (ZAK 7/4166, document 42).

[128] Meeting in Eisenach, February 24–26, 1941 (ZAK 7/4166).

[129] Grundmann, Report on Institute, typescript dated September 16, 1941 (LKA Eisenach DC III 2a), 1.

loyal adherence to the Führer, that the churches and all that is linked to their sterility and narrowness, their Jewish rigidity, are doomed to destruction.[130]

Conferences were organized by the Institute in different regions of the Reich. At the first, held in Wittenberg March 1–3, 1940, the noted völkisch theologian Wilhelm Stapel delivered a paper on "Wilhelm Rabbe's Position Regarding Judaism."[131] Grundmann, Meyer-Erlach, and Eisenhuth were invariably the keynote speakers at Institute conferences. At conferences in Schneidemühl and Rostock, Meyer-Erlach repeated his argument that England had been judaized. At a two-day pastors' meeting of the Thuringian and Saxonian churches, held in Eisenach, December 4–5, 1940, Eisenhuth delineated the differences among the Teutonic, Jewish, and Germanic ideas of God.[132]

In addition to participating in the conferences, Grundmann and Meyer-Erlach were frequently invited to lecture about the Institute to church groups and universities. Meyer-Erlach lectured in Graz in 1940, at the suggestion of the Thuringian SS; a report lauded his defense of Protestantism in Catholic Graz and his strong opposition to the Confessing Church.[133] Hugo Odeberg, a member of the Institute and a noted scholar of rabbinic literature, invited Meyer-Erlach to deliver a series of lectures in Sweden in the fall of 1941; he spoke in Lund (where Odeberg was a professor), Malmoe, Gothenburg, and Stockholm.[134] Otto Riedel, professor of Protestant theology at the University of Vienna, invited Grundmann to speak in March of 1941. The event was held in the largest hall of the university. His speech opened with the declaration, "Our Volk is in a struggle against the satanic powers of world Judaism, but cannot fight against the Jews and open its heart to the king of the Jews"; he proceeded to argue that the History of Religions school demonstrated the distinction between the Old Testament's messianic hope for Jewish world domination and

---

[130]Letter from Meyer Erlach to Zintzsch, dated January 1, 1941 (BDC Wi 2003).

[131]Grundmann, Report on Institute Work, dated September 16, 1941 (LKA Eisenach DC III 2a), 3. Stapel also lectured for the Bremer Bibelschule at its fourth Bibelkurs; see *Kommende Kirche* Nr. 15 (April 9, 1939); ZAK 50, Z 135, cited by Buss, *Die nordelbischen Landeskirche*, 114 fn 471. On Stapel, see Keinhorst, *Wilhelm Stapel*.

[132]Programs for the meetings are in the archives, LKA Eisenach.

[133]"It is entirely to be welcomed that this Protestant theologian and university professor is lecturing in a Catholic city such as Graz. Politically Meyer-Erlach can be judged entirely positively and regarded as a strong and formidable opponent of the Confessing Church" (SD-Aussenstelle Jena 29/91, Blatt 290–93; report dated October 29, 1940; Meyer-Erlach's November 16 speech was entitled "The Influence of Judaism on English Christianity").

[134]Letter from Meyer-Erlach to Reich Ministry of Education, dated September 6, 1942 (AA 3/4, R98796).

the spiritual messianism of Jesus, based on "peace and justice."[135] While in Vienna, Grundmann also addressed a group of Catholic priests on the significance of "Germanness" for theology; he then traveled to Salzburg, where he lectured on the Germanic nature of Luther's Reformation.[136] The following month, Theodor Odenwald, dean of the theological faculty at the University of Heidelberg and a member of the Institute, organized a conference at Heidelberg that included talks by several Institute members.

Conclusion

The Institute was extraordinarily energetic and productive. Its members were enthusiastic and willing to devote themselves to conferences, lecture tours, working groups, and publications. Church politics and divisions within the German Christian movement did not hinder the Institute, and while the unity of the regional churches that was supposed to occur was never achieved, the vitality of the Institute overrode any objections of its opponents. Each profession and academic field in Nazi Germany had one or more pseudoscientific "research" centers that were efforts at demonstrating support for National Socialism, and many were nothing more than antisemitic propaganda machines; the Institute was the theologians' outlet.

In addition to its frequent conferences that helped spread its message and bolster the careers of its members, the Institute's impact came through dissemination of its ideas in publications, both scholarly books and popular pamphlets. Most important were the publications intended for use in churches: its dejudaized New Testament, hymnal, and catechism. Those publications, undertaken in cooperation with the German Christians of Thuringia, translated

[135] Grundmann, "Das Messiasproblem," 379–412. Letter from Riedel to Liebe Kameraden, dated March 27, 1941, about planned visit by Grundmann (LKA Eisenach, CIV4: Ostmark).

[136] Grundmann was also invited to lecture in Prague, at a conference of pastors, by Erich Wehrenfennig, president of the German evangelical church of Bohemia, Moravia, and Silesia, but it is not clear if the Prague visit took place. Letter from Erich Wehrenfennig, no addressee, dated March 21, 1941 (LKA Eisenach). In a letter dated March 29, 1941, Grundmann was told that Wehrenfennig did not want the lecture to become an Institute event. Grundmann spoke at a conference of the German Protestant church of Sudetenland, held in Bodenbach, Bohemia, April 30–May 1, 1941. The other speaker was Werner Elert, professor of systematic theology at the University of Erlangen (conference program, LKA Eisenach). Grundmann also lectured in Salzburg and his visit to Vienna included a talk to a group of Catholic priests on the significance of "Germanness" for theology and the church. Letter from Grundmann to Riedel, dated March 27, 1941 (LKA Eisenach). In Salzburg, Grundmann spoke on "The German Character of Luther as Overcoming Jewish Elements in the Historical Development of Christianity."

the "scholarly" results of the Institute's working groups into concepts accessible to laypeople, soldiers, and, Institute leaders hoped, Nazi leaders who were skeptical of Christianity's relevance to their anti-Jewish campaign. The removal of the "Jewish" from Christianity first required a definition of its scope. Defining what was "Jewish" within Christianity was not easy. The Old Testament, the Pharisees, Jesus, Paul, concepts such as messianism, and so forth, were debated endlessly at Institute conferences. What was agreed by all was that Judaism was a violent, degenerate, and threatening force that sought the destruction of Christians and stood behind the war; Germany, the Institute proclaimed, was fighting a defensive, life-or-death struggle against the demonic Jews. Eradication of the Jewish, however, was not enough. The Institute proclaimed a positive message as well, not only in the teachings of Jesus—which they sought to recover in their pristine form, untainted by Jewish influence—but also in Teutonic myths that they incorporated into Christian settings, including prayer. The goal was to demonstrate that the teachings of Jesus and those of the Teutonic myths were essentially the same; the essence of Christianity was Aryan, Germanic religion.

Projects of the Institute

AN ARYAN NEW TESTAMENT: *DIE BOTSCHAFT GOTTES*

THE FIRST AND MOST SIGNIFICANT project of the Institute was eradicating "Jewish influence" from the Bible. The Old Testament was simply eliminated from German Christian religious worship, but the New Testament posed complex challenges for the Institute's dejudaization of Christianity. In the gospels, Jesus is called a rabbi. He attends synagogue and holds heated debates over interpretations of Jewish religious practice with Pharisees. In some verses, the New Testament speaks highly of Jews. For example, John 4:22 states, "Salvation comes from the Jews." In a 1938 article, Grundmann discussed that verse, arguing that it must have been a later interpolation into the original text of the John's gospel, which was otherwise anti-Jewish, identifying Jews not as the source of salvation, but as murderers of Christ, descendants of Satan, and opponents of Jesus. He called on the church to ban sermons based on John 4:22.[1]

More effective, from Grundmann's point of view, was a thorough revision of the New Testament. Pro-Jewish verses would be eradicated, while passages condemning Jews would be retained. Scholars would restore the original, pristine text of the New Testament, which, Grundmann argued, was surely an anti-Jewish text. Publication of a dejudaized version of the New Testament in 1940, *Die Botschaft Gottes* (*The Message of God*), constituted the Institute's crowning glory. Produced by a committee of noted New Testament scholars and pastors, *Die Botschaft Gottes* reshaped the four gospels into a single narrative. A more difficult problem was what to do with the Pauline epistles. Since Paul identified himself as a Jew, he could not be reconstructed as an Aryan. Instead, the editors of *Die Botschaft Gottes* eliminated Paul's autobiographical texts altogether, and selected passages from his epistles, which they mixed with excerpts from the Gospel of John in order to present early Christianity as a repudiation of Judaism. While not the first Nazi-era revised New Testament, it became the most widely known.

[1] Grundmann, "Das Heil kommt von den Juden," 1–8. In the Institute-sponsored version of the New Testament, verse 22 was simply omitted from the narrative of John 4. *Die Botschaft Gottes* (Leipzig: Otto Wigand, 1940), 109–110.

Nazi-Era Bibles

Smaller-scale efforts to revise the New Testament in the spirit of National Socialism had already been undertaken by theologians during the 1920s and '30s.[2] In 1934 Hans Schöttler, later the director of the German Christian movement's Bible school in Bremen, had published *Gottes Wort Deutsch* (*God's Word in German*), which included selected New Testament texts retold using Nazi language (for example, using the term "Führerpflichten," obligations to the Führer, in translating Matthew 5:13–16, and describing Jesus's "Kampf" in Jerusalem).[3] Two years later, Reich Bishop Ludwig Müller's version of the Sermon on the Mount omitted references to the Old Testament, and revised the Ten Commandments: "You shall do no murder. . . . But whosoever tries to ruin him morally, or threatens to assault him, destroys the national fellowship and makes himself deserving of the severest punishment before God and men."[4]

An anti-Jewish revision of the Gospel of John was undertaken in 1936 by the German Christian movement in Bremen, under the leadership of Bishop Heinz Weidemann, with Emmanuel Hirsch acting as scholarly advisor. Weidemann's Germanized version, published as *Das Evangelium Johannes deutsch*, presented Jesus as fighting against Judaism. It omitted all named references to Moses and to Hebrew prophets and all Hebrew place names. Weidemann's Gospel assumes that the Galilee was inhabited by Gentiles, and it omits references to both sin and grace. John 1:47—"Behold an Israelite indeed, in whom there is no guile!"—is changed to "Thou art a true man of God in thy nation." "Hosanna" in John 12:13 is changed to "Hail" ("Heil"), and "king of Israel" to "king." At the same time, the Weidemann version is not as hostile toward Jews as the texts later produced by the Institute. For example, John 4:22, "salvation comes from the Jews," is changed to "The Jews at least know of the God from whom alone salvation comes." John's emphasis on the Jews' responsibility for the death of Jesus is retained, while John 21, describing Jesus's post-resurrection appearance to the disciples, is omitted. In 1942, Weidemann explained his efforts as recapturing the original intention of the text by purging it of the language that was used in the first century's Jewish context and recasting it in language that would appeal to National Socialists.[5]

---

[2] There was also Artur Dinter's version of the gospels, published in 1923 as *Das Evangelium unseres Herrn und Heilandes Jesus Christus*. Dinter was already an avid supporter of Hitler in 1923.

[3] Heinonen, *Anpassung und Identität*, 217.

[4] Ludwig Müller, *Deutsche Gottesworte: Aus der Bergpredigt Verdeutscht*; see also the English translation, *The Germanisation of the New Testament*.

[5] "What can a National Socialist, an SA man, a German child of our day do with a gospel where [John] chapter 1:17 reads: 'For the law was given by Moses, but grace and truth come by Jesus

Whereas Weidemann's revision was limited to the Gospel of John, the Institute's New Testament project had a more ambitious goal: to uncover an "authentic" gospel from under the many layers of later accretions within the text. The Institute equated the "authentic" with the original words and deeds of Jesus; the oldest version of the text and its recovery required intense historical research by New Testament scholars. To that end, scholars, pastors, and even a German poet were engaged in the project. The Institute's New Testament project was ambitious in another sense as well: its goal was to reach a popular—and not simply scholarly—audience. "The creation has to be scientifically proper, practically applicable, and linguistically without blemish,"[6] wrote Grundmann in the Institute's first issue of *Verbandsmitteilung* (its quarterly newsletter).[7] Propagandistic in tone, the newsletter presented Institute "scholarship" in popularized form, with heavy emphasis on antisemitism.

The Institute's working group preparing a new edition of the New Testament, called a Volkstestament, a gospel for the German race, was chaired by Grundmann and Herbert Preisker, professor of New Testament at the University of Breslau, and included two pastors from Thuringia as well as a graduate student in theology at the University of Jena.[8] They reported on its progress at a conference in Wittenberg in March 1940. The project was intended to proceed in three stages: the synoptics; John; then the remainder of the New Testament. The synoptics were to be purged of positive Jewish references, Paul was to be downplayed so that some of his ideas were retained but autobiographical and biographical information eliminated, and the Gospel of John, with its strong anti-Jewish motifs, was to be highlighted, both as the most reliable source for the historical Jesus and as a theological substitute for Paul—this despite the awareness among scholars since the 1820s that John was not a reliable historical source.

Christ'?" Weidemann, "Mein Kampf um die Erneuerung des religiösen Lebens in der Kirche: Ein Rechenschaftsbericht," manuscript, 1942 (BA Koblenz R 43 II/165, fiche 4, p. 321), 4. Cited by Bergen, "*One Reich, One People, One Church*," 480. In the fall of 1939 Weidemann also began work on a collection of the major texts of the New Testament, tentatively entitled the Christustestament, but it never materialized. Heinonen, *Anpassung und Identität*, 228.

[6]Grundmann, "Unsere Arbeit am Neuen Testament," 9.

[7]The *Verbandsmitteilung* appeared irregularly, and it is not clear how many issues were ultimately published nor how many copies were printed. The financing of the newsletter is also not clear; it contained advertisements for publications of the Deutsche Christen Verlag in Weimar, which may have subsidized printing costs; the cost of mailing the *Verbandsmitteilung* to Institute members remains unclear.

[8]The graduate student, Heinz Günkel, a member of the NSDAP and the SA, completed a dissertation at the University of Jena on the origins of the Sermon on the Mount in 1939 and was awarded honors by Gerhard von Rad, professor of Old Testament, and Grundmann.

The Gospel of Mark served as a structural basis for the synoptic harmonization of the first part of the *Botschaft Gottes*, but the big problem was the Gospel of Matthew, long recognized as the most pro-Jewish of the gospels.[9] According to Grundmann, Matthew's image of Jesus was a distortion concocted by early Jewish Christians, in order to place Jesus in the context of the salvation history traditions of the Old Testament, and the gospel does not present "the true picture of Jesus."[10] Grundmann wrote to Kerrl on March 23, 1940, about his criteria for treating this section: remove all legendary material except those stories related to Christmas, which are deep in the consciousness of the German Volk; remove reports whose historical kernel was distorted by later formulations; and eliminate secondary sayings and obvious duplications within the text. The harmonization of the synoptics was intended to recreate the earliest strands of traditions about Jesus, eliminating thereby the later accretions in the text that stemmed from Jewish Christians. Grundmann wrote, "The oral tradition that the gospel authors encountered was painted over in a Jewish-Christian way and superimposed with superstition."[11]

The completed edition of the New Testament, *Die Botschaft Gottes*, published in 1940, was divided into four sections, which in turn were divided thematically. Section 1, "Jesus the Savior" ("Jesus der Heiland"), is a life of Jesus based on excerpts from each of the synoptic gospels, reorganized to present a story of triumph—its last three units describing ""His Struggle, His Cross, His Victory" ("Sein Kampf, Sein Kreuz, Sein Sieg"). Section 2, "Jesus the Son of God" ("Jesus der Gottesohn"), forms the theological backbone of the work, and presents a slightly condensed version of the Gospel of John, less about Jesus's actions than their theological significance. Section 3, "Jesus the Lord" ("Jesus der Herr"), contains brief excerpts from the various epistles, organized according to religious teachings, such as hope, comfort, community of God, and so forth. Section 4, "The Emergence of the Christian Community" ("Das Werden der Christusgemeinde"), presents an account, based on Acts and the Pauline epistles, of Paul's mission to the Gentiles and his break with the judaizers of Palestine. Paul is acknowledged as a Pharisee to whom God revealed Jesus, and who was persecuted by Jews who hated him and sought to kill him.[12]

Die Botschaft Gottes retells Jesus's life with an emphasis on his triumph rather than defeat through death. References to Jewish names or places, as well as citations from the Old Testament, are retained only as long as they expressed a negative view of some aspect of Judaism. Cut from *Die Botschaft*

---

[9] Grundmann, "Die Arbeit des ersten Evangelisten," 55–78.

[10] Ibid., 77–78.

[11] Grundmann, "Unsere Arbeit," 9.

[12] *Die Botschaft Gottes*, 253, 274–75.

Gottes are the genealogy in Matthew and Luke linking Jesus to Old Testament figures; the hymn of Mary; John the Baptist; Herod's killing of the children and the flight to Egypt; Zecharias and Hanna; the story of the wise men from the Orient; and the title "King of the Jews." Deleted, too, is any fulfillment in Jesus of an Old Testament prophecy, although the fact that Jesus knew of Jewish ways is preserved. For example, when Jesus taught in the Temple and asked the people why the scribes believed that the messiah had to be the son of David, the text continues, "The Volk listened to him gladly, as he hit the Scribes with their own weapons."[13] Whereas the Temple is not absent, the text refrains from mentioning religious offerings brought to it. Instead, "the parents came with the Jesus child, in order to bring him before God."[14] Jesus is not circumcised but is simply given a name. Other linguistic changes are notable: the Sabbath becomes "holiday," (Feiertag), and Pesach is called "Easter" (Oster-fest). Apocalyptic ideas are removed, as well as doctrinal concepts such as sinner, righteous, and penance (Sünder, Gerechte, Busse). The Jews' celebration of Passover is mentioned, but Jesus and his disciples simply gather for a meal, without any connection to Passover.

Die Botschaft Gottes treats Jesus's racial identity gingerly. Identified as neither a Jew nor an Aryan, he is simply a resident of certain regions, though the Galilean-Aryan equation would have been understood by readers. The text identifies Jesus with Galilee, both in origins and activities, and associates Judea with menace. Jesus has to leave Judea out of fear of the Pharisees[15] and move to Galilee, thus retaining the New Testament's tension between Galilee and Jerusalem (John 1:46; 7:41–43). The latter locale is identified with peril: " Only in Jerusalem do the prophets die."[16] In John 4:1–42, describing Jesus's encounter with the Samaritan woman, the exchange follows the text of John's gospel, but the word "messiah" ("Messias" in the Luther Bible, John 4:25) is changed to "Verheissene" (promised one).[17]

The Sermon on the Mount appears early in *Die Botschaft Gottes* and mixes the texts from Luke's gospel with the version in Matthew. The text is not as militarized as other nazified versions, such as Ludwig Müller's, but there were some notable changes to key terms. For example, "kingdom of God" (Luke 6:20) is changed to "God comes to you";[18] other classic terms, such as "compassionate" (Matthew 5:7), are simply omitted.

[13] Ibid., 79.
[14] *Die Botschaft Gottes*, 4.
[15] Ibid., 109
[16] Ibid., 74.
[17] Ibid., 110.
[18] Ibid., 21.

The description of the arrest and crucifixion is extended considerably.[19] The account follows John's narrative fairly closely, although the language is simplified from Luther's version. Loosely following Mark 14 and Luke 22–23, Jesus is asked by the high priests if he is a messiah, and he gives an ambiguous reply. When he is then asked, "So are you the Son of God?" he replies, "I am."[20] The references to him as messiah (Matthew 26:68, 27:17, 22; Luke 22:67, 23:2) are omitted.[21] Still, Jesus's citation of Psalm 22:1 is retained, though in German only and not in Aramaic (Matthew 27:46; Mark 15:34).

Printing *Die Botschaft Gottes* proceeded unhindered. Paper was not easily available if a project was deemed contrary to wartime propaganda, but while other publications in Germany were shut down by the Reich on the stated grounds of a paper shortage, the Institute faced no such difficulties. Its benefactor, Werner, had hoped for a publication of *Die Botschaft Gottes* in time for Easter 1940, to be distributed to all candidates for confirmation.[22] That deadline was not met. By the end of 1941, however, the Institute was pleased to announce that 200,000 copies had been sold or distributed, a sign—according to the Institute's newsletter—of how important the new "Germanization" was.[23] Heavily subsidized, the volumes were sold individually (from 30 pennies for *Jesus der Heiland*, the smaller collection of excerpts from the synoptic gospels), or 1.50 RM for the entire edition, not enough to recoup printing costs.

RECEPTION OF THE DEJUDAIZED NEW TESTAMENT

What kind of impact was achieved by the dejudaized Bible? The Institute certainly spared no effort to send copies wherever possible. Institute business manager Heinz Hunger, who was among thosed who signed the foreword, claimed to have sent a copy to all soldiers who were members of the German Christian movement.[24] In Lübeck, *Die Botschaft Gottes* was introduced to religious services and Bible study,[25] while in Weimar, German Christian pastors presented a copy to young people at confirmation, and in Altenburg it was

---

[19] The arrest and crucifixion account extends from p. 74 to 98, drawing from the synoptics, and is retold on pp. 152–66 following the Gospel of John's account.

[20] *Die Botschaft Gottes*, 88.

[21] Ibid., 88.

[22] Letter from Werner to D. Hymmen, dated January 22, 1940 (ZAK 7/4166).

[23] *Verbandsmitteilung* 4 1941.

[24] Jerke, "Wie wurde das Neue Testament," 228.

[25] Thierfelder and Röhm, eds., *Evangelische Kirche*, 43.

given to wedding couples.[26] A large number of church congregations purchased copies and presumably used the so-called "Volkstestament" for their
weekly scriptural readings. How many regional churches altered their lectionary to accord with the new version is not known.

The reception by Confessing Church members was mixed. Hans von
Soden, professor of New Testament at the University of Marburg, published
a pamphlet accusing the editors of the Volkstestament of acting like "Pharisees," emending the biblical text and thus creating a new canon.[27] His critique exemplifies the spirit of competition between the Confessing Church
and the German Christian movement over who could be more strongly anti-
Jewish. The assertion that Jesus opposed the allegedly degenerate Judaism of
his day was a point shared by both. In 1940, Karl Fischer, a Confessing
Church pastor in Dresden, published a pamphlet against *Die Botschaft Gottes*,
printed by the Confessing Church of Saxony, noting that *Jesus der Heiland*
makes Jesus "no longer the fulfiller but the destroyer . . . the great revolutionary, who gave only a clear No to his era."[28] The New Testament scholar Ernst
Haenchen, professor at the University of Giessen, called the project unscholarly, its choice of texts tendentious and unscholarly; it was a "miscarried
effort."[29]

The concern of the Confessing Church (and, to a great extent, the Catholic
Church) to preserve intact the canon of Scripture marks one of its sharp con-
trasts to the German Christian movement. And yet a commonality exists here
as well, not only over the anti-Judaism that they shared, but also over their use
of racial imagery. The German Christians sought to create what they considered a racially pure Bible, that is, a Bible without any Jewishness. The concern
of the Confessing Church was protecting the "body" of the canon against the
threat of what they termed the "Pharisaic" theological corruption of the German Christian movement. From the perspective of the German Christians, the
Bible was a body that had to be purified of Jewish corruption. For the Confessing Church, if Scripture was the body, it was the German Christian movement that, in its violation of the integrity of Scripture, represented the spirit of
Jewishness that was threatening Christianity. In both cases, the Nazi prohibition

[26] Letter from Säuberlich, Etzdorf über Eisenberg, to Superintendent Martin Albertz, Berlin-
Spandau, dated July 26, 1940 (LKA Eisenach DC III 2f).

[27] Soden, "Die synoptische Frage und der geschichtliche Jesus."

[28] Fischer's critique of the Volkstestament is cited by Jerke, "Wie wurde das Neue Testament zu
einem sogennanten Volkstestament 'entjudet'?," 215. See also Grundmann, "Das Messiasproblem," 7.

[29] See Ernst Haenchen, *Gottes Wort Deutsch*, 120f, cited by Heinonen, *Anpassung und Identität*,
229.

against "Rassenschande," sexual relations and miscegenation of Aryans with non-Aryans, was transferred to the scriptural level.

HYMNS AND PRAYER

The German Christian movement attempted not only to reconceive the theology but to alter Christian worship in keeping with Nazi racism, militarism, and hypermasculinity. Like the German Christians, the Institute also had the goal of creating a Reich church that would transcend denominational differences, whether Catholic, Lutheran, or Reformed. Such a church would require alternative liturgical texts acceptable to all, but also a new interpretation of worship. Should a Eucharist be celebrated, and, if so, what would its theological meaning be? Gerhard Delling, one of Grundmann's close friends, described the difficulties he had as a military chaplain in creating new forms of worship that appealed to Catholics as well as Protestants and, in particular, to soldiers. At the war's front lines, Delling wrote, church politics were irrelevant, and so was religiosity. What mattered was the practical relevance of a living, helping God who, he added, "had to be as real as the incomprehensible reality of war."[30]

Yet in creating a dejudaized Christianity for the domestic war front, the Institute discovered that it had to reconceive the religiosity of Christian practice. Nazism and prayer, however, were difficult to reconcile. How should a Nazi pray, if prayer implies an attitude of supplication and pathos directly at odds with the manly, militaristic posture promoted by Hitler? The nature of prayer during the Third Reich had to be reconfigured as praise and affirmation rather than atonement and petition. Prayers of repentance and requests for divine forgiveness also seemed out of place; Der Schwarze Korps, the newspaper of the Sturmabteilung (SA, the so-called brownshirts), objected to sinners confessing and asking forgiveness of God on behalf of the Volk.[31] Some Nazis formulated short verse as substitutes for Christian liturgy, directed not to God but to Hitler, primarily as expressions of praise for the Führer's beneficent leadership. German Christians wanted to demonstrate that Christian liturgy could be comparably nazified. They suggested, for example, that religious services should no longer be called "Gottesdienst" (divine service) but rather "Gottesfeier" (divine celebration), because "service" was Old Testament–Jewish,

---

[30]Four-page, single-spaced letter from Gerhard Delling to Grundmann, dated June 3, 1942 (LKA Eisenach NG 44, II).

[31]Das Schwarze Korps, October 27, 1938; cited by Helmreich, The German Churches under Hitler, 230.

while "celebration" was German. Yet such linguistic changes did not resolve all the problems. Should one pray for Germans and Germany, or for all Christians, even those in countries opposed to the Reich? Could there be prayers for peace, a central theme in Christian scripture and liturgy, when Germany was preparing for war or even at war? If prayer included entreaties, would that transfer German fate to God's hands?

Elements of Nazi imagery and language were first brought into the Christian hymnal in the late 1920s, not simply to change the text but to create a new aura. Songs of the SA and the Hitler Youth were included with church hymns and older German nationalist verse, including some by Ernst Moritz Arndt, the nationalist writer Ricarda Huch, and the German Christian poet Heinrich Anacker, in the first hymnal issued by the German Christians of Thuringia, *Unsere Kampflieder* (*Our Fighting Songs*).[32]

The Institute's dejudaization of the liturgy was not innovative, but followed previous efforts within the German Christian movement. At German Christian rallies prior to late 1933, passages from the Old Testament, such as psalms, and even Hebrew words, had been included. Following the November 1933 German Christian rally at the Sports Hall in Berlin, however, such "Jewish" language was no longer acceptable. Moreover, while the place of the Old Testament in the Christian Bible became a central point of contention between German Christians and the Confessing Church, removing Hebrew and Old Testament references from the hymnal was, at least theoretically, a point on which German Christians and many members of the Confessing Church were in agreement.

In 1933 Wilhelm Caspari, a professor of Old Testament at the University of Kiel who became a member of the Confessing Church, called for the eradication of some Old Testament references and Hebrew words from the hymnal, but the retention of others. Jehovah, messiah, son of David, Bethlehem, Judea, Sabbath were among the terms Caspari argued should be removed from the hymnal, while Amen, Halleluia, Hosanna, and Jerusalem should be retained, since they appear in the New Testament.[33] Caspari, a theologically conservative scholar of ancient Israelite religion, lost his professorship at Kiel in 1936 under the Nazi racial laws.[34]

Emanuel Hirsch, professor of systematic theology at the University of Göttingen, had radically different political and theological views from Caspari, yet agreed substantially with him regarding the hymnal. Hirsch, a Nazi and a

---

[32] Heinonen, *Anpassung und Identität*, 181.

[33] Caspari, "Über alttestamentliche Bezugnahmen," 169–79. See also Caspari, *Die alttestamentliche Schicksalsfrage.*

[34] *Displaced German Scholars.*

major theologian of the German Christian movement, also called for the hymnal's dejudaization in his 1939 book defining Jesus as Aryan, *Das Wesen des Christentums*.[35] Hirsch urged removal of all traces of the Old Testament and purging the hymnal of Hebrew; for example, he proposed that the Hebrew word Halleluia be replaced by "Gott sei gelobt" ("God be praised"). Such dejudaizations were never fully implemented, nor were angry denunciations of Jews introduced into the hymnal.

Several new hymnals were published during the Third Reich, both by church officials and by the military. In early 1934, the German Christians published a hymnal, *So singen deutsche Christen*, containing German Christian poems set to familiar melodies. The fifty-one songs of the hymnal were divided into categories of "struggle," "work," and "meditation."[36] By 1935 not only were the German Christians agitating against Hebraisms in church music, which included Hebrew words and Jewish composers, but even ranted against Gregorian chants as influenced by Hebrew melodies.[37] Yet the popularity of the music and the nostalgia felt for melodies learned in childhood prevailed, and the changes were conservative. What characterized the new hymnals most prominently were their militaristic and racist themes and the absence of Jewish and Hebrew references. The militarism itself was not entirely new; nineteenth-century hymnals such as the *Liederbuch für deutsche Studenten* (*Hymnal for German Students*), published in 1898, were filled with hymns about war, soldiering, and the "fatherland,"[38] and the World War I era also introduced militaristic hymns. But the call for a radical removal of so-called Jewish elements began with the Third Reich.

In October 1939 Bishop Weidemann published a hymnal, *Lieder der kommenden Kirche* (*Songs of the Coming Church*), that reduced the number of pietistic hymns and added twentieth-century folksongs, but it did not include overt anti-Jewish sentiments, in sharp contrast to his version of the Gospel of John, published in 1936.[39] Intended as the kernel of a national hymnal, it circulated to regional bishops affiliated with the German Christian movement as well as to congregations in Bremen. While it sold tens of thousands of copies, it never became the standard hymnal of the Bremen congregations, but it did establish

---

[35] The book was commissioned by Weidemann's Bibelschule. For a discussion of Hirsch's involvement with Weidemann, see Heinonen, *Anpassung und Identität*, 187. On Hirsch, see Ericksen, *Theologians under Hitler*; Forstman, *Christian Faith in Dark Times*.

[36] *So singen deutsche Christen*, ed. Albert Protz, cited by Bergen, *Twisted Cross*, 281 fn 116.

[37] Bergen, "Hosanna," 148.

[38] Of 305 hymns, 28 were "Vaterlandslieder," 37 were "Freiheits- und Kriegslieder" and 21 were "Soldatenlieder," notes Seidel, *Im Übergang der Diktaturen*, 29.

[39] Bergen, "Hosanna," 149–50. See also Bergen, "One Reich, One People, One Church," 508.

an approach that was copied.[40] Its influence was extended over the subsequent hymnals produced by church groups and by the military. The military's revised hymnal, *Feldgesangbuch* (*Military Field Hymnal*), lifted nearly three-quarters of the songs and many of the lyrics from the Bremen book. Needless to say, the two million copies of the military hymnal eliminated all Jewish references.[41] Yet Weidemann's hymnal was not appreciated everywhere. Some complained about the changes, and it was not adopted for religious instruction in Bremen.[42]

The motivations for changing the hymnal were, as always, a mixture of politics, theology, and aesthetics. As fascism is about the aestheticization of politics, essential to that relationship, Emilio Gentile argues, is creating an aura of sacrality around the political.[43] Cultural ties to familiar hymns, both their music and words, were strong enough to hinder full acceptance of altered hymnals, and no one hymnal was ever adopted for use on the national level. There was some effort to wean churchgoing Germans from the old hymnals—witness a German Christian liturgical guide in 1935 criticizing some church music as "borrowed from the synagogue."[44] By and large, however, as Bergen has noted, "churchgoers were simply not willing to part with all those beloved songs."[45] Certain hymns, having been sung over and over, often committed to memory, can be assumed to have been associated with nostalgic moments in the calendar, such as Christmas, and frequently with childhood experiences as well. At the same time, the nostalgia associated with certain hymns that were preserved in German Christian church services served to allow more radical changes in other elements of the service, reassuring churchgoers that the Institute was promoting a dejudaization not as a radical departure from Christian theology, but as a return to the anti-Jewish Christianity practiced in the days of Jesus and the earliest Christians, before Christianity was judaized. Familiar hymns and music set the background for altered scriptures and sermons that were far more direct and forceful about anti-Jewish politics without seeming to introduce a new and jarring note.

The Institute spearheaded development of a new hymnal collaboratively with the German Christian faction of Thuringia (KDC). Appointed as editor of the project was Kurt Thieme, whose qualifications were more political than

---

[40] Heinonen notes other hymnals, including *Singt Lob und Dank*, prepared by the Reichsverband für evangelische Kirchenmusik.

[41] Heinonen, *Anpassung und Identität*, 198.

[42] Ibid., 195.

[43] Gentile, "The Theatre of Politics in Fascist Italy," 73.

[44] Bauer, *Feierstunden Deutscher Christen*, cited by Bergen, "One Reich, One People, One Church," 496.

[45] Bergen, "Hosanna," 151.

theological. A schoolteacher in Thuringia and a member of the Nazi Party and the German Christians, Thieme wrote that the hymnal would demonstrate the church's "struggle against everything racially foreign . . . this struggle against the Jewish deadly enemy."[46] Although he had no formal theological training, Thieme was given the title of "pastor" in 1940 by the German Christians and was formally ordained in 1943.[47] The model for the hymnal was Jesus himself, who had fought, Thieme wrote, "a singular declaration of war against the Jewish race."[48] Issues of dogma and poetic unsuitability paled before the central concern of the hymnal, eradicating all Jewish elements, Thieme continued: "The decisive task in the revision of the hymnal . . . is the eradication is the eradication of all that is of Jewish origin or serves the advancement of the Jewish essence. The entire collection of hymns had to be examined and revised in light of our return to our own essence."[49] A working group to prepare the hymnal was appointed by Leffler in March of 1939, before the Institute was formally opened, at a meeting of German Christian leaders. Ultimately, the project was run by members of both the German Christians and the Institute (whose memberships overlapped considerably).

At a conference of the Institute held in Eisenach on July 6–7, 1939, a report was presented on the state of the German Protestant hymnal by Paul Gimpel, another schoolteacher.[50] He and several colleagues had surveyed all thirty hymnals at use in Reich churches, examining over 2,300 hymns. Most hymns—1,971—they denounced as Jewish in either language or thought, as well as dogmatic, sentimental, tasteless, self-denigrating, or poetically unacceptable.[51] Of the rest, 102 were accepted without further alteration as "valuable German cultural property," while 263 were identified as worth considering further.[52] The anti-Jewish criteria were clear, as was the necessity for

---

[46] Project Report Thieme, June 13, 1940 (LKA Eisenach Bestand DC, C VI2a, p. 1), cited by Buss, "Entjudung der Kirche," 77.

[47] Seidel, ed., *Thüringer Gratwanderungen*, 293. After the war, Thieme (1899–1971) served as pastor in Silesia and in Brandenburg; he retired in 1969.

[48] Project Report Thieme, September 1940 (LKA Eisenach Bestand DC, C VI2a, p. 3), cited by Buss, "Entjudung der Kirche," 77.

[49] Ibid., 78.

[50] "Bericht über die Tagung der landeskirchlichen Referenten zum 'Institut zur Erforschung und Beseitigung des jüdischen Einflusses auf das deutsche kirchliche Leben' am 6. und 7. July 1939 in Eisenach," signed by Hugo Pich, with report from Gimpel (ZAK Berlin 1/C3/174).

[51] The three categories for judging the contents of the hymns were Jewish content, dogmatic content, and poetic quality. See Buss, "Entjudung der Kirche," 76–77, and 77 fn 313.

[52] Report on the meeting of the state church consultants concerning the "Institut zur Erforschung und Beseitigung des jüdischen Einflusses auf das deutsche kirchliche Leben" (LKA Eisenach, DC III/2f).

reform. Meanwhile, concern was expressed that the Institute's direct involvement in publishing the hymnal might be a tactical error.[53] While the hymnal was ultimately a joint product of the National Union of German Christians, the Working Group of German Christian church leaders, and the Institute, the Institute's name was not included on the title page. The institutional distinction was only a formality, since the actual membership of the three groups overlapped.[54] Indeed, the head of the Institute's finance committee, Johannes Sievers, was ultimately responsible for bringing the hymnal to publication.

The hymnal was published in June of 1941 under the title *Grosser Gott wir loben dich!* Its publisher was a Weimar house with close connections to the German Christian movement, Der neue Dom, run by Pastor Heinz Dungs, a member of the Institute. Publication of *Grosser Gott* was occasion for a public celebration in the Wartburg chapel on June 13, 1941, nine days before the Nazi invasion of the Soviet Union, with speeches by Grundmann and Dungs; Dungs proclaimed that Germans were engaged in a final solution of the Jewish question and could no longer tolerate a Jewish-Christian spirit at prayer.[55] The new hymnal contained 284 hymns for church liturgy, plus a smaller section, entitled "Von frommer deutscher Lebensart" ("Pious German Ways of Life"), containing prayers and songs for family use, and a collection of thirteen "Lieder der Kameradschaft" ("Hymns of Friendship"). All were purged of references to the Old Testament or Judaism. Of the hymns, only 150 were taken from the 500 hymns included in German Lutheran hymnals, and all but 22 of these were altered. The remaining 134 hymns were drawn from modern poetry and songs, including völkisch verse referring to the Führer and asking for God's "strong hand" on "our Volk and Fatherland."[56]

The title hymn, "Grosser Gott, wir loben dich" ("Holy God, We Praise Thy Name"), an old and popular one, was originally Catholic, translated into German from the Latin "Te Deum, Laudamus Te," adopted by the Protestant hymnal, and had become one of the favorites of Stormtroopers and the SS, evoking both church and nation.[57] It was purged of reference to cherubim and seraphim in its second stanza and instead proclaimed: "Heilig, heilig, Herr der

---

[53] Letter from Dungs to Sievers, May 8, 1940 (LKA Eisenach, Bestand DC, VI, 21), Cited by Buss, "Entjudung der Kirche," 76 fn 312.

[54] Gregor argues that the hymnal was not the product of the Institute, while Buss rejects that claim, noting the overlapping membership and the tactical reasons for keeping the Institute's involvement quiet. Gregor, "Von jüdischem Einfluß befreit," 124–42.

[55] Heinz Dungs, lecture held on June 13, 1941 (LKA Eisenach DC, C VI 2a, Blatt 301); cited by Buss, "Entjudung der Kirche," 173.

[56] *Grosser Gott*, 415.

[57] Bergen, "Hosanna," 148.

2. Wir aus Erde, staubgeboren, sind von heilger Lust durchbebt durch das Licht der reinen Sehnsucht, das aus deinem Wesen lebt.

3. Was von deinen Erdgeschenken du uns gabst, war heilig Gut: Weib und Bruder, Volk und Freiheit, heilig durch der Liebe Glut.

4. Nur, was irdisch und vergänglich, senkt sich dem Verderben zu. Aber du, du heilge Flamme, unsre Sehnsucht, glühe du! Heinrich Lersch, 1889–1936

Figure 3.1. The hymn "Heilig Vaterland" ("Holy Fatherland"), with an illustration of a soldier with a mother and children. (All the illustrations in chapter 3 are from the hymnbook *Großer Gott, Wir Loben Dich* [Weimar: Georg Wigand, 1941]; this is from pages 46–47.)

Figure 3.2. Martin Luther's hymn, "Ein feste Burg," retitled as "Heilig Vaterland: Volk vor Gott" ("Holy Fatherland: Volk before God"), with an illustration of a castle on a mountain (*Großer Gott, Wir Loben Dich*, pages 48–49).

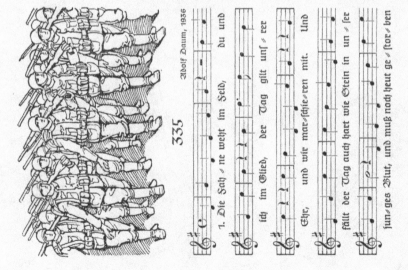

Figure 3.3. The hymn "Die Fahne Weht im Feld" ("The Flag Flies in the Field"), with an illustration of a troop of soldiers (*Großer Gott, Wir Loben Dich*, page 492).

2. Nur die Falſchen ſterben, die Feigen verwehn, die
können nicht durch das Feuer gehn, die können nichts
tragen durch die Glut, ſie hüten kein Erbe in ihrem Blut.

3. Das Feuer iſt jung, das Feuer iſt alt. Das Feuer
hat von Gott Gewalt. Im Feuer geboren ward die Kraft,
die dem Deutſchen das Heil und das Ewige ſchafft.

Hermann Ohland, geb. 1888

Figure 3.4. Opening of a hymn, illustrated with a knight (*Großer Gott, Wir Loben Dich*, page 494).

Kinder beten

Gib, daß nicht bet allein der Mund,
gib, daß es geh von Herzensgrund.
Luther

Ich danke dir, mein himmlischer Vater, daß du mich diese Nacht vor allem Schaden und Gefahr behütet hast, und bitte dich, du wollest mich diesen Tag auch behüten vor Sünde und allem Übel, daß dir all mein Tun und Leben gefalle. Denn ich befehle mich, meinen Leib und Seele und alles in deine Hände. Dein heiliger Engel sei mit mir, daß der böse Feind keine Macht an mir finde.   Luthers Morgensegen

Schütze, Gott, mit starker Hand
unser Volk und Vaterland!
Laß auf unsres Führers Pfade
leuchten deine Huld und Gnade!
Weck im Herzen uns aufs neue
deutscher Ahnen Kraft und Treue.
Und so laß uns stark und rein
deine deutschen Kinder sein.
Aus dem Amtsblatt des Thür. Ministeriums für Volksbildung

Herr, im tiefsten Herzensgrunde
tragen wir dein heilig Gut.
Mach uns reif zu jeder Stunde,
treu und adlig, stolz und gut,
daß wir für des Volkes Ehr
willig leben, kämpfen, sterben,
daß wir für des Volkes Wehr
unsre Kräfte einst vererben. Hermann Ohland

Wie fröhlich bin ich aufgewacht,
wie hab ich geschlafen so sanft die Nacht!
Hab Dank, im Himmel du Vater mein,
daß du hast wollen bei mir sein.

Figure 3.5. The Children's Prayer (*Großer Gott, Wir Loben Dich*, page 415).

Kriegesheere, starker Helfer in der Not" ("Holy, holy, majestic God, lord of war, strong friend in need"). Another popular hymn, "Wachet auf, ruft uns die Stimme " ("Wake, Awake, a Voice Is Calling"), was drastically altered to eliminate the first two stanzas entirely, with their references to Jerusalem and Zion, and the use of the word "Halleluja." In the third stanza "Halleluja" was replaced with "Lob und Danklied" "Hymn of Praise and Gratitude"). "Stille Nacht" ("Silent Night") retained its reference to Bethlehem, since Grundmann had determined that a second, non-Jewish village of Bethlehem existed in Gentile Galilee.

No foreword or explanatory materials were included, and the hymns clearly not only were dejudaized, but expressed an ethos appropriate to the Reich. Hymns authored by non-Aryan Christians were eliminated.[58] Words such as Psalm, Jehovah, Yahweh, and Immanuel were removed, as were evocations of Old Testament terms such as "psalters and harps."[59] Other phrases from the Old Testament, however, remained intact, including well-known verses from the psalms, such as "Lobe den Herrn, o meine Seele" ("Praise the Lord, O My Soul"). In the Institute's hymnal, the second stanza of Luther's famed Reformation song, "Ein' feste Burg" ("A Mighty Fortress"), was purged of the words "Herr Zebaoth" ("Lord of Hosts") and "der Retter in Not" ("knight in shining armor") was substituted. The hymn itself was entitled "Heilig Vaterland" ("Holy Fatherland"), and the accompanying drawing of a castle bore the inscription, "Ein' Feste Burg ist unser Gott, ein gute Wehr und Waffen" ("A mighty fortress is our God, a trusty shield and weapon"). In the seventeenth-century hymn "Die güldne Sonne" ("The Golden Sun") the words "Weihrauch und Widder" (frankincense and ram) were removed as symbols of Jewish sacrificial offerings.

Some of the household prayers and hymns included for life cycle events gave direct support to racial language. For example, a baptismal hymn composed for *Grosser Gott* was "Tender Child of German Blood." Christ, his blood, and his resurrection were de-emphasized, as in the baptismal formula, "We baptize you that you may be consecrated and brave in life, faithfully committed to the Volk in a new time in truth."[60]

Illustrations for the hymnal were done by Emil Ernst Heinsdorff, a völkisch artist who had illustrated two volumes of Wilhelm Kotzde-Kottenrodt's 1916

[58] A sole exception was the hymn "Wir treten zum Beten," originally a Dutch hymn that had been translated into German by the 19th-century Austrian writer Joseph Weyl, a non-Aryan. See Gregor, "Von jüdischem Einfluss befreit," 213f.

[59] Bergen, "One Reich, One People, One Church," 169.

[60] Gregor, "Von jüdischem Einfluß befreit," 138.

völkisch book for youth, *Deutsches Jugendbuch*.[61] Clearly intended to give hymn-singing a forceful, wartime atmosphere, the hymnal's drawings are highly militaristic, showing troops of soldiers with rifles over their shoulders; a contemplative knight in armor standing with a large sword; a soldier in uniform greeting his wife and two small children; and a knight in full armor, surrounded by flames.

The first printing of the hymnal was 55,000, with many copies distributed free of charge, but a second printing was necessary to meet the demand of another 50,000 copies that had been requested; copies were sold for 3.5 RM each.[62] Ten thousand copies were purchased by the Thuringian church, which sent one to each church community within Thuringia, to decide whether to purchase copies for its congregation.[63] The Red Cross in Weimar ordered 100 copies. There were also copies sent to soldiers on the front. In early 1941 a new printing produced another 100,000 copies. Judged by sales alone, the hymnal was a great success. Subventions of 1,500 RM from the Ministry for Church Affairs and 3,000 RM from the Thuringian church assisted with printing costs.[64] Other subventions came from various regional churches, but the crucial financial support was a credit extension of 60,000 RM to the publishing house, arranged by Sievers, who held a governing position within the church of Lübeck.[65] Sievers's crucial assistance in bringing the hymnal into being was proclaimed by Heinz Dungs at the celebration of the hymnal's publication.[66]

The reception of the hymnal, *Grosser Gott*, is difficult to judge. A review in the respected journal, *Theologische Blätter*, complained about its reduction in the number of hymns from 500 to 300 and criticized it for divisiveness at a time when the "unity of the Church is felt to be an especially pressing task," but did not criticize its dejudaization.[67]

[61]*Deutsches Jugendbuch*, ed. Wilhelm Kotzde (Mainz: Scholz, 1909–13), vols. 1–5. Kotzde (1878–1948) was one of the most prominent early promoters of "fatherland ideology" in youth literature. Heinsdorff (1887–1948) illustrated vols. 4 and 5.

[62]Letter from Dungs to Bartosch, dated January 14, 1942 (LKA Eisenach). Dungs writes in his letter that the publication had received a positive recommendation from Hans Kerrl and from Alfred Rosenberg and his Frankfurt Institute.

[63]This was announced in the *Gesetzblatt* of the Thuringian church, signed by Sasse. *Gesetzblatt* 15 (July 23, 1941), 111 (LKA Eisenach DCIA).

[64]Gregor, "Von jüdischem Einfluß befreit," 130.

[65]Buss, "Entjudung der Kirche," 177 fn 39. After the bishop of Lübeck, Erwin Balzer, another active supporter of the Institute, was drafted, Sievers, a senior church councillor, became head of the governing council of the church.

[66]"His name will forever remain bound up with the history of the hymnal" (LKA Eisenach, Bestand DC, C VI 2a, Blatt 301).

[67]Bertheau, review of *Grosser Gott wir loben Dich* in *Theologische Blätter*, 96.

Dejudaizing the Catechism

After the New Testament and hymnal, the third in the triad of liturgical materials to be nazified was the catechism. The commission established to create a new catechism was chaired by Grundmann and included several pastors as well as a professor of religious pedagogy from Dortmund, Hermann Werdermann.[68] The commission met frequently, and the fruit of its labor was produced by the Institute in 1941 under the title *Deutsche mit Gott: Ein deutsches Glaubensbuch* (*Germans with God: A German Catechism*). The chosen title itself is instructive—the word "Christian" does not appear, presumably either because German faith was self-evidently Christianity, or because the Institute was beginning its shift toward a greater inclusion of non-Christian Teutonic religious themes.[69] Indeed, the foreword states that the present generation "is searching for its way with God," and that answers to the search can be found "out of the rich history of German piety." The catechism, which was supposed to include a teacher's guide that was never completed, is divided into forty-three brief sections, with titles such as "The Reich of the Germans, our Divine Obligation," and "The Victor on the Cross," as well as traditional concerns, such as thanks and joy, faith, sin, and homecoming.

Jesus was defined as "savior of the Germans" with the following explanation:

> Jesus of Nazareth in the Galilee proves in his message and behavior a spirit that is in opposition to Judaism in every way. The struggle between him and the Jew became so bitter than it led to his deadly crucifixion. Thus Jesus cannot have been a Jew. Until this very day the Jews persecute Jesus and all who follow him with unreconcilable hatred. By contrast, Aryans in particular found in Jesus Christ the answer to their ultimate and deepest questions. So he became the savior of the Germans.[70]

The catechism omitted traditional doctrinal positions regarding miracles, virgin birth, incarnation, resurrection, and so forth, in favor of positioning

[68]Others on the committee included Max-Adolf Wagenführer, Grundmann's student and academic assistant at the University of Jena, Pastor Wilhelm Büchner (Jena), Paul Gimpel, a teacher in Eisenach, Pastor Hans Pribnow (of Lauenburg, in Pomerania), Kurt Thieme, a teacher in Eisenach, and Pastor Heinrich Weinmann (Pfaffendorf, near Koblenz). Both Heinz Hunger and Erich Fromm, Thuringian pastors and members of the DC and the Institute, had also been members of the commission, but were drafted into military service during its preparation.

[69]A brief but helpful description of the considerations of the commission is contained in an unsigned letter to Hans-Joachim Thilo, most likely written by Max-Adolf Wagenführer, dated April 9, 1941 (LKA Eisenach NG44, I).

[70]*Deutsche mit Gott*, 46.

Jesus as a human being who struggled on behalf of God and died not only as a martyr but also a "victor" on the cross, despite being a victim of the Jews. He functioned, in that way, as a figure with whom Germans could identify in their own struggle against the Jews on behalf of God. This identification is given further impetus in the "Twelve Commandments" presented in the catechism, which include "Keep the blood pure and the marriage holy!" and "Honor Führer and Master!" but omit mention of murder, theft, and, of course, Sabbath observance.

The language of the catechism was subtle by comparison to other Nazi-era catechisms. For example, a 1940 catechism, *Ruf an den jungen Morgen*, taught:

> Who is the enemy of the German essence? The enemy of the German essence is the eternal Jew. . . . Was Christ a Jew? It is the greatest lie that the Jews have brought into the world, that Jesus is a Jew. . . . What obligations do we have? Jesus's life and teaching is a great challenge against the Jewish spirit. . . . What do we think of the Old Testament? Just as in a field grain and weeds grow together, so the Old Testament contains good and evil. We have reverence for its eternal truths about God, but we exterminate its Jewish spirit root and branch.[71]

Whether the catechism was introduced in many churches remains unclarified; there is evidence, however, of discussions of catechetical reform in churches affiliated with the German Christian movement.[72]

Related to the catechism was another planned book, *Der Ruf des Lebens* (*Call of Life*), an anthology of German texts intended as a book of household prayers and readings "from the standpoint of German piety." Due to a paper shortage, however, *Der Ruf des Lebens* was never printed.[73] The Institute also planned a series of inspirational books under the general title *Die Geschichte Gottes mit den Deutschen und der Deutschen mit Gott* (*The History of God with the Germans and that of the Germans with God*), to be produced by a commission of German poets under the direction of the völkisch writer and Institute member Kotzde-Kottenrodt, with assistance from another Institute member, Wilhelm Stapel, a noted völkisch writer on religion. The volumes would provide texts describing

---

[71] Gruber, *Rufe an den jungen Morgen* (1940), 1, 4, 11 (LKA Eisenach DC III 2c).

[72] See various documents regarding catechism instruction in the archive of the NEK, Kirchenkampf Lübeck. Grundmann received letters commenting, positively and negatively, on the catechicsm (LKA Eisenach Grundmanns Briefe, 25.1.1940–27.7.1942: Signatur NG44, I).

[73] Undated eight-page summary of the Institute's projects by Grundmann, YIVO. The paper shortage is also blamed in an unsigned letter to Grundmann dated August 20, 1942 (LKA Eisenach, NG44, II).

"how German human beings went along their path with God, how God became the strength for affirming life and shaping life." The plan was for four books aimed at children, youth, families, and, lastly, a "German Psalter."[74] The imagined multivolume set was to have been similar in content, if not length, to Wilhelm Schwaner's *Germanen-Bibel*, a compilation of texts about German identity, ranging from Tacitus to Hölderlin, Lagarde, and Hitler. First published in 1904 and reissued in 1934, it was intended as a collection of holy scriptures that would replace the "Jewish and Christian Bible"[75] and revitalize Germans by making Christianity compatible with Germanic nature. A foretaste of the Institute's project was delivered as a lecture by Kotzde-Kottenrodt, "Eine Deutsche Gottes- und Lebenskunde," at an Institute meeting held at the Wartburg Castle in July of 1941, but the project was never completed. In his lecture, Kotzde-Kottenrodt stated that "Juda [sic] had removed God from the world. It could not comprehend the higher thinking of Nordics, that the world is filled with God." He went on to explain that we cannot know if we have the authentic Old Testament because the Jews have distorted it through the centuries to meet their own purposes.[76]

THE 1941 SHIFT

The spring of 1941 began the heyday of Institute conferences and Grundmann's popularity as a speaker. Both exhaustion over the ongoing internal church political conflict between German Christians and the Confessing Church and the course of the war required a reconceptualization of the Institute. Grundmann and his colleagues were now viewed in certain circles not as representing the politicized German Christian movement, but as an alternative to it. In his lectures and publications, Grundmann presented himself as an independent-minded scholar whose analyses of Christian origins were not motivated by church political interests, but by a search for historical truth. Moreover, Grundmann had succeeded in presenting the Institute's work as strictly scholarly. Thus, invitations to lecture arrived with the caveat that speakers were to avoid German Christian political concerns in order to unify a divided pastorate. Typical of that was the invitation to lecture in Prague to a closed,

[74]Undated eight-page summary of the Institute's projects by Grundmann, YIVO.

[75]Schwaner, ed., *Germanen-Bibel*; reprints appeared in 1905, 1909, 1918, and 1921. See Schwaner's introduction.

[76]A copy of the lecture is at LKA Eisenach. See p. 6 for the quotation: "Juda hat die Welt entgottet."

two-day meeting of fifty pastors.[77] Grundmann, meanwhile, also spoke at a three-day Institute conference held at the University of Heidelberg in mid-April 1941, co-organized with Theodor Odenwald, an Institute member who was professor of systematic theology and dean of the theological faculty there.[78]

The message of Grundmann's lectures did not change—Judaism was degenerate and Jesus was not a Jew. In a letter he wrote to the Reich Minister for Church Affairs in July 1942, he made his purpose clear: "Strong Jewish influence has penetrated the Western world through certain forms of Christianity that have to be unmasked."[79]

INSTITUTE ACTIVITIES OUTSIDE GERMANY

Through its antisemitism, which was in no way mitigated by the shift from politics to scholarship, the Institute also helped to define "ethnic Germans" in Eastern Europe. As Bergen has made clear, this much-prized Nazi designation was constructed by Nazi authorities during the course of the war.[80] Obtaining "ethnic German" status required not simply demonstration of Germanic acculturation, for which one piece of evidence was membership in a German— that is, Protestant—church, but active support of Nazism, for which involvement in the Institute's program of dejudaization and antisemitism offered proof. The desirability of ethnic German status during the war helped stimulate the receptivity in the east to Institute efforts at outreach.

The Protestant Church in Hermannstadt (as the Germans renamed Sibiu), Romania, in particular, responded enthusiastically to Hugo Pich's initial contact, made in 1941, with Bishop Wilhelm Staedel.[81] Staedel himself had a background that made him well disposed towards this overture. Born in 1890

---

[77] Letter to Grundmann from senior church councillor Piesch, Prague, dated April 17, 1941, regarding his participation in a pastors' conference on April 30 and May 1, 1941. Piesch writes about the forthcoming lecture, "Aber es darf kein DC Sache daraus warden!" (LKA Eisenach, III 2f).

[78] LKA Eisenach, Program for Institute conference in Heidelberg April 15–17, 1941; also at UAH PA25: Personalakten Theodor Odenwald.

[79] Five-page letter from Grundmann to Reich Minister of Church Affairs Hermann Muhs, dated July 16, 1942 (LKA Eisenach, DC III 2f).

[80] Bergen, "Nazi Concept of 'Volksdeutsche,'" 569–82.

[81] After World War I, Sibiu was ceded to Romania as a result of the peace treaties. In 1940 Sibiu was not included in the territory of Northern Transylvania ceded to Hungary by Romania. The region was restored to Romania after the close of World War II in 1945.

in Siebenbürgen, a German enclave, he had studied theology in Jena, Budapest, and Berlin, served in World War I as a field curate, and become a pastor in 1919. He later worked with a German youth group in Romania, transforming it along National Socialist principles, and, as a member of the fascist Deutsche Volkspartei in Rumänien (DVR), attempted a restructuring of the Romanian Protestant church in 1936.[82] These initial efforts led to his removal from his pastoral position in 1937, as Viktor Glondys, bishop at the time, was opposed to clerical involvement in Nazi politics.[83] Four years later, however, after the Nazi Party was well established in Romania, Nazi sympathizers among the clergy succeeded in reinstating Staedel and electing him bishop on February 16, 1941, just weeks after the Iron Guard unleashed a major pogrom in Bucharest, destroying two major synagogues, attacking, arresting, and murdering Jews.[84]

One of Staedel's first acts as bishop was to travel to Germany in April 1941, shortly before the outbreak of war between Germany and the Soviet Union, to meet with Grundmann about creating a new kind of church in Romania, based on "the purity of the divine truth of Christ."[85] Some six months later the regional consistory of the Evangelical church in Romania decided to establish a branch of the Institute, after receiving a petition signed by 39 pastors requesting a dejudaization of the church.[86] "The goal of dejudaization of teaching and life should be our earnest and serious obligation."[87] An opening conference was held March 4–5, 1942, in Hermannstadt at which participating pastors were divided into six working groups, coordinated with those of the

[82] Böhm, *Das nationalsozialistische Deutschland*, 42; for a brief sketch of the German evangelical church in Romania during the war, see pp. 136–47.

[83] Glondys, *Tagebuch*.

[84] Staedel assumed the office of bishop on March 23, and held it until 1944, encouraging a transformation of the church along a German Christian model. From 1944 to 1946, Staedel was imprisoned by the Communists. After his release, he served as a hospital chaplain in Minden, West Germany, where he helped establish an archive for former German Christian members, until his retirement in Marburg in 1959. See Böhm, *Das nationalsozialistische Deutschland*; Böhm, *Die Gleichschaltung der deutschen Volksgruppe*. Staedel's views corresponded to those of other Germans in Romania. See Markus, "Altbischof Wilhelm Staedel," 10.

[85] Letter from Staedel to Grundmann, dated April 7, 1941 (LKA Eisenach). Even as Staedel planned a dejudaization of the church, Romania itself was being emptied of Jews. During the first months of Operation Barbarossa, half of the 320,000 Jews of Bessarabia, Bukovina, and Dorohoi were murdered; ghettoization and deportation began shortly thereafter.

[86] The church's decision was reported in the *Siebenbürgisch Deutsches Tageblatt* of March 17, 1942; cited by Böhm, *Das nationalsozialistische Deutschland*, 144. On the petition, see *Südost-deutsche Tageszeitung*, March 15, 1942, p. 3. See also Ekkehart Lebouton, *Die evangelische Pfarrgemeinde A. B. Czernowitz*.

[87] Report by Ekkehart Lebouton, undated (LKA Eisenach).

Institute; for example, a commission to collect an "archive of German piety" was established. The meeting ended with a reading from *Die Botschaft Gottes* and the papers presented were published as a volume.[88] The antisemitic propaganda generated by the church under Staedel found a receptive response among Germans in Romania, in part no doubt because noncooperative pastors were threatened.[89]

Staedel maintained close ties with Grundmann and the Institute, attending Institute conferences in Germany and inviting Institute members to lecture in Romania, including Georg Bertram, from the University of Giessen,[90] together with Heinz Eisenhuth, a member of the Institute and professor of systematic theology at the University of Jena, in the spring of 1943.[91] In a letter to Grundmann after an October 1942 conference held in Weissenfels, Saxony, Staedel expressed his hope that the Institute's work would be expanded to reach larger circles, including his own church.[92]

Staedel, like Leffler and Leutheuser a recognized "Alter Kämpfer" in the Nazi Party, hoped his Nazi ties would allow him to lobby successfully for elevated rights for ethnic Germans in Romania. A privileged political status ought to be given to ethnic Germans over other ethnic groups, he argued, based on the Romanian Germans' fascist and antisemitic activities, to which the Evangelical church was making a strong contribution. Staedel's exploitation of Lutheran Protestantism to transform Romanians into ethnic Germans fell victim to a more general scorn of Christianity. In the summer of 1943, a luncheon of church leaders in Romania was interrupted by a sardonic choir singing, "You didn't see Jesus? He's supposed to roll cigarettes for us!"[93] If not a Jew, Jesus could still be mocked as a servant.

Some pastors remained voices of moral and political authority. Fewer Romanians from communities whose pastors opposed the Nazi movement joined the Waffen-SS, and fewer SS actions occurred than elsewhere.[94] Membership

---

[88]See Scheiner, *Das Dogma der evangelischen Landeskirche.*

[89]Böhm, *Das nationalsozialistische Deutschland,* 147. Leadership of the Romanian Institute was in the hands of Bishop Staedel together with two pastors, Andreas Scheiner and Ekkehart Lebouton, both active in the DC and Nazi Party. Lebouton joined the Waffen-SS on July 25, 1943; see Glondys, *Tagebuch,* 362. After the war, Lebouton became a pastor in Austria.

[90]Bertram was appointed tenured professor for New Testament at Giessen in 1925. His doctoral students, twenty-five between 1925 and 1943, included Karl Euler (1934) and Theodor Ellwein (1935), both Institute members.

[91]Letter from Reich Minister for Education to Bertram, with copy to the rector of the University of Geissen, dated April 6, 1943 (UAG, Georg Bertram: Personalakten).

[92]Letter from Staedel to Grundmann, undated (LKA Eisenach).

[93]Böhm, *Das nationalsozialistische Deutschland,* 194.

[94]Ibid., 195.

in the Institute, by contrast, signaled support for Nazi antisemitism. Thus, eight pastors who were members of the Romanian branch of the Institute were sent by the SS to Poland in 1944, selected because they were viewed as reliable Nazis who would strengthen antisemitism through their religious ministry.[95] Thus, Christian influence could either hinder or promote involvement with the SS and its antisemitism.

VIENNA

The Institute also established itself in Vienna. Of the small Protestant theological faculty at the University of Vienna, four of the six professors became active members of the Institute: Gustav Entz (practical theology), Richard Hoffmann (New Testament), Fritz Wilke (Old Testament), and Hans Opitz (church history). With the support of the government, the university presented itself as an institution on the border between the Reich and the Eastern occupied territories with their mixture of ethnic populations. Half of the 200 students of theology in 1932 came from areas outside pre-1938 Germany, including Austria, Poland, Hungary, and Yugoslavia. In 1938 Entz proposed transforming the Protestant theological faculty into a center for training ethnic Germans of eastern and southeastern Europe.[96] The Nazi Party district leader of Vienna at that time, Odilo Globocnik, was sympathetic to Entz's proposal, and it received added significance when Gerhard Kittel arrived in Vienna 1940 as a visiting professor of theology. Entz wanted to transform the Ostmark from being viewed as a "conquered province" into a model of diasporic German Christianity.[97] The Vienna faculty of Protestant theology brought Grundmann for a lecture tour in 1941 to describe the work of the Institute.[98] However, the transformation of the Vienna theological faculty did not occur. Entz's proposals were vetoed at the Reich level in 1942 by Martin Bormann. After Entz again failed in 1943 to gain permission for two new professorships, in diaspora studies and church history, with an emphasis on southeastern Europe, Kittel gave up and in early 1943 returned to Tübingen.

[95] Bergen, "Nazi Concept of 'Volksdeutsche,'" 578.

[96] Schwarz, "'Grenzburg' und 'Bollwerk,'" 9; Schwarz, "Eine Fakultät für den Südosten."

[97] Schwarz, "'Grenzburg' und 'Bollwerk,'" 25.

[98] One of Grundmann's lectures in Austria was "The Breakthrough of Germanness in Life and Thought in Its Significance for Theology and Church," presented to a group of Catholic clergy. In Salzburg he spoke to a community gathering on the topic of "The German Character of Luther as Overcoming the Jewish Elements in the Historical Development of Christianity." At the University of Vienna his topic was "The Problem of the Messiah." Letter to Riedel from Grundmann, dated March 27, 1941 (LKA Eisenach, DC III 2f).

ON CATHOLICISM

The Catholic Church was a problem for German Christians. Their ideology insisted that only Protestantism could be the national religion of Germans, and yet they also sought to win Catholic members for the German Christian movement.[99] Just as importantly, they sought to undermine the position of the Catholic Church within the Nazi Reich, which they did by tarring it as "Jewish." Within Institute discussions and publications, Catholicism was praised for initiating antisemitic measures over the centuries, while on the other hand, it was reviled, blamed for bearing the mantle of Jewish Christianity, proof that only Protestantism could be truly "judenrein." Catholicism was most often portrayed within the Institute as a vehicle for the transmission of Judaism to Christianity, thus being a "Jewish" religion itself, a portrayal that only served to stimulate German Christian hostility toward Catholics.

While priests and professors of theology within the German Catholic Church never engaged in the sort of formal dejudaization project promoted by the Institute, some Catholic theologians formulated arguments close to those of Grundmann and his colleagues. For example, in 1943 Karl Adam, professor of theology at the University of Tübingen and one of the leading Catholic theologians of his day, published an essay arguing that Jesus was racially not a Jew. His claims were similar to those of Grundmann: Jesus came from Galilee, which was populated by non-Jews; Mary was conceived immaculately and thus did not possess Jewish moral or physical traits; and Jesus himself rejected Jewish law.[100] Other Catholic thinkers, some of whom were priests, like Adam, formulated justifications for antisemitism, eugenics, and the immutable racial identity of Jews that could not be erased by baptism.[101]

A working group on Catholicism organized by the Institute met during the summer of 1940, subsuming a German Christian "Specialized Division for Catholic Questions" that was founded in Thuringia on August 15, 1938, to encourage Catholics to join the German Christians in establishing a national, nondoctrinal, supraconfessional church, an effort that produced no significant results.[102]

---

[99] Circular of the DC Nationalkirchliche Einung, no. 2, Division of the Catholic Church, dated June 6, 1942 (LKA Eisenach, DC III2f).

[100] Adam, "Jesus, der Christus, und wir Deutsche," 10:73–103. See the discussion of Adam's article in Denzler, "Antijudaismus und Antisemitismus," and Krieg, *Catholic Theologians in Nazi Germany*.

[101] Connelly, "Catholic Racism and Its Opponents."

[102] See the discussion in Bergen, *Twisted Cross*, 110.

A former Catholic priest from Freiburg, Friedrich Kapferer,[103] chaired that group; in 1939, he had published a pamphlet explaining German Christian ideology to Catholics, *An die Katholiken Deutschlands: Die sieghaften Ideen der Deutschen Christen*. Kapferer's goal was spreading German Christian ideas among Catholics, but also formulating a German Christian position regarding Catholicism. By 1941, the Institute's working group reported that it was studying the biological relationship between Judaism and Catholicism, the sociological influence of Judaism on the Catholic Church, and the problem of Judaism's spiritual influence on Catholicism.[104]

The working group on Catholicism attracted a few new members to the Institute, including some Catholic theologians,[105] and gathered for a conference on December 9, 1941, in the Elgersburg Castle, in the Thuringian forest, under the leadership of Heinz Dungs.[106] His brother, Karl Dungs, chaired a commission established by the Institute to investigate the influence of Judaism on Catholicism, "in blood-racial and spiritual-religious respect," to uncover Germanic elements in Catholicism, and to delineate the essential "Christian" within Catholicism. Smaller working groups were also organized in Vienna, Cologne, and Weimar, and the meeting in Elgersburg was to formalize their theological direction under the guidance of the Institute.

Antisemitism was thus mobilized to undermine the status of the Catholic Church and, at the same time, to win Catholic members for the Institute. Catholicism's own antisemitism became the key to rejecting the church and accepting its adherents. German Christians had earlier debated whether the Old Testament was a Jewish book or an anti-Jewish book. Now the question was whether Catholicism was a Jewish form of Christianity or, rather, contributed significantly to anti-Judaism. At the Institute conference on the Catholic question held in 1941, Fritz Schmidt-Clausing, a student of Grundmann's at the University of Jena and a former Catholic who had become a Protestant pastor, gave the keynote address arguing that Catholicism was to be lauded for its

---

[103]Kapferer also published a brochure, *Die Bergpredigt als Kampfansage gegen das Judentum* (1944). See Bergen, "One Reich, One People, One Church," 486–87.

[104]Report presented by the Working Group on Questions of Catholicism, September 25, 1941 (YIVO G135).

[105]These included Alois Closs, instructor in Catholic theology at the University of Vienna. Report of the Administrative Board of the Institute held July 17, 1940, in Hotel Thüringer Hof (LKA Eisenach, DC III 2a). Another was Father Richard Kleine, a religion teacher. See Spicer, *Hitler's Priests*,182–84.

[106]Dungs substituted for Gerhard Ohlemüller, who was unable to participate. Ohlemüller was the author of *Politischer Katholizismus* (1936). Others present included Karl Dungs, van Beuningen, Buch, Grell, Kapferer, Schmidt-Clausing, Seidl, and Würzinger. See the meeting report written by Schmidt-Clausing (ZAK 7/4167).

anti-Judaism of earlier eras, but that it had outlived its purpose because the Church had been infiltrated in the modern era by Jewish thinkers. Following closely Grundmann's own schema of Christian origins, he argued that the post-apostolic division was not between Pauline (Gentile) and Jewish Christianity, but rather between Paul's Jewish Christianity and Stephen's (Gentile) authentic version of Christianity. Like Grundmann, he argued that Paul, as a Jew, had failed to take up the two central teachings of Jesus, the sonship of Christ and the kingdom of God. Jews had been responsible for the Roman Empire's persecution of the early Christians, so that Christianity in the first centuries had been anti-Jewish. Jewish Christianity died out in 200 CE as the church became Gentile Christian. Even the Jewish historian Heinrich Graetz, noted Schmidt-Clausing, wrote about the hatred Jews felt toward the church fathers, who were in the truest sense, he said, the prophets of the new covenant.

Turning to the anti-Judaism of the Catholic Church, Schmidt-Clausing reminded his audience that ever since the Council of Elvira in 306 CE, the Catholic Church had taken canonical measures against the Jews, including early edicts demanding that Jews mark themselves by wearing a Jewish star.[107] Jews collaborated with the Church's enemies, such as the Arians and Donatists, but also infiltrated the Church to become dangerous figures, such as the great inquisitor, Tómas de Torquemada. Until shortly before the Tridentine reforms, the Church remained fundamentally opposed to Jews, but since then, he continued, Catholic theology had been influenced by Jewish thinkers such as the medieval Jewish philosopher Moses Maimonides and the Enlightenment philosopher Moses Mendelssohn. Their influence, combined with the impact of the Council of Trent, led, Schmidt-Clausing argued, to a Jewish triumph over the Vatican, turning Catholicism from an anti-Jewish to a Jewish-dominated church. Germany's defeat in the Great War represented the final victory of the Jews, launching an outrage on the part of priests against Germany's domination by Jews, while the church itself, Schmidt-Clausing concluded, remained torpid.[108]

Ideologically, Schmidt-Clausing's construction of Catholicism sought to appeal to Catholics to join the German Christian movement, while rejecting the Catholic Church as a foe of National Socialism for its "Jewishness."

---

[107] The Council of Elvira did not mandate that Jews wear a star, although it prohibited Christians from eating with Jews and committing adultery with Jews, and told landlords to keep Jews from blessing their crops.

[108] Six-page report of Schmidt-Clausing's speech in ZAK 7/4167. The so-called Working Group for the Catholic Question continued at least until January 1943, holding a meeting in Eisenach January 26–27 under the direction of Karl Dungs of Essen (UAH, Personalakten: Theodor Odenwald).

Theologically, he aligned himself with the efforts of those within the Institute who were attempting to eliminate the New Testament writings of Paul from the new Christianity that the Institute was constructing. For Schmidt-Clausing, Paul had misunderstood Jesus's fundamental teachings, which were utterly un-Jewish, and Paul's writings were not to be considered foundational for Christian theology.

The Institute conference was held in the wake of a similar meeting, on "The Catholic Church and the Jewish Question," sponsored by Walter Frank's Reich Institute for the History of the New Germany in 1940. At that meeting, Josef Roth, a priest who was also an assistant to Hanns Kerrl in the Reich Ministry for Church Affairs, presented a paper arguing that, despite its long history of anti-Jewish regulations and teachings, Catholicism had been permeated by Judaism to its very core. Roth's rant was both antisemitic and directed against the Church, concluding that "The Catholic Church will never come to a clear and determined struggle against Judaism and will never become an ally in the national ideological struggle because it would have to give up its own mission and its own spiritual substance."[109] As was so often the case, the Institute used the Catholic question as a tool of competition with Nazi functionaries: who were the more committed, effective antisemites—Institute members, with their training in Christian theology and their assumed expertise on Judaism, or Nazi ideologues?

Incorporating the Teutonic

Competition between the German Christian movement and the numerous, far smaller neo-pagan movements that arose even before the Third Reich revolved during most of the 1930s around the question of Christianity's suitability for Nazi Germany. One of the major neo-pagan polemics against the German Christians was that Christianity was a Jewish religion. While never resolved, the conflict was mitigated during the war years with the elimination of Jews from the Reich. As Jews disappeared, first isolated and then deported, German Christians shifted their rhetoric to embrace Germany's Teutonic heritage—even as they blamed Jews for having obscured that heritage from Germans.

Over the course of 1941, Institute publications began to speak increasingly about the Teutonic and Nordic sources of German religiosity that had been

[109]Roth, "Die Katholische Kirche und die Judenfrage," 163–76. See the discussion in Spicer, *Resisting the Third Reich*, 142.

concealed and forgotten as a result of Jewish philosophical influences in the modern era. Grundmann blamed the Jewish philosophers Benedict Spinoza and Moses Mendelssohn for undermining authentic German—and Christian—religiosity. The loss of faith in the God of love following World War I was not a loss of faith in the Christian God, he argued, but in the Enlightement God of Mendelssohn.[110] The attacks on Christianity from certain Nazi quarters were errors rooted in Mendelssohn-inspired beliefs that Jesus was a Jew; apparently for Grundmann, even Nazis could be duped by Jews. Meyer-Erlach contributed the argument that while north Germanic tribes had retained Thor, Odin, and other gods, the southern Germans had demonized them, causing a break in the souls of the south Germans, as the nineteenth-century Danish Lutheran bishop Nicolai Frederik Grundtvig had shown a century before, by causing them to become Catholic.[111]

During a visit to Sweden in 1941 Meyer-Erlach formed a new organization, Arbeitsgemeinschaft Germanentum und Christentum, with his friend, Hugo Odeberg, professor of theology at the University of Lund, to bring Swedish writers, theologians, and students to Germany for Institute-sponsored meetings. Odeberg, the most distinguished scholar of Judaism to join the Institute, was already involved in pro-Nazi activities in Sweden.[112] He had a close personal relationship with Meyer-Erlach.[113] Meyer-Erlach explained, in a letter to the German Foreign Ministry, that his work with Odeberg had the purpose of liberating the Nordic peoples from the influence of the Jews and their vassal,

[110]Letter from Grundmann to Heinz Dungs, dated December 18, 1942 (LKA Eisenach, DC III 2f), p. 6.

[111]Letter from Meyer-Erlach to Odeberg, on letterhead "Arbeitsgemeinschaft Germanentum und Christentum," dated January 26, 1942 (UAL, Odeberg files). On Grundtvig, see Knudsen, "One Hundred Years Later, 71–77; Skarsten, "Rise and Fall of Grundtvigianism in Norway," 122–42; Sneen, "The Hermeneutics of N.F.S.G.," 42–61.

[112]At Swedish universities, a significant number of faculty were sympathetic to Nazism, Sverker Oredsson has found. Odeberg not only was one of the major Nazi academics, but became one of the leading Nazis in Sweden, serving 1941–43 as president of the pro-German Riksföreningen Sverige Tyskland and editor of its periodical *Sverige-Tyskland*. Oredsson, "Svenska teologer under nazitiden," 167–78, which is drawn from the author's book, *Lunds universitet under andra världskriget*. Odeberg resigned from Sverige Tyskland in early 1943, for reasons that remain unclear. Such ties between Germans and Scandinavians were encouraged by Hitler after the occupation of Denmark and Norway, and by Alfred Rosenberg in connection with the search for alternative religious forms to Christianity. See Bohn, ed., *Die deutsche Herrschaft*, and Locke, "Zur 'Grossgermanischen Politike' des Dritten Reiches," 39.

[113]The friendship was not merely collegial; children of each the two families took their vacations with the other. Letter from Meyer-Erlach to Odeberg, on letterhead "Arbeitsgemeinschaft Germanentum und Christentum," dated January 26, 1942 (UAL, Odeberg files).

England.[114] In November 1941, the Swedish organization Odal, together with the Arbeitsgemeinschaft Germanentum und Christentum, sponsored a conference in Weissenfels, a city in Saxony that had served as headquarters of the great Swedish king, Gustavus Adolfus, prior to his death during the Thirty Years War at the battle of Lützen in 1632. The purpose of the meeting, as Grundmann wrote in his foreword to the volume of conference proceedings, was to examine the shared foundation of blood of Germanic peoples after the era of the Reformation, recognizing that "the shape of faith and religion is determined by the idiosyncracy of the Volk's character."[115]

At the conference, in which twenty Swedes took part, Odeberg spoke on Hellenism as a Greek culture corroded by the Jews, and compared it to contemporary American and English culture, which he viewed as similarly disfigured by Jews.[116] Other speakers described the Germanic piety that gave the German Reich a particular mindset, and its positive influence on Scandinavia. A Swedish speaker warned of the "English-Jewish sects" that were undermining collaboration between Sweden and Germany.[117] Such collaborative conferences of Germans and Scandinavians required Reich approval that was always forthcoming. Although doubt was expressed within the German Foreign Ministry about the effectiveness of Meyer-Erlach's theological rhetoric and Sweden's resistance to German Christian theological directions, obstacles were never erected to the Institute's work.[118]

Even as the Institute sought to eradicate the Jewish from the Christian, it attempted to introduce Teutonic myths and rituals as proto-Christian. Papers presented at Institute conferences argued for similarities in the religiosity underlying Teutonic and Christian faith, both of which were Aryan, according to Institute analyses. These were part of broader efforts by German scholars in the field of "Nordic studies" to understand the underlying religiosity of myths.[119] The goal of the Institute was to meld Teutonic ideas into Christianity. To that end Institute members argued that Jesus did not emerge out of Judaism, but represented an essentially Nordic or Aryan religiosity with either Teutonic roots or close parallels with Teutonism. Nazism's revival of Teutonic traditions did not contradict Christianity, but as presented by the Institute, they were united in their goal of destroying Jews and Judaism.

---

[114]Meyer-Erlach to Büttner, dated August 8, 1942 (AA R98796: 1949: Inland I-D, 3/4).

[115]Grundmann, *Die völkische Gestalt des Glaubens*, foreword.

[116]Odeberg had articulated those views in an earlier article, "Ist das Christentum hellenistisch oder jüdisch?," 569–86.

[117]Report on the conference (BA Potsdam 49.01; 2966/4).

[118]Memo signed by Roth, dated September 22, 1942 (AA R98796, 1949: Inland I-D, 3/4).

[119]See Mees, "Völkische Altnordistik," 316–26.

Interest in the Teutonic brought new alliances for the Institute, making it an axis for uniting a wide range of völkisch thinkers and scholars with Christian theologians. The Institute formed a working group on Teutonism and Christianity in 1941 under the joint leadership of Meyer-Erlach and Odeberg.[120] That, in turn, brought Swedish writers and theologians to Germany for Institute-sponsored conferences. Institute theologians gained a positive reputation among advocates of neo-paganism. Friedrich Knorr, editor of the racist journal *Zeitschrift für deutsche Geisteswissenschaft*, contacted Grundmann in 1943 to establish a working collaboration, and invited him to contribute to the journal.[121] The Houston Stewart Chamberlain Vereinigung, based in Dresden, also initiated contact with Grundmann in 1943, expressing hope for jointly sponsored conferences and lectures.[122] In April 1942, Grundmann received a friendly letter from Wilhelm Hauer, professor at the University of Tübingen and, until 1936, head of the Deutsche Glaubensbewegung (German Faith Movement), a neo-Teutonic religious movement, proposing collaboration.[123] Grigol Robakidse, a prominent Georgian writer who fled to Germany after the Soviets took control of Georgia in 1921, was also in contact with Grundmann, Meyer-Erlach, and Eisenhuth, as well as students in the theological faculty of the University of Jena. Enamored of Hitler, Robakidse, who lived in Jena, was part of the circle of völkisch writers in Thuringia and wrote popular novels and plays in Georgian as well as pamphlets in German extolling Hitler and Mussolini.[124]

---

[120]Odeberg's antisemitic, pro-Nazi publications and activities are delineated by Gerdmar, "A Germanic Jesus on Swedish Soil."

[121]Letter from Knorr to Grundmann, dated February 20, 1943 (LKA Eisenach CIV4: Ostmark). The article was Walter Grundmann, "Luther in der Sicht der Reichsidee," *Zeitschrift für deutsche Geisteswissenschaft* 5 (1942/43) 19–32. The journal, which was printed at the Dietrichs Verlag, a völkisch publication house in Jena, from 1938 to 1944, published pseudo-scholarly articles on topics such as medieval Teutonic literature, music, modern Germanic philosophy and literature, and racial approaches to scholarship. The journal articles are listed at http://www.phil.uni-erlangen .de/~p1ges/zfhm/geist.html.

[122]Letter from Felix Eichler to Grundmann, dated February 6, 1943 (LKA Eisenach CIV4: Ostmark).

[123]Letter from Hauer to Grundmann, dated April 14, 1942 (LKA Eisenach, DC III 2f). The organization renamed itself the Kampfring Deutscher Glaube (Fighting Circle of Germanic Faith). On Hauer, see Junginger, *Von der philologische zur völkischen Religionswissenschaft*; Poewe, *New Religions and the Nazis*; Dierks, *Jakob Wilhelm Hauer*.

[124]See Robakidse, *Adolf Hitler*, and *Mussolini*. Information on his contact with the theological faculty from Hans-Joachim Thilo personal interview, Lübeck, July 20, 1995. Thilo claimed that Robakidse had received an honorary doctorate from the University of Jena, but I have been unable to substantiate that. A private university in Tblisi, Georgia, "Alma Mater," was opened in 1991 and renamed for Robakidse in 1995.

Eradicating the Jews

The deportation of German Jews began in the fall of 1941, along with regulations marking their clothing with a star and further limiting their ability to move about in the public domain. Those last months of 1941 also saw significant shifts in the public rhetoric regarding Jews: "The restraint of the previous months gave way to an explosion of the vilest anti-Jewish invectives and threats," as Saul Friedländer writes. In a speech on October 2, 1941, Hitler declared that the enemy poised to "annihilate not only Germany, but the whole of Europe" was "Jews and only Jews!"[125] The decision to exterminate the Jews was communicated by Hitler to his closest colleagues on October 19, 1941. During that same week, Hitler ranted in the same kind of language as the Institute: Jesus was not a Jew, Paul falsified the gospels, and the Jews were seeking the destruction of Aryans through racial contamination. Similar tirades by Hitler against the Jews continued well into November, both in public and private, explicitly referring to the extermination of the Jews,[126] and his claims about Jesus and Paul were repeated during the war years in private conversations.

The Reich regulations limiting Jews' presence in public did not include the churches; instead, the churches issued their own regulations. On December 17, 1941, seven regional churches governed by members of the German Christian movement issued a joint declaration stating that baptized Jews—that is, Christians who were non-Aryan, according to the Nazi racial laws—were unwelcome at church and not to receive pastoral care from clergy. That decision was made after the churches had solicited a theological opinion from Eisenhuth, who declared: "Jewish Christians are to be excluded from religious congregations as enemies of the Reich; German pastors may not extend their official services to Jewish Christians; church taxes may not be collected from Jewish Christians." Eisenhuth justified the exclusions by reference to Martin Luther: "Luther saw the Jews above all as murderers of Christ. We see in them destroyers of God's creation, whose defense is the duty of all Germans and also of the German Protestant church."[127] The declaration was given further weight in a ruling from the national governing board of the entire Protestant church, published three days before Christmas, upholding the new regulations. The exclusion of Jews forged a link among otherwise warring factions within the

---

[125] Cited by Friedländer, *The Years of Extermination*, 272.

[126] Ibid., 281.

[127] Heinz Erich Eisenhuth, "Gutachten über die Stellung getaufter Juden in der Kirche," cited by Prolingheuer, "Der Lutherisch Deutsch-Christliche Weg," 79, 91 fn 42. See also Schenk, "Der Jenaer Jesus."

church, but not all were willing to accept the decree. For example, Bishop Theophil Wurm of Württemberg, one of the three Protestant bishops who presented themselves as "neutrals" in the church struggle between the German Christians and the Confessing Church, supported the right of the state to enact racial laws to protect the purity of the German race.[128] Yet Wurm, writing in February 1942, claimed that the church should treat baptized Jews as "our brethren in Christ"; for the church to exclude them would be to act "like the Pharisees" and to abandon the belief that baptism brought salvation.

Hitler's message of extermination of the Jews opened the year 1942. His public speeches and private comments used the same language and were reported in the press. Thus, by early 1942 Germans, but also Jews trapped in the Reich's clutches, "knew that the Jews were being pitilessly murdered."[129] This became the year when the greatest number of European Jews were murdered, and it was a busy and productive year for the Institute. As Europe was being rid of its Jews, the Institute was creating a Christianity rid of its Jewishness. Conferences, publications, and lecture tours made the work of the Institute widely known and brought new members. As Hitler murdered the Jews, the Institute removed the word "Eradication" from its formal name, as if to indicate that the goal was achieved. The problem facing Institute members was determining precisely what constituted the Jewish within Christianity, a problem that was debated endlessly at its conferences. Once a Jewish element was identified, another problem became weaning Christians from words and ideas that had come to seem quintessentially Christian—for example, certain hymns, and Hebrew words such as "Hallelujah."

The Institute's central concern with eradicating Judaism did not disappear nor become supplanted by the new interest in the Teutonic; Grundmann continued to lecture on dejudaization, viewing it as a basis for his alliances with Teutonic groups.[130] By 1942, the German Christians had apparently succeeded in altering religious discourse in Germany. The Institute's campaigns had succeeded in creating such widespread hostility toward the Old Testament that Heinrich Weinmann, a pastor on an Institute commission, wrote that "today one does not dare to bring something from the Old Testament to the Volk."[131] A commission was established by Grundmann in 1942 to uncover those passages in the Old Testament that were not Jewish and might give Germans

[128] Gerlach, *And the Witnesses Were Silent: The Confessing Church and the Persecution of the Jews*, 195–96

[129] Friedländer, The *Years of Extermination*, 334.

[130] Letter from Grundmann to Günther Geissler, dated February 11, 1943 (LKA Eisenach CIV4: Ostmark).

[131] Letter from Weinmann to Grundmann dated February 12, 1942 (LKA Eisenach).

strength and comfort.[132] It was led by Karl Euler, a Nazi Party member, who was an instructor in theology at the University of Giessen, where he had earned a doctorate under Georg Bertram.[133] The commission was ambivalent about continued use of the Old Testament. At best, Weinmann argued, the material could be presented as excerpts from Luther, but not as Old Testament. In a talk on behalf of the Institute, Theodor Odenwald, professor of systematic theology at the University of Heidelberg, argued similarly that the Old Testament was to be avoided. At stake was not simply Nazi Party hostility toward the Old Testament, he said, but a theological consensus that the Old Testament aroused annoyance.[134]

Institute members actively contributed propaganda to the war effort. Grundmann described the Institute's conferences as an effort to reconfigure the consciousness of Europe, presumably to challenge the link Germans might feel with other European nations through their common Christianity.[135] Meyer-Erlach, always the popular propagandist, went on lecture tours to speak to Wehrmacht troops in France, Finland, Ostland, and Ukraine.[136] In pamphlets published in 1940 and 1941 based on his lectures, he denounced England as judaized through its Calvinist Reformation that placed excessive emphasis on the Old Testament, a charge encouraged by the Propaganda Ministry, which published similar charges against England in its own pamphlets.[137]

A March 1942 Institute newsletter declared: "Julius Leutheuser once wrote from the front that the hatred of Christ is in the deepest sense a form of spiritual resistance against the Jews on the part of the German people; develop-

---

[132]Examining the Pentateuch were Hermann Werdermann (Practical Theology, Rostock) and Grundmann; Prophets, Wagenführer and Büchner; Psalms, Pribnow and Gimpel; Historical books, proverbs, etc, Weinmann and Thieme. Memorandum from Grundmann dated January 8, 1942; LKA Eisenach). None of those participating was a scholar of the Old Testament; Hempel, the Institute's most distinguished Old Testament scholar, had already left for military service as a chaplain.

[133]NSDAP May 1, 1937, no. 5575607 (BDC, Karl Euler materials).

[134]Letter from Weinmann to Grundmann, dated February 12, 1942 (LKA Eisenach, DC III 2f).

[135]Fourteen-page report sent to Buettner at the Auswärtiges Amt and to General Consul Wuester (AA R98796, 1949, Inland I-D, 3/4).

[136]Unsigned report of conference in Weissenfels, undated typescript (AA R98796, 1949, as in preceding fn).

[137]Meyer-Erlach, *Der Einfluss der Juden auf das englische Christentum,* and *Ist Gott Engländer?* Jeffrey Herf notes that Goebbels, in his article, "Im Gelächter der Welt, 16. February 1941" (published in *Die Zeit ohne Beispiel,* Munich: Eher, 1941, 394–95), declared that the English were "the Jews among the Aryans." Herf also calls attention to other publications of the Propaganda Ministry on affinities between English Puritans and Jews, including Meyer-Christian, *Die englisch-jüdisch Allianz.* Meyer-Christian was director of the Reich Press School in Berlin and worked closely with Goebbels. Herf, "The 'Jewish War,'" 51–80.

ments in the political sphere have demonstrated this fact quite impressively. The foundations required to arrive at the same position in a scholarly way are being created by the Institute today in the midst of the war."[138] Six weeks later, on April 14, 1942, the first deportation from Thuringia left for Majdanek, with 148 Jews from various towns, excluding Erfurt; no one survived that deportation.[139] Later that month, Grundmann received an admiring letter, thanking him for his lecture in Tübingen: "Your explications in Tübingen are still resonating in their great dynamism."[140]

Feeling energized, Grundmann in May 1942 requested additional funding for the Institute from the finance department of the German Protestant church.[141] He claimed that fifty professors had become members of the Institute, and that funds were necessary to establish additional working groups for them. His request received approval from Kerrl,[142] but some member church leaders objected. Until that point, only the Lutheran academy in Sondershausen (Thuringia) had received a subvention, leading Kipper, president of the church in Nassau-Hesse, to reply that the Institute ought to receive a higher subsidy than the Lutheran academy.[143] Grundmann did not ask for a specific amount, but the Institute received 3,000 RM in October 1942.[144]

Grundmann's funding request came just days after the May 9–10, 1942, deportation of Jews from forty Thuringian towns and villages to Leipzig. Together with a group of Leipzig Jews, they were then deported to Belzyce, in eastern Poland. Most were held briefly, then sent to the Majdanek death camp on May 22. Those who remained in Belzyce were shot by the SS in May 1943.[145] Deportations of Jews from Thuringia to Theresienstadt, Auschwitz, and Ravensbrück continued relentlessly; as late as the end of February 1945, after Auschwitz had already been liberated, a transport of Jews married to Aryans left Thuringia for Theresienstadt.

The summer of 1942 saw an extension of the Nazi extermination program. The geographic net expanded to include deportation of Jews from areas of

[138] DC Nationalkirchliche Einung, Information Service, Weimar, March 1, 1942 (LKA Eisenach, DC cl4).

[139] Liesenberg, ""Wir täuschen uns nicht," 455.

[140] Letter from Werner Kocher, Reutlingen, to Grundmann, dated April 28, 1942(LKA Eisenach, DC III 2f).

[141] Letter from Grundmann to the finance department of the German Protestant church, dated May 19, 1942 (ZAK 1/C3/174).

[142] Letter from the finance department of the German Protestant church, dated June 27, 1942 (ZAK 1/C3/174).

[143] Letter from Kipper to Werner, dated July 6, 1942 (ZAK 1/C3/174).

[144] Receipt signed by Brauer, dated October 23, 1942 (ZAK 1/C3/174).

[145] Liesenberg, "Wir Täuschen uns nicht," 455.

western and eastern Europe, and the murder rate in the death camps was also increased. Within Germany, awareness of the deportations and murder of the Jews undoubtedly gave rise to some moral qualms that the Institute sought to reassure. In the foreword to a 1942 book he coauthored with Euler, Grundmann wrote, "A healthy Volk must and will reject the Jews in every form. This fact is justified before history and through history. If someone is upset about Germany's treatment of the Jews, Germany has the historical justification and historical authorization for the fight against the Jews on its side!"[146] The Institute's affirmation of the Teutonic did not distract from its antisemitic propaganda, now focused primarily on the war, which it defined as Germany's defense against Jewish efforts to destroy it: "We know that the Jews want the annihilation [Vernichtung] of Germany," Grundmann wrote.[147]

In June of 1942, at an Institute conference in Nuremberg,[148] dejudaization was discussed in terms of both popular liturgy and the problem of the apostle Paul. Werdermann, now serving as professor of practical theology at the University of Rostock, warned of the "danger of judaization" in religious instruction that included the Old Testament and Matthew's gospel. The children's prayer, "I am small, my heart is pure, noone should reside in it except Jesus," based on Psalm 51:10, was condemned by Werdermann: "Through that children's prayer a small, self-righteous Pharisee will be raised!"[149] He reiterated those warnings at a meeting in Jena in January of 1943 of the religious pedagogy working group, urging that race as the "order of creation" be recognized as the basis of Christian truth and that Jesus be viewed "with German eyes" to see his opposition to Judaism.[150] Theodor Pauls, an Institute member and professor of pedagogy, who edited several volumes of Luther's texts, lectured on the "destructive Jewish intellect" and "racial mixture" of Jews that Luther

---

[146] Foreword to Grundmann and Euler, *Das religiöse Gesicht des Judentums* (unpaginated).

[147] Grundmann, "Das Heil kommt von den Juden," 1–8.

[148] The conference took place June 8–10, 1942, at the Hotel Deutscher Hof, postponed from a March date due to war exigencies (notice from Grundmann about postponement, February 25, 1942, UAL Odeberg materials). Because of the war exigencies, this conference was open only to members. Its tone was also different. No papers were delivered about Jesus, for the first time, and instead, there was extensive presentation of Nordic literature, with two lectures on Icelandic myths. In addition to theologians, several writers with völkisch connections spoke: Åke Ohlmarks, Hans Franck, and Wilhelm Kotzde-Kottenrodt. Ohlmarks, a Swede, held a visiting appointment at the Moritz Arndt University in Greifswald. See Ohlmarks and Åkerberg, *Thomas Thorild als Vorläufer der neuzeitlichen Religionswissenschaft*.

[149] Hermann Werdermann, "Die Gefahr des Judaisierens," 217–48.

[150] Five-page report from the Institute, press liaison Pastor Heinz Dungs, Weimar, dated May 13, 1943 (UAH, PA25: Personalakten: Theodor Odenwald).

himself had warned against.[151] Meanwhile, Odeberg lectured at Nuremberg on Aramaic as Jesus's mother tongue, a language he distinguished from Hebrew and identified as modern, worldly, and close to German.[152] The argument followed Grundmann's claim, in *Jesus der Galiläer*, that the inability of Galileans to speak the guttural sounds of Hebrew was evidence that they were "not true Semites."[153] Thus, even from a linguistic point of view, Jesus could not have been a Jew.

THE PROBLEM OF PAUL

Perhaps the most significant Jewish element within Christianity was the figure of Paul, whose theology was foundational to Christianity and deeply admired by Martin Luther, and yet whose Jewish identity could not be denied. The problem of Paul's Jewishness remained unresolved and not often discussed directly by Institute members. Initially, at least some supporters had apparently expected strong action against Paul, as suggested by Bishop Heinrich Oberheid's 1936 fulmination, "We will get rid of the Old Testament, we will critically examine the New Testament. The Jew Paul can be as negligibly canonical for us as any other confessions of the past. We will also place many, many passages of the New Testament before the seat of judgment."[154] In the end, the Institute removed the Old Testament from the Christian Bible, declared Jesus an enemy of the Jews, but never resolved the problem of Paul's Jewishness.

The Institute's conference of June 1942 addressed the problem of Paul's Jewish identity and the Judaism that infused his theology. Paul was of mixed race and mixed thinking, combining Pharisaic closed-mindedness with Hellenistic open-mindedness. Unable to free himself from Jewish ways of thinking, he still managed to preserve the gospel of divine sonship, though in distorted form. The conclusion, according to Grundmann, was that "a German faith cannot be based on Paul, because it would then be deformed through his Jewish system of coordinates, and the necessary Germanic foundations would not be able to come into effect."[155] Yet the next logical step—eliminating Paul and

---

[151] Pauls, "Die Ursprünglichkeit des Gotteslobes bei Luther," 137–92.

[152] Odeberg, "Die Muttersprache Jesu," 69–82.

[153] Grundmann, *Jesus der Galiläer*, 165.

[154] Heinrich Oberheid, in *Luther Kirchenzeitung*, no. 29 (July 1936).

[155] Two-page report by Grundmann, "Zur grundsätzlichen Bedeutung der 3. Gesamtmitarbeitersitzung," undated (ZAK 7/4167, files). Conference proceedings were published as Grundmann, ed., *Germanentum, Christentum und Judentum*, vol. 3.

his Jewishness from the Bible—was not taken nor even formally proposed until 1944.

In August of 1944, the Thuringian pastor Hugo Pich, one of the original founders of the Institute, circulated a memorandum calling for a more thorough dejudaization of the church by eradicating Paul and his theology. The German Christians, he wrote, were holding onto a "Jewish Christianity"[156] by retaining Paul. What was needed was the "faith in God" of Jesus, "for which he, in battle against Judaism, went to his death."[157] The church should reject the Old Testament in favor of the history of the German Volk and God's revelation in it, but should also reject the "Jew Scha-ul [Saul] with his Jewish-messianic 'Christ'-proclamation."[158] Pich argued that the church remained a "breeding ground" for Jewishness, and he blamed Jews for the attempted assassination of Hitler on July 20, 1944, and for the German war dead, concluding that the war was a battle of the German nation against a world Jewry bent on its destruction.[159]

Reactions were negative. Hugo Rönck, who had served as president of the Thuringian church since the death of Bishop Sasse in August 1942,[160] told Pich that in attacking Paul, he was giving ammunition to the Confessing Church, which long claimed that the German Christians had abandoned Christianity.[161] Johannes Sievers, who had replaced Leffler as executive director of the Institute, replied that Germany's state of total war had become so drastic that no reconfiguration of the church could be considered at present.[162] Bishop Walther Schultz of Mecklenburg, one of the early and most enthusiastic supporters of the Institute, described Pich as a theological hysteric and urged that his proposal not be adopted as an official Institute policy.[163] Furthermore, Schultz wrote to Rönck, "I consider Pich's observations completely erroneous and moreover an insult to our nation, which is blamed indirectly for having been duped, in its hopeless stupidity and lack of instinct, by some stinking Jew for 1,500 years [verschwitzem Juden auf dem Leim gekrochen]."[164]

[156]Hugo Pich, "Der Weg zur entjudeten deutschen Reichskirche in der Glaubensgefolgschaft Jesu" (LKA Eisenach, DC III 2a), 3.

[157]Ibid., 5.

[158]Ibid., 6.

[159]Ibid., 1.

[160]He was made president, rather than a bishop, as mandated by Thuringian church laws dated Feburary 1943, which state that the position of bishop would remain unfilled throughout the war.

[161]Letter from Rönck to Pich, dated August 18, 1944 (LKA Eisenach, DC III 2a).

[162]Letter from Sievers to Pich, dated August 15, 1944 (LKA Eisenach, DC III 2a).

[163]Letter from Schultz to Bertram, dated August 9, 1944 (LKA Eisenach, DC III 2a).

[164]Letter from Schultz to Rönck, dated August 2, 1944 (LKA Eisenach, DC III 2a).

Nordic and Jewish Influences

One of the largest conferences sponsored by the Institute was a "Nordic Working Conference" held October 7–13, 1942, at Weissenfels.[165] Many of the participants were Scandinavians, including Swedes, Finns, and Norwegians,[166] and the papers "began with the obligatory recognition of the racial-völkisch approach for all scholarly work, with the knowledge of the common Germanic blood and cultural traits and with the consciousness of the fateful significance that is bound up with the name of Luther for the Germanic Nordic people and for the German Volk."[167] The conference received government support[168] to bring the Scandinavians, selected by Odeberg.[169] Lectures tended to focus on Nordic and Germanic literature, rather than New Testament and Jesus. For example, Wilhelm Koepp, professor of systematic theology at the University of Greifswald, spoke on Thule, a Nordic mythical place popularized by the Nazis. The medieval Teutonic "Heliand" text was discussed by Erik Rooth, professor in Lund. Hans Heinrich Schaeder, a scholar of Persian religion and professor at the University of Berlin, called in his lecture for solidarity between Christians and Muslims against England. The Teutonic, the conference participants concluded, had brought into being a "natural Christianity," and it was Germany, Meyer-Erlach emphasized in his opening address,

[165] This was the largest conference organized by the Institute. Its official sponsor was the Arbeitsgemeinschaft Germanentum und Christentum, which received its support from Reich offices; Meyer-Erlach claimed approval from the Gestapo, the Foreign Offie, and Kerrl. Letter from Meyer-Erlach to Reich Minister for Church Affairs, dated July 9, 1942 (AA R61690).

[166] A list of the names and addresses of the Scandinavians can be found in in ULA, Hugo Odeberg files. A list of the participants can be found at LKA Eisenach C III, 2a.

[167] Letter from Grundmann to AA, dated January 23, 1943 (AA Inland I-D, 3/4: R98796, 1949).

[168] Meyer-Erlach also attempted to receive permission from the AA for three Norwegians to attend, but was turned down. The three were the Norwegian Minister for Church and Educational Affairs in the Quisling government, Ragnar Skancke, the bishop of Trondheim, and the bishop of Oslo. The rector of the Swedish-language theological academy at Turku, Finnland, Otto Andersson, was also invited, but could not attend at the last minute. The Dutch theologian H. W. van der Vaart-Smit was also invited but did not attend. Letter from Meyer-Erlach, dated July 9, 1942 (AA Signatur R61690). See Vaart-Smit, *Kamptoestanden 1944/45 bis 1948*; see also Vaart-Smit, *De Duitsche kerkstrijd*. A list of the names and addresses of the Swedish participants is in ULA, Odeberg files.

[169] In June 1942, Odeberg wrote to thank Grundmann for their work together at the November 1941 Weissenfels conference, to which he had brought twenty students from Scandinavia, and emphasized how impressed he was with the theological scholarship underway in Germany: "one could see that in your community one works in a strictly scholarly way . . . (1) First one could

that was the "linchpin of the history of the nations." One outcome of the conference at Weissenfels was strengthening links with Odal, a the Swedish organization directed by Odeberg that explored Teutonic and Nordic culture as bases for contemporary German identity.[170]

A few weeks later, Heinz Eisenhuth, professor of systematic theology at the University of Jena, presented a paper to an Institute-sponsored working group on the philosopher Spinoza, which was examining how Spinoza's Jewishness had infiltrated modern thought under the guise of secularism. What characterized secularism, Eisenhuth argued, had come from Judaism via Spinoza: a lack of faith, an absence of a sense of "Heimat" (home), and an anti-Christian hostility.[171] Grundmann recapitulated Eisenhuth's arguments in a ten-page memorandum written in November 1942 calling for a "fundamental change" in accord with the "new order." Germany's problems originated in Jewish degeneracy, he wrote, exemplified by Spinoza, who destroyed Aryan thinking, and Moses Mendelssohn, who destroyed religion and myth by insisting on reason and denying revelation.[172]

RELATIONS WITH THE NAZI REGIME AND THE RIVAL CONFESSING CHURCH

German Christians who hoped to see a German Christian–led Protestant church transformed into a virtual branch of National Socialist ideology needed an explanation for the ongoing hostility of influential factions within the Nazi Party toward their efforts, and toward Christianity in general. Like all organizations, the Institute was monitored by the Reich, but its members were never threatened nor its work hindered, though its efforts were at times mocked. Friedrich Wieneke, one of the early members of both the German Christians and the Nazi Party, was sarcastic in reports he filed about Institute confer-

---

therefore disprove the lie widespread by the Jewish student body that in the new Germany scholarship is no longer pursued. (2) Second it is clear that we can therefore resist foreign influences in our work particularly because we work in a scholarly fashion while in Jewish cultural circles scholarship is only tolerated when it acts in accordance with orders and in alliance with their interests." Letter from Odeberg to Grundmann, dated June 21, 1942 (LKA Eisenach, DC III 2f).

[170]Lectures from the 1941 and 1942 conferences at Weissenfels were included in a volume edited by Grundmann with Hugo Odeberg and Wolf Meyer-Erlach, *Die völkische Gestalt des Glaubens*. In his foreword to the volume, Grundmann explained that "the configuration of faith and religion is determined by the idiosyncratic character of the particular race."

[171]Eisenhuth's lecture is summarized in a five-page report by Heinz Dungs, dated May 13, 1943 (UAH, Personalakten 25: Theodor Odenwald).

[172]"The Necessity of a Managed Reform of the Religious Situation," unsigned, undated memorandum (LKA Eisenach III 2a).

ences, in which he described the simpleminded level of the discussions.[173] Gestapo reports ridiculed Meyer-Erlach for having attended the dedication of a new synagogue in Würzburg in 1929; he was called "der Synagoge-Meyer." The home of Heinz Dungs was searched in May 1939.[174] There is no evidence, however, of Gestapo threats to Grundmann, Leffler, or other leaders of the Institute, despite their insistence after the war that they had been persecuted by the Nazis for their efforts to "preserve" the church.

The Institute, like all groups sponsoring public gatherings, was under secret service (Sicherheitsdienst, or SD) surveillance, and SD offices in Eisenach monitored its *Verbandsmitteilungen*, the occasional newsletter sent to Institute members.[175] Contributing to the surveillance was Thuringian church council member Paul Lehmann, a member of the Institute, who also served as an informant to the SD concerning activities of church officials. According to an April 1940 SD report, Lehmann was coming under suspicion within the church for spying, especially from Erwin Brauer, the Institute's managing director. The SD reports are neither critical of the Institute's efforts nor sarcastic in tone, commenting instead matter-of-factly that the German Christians were not reaching their goal with their present-day efforts.[176]

The reception of the Institute by the Reich and the Nazi Party varied. On the one hand, Martin Bormann, head of the Reich Chancellery and opposed to any attempted synthesis of Christianity and National Socialism, informed State Secretary Muhs of the Ministry for Church Affairs on September 25, 1942, that the Institute was not entitled to recognition or aid from the party and that all references to support from the party must cease.[177] On the other hand, government officials allowed the Institute to hold its conferences and publish its materials well into 1944, despite paper shortages and directives that conferences and institutes unrelated to the war effort should cease activities.[178] Grundmann's major disappointment was lack of permission from the Reich Press Office and the Propaganda Ministry to publish a scholarly theological

[173] Friedrich Wieneke, "Kirche und Weltanschauung 1933 bis 1945," typescript (ZAK 7/4166), 49–53.

[174] Helmreich, *The German Churches under Hitler*, 337.

[175] See, for example, the notice sent by SD offices in Eisenach to SD offices in Weimar, April 17, 1940, that the investigation of the Institute could not yet be closed (USHMM archive, RG-11.001M Reel 80, from Osobyi Archive (Moscow) records, 1932–45; 1993.A.0085 UC).

[176] See the report from SD Eisenach to SD Weimar, April 22, 1940 (USHMM archive, RG-11.001M Reel 80, from Osobyi Archive (Moscow) records, 1932–45; 1993.A.0085 UC).

[177] Letter from Bormann to Muhs, Berlin, dated September 25, 1942 (BA Koblenz R 43 II/151), 44–46.

[178] See the documents in BA Koblenz, Reichskanzlei, R 43 II/151, pp. 44–46. See also Ehrenfort, *Die schlesische Kirche*, 198, and 517 fn 156.

journal that would contain "scholarly conclusions from the racial-völkisch epistemology of National Socialist worldviews." [179] He continued to apply through the spring and summer of 1941,[180] but was finally informed by an official in the Propaganda Ministry that while his efforts were well intentioned, "there is no interest in synthesizing Christian teachings with National Socialism, nor proving that a reshaped Christianity is not fundamentally Jewish." [181] Approval in principle of the journal came from the Ministry for Church Affairs in March of 1942, but the journal itself never came into being.

Yet Meyer-Erlach and Grundmann were successful in forcing the resignation of an SS officer, Friedrich Murawski, from his post as advisor on church matters within the Reich Security Main Office (RSHA), on the grounds that Murawski had defamed Christianity by claiming it was a Jewish religion.[182] Grundmann accused Murawski of having plagiarized the work of a Jewish scholar, Robert Eisler, when he attacked Jesus as a revolutionary messianist and Christianity as a Jewish religion. It was not the plagiarism, but the fact that Murawski took his ideas from a Jew that incensed Grundmann, who took it as proof that Jewish thinkers were responsible for convincing certain Nazi leaders that Christianity was a form of Judaism. He also accused Murawski of being unreliable because in 1925 he had published a pamphlet opposing antisemitism.[183] As a result of Grundmann's charges, Murawski was expelled from the SS and dismissed from the RSHA; he then committed suicide in 1945.[184]

Despite all the influence he exerted, Grundmann suffered mightily from what he viewed as a lack of public appreciation from the Nazi Party and Reich officials for his work, acknowledging in private correspondence that his support for National Socialism was an unrequited affection. He complained that

[179] Letter from Grundmann to Gielen, Propaganda Ministry, Berlin, May 31, 1941 (LKA Eisenach DC III 2f and YIVO G135).

[180] In a letter to the Propaganda Ministry, June 24, 1941, Grundmann refers to a letter of June 12 rejecting his proposal. He intended to call the journal *Religionswissenschaftliche Blätter* (memorandum by Grundmann, April 29, 1942, YIVO, G135).

[181] Letter from Schmid-Burgk to Berndt, January 13, 1942 (YIVO, G135).

[182] Murawski is discussed in Dierker, *Himmlers Glaubenskrieger*, 556. The plagiarism was brought to Grundmann's attention by one of his students at the University of Jena, Max-Adolf Wagenführer. Robert Eisler, a noted scholar of the Hellenistic era, emigrated from Germany before the war, after imprisonment in Dachau and Buchenwald, and spent his last years in Great Britain; he died in 1949. He is best known for his argument that Jesus was a Zealot, one of the passionate first-century Jewish opponents of the Roman occupation of Palestine.

[183] Murawski, *Die Juden bei den Kirchenvätern und Scholastikern*.

[184] While his dismissal from the RSHA was a victory for Meyer-Erlach and Grundmann, they both subsequently used the experience as evidence that it was they who had been persecuted as a result of their complaint against Murawski. In his 1969 unpublished memoir, Grundmann

the Nazi Party was attempting to take over all religion and that the difficulties in the religious realm facing Germans was a result of destructive Jewish activity.[185]

In a personal letter written to his student, Hans-Joachim Thilo, on November 18, 1942, Grundmann bemoaned his situation. There are only two alternatives, he wrote, the old church or a germanic paganism promoted by the Nazi Party: "I cannot return to the old church; I cannot give my good name to a religious nihilism, hence there remains nothing else than to confine myself in the corner and take up another profession as a Germanist or a historian. . . . I am quite aware of the fact that with submission to the Party there is nothing to be gained."[186] At the same time, Grundmann held out hope that the Institute would at least win broad popular support among German soldiers, as he wrote to another Institute member and close friend, Gerhard Delling, who was serving in 1942 as a military chaplain.[187] His hope was fed by letters he received from soldiers at the front, thanking him for his work. Günter Geissler, a student of theology serving in the Wehrmacht, wrote to Grundmann that *Die Botschaft Gottes* was furthering Luther's work. War, he wrote, was "a measure of God's word." Most important about the Institute was its effort to understand Jesus within the framework of "historically conditioned perspectives and speculations that are historically as well as psychologically more intelligible."[188] In his reply, Grundmann wrote that historical investigation cannot make faith decisions, but it can distinguish between genuine searching for God that is expressed in "Indo-Germanic and Aryan fragments within the Old Testament and the clearly Jewish and Israelite material." The Institute's job, he wrote, was to make that distinction clear. "Until now the question of the Old Testament had not been resolved, not to avoid the question, but because of the war conditions and the drafting of many Institute members."[189]

---

claimed that as a result of his attack on Murawski he was drafted into military service in 1943, through the machinations of Astel, rector of the University of Jena ("Erkenntnis und Wahrheit," 48. Murawski was a well-published author of popular religion books and pamphlets. Murawski's text that Grundmann challenged, *Jesus der Nazoräer, der König der Juden*, was published in 1940 by Theodor Fritsch Verlag, an antisemitic press.

[185] Letter from Grundmann to Schmidt zur Nedden, November 17, 1942, enclosing memorandum, dated April 27, 1942 (LKA Eisenach, Personalakten, Grundmann).

[186] Letter from Grundmann to Hans-Joachim Thilo, dated November 18, 1942 (LKA Eisenacht NG44, II, Briefe August 1942–April 1943).

[187] Letter from Grundmann to Delling, dated November 5, 1942 (LKA Eisenach, NG 44, II), responding to the four-page, single-spaced letter from Delling to Grundmann, dated June 3, 1942. The two men were on a first-name basis.

[188] Letter from Geissler to Grundmann, January, 1943 (LKA Eisenach, NG 44, II).

[189] Letter from Grundmann to Geissler, dated February 11, 1943 (LKA Eisenach, NG 44, II).

WALTER GRUNDMANN'S JESUS

For academic theologians, three elements were central to the Aryan Jesus argument. First was the question of Jesus's ancestry: the racial and religious identities of his parents. That question was answered primarily in terms of the historical settlement of the Galilee by non-Jews, some of whom had converted to Judaism but were nonetheless not Jews by "race." Second was the nature of Jesus's teachings: the extent of his religious affinity with Old Testament and other Jewish teachings, and the extent to which his teachings expressed Aryan sensibilities. Third was the perception of Jesus by those who immediately followed him: whether he was viewed in the post-apostolic era as a Jewish or an anti-Jewish figure. All three elements were addressed by Grundmann in his various publications. His argument was not based on biology or physiognomy, but on "race" in terms of spirit and religiosity.

In 1933, when Grundmann composed the "Twenty-Eight Theses" of the German Christian movement, he stated that Jesus transcended human categories such as race and thus could be labeled neither as Jew nor as Aryan. Over the course of the subsequent years, Grundmann presented Jesus's teachings as standing in absolute opposition to Judaism; theirs was a religion of law, his was a religion of intimacy with God. The goal of Jesus, he claimed, was to bring an end to Judaism, but instead he fell as victim to the Jews, a violent and degenerate people. Grundmann did not engage in any new research or present new evidence in making his claims, but rather drew on existing arguments by scholars and demagogues, despite knowing that those arguments did not meet scholarly standards. Yet there were enough theologians of importance who had participated in the discussions about Jesus as Aryan to make it possible for Grundmann to rest his case on their shoulders.

At the end of the decade, in 1940, Grundmann presented his version of the life of Jesus, and the question of Jesus's race was central. The title of his book was *Jesus the Galilean*, not Jesus the Aryan. "Galilean" had long been a code word for "Aryan," but the former was the more acceptable academic term, as the latter had come to be associated with propagandists, and Grundmann was always anxious to be perceived as a serious scholar and his Institute as an academic research center. His book's goal was to demonstrate that Jesus was most definitely not a Jew (although his racial identity was not determined with comparable assurance) but the Jews' greatest enemy. The book synthesized the many strands showing Jesus's antagonism toward Judaism and built its case by resting on both demagogic and scholarly claims published by respected scholars in the preceding decades, not all of whom were Nazis or antisemites.

Thanks to the work of Walter Bauer situating Jesus in Galilee, Grundmann could easily present Galilee as standing in opposition to Judea; thanks to Assyriologists such as Paul Haupt (and ignoring Albrecht Alt), he could claim that Galilee had been populated by Aryans who had been forcibly converted to Judaism by the Hasmoneans, but who were not racially Jewish; thanks to Wilhelm Bousset's argument that the "son of man" was "Oriental," not Jewish; and thanks to Ernst Lohmeyer's argument that Jesus taught a Galilean eschatology, Grundmann could claim that Jesus was not the expected Jewish messiah or fulfilling Old Testament messianic expectations, but represented a new kind of non-Jewish eschatology. That the Jews rejected Jesus was used by Grundmann as further proof that he was not a Jew. Indeed, Grundmann drew on a hoary rabbinic legend that Jesus's father was not Joseph but rather a Roman soldier, Pantera, to establish a non-Jewish genealogy for Jesus and then argue that the genealogy in the opening chapter of the Gospel of Matthew was a Jewish interpolation, falsifying the true gospel of Jesus's Aryan origins. Each argument provided building blocks for Grundmann to construct his case, racializing the antinomies and claiming that Jesus could not have been a Jew. Typological distinctions were used by Grundmann in his attempts to link geography, race, and faith, and his arguments recapitulate the material of preceding decades rather than providing new proof.

Central to his work was defining Jesus not simply as a non-Jew, but as the anti-Jew, and making a sharp opposition between the religiosity of Jesus and that of Judaism by equating the racial with the spiritual. He embraced History of Religions methods as key to the distinction. By obviating doctrinal considerations, those methods, Grundmann argued, demonstrated that the Old Testament's God reflected the authors' tribal and national henotheistic beliefs that had nothing to do with Jesus's understanding of God. The fundamental law of Judaism, Grundmann insisted, "is hatred of non-Jewish races and the quest for their subjugation."[190] Old Testament messianism called for the political world rule of Jews, whereas Jesus called for peace and justice in a spiritual sense not bound to Palestine and thus was not a Jewish messiah, even if some early Jewish Christians, including the author of Matthew's gospel, falsely claimed that he was.[191] Instead, Matthew and others had falsified the Jesus story in order to

---

[190]Grundmann and Euler, *Das religiöse Gesicht*, 63. Grundmann here cites, approvingly, the work of Karl Georg Kuhn, "Ursprung und Wesen."

[191]Grundmann, "Das Messiasproblem." The rejection that Jesus was a Jewish messiah was also discussed by Grundmann in his 1938 book, *Die Gotteskindschaft in der Geschichte Jesu*, which aroused some debate in contemporary theological periodicals in Germany. See, for example, Wilhelm Michael in *Deutsches Pfarrerblatt* 44 (1940), 122; Friedrich Büchsel, in *Evangelisches Deutschland* 16 (1939), 24; Grundmann's response in *Evangelisches Deutschland* 17 (1940), 3. See also

make him fit messianic expectations, whereas Jesus himself, Grundmann claimed, placed no worth on being descended from the line of King David and denied he was a Jewish messiah.[192]

Grundmann argued that Galilee was not simply Gentile, but represented a non-Jewish religiosity that stood in polemical opposition to the Jews of Judea, whom he lumped together as a group.[193] Galilean Gentiles, among the many non-Jewish populations that had moved into northern Israel after the Assyrian conquest, embraced Jesus because they knew he was one of them, while Judean Jews rejected him because they knew he was not one of them. Jesus appealed to Gentiles, rather than Jews, because they understood his intimate relationship with God, Grundmann argued, exemplified by Jesus calling God "Abba" ("Daddy" in Aramaic), a theme Grundmann developed in his 1938 study on divine sonship and that became widely influential among Protestant theologians in subsequent years.[194] From that intimacy of child with father stemmed a new understanding of the nature of the divine and the human, and, especially, of ethics. Love was Jesus's guiding ethical principle and overrides, Grundmann claimed, divine commandments of law. Jews—including the prophets of the Old Testament—view themselves as slaves in relation to a God,[195] which marks their contrast to Aryans, whose piety leads them to view the covenant with God as a "grace of being."[196]

Throughout, the argument about Jesus was informed not by biological or genealogical claims, but by defining the nature of his alleged religiosity in contrast to the alleged degeneracy of the Jews. Indeed, Nazi propaganda itself

---

Leipoldt, "Jesu Verhältnis zu Griechen und Juden," 98–101, and Grundmann, *Aufnahme nd Deutung der Botschaft Jesu,* 3:20ff.

[192] Grundmann, *Jesus der Galiläer und das Judentum.*

[193] See the long footnote on Galilee, summarizing the position of Albrecht Alt, in Grundmann and Euler, *Das religiöse Gesicht,* 65.

[194] Grundmann, *Die Gotteskindschaft in der Geschichte Jesu.* Gerhard Kittel discussed "Abba" in the *Theological Dictionary of the New Testament* that he edited, but did not draw the same conclusions. Joachim Jeremias's widely read book *Abba,* published in 1966, makes an argument very similar to Grundmann's about Jesus's intimacy with God, though he does not cite him. A sharp critique of the anti-Judaism at the heart of Jeremias's book was formulated by Sanders: "Jesus and the Kingdom"; "Defending the Indefensible." A rejoinder to Sanders in defense of Jeremias is found in Meyer, "A Caricature of Joachim Jeremias." In response to Meyer, see Sanders, "Defending the Indefensible." For a superb analysis of the Abba debate, see D'Angelo, "Abba and 'Father.'"

[195] Grundmann and Euler, *Das religiöse Gesicht,* 93 and 105.

[196] Ibid., 94. In fn 113, Grundmann cites Kurt Leese, *Natürliche Religion und Christlicher Glaube: Eine theologische Neuorientierung* (Berlin: Junker und Dunnhaupt, 1936) for a definition of the "Aryan fundamental experience of religion."

made similar arguments. An article in a 1938 issue of *Der Stürmer* asking "War Christus Jude?" answered by arguing that "a teaching that does not come out of Nordic blood and carry Nordic spirit cannot spread itself among Nordic races." Since Christianity had become a successful religion for two thousand years only among Nordic races (not among Jews), and Christian ideas were the greatest culturally creative force in human history, it was simply impossible that Christ, the driving force of Christianity, could have been a Jew.[197]

Similar logic informed Grundmann's magnum opus, *Jesus der Galiläer*, published in 1940. Proving that Jesus "with the greatest probability"[198] was no Jew but belonged instead to one of the various Gentile races within the Galilee (though which race remained uncertain, according to Grundmann) involved a range of claims primarily about his faith but also concerning his parentage and the history of the Galilee.[199] Mary was not a Jew and Jesus's father was actually a Roman named Panther, Grundmann claimed.[200] He drew on arguments that Galilee was free of Jews one hundred and fifty years before Jesus's birth, populated instead by Gentiles. The argument of a Gentile Galilee is old in New Testament scholarship, from Renan to Chamberlain to Grundmann, and is based on vague assumptions: equating with "non-Jews" the reference to "nations" in the phrase "Galilee of the nations" ("Galil HaGoyim" in Hebrew; Isaiah 8:23 and 9:1, and cited in Matthew 4:15); confusing the distinct regions of northern Israel (which had varied histories of conquest and ethnic settlement); and drawing on evidence of Hellenism in the Galilee that was then misinterpreted as paganism. To this were added claims found in Jewish texts, from rabbinic literature to the nineteenth-century historian Graetz, that Galilean Jews were unlettered, susceptible to apocalyptic fantasies, and removed from the control of Pharisaic and Temple authorities in Jerusalem.

Jesus's religious quest, Grundmann further argued in *Jesus der Galiläer*, was shaped by the non-Jewish teachings current in the Galilee and that are reflected in other contemporaneous literature. As evidence, he pointed to 1 Enoch, a frequently cited source in German Christian–authored scholarship thanks to its "son of man" passages in chapters 37–71 and the assumption that the text reflected Iranian, not Jewish, influences. Grundmann interpreted the birth narrative in 1 Enoch 105 as describing a Nordic savior.[201] Drawing on

[197] Holz, "Was Christus Jude?"

[198] Grundmann, *Jesus der Galiläer und das Judentum*, 199–200.

[199] Ibid., 175.

[200] Ibid., 196–97. Grundmann justified his argument about the father of Jesus by reference to a rabbinic tradition that identified Jesus's father as a Roman soldier named Panthera.

[201] Ibid., 82f. "She became pregnant by him, and brought forth a child, the flesh of which was as white as snow, and red as a rose; the hair of whose head was white like wool, and long; and

earlier scholars, Grundmann wrote that Jesus's eschatology was not the messianism of the Old Testament's Jewish prophecies because Jesus did not use the title "messiah,"[202] but rather "son of man," which "had nothing to do with Judaism, but signified rather the replacement of the Jewish religious world."[203] Indeed, the Judaism of Jesus's day, Grundmann wrote, did not recognize a description of the expected messiah as a son of God, and in later years Judaism's God declared, "I have no son."[204] Nor did Jesus's message come from Judaism; the idea of divine sonship was taken from Hellenism, and the idea of a kingdom of God was taken from Zoroastrianism. Grundmann's colleague, Johannes Hempel, had argued in a 1938 article that the monotheism of Jesus had not stemmed from the Old Testament but from Zoroastrianism and Hellenism; Jesus had a fundamentally different approach to the Old Testament, and his monotheism did not demonstrate any linkage.

That Jesus rejected the teachings of Judaism, including its messianism, was further demonstrated, Grundmann argued, by the Jews' rejection of him, a rejection that then motivated the Jews to seek his death, and to defame and fight against early Christians. Such views were translated for Christian education in a 1937 guide to religious instruction, prepared by Grundmann's former teacher, Johannes Leipoldt. Grundmann's views were also reflected in an article by his doctoral advisor, Kittel, who urged that the tie between New and Old Testaments be broken, and that Jesus could no longer be viewed as racially Jewish. [205]

What was decisive for Grundmann was not a doctrinal conclusion regarding christology, but rather a new understanding of the nature of religiosity, as taught by Jesus, that stood in opposition to that of Judaism. "With the announcement of the kingdom of God as a present-day intervention of God comes a new experience of God and a new understanding of God that became a reality within him [Jesus] and to which he calls mankind." [206] According to Grundmann, the Jewish notion of a messiah was political, not religious, and

---

whose eyes were beautiful. When he opened them, he illuminated all the house, like the sun; the whole house abounded with light" (1 Enoch 105:2). Enoch was believed by Grundmann to have stemmed from the so-called "Amei Ha'Aretz" of Galilee, whom he defined as non-Jews opposed to the Jerusalem circles of rabbis and Pharisees.

[202] Grundmann, *Die Gotteskindschaft in der Geschichte Jesu*, 155.

[203] Ibid., 162.

[204] Exodus Rabbah 29; 88d; see Strack and Billerbeck, *Kommentar zum Neuen Testament aus Talmud und Midrasch*. Grundmann, *Die Gotteskindschaft in der Geschichte Jesu*.

[205] Kittel, "Die Wurzeln des Englischen Erwählungsglaubens."

[206] Grundmann, *Die Gotteskindschaft in der Geschichte Jesu*, 162.

was bound up with the idea of "rule," in the sense of both law and divine governance, whereas Jesus's message was that of a servant. Jesus's "cleansing" of the Temple was not a measure of reform of Judaism, but an absolute rejection of the Temple and the Judaism it represented. [207] The notion that Jesus was the fulfiller of the law sent to the house of Israel was a false Jewish-Christian invention not based on historical evidence, but resulted from falsifications of the gospels by Jews. [208] Jerusalem was the center of opposition to Jesus and Jesus's hostile reception there, Grundmann argued, demonstrated not only the unpleasant Jewish nature of the city but the non-Jewish identity of Jesus and the anti-Jewish nature of his message. [209] Jesus was a fighter, engaged in a prolonged struggle against Judaism, and fell as victim to the Jews' wrathful violence. [210] Their hatred of Jesus is further proof that he was not one of them.

Jesus, Grundmann wrote, called God "Abba," a name that was not used by Jews to address God. [211] Rather, Jesus's experience of intimacy with God was derived from Hellenism, [212] a theme Grundmann had developed in an article he wrote for Gerhard Kittel's *Theological Dictionary of the New Testament*: "It is not the knowledge of magic media and formulae, but the personal relationship between God and Jesus on the one side and Jesus and men on the other which works the miracle with no magical compulsion." [213]

Descriptions of Jesus as the lamb of God and his teachings emphasizing meekness were a problem for Nazi theologians. Leipoldt, professor of New Testament at the University of Leipzig and a member of the Institute, argued that the oldest traditions about Jesus presented him as a figure in a warrior movement, and that only later did the text of the suffering servant of Isaiah 53 and the ideals of Greek philosophy distort the warrior Jesus. [214] Once again, the theologians sought the "real Jesus" in a lost original gospel whose message had been distorted.

---

[207] Grundmann, *Jesus der Galiläer und das Judentum*, 30.

[208] Ibid., 26; see also Grundmann, "Das Problem des Hellenistischen Christentums," 45–73.

[209] Grundmann, *Jesus der Galiläer und das Judentum*, 76.

[210] Ibid., 150–64. Grundmann sees those struggles reflected in passages in the Gospel of Luke 7:36; 14:1; 17:7–10; 12:47–48; 15:6, 10, 23, 32.

[211] Grundmann here cites Kittel's article, "Abba," in the *Theologische Wörterbuch zum Neuen Testament* (henceforth: TWNT) and develops the theme in his book, *Die Gotteskindschaft in der Geschichte Jesu*.

[212] This argument anticipates Johannes Leipoldt's study, "Jesu Verhältnis zu Griechen und Juden." The Abba traditions were developed after the war by Jeremias in *Abba*. See the discussion of the theme in D'Angelo, "Abba and 'Father.'"

[213] Grundmann, "Dunamai," TWNT, 302.

[214] Leipoldt, *Gegenwärtsfragen*.

The story of Jesus was retold to mesh with Nazi propaganda, linking the innocence of Jesus with the innocence of Germans fighting an implacable, violent enemy: "They hate us, and so we therefore must hate them," Hitler stated of the English in January 1942.[215] As Hitler shaped a grand political narrative of a fight to the death between Aryans and Jews, the Institute gave the story religious significance. Just as Joseph Goebbels, head of the Propaganda Ministry, denounced "sentimentality,"[216] the German Christians spoke of a manly Jesus. Nazi antisemitism was a doctrine of political paranoia and fanaticism, as Jeffrey Herf has written, convinced that the Jews, "with extraordinary powers of control and manipulation," were waging a war against Germany.[217] That message was reflected in Institute propaganda as well. Paranoia about Jewish power over Christianity was regnant in their theology; the Jews had falsified the message of Jesus, judaizing the gospels with their interpolations of Jewish teachings that went contrary to the anti-Jewish campaign launched by Jesus. Christianity required purification from Jewish influences in order to recover its original, true meaning, but even more: it required a destruction of the enemy, Jews, who have sought the annihilation of Gentiles since antiquity.

A study of Jewish violence against non-Jews was published by Grundmann and Karl Euler in 1942. Their book, *Das religiöse Gesicht des Judentums*, is filled with wild assertions: "The law to which the Jews accede is hatred for non-Jewish peoples and the striving for their subjugation."[218] When the Jews conquer a land, they forcibly judaized the non-Jewish population through circumcision;[219] whoever is not a Jew goes against Yahweh and must be destroyed [vernichtet]."[220] Jesus stood in total and unbridgeable opposition to the religion of Judaism, overcoming the uncreative legalism and rationalist preoccupation with retaliation of Judaism with a new view of God as creative and indissoluble love.[221] Drawing on race theorists Eugen Fischer and Hans F. K. Günther, Grundmann and Euler asserted that Jewish degeneracy derived from their racial mixture of Oriental, Mediterranean, Near Eastern, and Nordic elements, in contrast to Arabs, who belonged to the Oriental race without any foreign elements.[222] To prove the violence of Judaism, Grundmann, following

[215]Hitler's annual speech to the Reichstag on January 30, 1942; cited by Jeffrey Herf, *The Jewish Enemy*, 143–44.

[216]Herf, *The Jewish Enemy*, 148.

[217]Ibid., 152.

[218]Grundmann and Euler, *Das religiöse Gesicht*, 63.

[219]Ibid., 65.

[220]Ibid., 67.

[221]Ibid., 117.

[222]Ibid., 60. See Fischer, "Rassenentstehung"; and Günther, *Rassenkunde des jüdischen Volkes*. On Günther, see Lutzhöft, *Der nordische Gedanke*, 28–41.

his teacher, Adolf Schlatter, drew meager evidence from the first-century historian Josephus that during the Hasmonean era, Hyrcanus "subdued all the Idumeans; and permitted them to stay in that country, if they would circumcise their genitals and make use of the laws of the Jews." [223] Aristobulus "compelled" the Itureans, according to Josephus, "to be circumcised and to live according to the Jewish laws." [224]

Grundmann also drew further evidence of Jewish violence against Gentiles from 1 Maccabees, which states that Mattathias, leader of the Maccabean revolt, forcibly circumcised "all the uncircumcised boys that they found within the borders of Israel" (1 Maccabees 2:46); yet those boys may well have not been Gentiles, but Jewish boys whose circumcision had been forbidden by Antiochus Epiphanes (1 Maccabees 1:48, 60–61). Since there are no earlier sources corroborating that Jews engaged in forced conversion through circumcision, the event is dubious.[225] The passages in Maccabees and Josephus concerning forced circumcision are not directly connected to issues related to the origins of Christianity, and received little attention from New Testament scholars until the Nazi era. During the Third Reich, however, the charge of Jewish violence was emphasized in the Christian theological litany of the degenerate Judaism, precisely at a time when it was, of course, Christians who were perpetrating violence against Jews.

Although forceful in its accusations of Jewish violence, Grundmann's work is pervaded by a theological caution that keeps him from asserting Jesus's Aryan race too emphatically; he wavers, insisting that Jesus is a non-Jew, a fighter against the Jews, but ultimately remains of undeterminable racial ancestry. In his writings prior to 1936, he claims that Jesus stands "above race," and that those who seek to determine his race have not fully grasped the nature of his being.[226] However, Jesus's antagonism to Judaism was absolute, and Grundmann consistently defines Christianity in opposition to Judaism. Yet here, too, there is occasional ambivalence. Grundmann sees Judaism in antiquity

[223] Schlatter, *Geschichte Israels*; Josephus, *Antiquities*, 13, 318f. Already in 1940, Grundmann had written: "The subjugation of the Galileans by the Jews succeeded through forced circumcision and forced conversion to the Jewish religion. Whoever resisted was driven out." *Grundmann, Jesus der Galiläer und das Judentum*, 169.

[224] Josephus, *Antiquities*, 13.257–58; on circumcision of the Itureans, see Josephus, *Antiquities* 13:318.

[225] See Weitzman, "Forced Circumcision and the Shifting Role of Gentiles in Hasmonean Ideology," 37–59. Weitzman notes that "forebearers of the Idumeans and Itureans, like other Syro-Palestinian peoples, were already practicing circumcision as early as the sixth century BCE" and that conversion may have "resulted from a more peaceful process of coalescence whereby local Gentiles were gradually, and largely voluntarily, absorbed into the Hasmonean state" (40–41).

[226] Grundmann, *Totale Kirche im totalen Staat*, 28.

emerging as a religion with a racial consciousness;[227] Christianity lacked that racial awareness and needs to establish it. The Jews sought the conquest of land and peoples, not unlike the goals of present-day Nazis. In some sense, then, Grundmann denounced Judaism and called for its eradication, yet also attempted to appropriate the racial exclusiveness and militarism that he defined as one of Judaism's central elements.

The reception of *Jesus der Galiläer* by scholars of New Testament was mixed. Friedrich Büchsel, professor of New Testament at the University of Rostock, gave a positive and respectful review of several of Grundmann's books on Jesus, disagreeing with some points but accepting the thrust of the arguments.[228] That Jesus was not a reformer but an opponent of Judaism was acceptable to Büchsel, since he agreed that Judaism was simply a legal system; but he disagreed with Grundmann's claim that Jesus was rejecting the Temple rather than attempting to purify it. That Jesus was not of Jewish heritage is discussed by Büchsel as plausible but insufficiently supported by the evidence.

In his mixed review of the book, Leipoldt, Grundmann's collaborator at the Institute, noted that the question of Jesus's racial identity stemmed from present-day circumstances. His major criticism concerned the Galilean origins of Enoch, which served as a major source for Grundmann in determining Galilean popular piety, and that Grundmann relied too heavily on the work of Rudolf Otto. Leipoldt considered Grundmann's stress on the charismatic character of Jesus's uniqueness overemphasized, and was skeptical of Grundmann's claims regarding Jesus's völkisch membership. He approved, however, of Grundmann's insistence on Jesus's sharp repudiation of Judaism.[229]

By contrast, Grundmann's *Jesus der Galiläer* received a sharp critique by Hans von Soden, professor of New Testament at the University of Marburg and a member of the Confessing Church.[230] He criticized the poor scholarship of Grundmann's book, but also accused him and the German Christians of being infected with "Jewishness" in their failure to understand religion properly. Not Christianity but the German Christians were "Jewish," according to von Soden, as illustrated by the dejudaization efforts called for in the Godesberg Declaration. Trying to dejudaize Christianity by banning the Old Testament and rewriting the hymnal and New Testament actually "threatens a spiritual Judaization" of the church. This "Jewishness," he wrote, "shudders

[227]Grundmann and Euler, *Das religiöse Gesicht*, 67.

[228]Büchsel, "Walter Grundmann, Jesus der Galiläer und das Judentum."

[229]Leipoldt, "Jesus der Galiläer und das Judentum, von Walter Grundmann," *Theologisches Literaturblatt* 61, no. 5 (1940).

[230]Soden, "Walter Grundmann, Jesus der Galiläer und das Judentum."

before every Hebrew word in the liturgy or hymnal, but has itself fallen victim to the Jewish-anti-Christian spirit." Von Soden reveals what was shared by the Confessing Church and the German Christians: both asserted that Jewishness represented a real threat to Christians but differed in their definitions of Jewishness. For von Soden, the threat came not from the Old Testament, Hebrew words, and other elements within traditional Christian theology, but from what he saw as an antispiritual, materialistic theology promoted by Grundmann and his German Christian colleagues. The shared assumptions about the evils of Jewishness illustrate what Uriel Tal has pointed out, the pervasiveness of racist ideas among theologians, such that supporters and opponents of Nazism cannot easily be distinguished.[231] Grundmann was outraged by von Soden's review and demanded that the journal, *Deutsches Pfarrerblatt*, print a rebuttal, which the editor refused.[232] Finally, Grundmann secured the intervention of the Reich Ministry of Propaganda, ordering the journal's editor to print a response from Grundmann.[233]

GRUNDMANN'S FAREWELL AND THE INSTITUTE'S FINAL YEARS

Grundmann was drafted into military service on the Eastern Front in March of 1943, a month after Goebbels delivered his notorious "total war" speech in Berlin that defined the war as the Jews' effort to destroy Europe, and declaring Germany's intention of eliminating the Jews.[234] Grundmann was initially replaced as academic director of the Institute by Eisenhuth (who was called to military service in November 1943). In a farewell letter to Institute members, dated March 25, 1943, Grundmann noted the difficulties caused by the declaration of total war, including the cessation of publication of the *Verbandsmitteilung*.[235] The major concerns of the Institute, he wrote, were now the Old Testament and the question of Paul, although some of the scholars best able to address those concerns were serving in the military. He seemed to assume that the Jesus question had already been resolved. The Weissenfels conference on "Germanendom and Christendom," he wrote, had emphasized the unique

[231] Tal, Religious and Anti-Religious Roots of Modern Antisemitism. See also Hering, *Theologische Wissenschaft und "Drittes Reich."*

[232] Grundmann's correspondence with Ludwig Seiler, editor of *Deutsches Pfarrerblatt*, is found in YIVO G135.

[233] Letter from Propaganda Ministry, Paffrath, to Ludwig Seiler, dated July 10, 1942 (YIVO G135).

[234] Friedländer, *The Years of Extermination*, 472.

[235] Grundmann and Pich, "An die Förderer des Institutes," March 25, 1943 (LKA Eisenach).

religiosity created by the encounter of Germanic tribes with Christ: "The decisive moment in the encounter between Germanendom and Christendom lies precisely at that point at which for the Teutons the all-powerful Fate, which had been absorbed into their pagan gods, changed into one almighty God whose enigmatic essence revealed itself, beyond all the terror of the reality of life, as the secret of an unbreakable bond of faith and of a creative love." The Institute had demonstrated, Grundmann continued, that Jesus's appearance represented an "anti-Jewish type [gegenjüdische Art]," and that the modern, rational God of Spinoza and Mendelssohn was nothing more than an "enlightened Yahweh" that had nothing to do with the Germanic soul and stemmed from the "arsenal of weapons of modern Jews."[236]

Appended to Grundmann's farewell letter were statements excerpted from German soldiers, thanking the Institute for its work. A pastor serving as a noncommissioned officer stationed in the Ukraine wrote that he read the *Verbandsmitteilungen* "with a glowing heart" and rejoiced over the Institute's "blessed progress." A lance corporal wrote: "Everyone has to be liberated from the Jewish delusion, because it is not possible that we in the Third Reich still have Jewish teachings. They must and will be destroyed, at whatever cost. Our struggle will be carried out in any way necessary. We were born as warriors and, if necessary, will die in battle. We want to open the eyes of our compatriots and liberate them from the Jewish spell, because this is about the wellbeing and future of our Volk. Our struggle has begun and it will be carried out until the final victory."[237] Just weeks later, on May 27, 1943, the bombing of Jena brought the war to the university.

With Leffler, Grundmann, and Eisenhuth all serving in the military by 1944, Georg Bertram became academic director of the Institute. Remarkably, considering the civilian bombings and military catastrophe unfolding for Germany, Institute activities continued. Just as Hitler's passionate antisemitic tirades continued in the face of Germany's defeat, and antisemitism grew unabated in the general German population, the Institute's antisemitic rhetoric followed suit, blaming Jews for the war, eradicating any Jewish remnants from Christianity, and seeking new ways to identify Christianity with Teutonism. Although most Jews in Europe had already been murdered, antisemitic passions remained on fire. The last conference organized by the Institute was held March 22–24, 1944, at the Thuringian Pastors' Training Seminary in Eisenach, despite the bombings that had reached the city, for the purpose of contributing to the "world historical conflict with Jewry for which all the powers of the

[236] Ibid.
[237] Ibid.

German soul have to be mobilized," as Bertram wrote.[238] The tone of the conference was shrill in its discussion of Jews, and speakers defined the purpose of the war not in terms of conquest of land or of Bolshevism, but as a war against the Jews. Bertram opened the meeting by declaring: 'This war is the struggle of the Jews against Europe.' That sentence contains a truth that is constantly being reconfirmed by the scholarly work of the Institute. In that way this work is not only a frontal attack, but also an effort to secure the stability of the home front to attack and to defend against all secretive Jews and Jewish essence that over the course of the centuries has infiltrated western culture."[239] As in the previous two years, the conference placed its emphasis on the Teutonic and on History of Religions methods. The assembled speakers were an impressive array of academics, including the theologians Johannes Leipoldt, Theodor Odenwald, Karl Euler, Walter Birnbaum, and Wilhelm Koepp, as well as the Egyptologist Siegfried Morenz and several prominent völkisch writers.

The Aryan identity of Jesus and the uniqueness of Germanic religiosity were main topics of the lectures. Friedrich Cornelius, who had recently published a study of Indo-Germanic religiosity, presented a paper arguing that early Christianity was a revolt against Pharisaism, and that a liberated understanding of the Aryan Jesus could be achieved within the context of Persian, Greek, and Indo-Germanic religions. The theologians Hans Ermisch and Wilhelm Koepp lectured on the piety of the Germanic soul, to show that on Indo-Germanic foundations a "belief in fate" grew up and subsequently entered Christian theology, strengthening Christian belief in God. Leipoldt, in collaboration with Morenz, emphasized Hellenism as the original cradle of Christian religious practice that was only later judaized by introducing readings from the Old Testament. Leipoldt and Morenz pointed to 1 Corinthians 14:26 as rejecting scriptural readings and 1 Timothy 4:13 as advocating them, for evidence of a shift from Hellenistic to Jewish contexts. Eliminating the Old Testament from Christian liturgy was a return to original Christian practice, they argued, not a change in it.[240]

Euler delivered a lecture justifying Nazi policies against the Jews. Echoing by-now familiar Nazi propaganda, he denounced Zionism, claiming that Jews sought a return to Palestine as a means to achieve "Jewish world rule," and sought equal rights within nations as a "process of destruction" that was the "precondition of the Jewish seizure of world rule." Either the world would be

---

[238] Report by Georg Bertram, 1944 (LKA Eisenach DC III 2a).

[239] Ibid.

[240] A summary of their lecture is presented in the "Rundbrief" dated March 28, 1944, sent to Institute members (LKA Eisenach).

"verjudet" or "entjudet," judaized or dejudaized, Euler concluded, and there was only one solution to the "Jewish question," and that was Germany's solution:

> We have thrown down the gauntlet with a clear resolution to settle the Jewish question for the entire future. Germany, the land of thinkers and scientists, poets and artists—this land is called by fate to fight to gain the world by fighting what is possible: The solution of the Jewish question! . . . the hour is coming when all choirs and orchestras of the world, together with all those who have lost their lives in the struggle with the Jewish Moloch, will become one in the last hymn of victory, "Wake up, the day is coming."[241]

Grundmann's final propaganda publication appeared in 1944 and was written while he was in the military on the Eastern Front, a pamphlet defending the Third Reich that was addressed to German troops with little explicit Christian theological content but with an unwavering loyalty to Germany and hatred of the Jews despite the clear evidence that the war was lost.[242] It opens by stating that "the Jew" is "the Antichrist [who] wants to unleash itself and overthrow the Reich."[243] He then presents Germany as the savior of Europe against the degeneration of both East and West. Russia disintegrated through military challenges and incompetent leadership centuries ago, while the West disintegrated as a consequence of its liberalism, which permitted the emancipation of the Jews. Thus the war is fought in self-defense against the Jews: "This Western belief system became the precondition for the Jews' breakout from the ghetto and their intrusion into Western society, with all the devastating consequences of internal and external corruption, of which the Jews are the carriers everywhere. Most of all they pursued the corruption of values and the destruction of awe before the mysteries of life."[244] Antisemitic propagandist to the very end, this was Grundmann's final statement before the Third Reich collapsed and he began constructing his Nazi past as a defender of the church and a victim of the Reich.

Conclusion

The Institute shifted Christian attention from the humanity of God to the divinity of man: Hitler as an individual Christ, the German Volk as a collective

---

[241] LKA Eisenach DC, III, cited by Buss, "Entjudung der Kirche," 175.
[242] Grundmann, *Das Reich der Deutschen*, 289.
[243] Ibid., 4.
[244] Ibid., 89.

Christ, and Christ as Judaism's deadly opponent. As Leutheuser pungently expressed it:

> The Reich of the Germans is for us similar to the eternal Kingdom of God. For us, belief in Germany is a touchstone of our faith in God. Our love of Germany is a measure of our love for the Eternal. . . . It was for us as if Christ had traveled through Germany and Adolf Hitler was his mouth.[245]

The theological shift from God's humanity to human divinity was not an abandonment of Christianity. Rather, it mirrored the Nazi supersession of Christianity: the incorporation of Christian motifs, even while the Nazis undermined Christian authority. The classic Christian theological effort at supersession of the Old Testament rehearsed the process of internalizing Jewish theological motifs within Christianity even as Judaism was declared old, rejected by God, and dead. Similarly, Nazism took over central elements of Christianity, incorporating its anti-Judaism and other theological motifs—messiah, redemption, resurrection—as an act of politico-theological supersessionism. Christianity might continue, but in its nazified form. The Institute's dejudaized Christianity was offered both to the Nazi Reich and to the church as a template out of which each could produce an ideology favorable to the other.

Yet the relationship between the two ideologies could never be entirely easy. Hitler could be called a savior or a Christ figure, and the German Volk could be proclaimed the divinely chosen Volk of the Old Testament, but a rivalry remained palpable, at least until the middle of the war, between leaders of the Reich and leaders of the German Christians. In part, it stemmed from a competition between Nazism and Christianity over the antisemitism at the heart of both systems, as Christina von Braun has argued.[246] Who was the more effective propagandist of antisemitism, the German Christians or the Nazis?

The Jew was the central pivot for both. In its eradication from Christianity of everything it could identify as "Jewish," the Institute identified an issue with which its members had no disagreements with the Nazi Reich. Academic members of the Institute considered themselves experts on Judaism, or joined the Institute in order to proclaim that expertise. Remarkably, the Institute granted them a prestige that lasted well into the postwar years, enabling its former members to declare they were scholars of Judaism rather than participants in an antisemitic theological effort, and defenders of the church against its Nazi detractors rather than Nazi antisemitic propagandists.

---

[245]Leutheuser, *Die deutsche Christusgemeinde*, cited in Zahn, "Thüringer Blick-Punkte," 247.
[246]Braun, *Der ewige Judenhass.*

The Making of Nazi Theologians

WHAT DREW THEOLOGIANS to join the Institute? There is no single demographic or intellectual profile that fits most of its members. Scholars of theology who joined the Institute represented a spectrum of generational and demographic patterns as well as areas of research within theology. Some were full professors, others were lower on the academic totem pole. Some were Nazi Party members of long standing, while others never joined the party. Neither age nor geographic location within the Reich seems to have been a determinative factor. What the Institute offered its members was career enhancement and the intellectual tools to racialize their theological positions.

Through the Institute members had the chance to link the theological anti-Judaism that had long pervaded German Protestantism with the racist anti-semitism promoted by the Nazis, and to link their historical claims of the allegedly degenerate nature of Jews in antiquity with the alleged degeneracy of contemporary Jews. Arguments about Jesus's relationship to Judaism were suddenly lifted from the narrow world of gospel interpretation and placed at the center of the Third Reich's politics: solving the "Jewish problem." Out of the obscurity and political irrelevance of the fine points of theological scholarship, Institute members transformed themselves into experts on the vital problem of ridding Europe of the Jews. The Institute was the theological version of the many racial "research" institutes that flourished in virtually every academic discipline during the Third Reich, creating a widespread project of "Judenforschung" that engaged scholars from a wide range of disciplines.[1] Walter Grundmann, as academic director of the Institute, was typical of its members in his academic and political background, and at the same time he was their inspiration and tireless driving force.

Precisely what academics seek was what the Institute offered: support for publications, conferences to present ideas, gatherings to meet colleagues, and a sense of self-importance. For members who were pastors, teachers of religion, or students of theology, the chance to gather with well-known professors from all over the Reich as well as Scandinavia was certainly of great appeal,

[1] Rupnow, "Judenforschung," 107–32.

especially since all expenses were paid. Opportunities to publish in Institute-sponsored books were also valuable, because paper and funding were scarce during the war years. The Institute's many working groups and publication committees brought together senior and junior faculty with students and pastors, alliances that are sought after in academic life, and that certainly opened opportunities for younger scholars.

For example, the Institute's committee to study the origins of Christianity "from a racial perspective" was chaired by two professors, Grundmann and Herbert Preisker (1862–1952), professor of New Testament at the University of Breslau, and included other academics along with several pastors who might otherwise not have been invited to work with scholars.[2] The committee was scheduled to produce ten volumes of research results; these did not materialize.[3] Preisker was ripe for such work, having joined the Nazi Party in 1933 and become active in the German Christian movement.[4] His career benefited from Nazi politics; he received his professorship of New Testament at the University of Breslau in 1936 after his predecessor, Ernst Lohmeyer, was expelled for his anti-Nazi stance.[5] From his student days onward, Preisker wrote on ethics, including a habilitation thesis in 1927 on "Marriage in Early Christianity."[6] After the advent of Nazism, he published a pamphlet attempting to reconcile the New Testament "work ethic" with that of National Socialism, and a small book attempting to reconcile the gospels with the *Heliand*, a ninth-century Saxonian text about a savior figure.[7]

In his major study of New Testament history published in 1937, Preisker presented Christianity as overcoming both Hellenism and Judaism through

---

[2] Other members of the committee had similar training in History of Religions methods and Hellenistic literature: for instance, Georg Bertram, a specialist on the Greek translation of the Old Testament and professor at Giessen. The committee also included Carl Schneider, professor of New Testament at Königsberg; Rudolf Meyer, a graduate student in Leipzig; Heinz Hunger, a pastor in Thuringia; and Gerhard Delling, a school friend of Grundmann's in Chemnitz and Tübingen and an instructor in Leipzig. Erich Fromm, a Superintendent from Altenburg; Wilhelm Büchner, a Superintendent in Eisenach; Heinz Hunger, a pastor from Sundremda and office manager of the Institute; and Heinrich Weinmann, a pastor in Koblenz-Pfaffendorf.

[3] That committee, included Bertram, Gerhard Delling, Rudolf Meyer, Carl Schneider, and Heinz Hunger, with Preisker writing on Johannine literature.

[4] Preisker joined the Nazi Party on July 1, 1933, receiving membership number 217516 (BDC, Preisker files).

[5] Hutter-Wolandt, *Die evangelische Kirche Schlesiens*, 251–53.

[6] Preisker, "Christentum und Ehe in den ersten drei Jahrhunderten." An ironic topic, given that Preisker abandoned his wife and two daughters when he fled Breslau after the war, taking only his female research assistant with him to Jena. See Hutter-Wolandt, "Herbert Preisker," 1174–83.

[7] Preisker, *Das Ethos der Arbeit im Neuen Testament*.

the figure of the resurrected Christ (not the Jewish Jesus of history); he wrote, "Arising on Jewish ground, *early Christianity is the radical overcoming of Judaism*,"[8] precisely what the Institute sought to achieve. The Institute modified Preisker's argument in two ways: the "radical overcoming of Judaism" became a "racial overcoming" of the Jews, and what Preisker traced in antiquity became a contemporary struggle between Christians and Jews as well. During the Third Reich, he worked on a commentary on the Gospel of John. While that project remained unpublished, he was able to express his anti-Judaism in other forums, including an article on Judas.[9]

As dean from 1936 to 1945, Preisker nazified the theological faculty at Breslau, so that it was one of very few not closed by Reich officials during the war.[10] Together with other colleagues at Breslau, Hans Leube (systematic theology) and Wilhelm Knevels (church history), Preisker became a vigorous member of the Institute from its inception, presenting papers at conferences and editing the Institute's dejudaized New Testament.[11] An Institute conference was held in Breslau on December 1, 1941, with papers delivered by Grundmann and Leube, among others, to an audience of 200.[12] Preisker's efforts were well regarded; in October 1942, he was proposed by Alfred Rosenberg's Office of Ideological Information to be one of several instructors for a course planned for pastors,[13] indicating that Preisker's good standing with the Reich was retained well into the war years and was in no way diminished by his Institute affiliation.

Indeed, Institute membership was respected by administrative officials at German universities, who granted requests for leaves of absence to faculty members attending Institute conferences. After the war, the relationships forged at those conferences remained close; Institute members provided false testimony for one another to help evade punishment for Nazi involvements and secure postwar employment. In later years Institute members wrote memorial encomiums for one another and published joint scholarly projects.

[8] Herbert Preisker, *Neutestamentliche Zeitgeschichte*, 297, italics his.

[9] Preisker, "Der Verrat des Judas und das Abendmahl," 151–55.

[10] Report from Martin Bormann, dated June 23, 1939, of a conference held April 6, 1939, on the consolidation of the theological faculties (Bundesarchiv Potsdam. 62Di1, 56/4).

[11] Preisker presented papers at the Institute's first conference, held July 15, 1939, in Leipzig, on "Johannine Literature and Theology" and "The Spread of Early Christianity: Asia Minor."

[12] Hutter-Wolandt, "Spagat zwischen Wissenschaft."

[13] The proposal regarding Preisker came from Wilhelm Brachmann, director of the division on the Study of Religion (Bundesarchiv Potsdam, 62Di1, 56/4). Report from Brachmann, Insitute director, dated October 1, 1942, concerning a plan for a course of instruction on the study of religion for instructors and teaching institutes.

Gerhard Delling (1905–86), another member, wrote the memorial encomium for Preisker, and Johannes Leipoldt (1880–1965) collaborated with Grundmann on a major three-volume study of early Christianity published in the early 1970s.[14]

Oddly enough, participating in the Institute offered some of its members protection against penalties leveled by the postwar denazification investigations. For example, Karl Euler (1909–60), an instructor at the University of Giessen, joined several of the Institute's working committees. Born in 1909, Euler received his doctorate at Giessen in 1934 under the direction of Georg Bertram, and remained at Giessen as an instructor until 1945; he joined the SA in 1933, the Nazi Party in 1937.[15] Through Bertram he became involved with the Institute, which led to career opportunities: he delivered papers at Institute conferences, and in 1942 he and Grundmann published a book on Judaism.[16] Thanks to that publication, and despite its antisemitic arguments, Euler was able to present himself after the war as an expert on Judaism and hence a supposed opponent of Nazism. The strategy worked; he was appointment pastor in Frankfurt in 1946, then chaplain at the University of Giessen hospital from 1949 until his retirement in 1967; he died in 1986.

Another member whose involvement in the Institute furthered his postwar career was Georg Biundo (1892–1988). Editor from 1925 to 1958 of a journal on Palatinate church history, he was an enthusiastic speaker at local Nazi Party rallies who came to be known as early as 1932 as a "Nazi pastor," though he claimed after the war to have been "untainted." His engagement in Institute activities facilitated Biundo's connections with colleagues in the field of theology and encouraged his academic aspirations. After the war, those connections helped him obtain a position as lecturer and, later, honorary professor in the faculty of theology at the University of Mainz from 1949 to 1968. The Institute's independence from the Nazi Party and its position as a church-sponsored organization allowed Biundo to declare after the war that he had never been a member of an organization belonging to the Nazi Party, but had been a loyal member of the church. Ironically, he was aided after the war by the former Nazi Ludwig Diehl, bishop of the Palatinate from 1934 to 1945, who had supported the establishment of the Institute. As Ronald Webster has

---

[14] Delling, "Herbert Preisker in memoriam," 181; Leipoldt and Grundmann, eds., *Umwelt des Urchristentums.*

[15] Euler joined the NSDAP on May 1, 1937, receiving membership number 5575607 (BDC, Euler materials). See also UAG, PrA Theol no. 2.

[16] Karl Euler and Walter Grundmann, *Das religiöse Gesicht des Judentums: Entstehung und Art* (Leipzig: Georg Wigand, 1942).

discovered, Biundo's successful denazification led other former Nazis to request his support for their own denazification.[17]

Postwar scholarly careers were enhanced, not hindered, by Institute involvement; Johannes Hempel (1891–1964), professor at the University of Berlin, retained his editorship of the most prestigious German journal of Old Testament studies, the *Zeitschrift für alttestamentliche Wissenschaft*, from 1927 to 1959, despite infiltrating the journal with racist ideology. He had removed the phrase "und Kunde des nachbiblischen Judentums" ("and Study of Post-Biblical Judaism") from its title in 1937 and wrote in a 1942 editor's column:

> The more strongly the racial and völkisch awakening takes hold and the more energetically in the political situation the opposition between the Third Reich and the Jews comes to the fore as a struggle over life and death, the sharper the view becomes of the political content of the religion of the Old Testament, especially its expectations of the future. [18]

Hempel also transformed the prestigious Institutum Judaicum in Berlin, which he directed from 1937 until 1945, and which had been an academic center for Protestant studies of Judaism, into a center for racially based scholarship.[19] Already a star in his field when he became involved in the Institute, Hempel used his membership to create new outlets for expressing the racism that was central to his scholarship. For example, he viewed the Old Testament as a record of Israel's moral degeneracy, as exemplified, for example, in its hatred of other peoples,[20] and described the Old Testament as the most antisemitic book of world literature.[21] While defending Christian retention of the Old Testament—after all, that was his field of study—he argued that it was not a Jewish book, but a critique of Jewish national and racial characteristics.[22] In 1938 Hempel urged the University of Berlin to hire both Gerhard Kittel and Karl Georg Kuhn to collaborate with him in his antisemitic studies of Judaism,

---

[17] Webster, "Dr. Georg Biundo," 92–111. On Diehl, see Reichrath, *Ludwig Diehl*. Diehl was a member of the Bund für deutsches Christentum and attended its meetings in 1938 that ultimately led to the Godesberg Declaration and the Bekanntmachung establishing the Institute. See EZA 1/A4/468, 7/4166, 1/A4/168.

[18] Hempel, "Chronik vom Herausgeber," 212.

[19] For a history of the Institutum Judaicum, see Golling and Osten-Sacken, eds., *Hermann L. Strack und das Institutum Judaicum in Berlin*.

[20] Hempel, *Fort mit dem Alten Testament?*

[21] Hempel, *Das alte Testament und die völkische Idee*, 8, cited by Weber, *Altes Testament und völkische Frage*, 301.

[22] Hempel, *Fort mit dem Alten Testament?*

but was turned down.[23] He then turned to Grundmann, assisting him in negotiating the political intricacies in Berlin to win approval for establishing the
Institute, and he joined a variety of Institute working committees. In a 1942
letter Hempel explained the importance of the Institute to his own scholarship, for example in studying the links between Christianity and certain
races,[24] and that same year he tried unsuccessfully to establish a racially based
Institute for the Study of Comparative Religion, modeled after Grundmann's
Institute, at the University of Göttingen.[25]

Several Institute members were older and had already achieved tenured
professorships, often at distinguished universities, such as Vienna, Heidelberg,
and Berlin, so that joining the Institute was not for the reward of a politically
influenced professorial appointment. The three senior professors of Protestant
theology at the University of Vienna who joined the Institute, for example,
were born between 1872 and 1893 and taught Old Testament, New Testament, and practical theology. Theodor Odenwald (1889–1970), professor of
systematic theology and ethics, served as dean of theology at Heidelberg, and
did not join the Nazi Party until 1937. Active in the Institute throughout the
war years, he participated in its conferences and publications as well as in its
governing committees.

In addition to scholarly projects, the Institute afforded its members the
chance to help forge German consciousness during a war that was touted as
determining the survival of the Aryan race. Propaganda was crucial to the
shaping of the Third Reich, and antisemitism, always central to Nazi politics,
intensified continuously after 1938. The message of the Reich to Germans, as
Jeffrey Herf has shown, was that they were fighting a defensive war against a
hugely powerful international Jewish conspiracy that had gained control of
American and British governments and that sought the total annihilation of
the German people, not simply the overthrow of the Hitler regime.[26] Grundmann proclaimed precisely that message over and over:

The decisive German struggle for the freedom and life of our Volk reveals
itself all the more clearly as a struggle against the degenerating and destructive powers in all realms of life. Everywhere behind these degenerative
powers the Jew is visible. The task of German humanities and religious

[23] Letter from Hempel to university trustees, dated November 16, 1938 (Humboldt Universitäts
Archiv, Humboldt, Akten: H 216/4: Johannes Hempel).

[24] Johannes Hempel to the dean, dated February 16, 1942 (Humboldt Universitäts Archiv,
Akten: H 216/4: Hempel).

[25] Weber, *Altes Testament und völkische Frage*, 148.

[26] Herf, *The Jewish Enemy*.

scholarship in this connection is becoming all the more important in this context. For the battle of the weapons accompanies the battle of the spirit. As our weapons smite the enemy, our spirit comes to know his means and the methods with which he penetrates to the inner life of the nation, how to see the enemy as he really is, and how to create the intellectual principles with which to defeat him. The Institute has been in the service of this task from the very beginning.[27]

The apocalyptic mood of Grundmann's theological propaganda was influenced by the Christian interpretations that circulated widely in Germany after World War I. At that time, the Jews were said to have betrayed Germany, stabbing it in the back in the waning months of the war, causing German defeat, undermining its economy after the war, and spreading a degenerate moral influence in Weimar culture, all the while enriching themselves. The story of Jesus's life was a parable for Germany: just as Jesus had sought the destruction of the Jews, but had instead fallen victim to them, Germans were today facing the same enemy that now, in the name of Jesus, they had to fight and conquer, while Jews were enriching themselves through that betrayal as modern-day avatars of Judas.

Nationalism was transmitted to Grundmann in his youth both by his family and by his teachers. His father, Emil, a railway stationmaster, born in 1873, was a self-taught, intellectually gifted man, active in his church, who delivered lectures on Luther and music and wrote articles for church publications. When he heard that the Kaiser had abdicated, Emil cried, according to his son's later recollection.[28] His father was also immersed in antisemitic völkisch ideology, later writing that "At that time, in 1918, . . . after four difficult, hard years of world war this heyday of the scoundrels arrived, Germany, deathly wounded, surrendered to the enemy through a miserable betrayal by Jews and their consorts."[29] Echoing his father's reaction to Germany's defeat in World War I, Grundmann, in a series of pamphlets published in 1935 and 1936, linked the German struggle for greatness with the passion of Jesus.[30] "Jesus follows the path of the cross with full consciousness. . . . Jesus offers his suffering at a particular historical moment in which the secret of his imperative is

---

[27] Grundmann, *Germanentum, Christenum und Judentum*, foreword.

[28] Grundmann, *Erkenntnis und Wahrheit*, 42f.

[29] Emil Grundmann, "Feierabendstunde Ewige Wacht," *Christenkreuz und Hakenkreuz* 11 (1937): 14.

[30] For example, Grundmann, *Die Losung* (1935); *Der nationalsozialistische Pfarrer im Kampf um die Volkskirche* (1935).

illuminated."[31] As Jesus suffered, so must Germans: "We know today that the way home for the German Volk to itself is an ineffable path of sacrifice," Grundmann declared in 1936.[32]

The German economic crises of inflation and depression in the late 1920s did not themselves give rise to antisemitism and to support for the nascent National Socialist movement. However, these economic problems were sometimes "explained" by reference to narratives of Christian suffering and betrayal that had long been invoked, in Germany and elsewhere, as a substitute for political analysis. The effectiveness of Christian mythic narratives in the political arena not only stimulated their use by Nazi propagandists, but also contributed to the conviction of religious Germans that they had an important political role to play. While aware that theologians were not part of the military machinery, Grundmann and his colleagues emphasized that the war against the Jews required both weapons and spirit, and that strengthening the German spirit for its deadly battle against the Jews would come about by translating the Nazi message into religious language. What the Institute promised was the skills of scholars of religion to prove that "the Jew" had always sought the destruction of Aryan spirit. For example, the Old Testament had poisoned England through its Puritan heritage, Meyer-Erlach argued, and the depravity of Judaism had created both capitalism and bolshevism, the two great enemies of Germany.[33]

Martin Redeker (1900–1970), professor of systematic theology at the University of Kiel, also became a Christian propagandist for Nazism. He delivered antisemitic sermons from the chapel of the university that were broadcast on radio; two months after Kristallnacht he preached, "We can see all too clearly how the satanical power of rot is consolidated in world-Judaism and materialism."[34] Nazism he viewed as the essence of Germanness and Christianity, and Christian theology had to revise itself accordingly. In a 1939 article he wrote: "Contemporary theology has to recognize that our new völkisch-political point of view forms the foundation and bedrock of the entire German scholarly spirit."[35] Similarly, Nazism expressed Lutheranism: "The contemporary fulfill-

---

[31] Grundmann, *Die Passion des Heilandes der deutschen Gegenwart verkündigt* (1936), 9.

[32] Grundmann, *Der Gott Jesu Christi* (1936), 56.

[33] Meyer-Erlach, *Ist Gott Engländer?*, and *Der Einfluss der Juden auf das englische Christentum.*

[34] Redeker, "Uns ist das Kämpfen und Sein ist das Siegen, radio sermon preached on January 15, 1939; in Redeker, *Rundfunkpredigten* (Bremen, 1939); cited by Buss, *Die nordelbischen Landeskirchen*, 128.

[35] Redeker, "Theologie und Weltanschauung," 395 (in a Festschrift for Wobbermin, in which also appears Grundmann, "Paulus und Luther").

ment of German politics and political leadership that we are enabled to experience in National Socialist Germany is the fulfillment of Ur-German themes that broke forth with Luther and through Luther experienced a religious and moral substantiation."[36]

An active Institute member with a well-established academic career, Redeker received his doctorate in systematic theology at the University of Göttingen under Georg Wobbermin, an active member of the German Christian movement who also became an Institute member; both joined the Nazi Party the same day, May 1, 1933. Redeker found several religious outlets for expressing his Nazism. In 1936, he joined Bishop Weidemann's German Christian-oriented Bible institute in Bremen,[37] lecturing at the first two Bible courses organized by Weidemann.[38] In 1937, Redeker received a professorship at the University of Kiel, two years after receiving an honorary doctorate from the theological faculty at Göttingen for his efforts to shape the "foundations of religious education and the awareness of the connections between humanity, peoplehood, and Christianity."[39] Redeker is known to this day for his studies of the nineteenth-century German Protestant theologian Friedrich Schleiermacher.[40]

Georg Bertram (1896–1979) came to know Grundmann through their participation in contributing articles to the *Theological Dictionary of the New Testament*, edited by Gerhard Kittel, Grundmann's doctoral advisor at Tübingen. Bertram had received his doctorate in New Testament at the University of Berlin in 1921, and a habilitation in 1923, and contributed fifteen articles to the first four volumes of the *Dictionary*, published from 1933 to 1942 under Kittel's editorship.[41] Still very young but well known as an expert on the Septuagint, he received a professorship at the University of Giessen at the remarkably young age of 29, in 1925, despite warnings about the poor quality of his scholarship.[42] Bertram's scholarship was centered on Hellenistic literature and

---

[36] Redeker, "Der britische Cant," 263.

[37] Buss, "Entjudung der Kirche," 128 fn 523.

[38] Heinonen, *Anpassung und Identität*, 209, 215.

[39] Mager, "Göttinger theologische Promotionen 1933–1945," 357–58.

[40] Redeker, *Friedrich Schleiermacher*.

[41] Bertram wrote another twenty articles for the remaining seven volumes of the dictionary, published after the war under the editorship of Gerhard Friedrich, professor of New Testament at the University of Erlangen.

[42] Rudolf Bultmann, professor of New Testament at the University of Marburg, wrote to the faculty at the time of Bertram's appointment:

> You know Bertram better than I do. His previous writings show that he is certainly talented but they don't thereby really prove how far that talent really extends (i.e., in scope and future potentiality). And on the contrary they show a regrettable immaturity in their one-sidedness, exaggerations, and excessiveness in assessments and observations, as well

informed by History of Religions methods. In a major 1922 study, for example, he argued that the passion narrative of the gospels was not a historical report, but was shaped as a projection of the experience of the early Christian community onto the life of its hero, Jesus.[43]

Long active in the Institute, Bertram moved to Eisenach and took over its leadership in 1943, after Grundmann and Eisenhuth had been drafted. A member of the Nazi teacher's association (NSLB), he did not join the Nazi Party. His antisemitism, however, was heated: he blamed Jews for initiating the war, and drew parallels between Jesus's life and the present-day struggle of Germans against Jews. Jesus was the "unconditional opponent and ruthless fighter against Judaism," the liberator of the ancient world from Judaism who serves as an "exemplary model for the struggle of our Volk today."[44] The war, he stated at an Institute conference in March of 1944, was the "world historical conflict with Jewry for which all the powers of the German soul have to be mobilized." Bertram's influence also passed to his numerous graduate students—he had twenty-five during the Third Reich, among them Theodor Ellwein (1897–1962) and Euler, both of whom joined the Institute as well.

THE MAKING OF WALTER GRUNDMANN

Walter Grundmann's religious, political, and academic background was typical of many of the Institute members. The most active members of the Institute were of the generation born between 1900 and 1909, too young to have fought in World War I but old enough to have had their youth affected by the war's aftermath and to come of age just when Hitler assumed power. It was a generation that witnessed the theological crisis wrought by the devastation of the war, and was imbued with a mood that demanded a radically new approach to Christianity.

Born in 1906, Grundmann grew up in Chemnitz, an industrial city in eastern Saxony near the Czech border, where he experienced the inflation and

---

as a nebulousness in conceptualization. Shouldn't we wait for him to develop a bit more? (even though I am on principle not at all against the appointment of a very young person). But you are in a postion, on the basis of personal knowledge/acquaintance, to judge that better than I." Letter dated January 16, 1925 (UAG, Georg Bertram: Personalakten). For a description of the university during the Third Reich, see Chroust, "Social Situation and Political Orientation," 36–85. On the theologians at Giessen, see Greschat, "Die evangelisch-theologische Fakultät in Gießen," 139–66. See also Chroust, *Gießener Universität,* vol. 1.

[43] Bertram, *Die Leidensgeschichte Jesu.*

[44] Report (LKA Eisenach).

unemployment of the Weimar era. Chemnitz, which was particularly hard-hit, became a breeding ground for a politics of resentment, nationalism, and racism. There were food riots and shop lootings in Chemnitz in 1915, bringing military intervention,[45] and in the "Chemnitz bloodbath" of August 1919, 9,000 military troops ruthlessly suppressed a peaceful protest against food shortages, leaving fifty people dead. A year later came the violent Kapp Putsch, which left hundreds dead in nearby Leipzig and Dresden.[46] In October of 1923, 60,000 Reichswehr troops sent to Saxony toppled the leftist government with brutality, resulting in many deaths. During the hyperinflation of 1922, when he was sixteen years old, Grundmann earned 600,000 RM for giving a single private lesson. Economic dislocations led Saxons both to communism and to Nazism. Like Thuringia, Saxony was considered a "red" kingdom in Grundmann's youth, the cradle of the German organized working class and a bastion of the Communist Party, and yet it gave early and strong support to the Nazis. In the November 1932 Reichstag elections, Chemnitz-Zwickau had the second-highest NSDAP vote in Germany, with 43.4 percent, but also one of the highest Communist Party votes.[47]

Grundmann decided at a young age to study theology.[48] He wrote, "one is a Christian out of a decision of the heart in facing the grace of God that comes to us."[49] He joined a Christian youth movement and participated in school Bible circles and Christian organizations of young men, while his father exerted a pietistic influence. The decisive moment in his commitment to theology, he reports, was reading Johannes Müller's book on Jesus and hearing him lecture in Chemnitz.[50] Müller, a popular speaker and promoter of an alternative, anticlerical, "new age" holistic Christianity, ran a resort center called Schloss Elmau, in a castle south of Munich, that addressed the "liberation of personal life," with attention to guests' combined spiritual, intellectual, aesthetic, and physical well-being.[51] What impressed Grundmann about Müller, he later wrote, was the latter's understanding of the figure of Jesus not as a divinity nor as a person, but as an appearance that "gives birth and shares the richness of life, heals lives that are incomplete, atrophied, and sick, and opens to all human beings the divinity of life,—and this connection with Friedrich Nietzsche and Christian dogma stayed with me; I continuously rediscover

---

[45] Noon, "Saxon Politics during the First World War," 313.

[46] Szejnmann, *Nazism in Central Germany*, 96.

[47] Ibid., 116–17.

[48] See his curriculum vitae, written at Tübingen in late 1930 or 1931 (UAT, Signatur 162/92).

[49] Grundmann, *Erkenntnis und Wahrheit*, 15

[50] Müller, *Jesus, wie ich ihn sehe.*

[51] Haury, *Von Riesa nach Schloss Elmau.* Müller's publications included a journal, *Grüne Blättter.*

how these insights have shaped me."[52] While Müller's work was not explicitly political or antisemitic, his independence from church doctrine and his comforting spirituality divorced from moral responsibility allowed its easy appropriation by völkisch adherents.

At the three universities where Grundmann studied theology—Leipzig (1926–27), Tübingen (1927–28), Rostock (1928), and again Leipzig (1928–30, where he completed his first theological examinations in the winter of 1929–30)—many of his professors of theology had outspoken right-wing political views. At the universities, Grundmann also participated in the rise of right-wing Christian student groups. When Grundmann arrived at the University of Leipzig in 1926, a group of students had just founded the National Socialist German Student Union. At Tübingen in 1927, he joined a German Christian student organization that viewed both liberalism and communism as threats to religion and hailed völkisch movements as efforts to revive Christian faith and the church. Grundmann's first publications, in 1931 and 1932, were under the auspices of right-wing student Christian groups.[53] At Rostock in 1928 he studied with the New Testament theologian Friedrich Brunstäd, a specialist on the Gospel of John, who had long been active in völkisch circles, having delivered an address to the Deutschnational Volkspartei (DNVP) gathering in Munich in September 1921.[54] Grundmann later reported that Brunstäd "awakened a passionate interest in the fate of his own people."[55]

At each university, Grundmann forged friendships with professors and students who subsequently became Institute members. At Leipzig, for example, he worked closely with Johannes Leipoldt (1880–1965), who later became one of the most prolific and influential Institute members, having published both academic and popular books on religion and trained several of the schol-

---

[52] Grundmann, *Erkenntnis und Wahrheit*, 15. Müller's book on Jesus first appeared as articles in the journal he edited, *Grüne Blätter* (the journal was published from 1914 to 1941), and was published as a book in 1930, *Jesus wie ich ihn sehe*.

[53] The anticommunist pamphlet *Im Kampf um Gott: Ein Wort zur Gottlosenbewegung* (1931), and *Die nationalsozialistische Bewegung und das Christentum: 10 Thesen* (1932). See Kupisch, *Studenten entdecken die Bibel*, 178, 284; Adam, "Der theologische Werdegang W. Grundmanns," 171–90.

[54] The Rostock university archive contains no extant materials pertaining to Grundmann's term of study there, neither a curriculum vitae nor the names of those professors whose lectures he attended (personal communication from Angela Hartwig, director of the archive). For a history of the theological faculty at Rostock, see Pauli, "Geschichte der theologischen Institute an der Universität Rostock," 309–65. He also became close to Gottfried Quell, professor of Old Testament, one of the contributors to Kittel's Dictionary, and also a postwar collaborator with Grundmann and Bertam on a small volume of essays: Quell, ed., *Sin*.

[55] Grundmann, *Erkenntnis und Wahrheit*, 24.

ars who joined the Institute. Leipoldt's numerous publications followed the politics of the moment. In 1918, the rise of feminism in Germany prompted Leipoldt to publish a pamphlet on Jesus's masculinity; in 1923 came a pamphlet questioning whether Jesus was a Jew, reissued in 1935.[56] Leipoldt's work became increasingly antisemitic during the 1930s.[57] Director of an Institute for Comparative Religion at the University of Leipzig, he emphasized Hellenistic mystery religions as the stew out of which Christianity emerged, distancing Christianity from Judaism and emphasizing Jesus's originality and the superior truth of Christianity.

Leipoldt was considered an authority on Judaism, and from 1925 to 1942 he published a journal of New Testament studies, *Angelos*, whose early volumes included significant studies of rabbinic literature by Jewish as well as Christian scholars.[58] Within the Institute Leipoldt was a constant presence, lecturing frequently at its conferences, including at its final meeting in March of 1944. The Institute gave him the opportunity to incorporate racial theory in his academic work, explaining the rise of Christianity in antiquity as an Aryan triumph that incorporated Teutonic ideas, as he argued in a paper on "The History of the Ancient Church in Racial Illumination," presented at an Institute conference in November 1941. The Institute also fostered a collegiality that led to collaborations; for example, Leipoldt joined with another Institute member, Siegfried Morenz, an Egyptologist, to produce an important study of the role of scripture in the Mediterranean basin of antiquity, ultimately published after the war, in 1953.[59]

Another of Leipoldt's protégés who overlapped with Grundmann's student years at Leipzig was Carl Schneider (1900–1977), who subsequently became a professor of New Testament at the University of Königsberg and a member of the Institute. For Schneider, who was active in the German Christian movement,[60] the Institute's views were congenial; he published a textbook on the New Testament in 1934 that included some strongly harsh words about the Pharisees and early Judaism and placed Jesus outside its realm of religious

---

[56] Leipoldt, *Die männliche Art Jesu*; Leipoldt, *War Jesus jude?*

[57] The protean nature of Leipoldt's theology is delineated by Leonore Siegele-Wenschkewitz, "Ablösung des Christentums vom Judentum?"

[58] *Angelos: Archiv für neutestamentliche Zeitgeschichte und Kulturkunde*, published by the Forschungsinstitut für vergleichende Religionsgeschichte at the University of Leipzig, which was directed by Leipoldt. Among the contributors were Lazar Gulkowitsch, G. Polster, Joachim Jeremias, Gerhard Kittel, and Paul Fiebig.

[59] Leipoldt and Morenz, *Heilige Schriften*.

[60] See his pamphlet, *Paulusfragen* (Bonn: Gebet Scheut, 1937), published as vol. 10 of the German Christian series, Aufbau im Positiven Christentum.

influence.[61] Membership in the Institute intensified Schneider's anti-Jewish arguments; in 1940 he published a pamphlet arguing that Jesus, a non-Jewish Galilean, had initiated Christianity as an antisemitic movement. Jesus's teachings were not Jewish legalistic casuistry, but spiritual teachings about man's relation to nature, experience of God, and ethics of love. Above all, Schneider wrote, Jesus stood in constant struggle against Judaism and fell as victim to it—language typical of Institute rhetoric.[62]

After his studies at the University of Leipzig, Grundmann went to study at the distinguished theological faculty of the University of Tübingen. He described his years there as "decisive for my thinking and my life,"[63] and they were indeed a turning point in his political and academic life. Tübingen, a small university town with a population of 23,000 in 1930, held Germany's largest Protestant theological department at the time, and was one of the country's most distinguished universities.[64] The university had an unusually homogeneous and provincial environment; with the departure of the physicist Alfred Landes, who emigrated to the United States in 1931, only one Jewish instructor remained, and he left in 1938.[65] Although Tübingen in those years had only a small number of NSDAP adherents, there was strong ideological antagonism among students and faculty toward the Weimar Republic. Few faculty members identified with the Republic, and many were involved in right-wing nationalist groups, although only a handful were members of the NSDAP prior to 1933.[66] The Nazi Party first appeared in the university town in 1929, and won early and enthusiastic student support. Within the theological discipline, support for Nazism came from the faculty as well as the students. Theodor Häring, Georg Wehrun, and Karl Heim all published articles in support of a Führer who would lead Germany.[67] By 1930, half of the university student body had joined the Nazi Party, Grundmann among them, signing up on December 1, 1930. His early party membership earned him the title of an "Alter Kämpfer"[68] and allowed him to wear a lapel pin, the Nazi Party's golden

[61] Schneider, *Einführung in die neutestamentliche Zeitgeschichte*, 149–84.

[62] Schneider, *Das Frühchristentum als antisemitische Bewegung*.

[63] Curriculum vitae, April 25, 1931 (UAT 162/92).

[64] The theology department at Tübingen had a student enrollment of 459 in 1924, 952 in 1933; the Berlin theology department, next in size, had only 237 students in 1924. Martin Elze, "Tübingen I. Universität," *Religion in Geschichte und Gegenwart* third edition, vol. 6, p. 1068; cited by Rieger, "Die Tübinger evangelisch-theologische Fakultät," 175.

[65] Adam, *Hochschule und Nationalsozialismus*, 31.

[66] Ibid., 29, 31.

[67] Rieger, "Die Tübinger evangelisch-theologische Fakultät," 176.

[68] He received the membership no. 382544 (BDC Grundmann files).

insignia, as well as other privileges. He became a "supporting member" of the SS on April 1, 1934 (no. 1032691), of the NSV on July 1, 1934 (no. 1827439).[69] Grundmann's Nazi and Christian commitments made him, as a young man, one of the major theorists of the German Christian movement.

Grundmann credited the grand old man of German Protestant theology, Adolf Schlatter (1852–1938), as his most influential teacher and mentor,[70] though his doctoral advisor was the noted scholar Gerhard Kittel (1868–1948). Starting in 1933 Kittel put his convictions to work on behalf of the antisemitic goals of the Reich.[71] Schlatter's commentaries on the gospels remained for decades the standard reference work used by Protestant pastors in Germanic lands to prepare their weekly sermons, ultimately replaced after World War II by Grundmann's commentaries. Kittel's critical editions of rabbinic texts were serious works of scholarship, and the *Theological Dictionary of the New Testament* that he edited remains to this day a standard reference work on early Christianity and its cultural environment, though highly controversial, given both its pervasive anti-Judaism and Kittel's own subsequent Nazi activities.[72] Both Schlatter and Kittel were professors at Tübingen and shared political convictions regarding National Socialism, antisemitism, and the political role of Christianity.

Two Major Teachers: Adolf Schlatter and Gerhard Kittel

Schlatter's academic work was combined with a commitment to political and pastoral guidance of his students. He was not an innovative, sophisticated scholar who made original discoveries, but one who straddled the line between synthesizing historical research and infusing scholarship with a firm Christian piety. After holding a position in systematic theology in Berlin, he was appointed professor of New Testament at Tübingen in 1898, which

[69] ThHStA PA Vobi—Thüringisches Volksbildungsminiseriums in Weimar PA Walter Grundmann, 8807, p. 68. Later, on January 1, 1937, he became a member of the editorial board of the Commission for Protecting National Socialist Writings. Questionnaire signed by Grundmann July 6, 1938 (ThHStA 3426, p. 68).

[70] Grundmann, *Erkenntnis und Wahrheit*, 15.

[71] McNutt, "Adolf Schlatter and the Jews," 360. On Kittel, see Ericksen, *Theologians under Hitler.*

[72] Vos, "Antijudaismus/Antisemitismus, 89–110. Scholarly debates on Kittel focus on whether his Nazi propaganda involvements, which were substantial, influenced his scholarship. See, for example, Siegele-Wenschkewitz, *Neutestamentliche Wissenschaft vor der Judenfrage*; Ericksen, *Theologians under Hitler*; Wassermann, *False Start.*

aroused mixed feelings among students at that time, some of whom viewed Schlatter "as a pious but unscientific Biblicist."[73] For others, Schlatter's appointment represented a counterweight to the nondoctrinal, critical approach of the History of Religions school. Indeed, in his inaugural address, Schlatter blurred the boundaries between science and dogmatics, calling for theological methods to be grounded in Christian faith.[74] It was not an auspicious beginning at a university known for the work of its respected nineteenth-century New Testament scholar, Ferdinand Christian Baur, who promoted nondoctrinal, scientific analysis of the New Testament. Yet Schlatter's affirmation of Christian commitments made him a beloved figure in the pietistic atmosphere at Tübingen. Throughout his years at the university, Schlatter continued to work both in biblical studies and dogmatics, as both scholar and *Seelsorger* (pastoral counselor) to the two generations of students he taught from 1898 to 1930.[75] Schlatter exerted a strong, inspiring influence, intellectual and personal, on the thousands of young people who studied with him, most of whom became pastors and teachers in the church of Württemberg. He also became advisor to the German Christian Student Union, of which Grundmann was a member, and preached regularly at the university church. Schlatter was at times critical of Nazism, but the link between state and church that he advocated also influenced Grundmann strongly in his support for the Nazi regime. In a 1933 pamphlet, Schlatter wrote, "We must live totally in the church in order to live totally in the state, and live totally in the state in order to live totally in the church," which found echoes in Grundmann's pamphlet, written later that year, *Totale Kirche im totalen Staat*, and in 1937 Grundmann declared, "Adolf Schlatter built the path for us from theology to National Socialism."[76]

The message that linked Schlatter's theological and political work in ways decisive for Grundmann was the accusation that the Jews, both in antiquity and the present day, were a force of decadence, the "gegen-Volk," both the opposite and opponents of Christians as well as Germans, and that Jesus had been the Jews' greatest opponent. The Jews' rejection of Jesus as their messiah

---

[73] Neuer, *Adolf Schlatter*, 107, 109.

[74] Ibid., 109.

[75] Stuhlmacher, "Adolf Schlatter's Interpretation of Scripture," 434. See also Martin Hengel's observation that "Adolf Schlatter . . . was next to Ferdinand Christian Baur . . . the most important Protestant theologian in Tübingen during the past 200 years." *Paulus und das antike Judentum*, ed. Hengel und Heckel, vii, cited by McNutt, "Adolf Schlatter and the Jews," 366 fn1.

[76] The quotation comes from Schlatter, *Der neue deutsche Art*, 16. See the discussion in Heinonen, *Anpassung und Identität*, 157, and in Tyson, *Luke, Judaism, and the Scholars*. Grundmann, "Adolf Schlatter: Ein Wort des Grußes und des Gedenkens zu seinem 85. Geburtstag am 16 August," *Kommende Kirche* 33 (August 15, 1937), unpaginated.

and their guilt for his death was an indication not simply of their religious conviction, but of their inherent degenerate character. Their rejection of Jesus made it necessary, Schlatter argued, for early Christians to distance themselves even from Jews who did become Christians.[77] He declared in a 1929 lecture, "The Goal of History," that the Jews' "soul-murdering poison of our culture confirms the judgment of Jesus."[78] Such ideas echoed throughout Institute publications.

Schlatter blamed the decline in contemporary Christian piety in Germany on Jewish influence: "In the sphere of our natural estate how does one escape the alternatives of gluttony and poverty produced by the Jewish Type? Go to the Father, Jesus said, I will make you children of God. *That means, however, not only a change in business and politics, but the end of Judaism.*"[79] At the same time, Schlatter also blamed the Jews for the Nazis' neo-paganism. Just a few months after the promulgation of the 1935 Nuremberg Laws disenfranchising Jews as Germans, he published a pamphlet entitled *Will the Jew Be Victorious over Us? A Christmas Message*, which quickly sold 40,000 copies.[80] In it Schlatter identified the anti-Christian attitudes of some Nazis with anti-Christian prejudices of some Jews: "Today, a rabbi can say with pride . . . we were [once] alone in trying to erase from public consciousness the mad message preached at Christmas. . . . Now [with the Nazis], however, we have . . . allies in our fight. . . ."[81] By making public observance of Christmas into a winter solstice celebration to unify Germans, and rejecting it as a Christian holiday celebrating the birth of Jesus the Jew, the Nazi regime had created a secular occasion that would allow Jews to participate alongside Christians, Schlatter argued, misunderstanding that Jesus was the enemy of the Jews. Nazi racism, he wrote, was similar to Jewish racism, and in undermining Christianity the Nazis were behaving like Jews.[82] Such arguments were also echoed by Grundmann in later years, who

---

[77] For a discussion of Schlatter's anti-Judaism, see Sanders, *Paul and Palestinian Judaism*, 33–59, and Tyson, *Luke, Judaism, and the Scholars*, 56.

[78] Schlatter, "Das Ziel der Geschichte," 353, cited by McNutt, "Adolf Schlatter and the Jews," 356.

[79] Schlatter, *Wir Christen und die Juden*, 16, emphasis his; cited in McNutt, "Adolf Schlatter and the Jews," 357. McNutt notes the parallel to Gerhard Kittel, who wrote that if "Judaism wants to remain Judaism, it cannot do otherwise than declare battle on the claims of Jesus. And whenever Jesus is recognized as reality and truth, there Judaism has found its end." Kittel, *Die Probleme des palästinische Spätjudentum*, 140. See also McNutt, "Vessels of Wrath."

[80] Schlatter, *Wird der Jude über uns Siegen?* See the discussion of Schlatter in Siegele-Wenschke-witz, "Adolf Schlatters Sicht des Judentums im politischen Kontext."

[81] Friedländer, *Nazi Germany and the Jews*: vol. 1, *The Years of Persecution, 1933–1939* 165. Schlatter, *Wird der Jude über uns Siegen?*

[82] For two conflicting interpretations of Schlatter's pamphlet, see Neuer, *Adolf Schlatter*, and Siegele-Wenschkewitz, "Adolf Schlatters Sicht des Judentums im politischen Kontext," 95–110.

maintained that opposition to Christianity as a Jewish religion indicated a victory of Jewish propaganda, which had long claimed Jesus as a Jew.

Schlatter claimed he was rejecting Nazi racism, yet his emphasis on the moral and religious degeneracy of the Jews was precisely the argument that lay at the heart of Nazi antisemitic propaganda. That theme of the moral degeneracy of the Jews persists in Schlatter's widely read gospel commentaries, as Joseph Tyson has pointed out; for example, commenting on Luke 17:11–19, in which Jesus heals ten lepers and only one, the Samaritan, thanks him, Schlatter writes that the pericope "shows the sin of the Jew, that he accepts God's gift without thanks."[83] As James McNutt has argued, while "Schlatter resisted the racial premise, he reached by another route the same conclusion of Jewish alienation by means of alleged spiritual deformity."[84] Judaism, for Schlatter, was an immutable product of a degenerate Jewish character that could also infect non-Jews.

A gifted speaker and a master exegete, Schlatter inspired his students with his rhetoric and with the ease of his biblical interpretation. He encouraged a theological engagement in politics, and was also a prominent spouter of the conventional anti-Judaism of the conservative Protestant theology of his day.[85] In the language of scholarship, Schlatter repeated age-old stereotypes regarding early Judaism: Jesus brought faith to his followers, whereas the Jews concern themselves with achieving righteousness through unrighteous deeds, dogged by a fear of transgression; the Jews forced Pilate to carry out the crucifixion, which was approved by Rabbi Gamaliel and formed the "climax" of the Jews' guilt.[86] The crucifixion was, Schlatter writes, "the act of the nation."[87] Galilee was the stage for the "new community," but Jerusalem was the decisive place and moment for Jews, as a group, to return to God and recognize their messiah, and their failure to do so condemned them as a people. As late as 1957, Grundmann praised Schlatter's work as "groundbreaking" for connecting his History of Religions methods with studies of the Palestinian environment of the gospel authors; through Schlatter's methods, the Gentile nature of Jesus and the New Testament was made clear.[88]

---

[83] Schlatter, *Das Evangelium des Lukas*, 389; cited by Tyson, *Luke, Judaism, and the Scholars*, 63.

[84] McNutt, "Adolf Schlatter and the Jews," 358.

[85] Siegele-Wenschkewitz, "Adolf Schlatters Sicht des Judentums im politischen Kontext," 95–110.

[86] Schlatter, *Die Geschichte der ersten Christenheit*; quotations are from Schlatter, *The Church in the New Testament Period*, 5, 13, 81–83.

[87] Schlatter, *History of the Christ*, 367. My thanks to James McNutt for calling my attention to this passage.

[88] Grundmann, *Die Geschichte Jesu Christi*, 13.

In early 1930, Grundmann left Tübingen to attend the Prediger College St. Pauli in Leipzig for six months of training in practical pastoral work required for ordination. He returned to Tübingen in October 1930 to write his doctorate and work as a research assistant in the theology department under the supervision of his doctoral advisor, Gerhard Kittel.

Kittel, who had served during World War I as a naval chaplain and as a lecturer at the University of Leipzig after the war, was appointed professor at Tübingen in 1926, becoming one of world's most distinguished scholars in his field in the late 1920s and early 1930s. His subsequent enthusiastic support for the Nazi propaganda machine, for which he was imprisoned after World War II, is ironic given his scholarly reputation in the 1920s as a specialist in rabbinics.[89] Fluent in modern as well as rabbinic and biblical Hebrew, unusual for a Christian New Testament scholar at the time, Kittel had working relationships with distinguished Jewish scholars, and helped spearhead a major German Protestant project of publishing critical editions of rabbinic texts, including both the Mishnah and the Tosefta, early rabbinic texts. He was also conversant with the scholarship that placed Jesus within a Jewish context and that emphasized the similarities between Judaism and early Christianity, conceding that the comparison of Jesus's teachings to Judaism undermined claims to their originality and singularity.[90] He followed Adolf von Harnack in arguing that Jesus's ethics are unique not in their content, but in being pristine, unadulterated by the concerns that overwhelm rabbinic literature.[91]

But however seriously his scholarship treated rabbinic Judaism, Kittel had long been politically on the right, becoming a member of the proto-Nazi Vaterlandspartei in the immediate post–World War I years and supporting the aborted Nazi coup d'ètat, the Kapp Putsch, in 1920. Already during the years of the Weimar Republic, Kittel's politics and his stance toward Jews were harsh. In a 1926 publication of a German Christian student group, he fulminated against assimilated Jews as a "people who no longer possess that which their inheritance once consisted of; [a] people who have lost their souls—and all that remains of them is the outward hulls of a human being foreign to us."[92]

---

[89] Kittel, *Jesus und die Rabbinen*.

[90] Gerhard Kittel, review of Joseph Klausner's *Yeshu ha-Notsri: zemano, hayav, ve-torato* (Jerusalem, 1922) in *Theologisches Literaturblatt* 44 (1923), 241–46, 257–63; cited by Wassermann, *False Start*, 176. Klausner's book was published in English translation in 1925, and in German translation in 1930.

[91] Harnack, *Das Wesen des Christentums*; Kittel, *Die Probleme des palästischen Spätjudentums*.

[92] Kittel, *Jesus und die Juden*, 4; cited by Wassermann, *False Start*, 180.

As Robert Ericksen has demonstrated, Kittel's decisive antisemitic turn came in a notorious June 1, 1933, public lecture in Tübingen on "The Jewish Question," delivered one month after he joined the Nazi Party, in which he called for Jews to be given "guest status" in Germany. Kittel arrived at that conclusion, he wrote, because the alternatives—extermination, Zionism, and assimilation—were not "expedient." His speech, published as a pamphlet, repeated standard antisemitic charges against Jewish intellectuals, lawyers, doctors, and businessmen, and called for the end of marriages between Jews and Germans to prevent further corruption of the German race. The uproar over the casual mention of extermination as an option (however inexpedient) caused Kittel to make a few changes in the second and third editions of the pamphlet; he added, for example, that extermination would not only be impractical but unchristian.[93]

For Kittel as for Schlatter, Jews possessed an immutable moral and spiritual degeneracy reflected in their religion, which in turn made Jesus's antagonism to Judaism not merely religious but also racial. The theological opposition between Christianity and Judaism led, Kittel argued, to a Jewish enmity toward Gentiles. For example, after interrogating Herschel Grynszpan several years after his imprisonment for shooting Ernst vom Rath in 1938, an act that ultimately led to the so-called Reich Kristallnacht pogrom, Kittel wrote a report for the Gestapo, concluding that Grynszpan, as a Jew, was obsessed with hatred of Gentiles because Judaism was a racist religion teaching contempt for non-Jews.[94]

Grundmann became Kittel's assistant in the fall of 1930, and their personal relationship became very close. Grundmann and his fiancée were frequently invited by Kittel and his wife for meals at their home in Tübingen, as well as to their summer home in Walchensee, Bavaria, where the Grundmanns spent their honeymoon. The topic of Grundmann's dissertation, "The Concept of Power in the Mental World of the New Testament," was suggested by Kittel during an exchange of letters after Grundmann had already left Tübingen and was serving his vicariate at St. Pauli in Leipzig.[95] The dissertation, which was received *summa cum laude*, was published as a book in 1932 in a scholarly series edited by Kittel and Albrecht Alt, professor in Leipzig.[96]

---

[93] Kittel, *Die Judenfrage*. Robert Ericksen has called attention to the shift that occurred in 1933 in Kittel's scholarly writing as well: "Before 1933 Kittel defended Judaism, afterwards he attacked it. . . . He now took pains to distinguish Old Israel from post-exilic Judaism." Ericksen, *Theologians under Hitler*, 59, 61.

[94] Junginger, "Politische Wissenschaft," 23.

[95] Grundmann, *Erkenntnis und Wahrheit*, 73

[96] Grundmann, *Der Begriff der Kraft*.

THEOLOGICAL DICTIONARY OF THE NEW TESTAMENT

While studying for his doctorate, Grundmann also assisted Kittel in the preparation of the first two volumes of the *Theological Dictionary of the New Testament*, published in 1933 and 1935, and contributed numerous articles to the *Dictionary*.[97] Through his work for the *Dictionary*, Grundmann formed friendships with other contributors, many of them colleagues and students of Kittel who later became active members of the Institute, including Preisker, Delling, and Georg Bertram. The *Dictionary* was a massive scholarly project, analyzing the Greek terms of the New Testament for their theological significance in antiquity, which generally meant delineating their meanings in Jewish and Hellenistic contexts. Kittel took pride in the large number of contributors—forty names were listed, including twenty-two tenured professors—and in what he viewed as their commitment to rigorous historical and philological method. The first volume of the *Dictionary* was published when Hitler came to power and around the time that Kittel gave his notorious speech of May 1933 calling for German Jews to be given "guest status." No Jewish scholars contributed to the *Dictionary*, nor were contributors warned against injecting political views into their articles.

Grundmann's involvement in the project was extensive; among other duties he edited many of the contributions and wrote twelve articles for the *Dictionary's* first two volumes. His contributions included several major pieces, including the articles on "Christos" (messiah), "Megas" (greatness), and "Kraft" (power). Not all of his articles indicate the radical split between Christianity and Judaism of his later published work. While contrasting the New Testament and Judaism, some of his articles maintain a link between the New and Old Testaments,[98] and draw connections between understandings of God,

---

[97] The first three volumes of Kittel's notorious *Theologisches Wörterbuch zum Neuen Testament* were published between 1932 and 1938; volumes 4–10 were published after the war under different editorship. The entire Dictionary was translated into English and remains a major reference work. Its notoriety is derived from its particularly denigrating descriptions of early Judaism, which are all the more striking given that Kittel, like some of the other contributors, was one of the first German Protestant theologians trained in rabbinic literature. On Kittel, see Ericksen, *Theologians under Hitler*; Steinweis, *Studying the Jew*, 64–76; Siegele-Wenschkewitz, *Neutestamentliche Wissenschaft vor der Judenfrage*.

[98] "Dynamai," TWNT 2:306:

> The power of Christ is the power of God. There is here developed a line of thought already present in the OT in respect of the kingly and prophetic power of the Messiah. . . . Thus in the NT there is distinctive adoption of the OT view of the power of God active in history, shaping history and setting it its goal. The OT modes of thought and outlook . . .

messianism, and other concepts in the Hebrew Bible and New Testament. Even in cases where he argued that the New Testament had transformed a concept, he still acknowledged its roots within the Old Testament: "In the new covenant the people of God throughout the world are taken up into fellowship with God. The promise of the prophets is thus fulfilled, not limited to the nation of Israel, but as a divine work of salvation for the cosmos. The people of Israel in the New Testament is the new humanity in Christ."[99] Other articles, however, draw more radical conclusions: Jesus's religion of love "carries with it the radical overthrow of Jewish nomism, and in some sense of Judaism itself as a religion."[100] He writes that Paul did not enjoy the freedom that Jesus had proclaimed because "his view of the law was rabbinic."[101] Grundmann's articles did not denigrate Jewish concepts as severely as some other contributors to the *Dictionary*.[102] He affirmed the God of Judaism[103] and presented Jesus as the Jewish messiah,[104] a claim he went to great lengths to deny later in the 1930s and '40s, but followed the pattern common to Christian scholarship of the era: contrasting Judaism and Christianity as two opposite religious tendencies whose divorce was completed by Paul. Yet J. S. Vos has pointed out that the language Grundmann used to speak of Christianity's "overthrow" of Judaism as a religion is the same he used when calling for the "overthrow" of world Jewry.[105] In contrast to Grundmann's articles, those by Georg Bertram, later an active member and director of the Institute, contained much sharper denunciations of Judaism as a religion and an insistent opposition between it and the message of Jesus.

The Institute was not the only vehicle for theological expression of Nazi commitments; parallel routes were also open. For example, Kittel himself did

---

recur in the NT and fashion the fact of Christ. In the Christ event the power of God which shapes history and leads it to its goal is active as an eschatological event. . . . The OT view of God is accepted. God is the Almighty.

[99] "Dexomai," *Theological Dictionary of the New Testament* (English version; henceforth TDNT) 2:57; TWNT 2:57.

[100] "Megas," TDNT/TWNT 4, 536.

[101] TDNT/TWNT 4:542–43 fn 36.

[102] The overriding thesis of the articles in the *Dictionary* places Jesus's teachings in a Greco-Roman intellectual framework and in opposition to Judaism.

[103] "Dynamai," TDNT 2:297: "The supremacy of God as the Creator and Lord of the world is maintained in Judaism even though angelic and demonic conceptions enter in and to some extent obscure the person of God. And the essence of God is found in His power."

[104] "Dynamai," TDNT 2:299: "There can be no disputing the link with the OT and Jewish picture of the Messiah."

[105] Vos, "Antijudaismus/Antisemitismus," 89–110. See also the discussion by Rosen, "Familiarly Known as Kittel."

not join the Institute because he had reached higher levels of Reich propaganda, including Joseph Goebbels's Ministry of Propaganda and Walter Frank's Reich Institute for the History of the New Germany, with its special division on the "Jewish Question." In his work for those organizations, Kittel often brought along his former student and disciple, Karl Georg Kuhn. A nontenured instructor at Tübingen, where he had earned a doctorate and habilitation in Semitic philology and rabbinics during the same years that Grundmann was a student there, Kuhn had also trained in Talmud at the rabbinical seminary in Breslau in the late 1920s. A contributor of ten articles to the *Dictionary*, Kuhn was in charge of articles dealing with rabbinics. Kittel promoted his career, nominating him in 1938, along with Grundmann, for membership in the highly prestigious international Society for New Testament Studies (SNTS). Under Kittel's auspices, Kuhn translated and wrote an analysis of the tannaitic (early rabbinic) commentary on Numbers, Midrash Sifre, published in 1933 and reprinted in 1997. He had joined the Nazi Party in 1932 and was a member of the SA from 1933 to 1945. As Alan Steinweis has shown, Kuhn came to serve as an expert on Jewish matters for the Reich, writing a report in 1942 at the behest of the Racial Political Office of the Nazi Party (Rassenpolitischen Amtes der NSDAP), for example, determining whether the Karaites of Crimea were Jews who deserved extermination, and he gave frequent antisemitic lectures to Nazi propaganda groups.[106]

What is striking is the academic trajectory of Kuhn compared to that of Grundmann. Both were students of Kittel, contributors to the *Dictionary*, members of the SNTS, and avid antisemitic propagandists. Whereas Grundmann received a professorship during the Third Reich that he lost after 1945 thanks to his early Nazi Party membership, Kuhn, just as devout a Nazi and antisemite, did not receive a professorship until after the Third Reich. Grundmann defined his academic expertise as a scholar of the New Testament, particularly the Gospels, whereas Kuhn, who also trained in New Testament, presented himself as an expert on Judaism. Kuhn's alleged expertise on Judaism facilitated his position as propagandist during the Third Reich, but hindered an academic appointment, since none was available in the field of Judaic studies. After the war, however, Kuhn's career flourished, since few experts on Judaism were left in Germany. Although initially suspended in 1945 from his instructorship in Tübingen, Kuhn was exonerated by a denazification board in 1948, and in 1949 he was given a temporary appointment to a chair in New

[106] On Kuhn, see Steinweis, *Studying the Jew*, 76–91. On Kittel's involvement with the antisemitic institutes and journals sponsored by Walter Frank and Joseph Goebbels, see Ericksen, *Theologians under Hitler*, 34, 41, 67; Weinreich, *Hitler's Professors*.

Testament at the University of Göttingen in 1949; in 1954 he received a permanent professorship in New Testament at the University of Heidelberg. Promoting himself as a scholar of Judaism and concealing his Nazi collaboration, Kuhn became a respected authority on the Dead Sea Scrolls, and when he retired in 1971 he was presented with an academic Festschrift published in his honor.[107]

By contrast, Grundmann, who held a university professorship from 1936 to 1945, was relegated to a position at a Protestant seminary after the war. Because he lacked the training in rabbinics, Grundmann could not present himself as a scholar of Judaism like Kuhn. His antisemitic writings on Judaism were irrelevant to his postwar career: Grundmann lost his professorship because he had joined the Nazi Party at an early date—1930—not because he had been engaged in antisemitic propaganda. If anything, both Grundmann and Kuhn were aided by their Nazi-era propaganda efforts, since that work brought them to the wider attention of other scholars in their fields and allowed them vehicles for publication that created their reputations as productive scholars.[108] In neither case was the antisemitic nature of the propaganda promulgated by each man during the Third Reich a hindrance to his scholarly success and reputation.

GRUNDMANN'S EARLY CAREER

As academic director of the Institute, Grundmann combined scholarly training with political cunning. After completing the second set of required theological examinations in 1932 at the University of Leipzig, he was given a brief appointment by the Church of Saxony as vicar of a church in the rural village of Oberlichtenau, beginning on April 1, 1932. The village was so small that it was not served by rail, and required a thirty-minute walk to the closest train station. Several months after his appointment, he married Annelise Optiz, a fellow Tubingen student, the daughter of a professor of mathematics at the state academy in Chemnitz, Paul Opitz, who was close a friend of Grundmann's father and fellow member of the Lutheran community of Chemnitz. The two families had often celebrated family occasions together and took joint

---

[107] Jeremias, Kuhn, and Stegemann, *Tradition und Glaube; das frühe Christentum in seiner Umwelt: Festgabe für Karl Georg Kuhn zum 65. Geburtstag.*

[108] Steinweis (*Studying the Jew*, 91) has made the important observation that the Festschrift honoring Kuhn upon his retirement did not include the usual biography and bibliography of Kuhn's publications, no doubt in an effort to avoid mentioning his Nazi involvements.

vacations.[109] Grundmann remained as pastor in Oberlichtenau during the first year of his marriage, but he did not enjoy his work, due to the provinciality of the village.[110]

Grundmann was less than a year in Oberlichtenau when Hitler came to power. His first sermon after January 30, 1933, described Hitler as fulfilling Isaiah's eschatological promise.[111] The passionate emotions that many Germans experienced when Hitler came to power were given a theological meaning in a pamphlet, *Gott und Nation*, that Grundmann published in February of 1933, in which he aligned the goals of National Socialism with those of the church.[112] Race was an ordained part of God's creation (a theme that had been popularized in theological circles by Wilhelm Stapel[113]); National Socialism was restoring divine will by sounding the death knell of the French Revolution and its pernicious legacy of political equality, which had meant "the destruction of all authority and community . . . [and the denial of divinely created] distinctions between nation and Volk and race and clan and class and gender."[114] Present-day Germany had fallen into a "destructive racial chaos" that was a "sin against the natural order of völkisch life established by creation and divine will."[115] Hitler's achievement was to have created a true "cathedral" in Germany, and his power, Grundmann wrote, was derived from God:

> Everyone on first meeting [our Führer Adolf Hitler] shockingly recognizes: that is a completely pure man! All of us see it thus. In this man there is nothing disunited. He is in himself completely one, completely simple, clear and true. We also know that the power of such a clear and truthful man does not derive from the earth, but rather out of that higher world that the Master, Christ, called the kingdom of heaven. We also know from men

---

[109] Grundmann, *Erkenntnis und Wahrheit*, 11.

[110] According to Mrs. Annelise Grundmann, personal interview at Amrastrasse 37, Eisenach, February 24, 1993. Grundmann nonetheless continued his scholarly writing: Grundmann, "Rechtfertigung und Mystik," 52–65.

[111] The lectionary text was Isaiah 1:26 ("And I will restore your judges as at the first, and your counselors as at the beginning. Afterward you shall be called the city of righteousness, the faithful city"), and Grundmann spoke of a message of hope Grundmann, *Erkenntnis und Wahrheit*, 56.

[112] Grundmann writes in his curriculum vitae (UAJ) that he wrote the book in 1931; it was published two years later as *Gott und Nation: Ein evangelisches Wort zum Wollen des Nationalsozialismus und zu Rosenbergs Sinndeutung*.

[113] Wilhelm Stapel (1882–1954) subsequently joined the Institute. On Stapel, see Graf, "Wilhelm Stapel."

[114] Grundmann, *Gott und Nation*, 15.

[115] Ibid., 83.

who are close to the Führer that he knows of his inner connection with
God. He knows himself to be the instrument of God and has the clear,
simple trust in God of a man who—as the Bible puts it—is reconciled
with God. Some people have said to Adolf Hitler that a magic power radi-
ates from him. I do not know whether one ought to put it that way.
When one experiences this man for the first time, he certainly feels one
thing: the deep humility of the man which is at the same time completely
consistent with his higher commission. This oneness of man with his
God is a symbol of what the old church teachers intended to say with the
Trinity.[116]

The Institute's Aryan Jesus was not yet Grundmann's message in 1933, but
the dissociation of Jesus from Judaism was, and so, too, was his link between
first-century Jews and those of contemporary Germany. He argued that Jesus
was a messiah, but not in the Jewish sense; his was the God of the Old Testament, but not as Jews understood God; Jesus was fulfilling Old Testament
piety, but in a way that led the Jews to crucify him, evidence that they stand
under God's curse. [117] Responding to Alfred Rosenberg's challenge that Christianity was not compatible with German identity because its central teachings
were Jewish,[118] Grundmann asserted that Jesus was not a Jew but the son of
God. Nazi suspicion of the Church misunderstands, Grundmann wrote, the
connection between the New Testament message and Judaism.[119] Paul, too,
was "the sharpest fighter against judaizing tendencies within Christianity."[120]
The Jews today, he concluded, remained under divine judgment—"marked by
the curse of God" for having failed to recognize Jesus as the son of God and
for having had him crucified—thus rendering Nazi efforts to protect the nation from the Jews' continued "demoralizing and destructive" influence wholly
legitimate.[121] Thus it was "necessary" for National Socialism to be anti-Jewish
and to exclude Jews from the German Volk by creating a "Fremdenrecht" (law
governing foreigners) for Jews.[122]

---

[116] Grundmann, *Glaube und Volk*, 1933; cited by Zabel, *Nazism and the Pastors*, 139. Similar
tributes to Hitler as a divine savior are expressed by Grundmann in his article, "Die Neubesinnung der Theologie," 39–54.

[117] For example, he wrote, "Jesus understood himself as the messiah and rejected the Jewish
messianic ideal." Grundmann, *Gott und Nation*, 119 fn 57.

[118] Rosenberg, *Der Mythus des 20. Jahrhunderts*. On Rosenberg, see Piper, *Alfred Rosenberg*.

[119] Grundmann, *Gott und Nation*, 119 fn 57.

[120] Ibid., 65 fn 53.

[121] Ibid., 65 fn 53.

[122] Ibid., 29f.

Figure 4.1. Walter Grundmann, during the Third Reich.

GRUNDMANN AND THE GERMAN CHRISTIANS: ACHIEVING A
NATIONAL PLATFORM

The antisemitism and racist scholarship that characterized the Institute, as
well as its enthusiasm for Hitler and National Socialism, took root in individual regional Protestant churches through political machinations but also
through numerous publications—pamphlets, church newspapers, and statements of theological principles. Grundmann himself first attained power
within the church of Saxony, which had more Nazi Party members in 1933
than any other German state, and was one of the earliest strongholds of the
Nazi movement.[123] The German Christian movement was strong in Saxony,
and declared itself "for Luther and Hitler in the name of faith and the German
people." On July 1, 1933, one of its members, Friedrich Coch, was appointed
bishop in an illegal maneuver similar to German Christian coups occurring in
many of the regional churches.[124] Prior to his appointment, Coch had been the
local liaison for church affairs with the Nazi Party, and head of an association
of Nazi pastors. Upon becoming bishop, Coch immediately fired seven church
superintendents and fourteen pastors who had criticized the church's conciliatory efforts vis-à-vis the Nazis, one of whom was denounced to the Gestapo.[125]
Coch replaced them with German Christian lackeys, including Grundmann,
who came to Dresden on September 1 as Coch's assistant, and was appointed
Oberkirchenrat (church official) of Saxony on November 1.[126] This was
Grundmann's first major political appointment, and it led quickly to a role
within the church on the national level.

Together with Coch, Grundmann founded and edited a new monthly journal, *Christenkreuz und Hakenkreuz* (*Cross and Swastika*), and dominated its
voice.[127] The journal insisted on a racial approach to Christianity, assuring

[123] Szejnmann, "The Missing Pieces," 398.

[124] Fischer, *Die sächsische Landeskirche*, 17. For a description of the situation of the church in
Saxony from the perspective of the Confessing Church, see Klemm, *Ich konnte nicht zuschauer
bleiben.*

[125] Fischer, *Die sächsische Landeskirche*, 117 fn 180.

[126] See Klemm, *Im Dienst der Bekennenden Kirche: Das Leben des sächsischen Pfarrers Karl Fischer
1896–1941* (Göttingen 1986), 180, 184. According to Klemm, Grundmann had already begun to
work in the Saxony church headquarters on September 1, 1933.

[127] The journal changed its name in 1937 to *Deutsche Frömmigkeit* (*German Piety*), most likely
because of a Nazi Party prohibition instituted in 1936 against using the swastika without party
approval—a prohibition protested by numerous pastors who had hung the swastika next to the
cross on the church altar. Heschel, "Church Protests during the Third Reich," 377–88.

readers that Nazism was not opposed to Christianity but wished to deepen it; and, always, it presented Jews as dangerous racial enemies of Germany.[128] In a 1933 pamphlet, *Religion und Rasse*, which appeared in abbreviated form in *Christenkreuz und Hakenkreuz* the same year, Grundmann spoke of "the syphilization of our Volk through sexual relations, miscegenation, and the hybridization of races" that was destroying its cultural-building capacities. He lauded Hitler's recognition of racial mixing as a "sin against nature and as injustice against the Creator."[129] Although the church's mission was to bring the "message of God to the whole world, to all peoples, to all races, to all human beings," each church was to remain racially distinct, so that "Germanic-Nordic Christianity" would be "different from other races and peoples."[130] Christianity was not dangerous for Germans; on the contrary, he argued, the Germanic tribes had been in danger of dissolution when Christianity arrived: "Christianity made the Volk of the Germans into the Volk of history. . . . Christianity conveyed the power of historical assertiveness. There was therefore an inner necessity for the Christianization of the Germans."[131] But Grundmann hastened to add that his position did not imply that Jesus was a Jew: Jesus called himself "son of man," a title that, Grundmann wrote, was an "expression of old, above all Persian—and that means Aryan—hope for a redeemer and creator of a new humanity."[132]

Synthesizing Christianity and racism was increasingly at the center of Grundmann's writings in 1933, though he still claimed that Jesus was a divine figure and could therefore not be labeled an Aryan. In *Totale Kirche im Totalen Staat*, a pamphlet written in November 1933 as part of the nationwide festivities marking Martin Luther's 450th birthday, Grundmann presented Jesus as a "miraculous new creation of the living God," making his racial identity irrelevant:

> People have often asked in recent years if Jesus was a Jew or an Aryan. This question does not touch on the reality of Jesus Christ at all. Whoever asks it has absolutely not yet understood what Jesus Christ really is. We can only understand Jesus Christ truly, if we recognize him and pray to him as the

---

[128] See, for example, Hanche, "Christliche Frauengedanken über Nationalsozialismus"; Börner, "Der Reichsparteitag," 5–6. For a detailed review of Grundmann's articles in *Christenkreuz und Hakenkreuz*, see Deines, "Jesus der Galiläer," 43–133.

[129] Grundmann, *Religion und Rasse*, 8; cited by Adam, "Die theologische Werdegang," 175. See also Grundmann, "Die nationale Bewegung unter dem Wort Gottes," (1932/1933), 321–27.

[130] Grundmann, "Religion und Rasse," *Christenkreuz und Hakenkreuz* 1 (Nov./Dec. 1933).

[131] Grundmann, *Religion und Rasse*, 21–22.

[132] Ibid., 20.

miraculous new creation of the living God, beyond all racial connections. Whoever wants to be a Christian has to have the courage to believe in a miracle.[133]

To those concerned that faith in Jesus implied faith in a Jew, Grundmann offered reassurance that "the belief in [Jesus] means not . . . racial depravity [Rasseverderbnis], but rather the fulfillment of race [Rassevollendung]. The message of Christ doesn't make us un-German, but fulfills our Germanness. Therefore the German religion of the Volk cannot be an un-Christian, pagan religion, but German Christianity alone."[134] The pamphlet, whose cover pictures a large cross intertwined with a swastika, argued that Christianity receives fulfillment in National Socialism, with the state calling Germans as God calls his prophets.[135] Grundmann further declared that Hitler was instituting a "Divine Order," and that in National Socialism the actual presence of God could be perceived: "Here God Himself is dealing with the German people."[136]

The next month, Grundmann presented a set of principles for the German Christian movement, its first systematic theological statement, commissioned by Coch. The so-called "Twenty-Eight Theses" were presented to a German Christian–dominated church synod of Saxony by Grundmann on December 10, 1933, and were unanimously adopted—open debate was prohibited—and published on December 13 in the *Gesetz- und Verordnungsblatt* of the Saxony church.[137] The *Theses* called for a "Rassenkirche," a racial church whose members were united by their "blood and race." Thesis 3 differentiated baptized Jews from "members of the Volk" ("Volksgenossen"), according them guest status in the church and forbidding them from serving in synods and other governing bodies and from filling church offices.

The *Theses* spoke of race as "a law of God's creation" and miscegenation as "an offense against God's will," of the church's "experience of race" as the "foundation of becoming a Volk," and of the need for a German national Christianity based on "blood and race."[138] Jesus was neither Jew nor Aryan

[133] Grundmann, *Totale Kirche im totalen Staat*, 28.
[134] Ibid., 29.
[135] Ibid., 41.
[136] Ibid., 71. The pamphlet concludes with an an extended critique of Ernst Bergmann, the Leipzig philosopher who had rejected Christianity as the source of Germany's misfortunes.
[137] Published as Grundmann, *Acht und zwanzig Thesen der sächsischen Volkskirche zum inneren Aufbau der deutschen evangelischen Kirche* (*Twenty-Eight Theses of the Volks Church of Saxony for the Inner Reconstruction of the German Protestant Church*). For a description of the synod, see Fischer, *Die sächsische Landeskirche*, 24f, and Adam, "Der theologische Werdegang W. Grundmanns."
[138] The text of the *Theses* appears in English translation in Conway, *Nazi Persecution of the Churches*, 353–57. See also Adam, "Der theologische Werdegang W. Grundmanns," 182.

because he was not human but "reveals in his person God's personality."[139] The *Theses* called for a church within the state, making Coch's recent actions—firing dissenting pastors and non-Aryans from the church—entirely legal and equating loyalty to church and state. The language used in the *Theses* combined traditional Protestant statements of faith with Nazi language and racial concepts: "The Volk Church confesses its faith in blood and race"; the verb "confess" (sich bekennen) comes from classical Christian doctrinal creeds. Indeed, there are "twenty-eight" articles of the classic Augsburg Confession of 1530, which forms the basis of all Lutheran denominations, and, like them, Grundmann's theses were written in the past tense, as if they had always been the guiding principles of the church.[140] While some objections were raised—by the theological faculty of Leipzig, for example, and by the Pastors' Fraternity (Pfarrbruderschaft) of the Rhineland[141]—the objections were primarily against the process of implementing the *Theses*. The Berlin theological faculty expressed approval, though not without dissenting voices,[142] and those regional churches that were under German Christian control adopted the *Theses*, including Braunschweig, Mecklenburg, Oldenburg, and Schleswig-Holstein.

With the *Theses*, Grundmann transformed himself from a pastor to a nationally recognized theologian.[143] In the *Theses* there was no conflict between Nazi racial politics and the traditional theological claims of Christianity that all human beings were equal in God's eyes. Theologically, Grundmann made Christian experience the foundation of National Socialism, and Nazism the fulfillment of Christianity. God's order of creation was intended to be racially ordered, finally brought into being by Hitler, and the belief in blood and race, taught by Christian faith, was the basis of the National Socialist state. Thus, at a German Christian rally in Jena on April 19, 1934, attended by 800 to 900 people, including large contingents of Hitler Youth and German Girls, the notorious racial theorist Hans F. K. Günther was invited to speak on "The Racial Hygiene of the German People and Christianity."[144] Talk of racial cleansing was not enough; some German Christian pastors wanted to be actively

---

[139] Conway, *Nazi Persecution of the Churches*, 356.

[140] Hahn, *Kämpfer wider Willen*, 41.

[141] See Gerlach (*Als die Zeugen schwiegen*, 122), who judges the Leipzig faculty response as weak. In June 1934, the Pfarrbruderschaft of the Rhineland published a response against the *Theses*; see *Junge Kirche* 2 (1934), 494–98.

[142] Seven-page statement from Reinhold Seeberg, representing the theological faculty in Berlin, dated February 8, 1934 (NEK DC1, Allgemeines, Landesleitung, 1934/35). The responses are discussed by Meier, *Kirche und Judentum*, 25; Meier, *Die theologischen Fakultäten*, 383–85.

[143] Adam, "Der theologische Werdegang W. Grundmanns," 188.

[144] Ernst Koch, "Thüringer Wege," 90.

Figure 4.2. Cross and swastika adorn the nave of the Christuskirche in Hamburg-Wandsbeck in 1940. The overhead motto reads, "Our faith is the victory."

involved in the forced sterilization program and began to arrange training for pastors in selecting victims.

In 1935, Walter Schmidt, a Thuringian pastor in Bad Sulza, wrote a private letter to Thuringian church leaders, observing that Germans were becoming afraid to consult their physicians, out of fear they would be turned over for sterilization. He suggested that the church could fulfill a needed function by training pastors to recognize those who ought to be sterilized. For that purpose, a seminar for pastors was organized at the Harnack House in Berlin on February 5–7, 1935, during which they received instruction in methods of detecting potential candidates for sterilization from some of the leading figures in racial hygiene, including Eugen Fischer, Otmar Freiherr von Verschuer, Leonardo Conti, Wolfgang Abel, Julius Friedrich Lehmann, and Friedrich Burgdörfer.[145] The seminar was designed to train pastors in the practical work of racial hygiene. Ultimately, according to a report sent to the regional church council of Thuringia about the seminar by Schmidt, the plan was to have pastors take part in the Erbgesundheitsgericht, the special Nazi court determining who would be forcibly sterilized. The theologians who joined the Institute may have had a similar desire to transform their antisemitic rhetoric into action, to take a role themselves in the eradication of the Jews.

During the first years of Grundmann's career, prior to his appointment to a professorship at the University of Jena, he achieved a leadership position within the church as a voice of enthusiasm for the Nazi regime. His passion for Hitler, whom he viewed as sent by God, was combined with an unquestioning affirmation of racial principles. His Christology, as late as the end of 1933, continued to affirm Jesus as more than human and hence beyond the reach of racial definition; he was neither Jew nor Aryan. Only later did Grundmann introduce a more sophisticated reinterpretation of Christian origins, according to which Jesus sought the destruction of Judaism, while the Jews of his day sought his annihilation. Assertions of Jewish degeneracy and violence, both in antiquity and in the present day, grew increasingly prominent in Grundmann's writings as the Nazis took harsher action against the Jews, particularly after 1938.

Antisemitism remained constant within Grundmann's writings, fed in part by denunciations of Bolsheviks as Jews, at least prior to the 1939 Molotov-

---

[145] Schmidt's letter is dated February 14, 1935 (LKA Eisenach A920: Akten des Landeskirchenrats der Ev.-Luth. Kirche in Thüringen über Eugenik und Rassenhygiene 1933/51, vol. 1). Fritz Lenz was scheduled to speak, but did not attend. The topics of the lectures ranged from "Racial Hygiene in the Racial State" (Conti) to "Heritability of Psychic Qualities" (Fischer) and "Heritability of Illnesses" (Verschuer). The archives do not indicate the number of pastors who attended the seminar, nor whether they all came from Thuringia.

Ribbentrop Pact, and by insistence on the greatness of the German race and its Teutonic traditions. Whatever the metaphor, the message remained the same: Germans stood in utter opposition to Jews and would avenge their murder of Jesus and purify their corruption of the Christian message.

A remarkable description exists of one of Grundmann's 1936 speeches at a German Christian rally in the woods in Saxony:[146] "After singing an old hymn, 'Wer jetzig Zeiten leben will' ['Who wants to live in current times'], with militaristic overtones,[147] there came a hushed pause, and then jubilant applause broke out to welcome the leader of the local German Christian district, Comrade Dr. Grundmann." Grundmann then narrated a heroic history, of how the German people were transformed under the Saxon king Heinrich I (876–936) into a Reich Volk (people of the German nation) by repelling barbarian invasions of Slavs and Magyars from the East. Today the Germans would rise and restore their heroic history; while Jesus may have fallen victim to the Jews, Germans would now avenge his death and destroy the enemy that pursued all Germans. "Once again," concluded Grundmann, "there is an assault against the West, unleashed by the Bolsheviks of the world, behind whom stands the Jew, and the Germans are once again the Reich Volk. . . . Our Volk has been chosen to halt the avalanche of the Bolsheviks and the Jews on behalf of the entire West—and therefore in its deepest sense the word receives its meaning: the German Volk are the Anti-Jews [Gegenvolk der Juden]!"

CONCLUSION

Given their diverse ages, career stages, and areas of research, Institute members were a group of academics who might not have come together if not for Grundmann and his energetic leadership of the Institute; he was its backbone and driving engine. Directing the Institute solidified his own career and influence in the absence of original scholarly research, making him widely known and respected within his field, a recognition that assured his career after the war as well. Grundmann's academic trajectory was entirely politicized, both during and after the Third Reich: thanks to his Nazi propaganda writings, he rose to the top of church hierarchies in Saxony and Thuringia and received a

---

[146] *Christenkreuz und Hakenkreuz*, 9 (September 1936): 11–12.

[147] Wer jetzig Zeiten leben will   Whoever wants to live today
Muß habn ein tapfers Herze,   Must have a brave heart
Es sein der argen Feind so viel   There are so many wicked enemies
Bereiten ihm groß Schmerze.   Ready to give him monumental pain.

tenured professorship in theology at the University of Jena despite never having written a habilitation thesis. Through the Institute, he had funds to pay for conferences and publications of selected colleagues, tools for extending his ideological agenda to the academic world, and the academic prestige to win power within the ecclesiastical realm.

Professors, instructors, and students who joined the Institute came from diverse backgrounds, but all benefited from the opportunities for lecturing and publishing provided by the Institute. Meeting colleagues and exchanging ideas was valuable to building an academic career, and the sense that political enhancement might also be achieved was certainly enticing. Members hoped for recognition within the Third Reich, but received it even after the Reich was defeated. Once having been involved in a church-related "research" institute dealing with Jews and Judaism, Institute members found it easy after the war to conceal its antisemitic intentions and present themselves as experts on Judaism. The connections they made with colleagues via the Institute were used to establish academic credentials, often by submitting a doctoral dissertation to the theological faculty at the University of Jena, which was dominated by Institute members, as will be discussed in the next chapter. In addition, Institute colleagues helped one another escape punitive sanctions after the war by writing letters attesting to each other's anti-Nazi credentials, as will be shown in chapter 6.

Indeed, had the theologians who joined the Institute been motivated primarily by a desire for careerist self-promotion or a wish to curry favor with Nazi authorities, they would have broadened their support for Nazi racial politics. Instead, the racism of the German Christian movement and of the Institute's own propaganda was limited to attacks on Jews and did not extend to the handicapped, people of color, Roma and Sinti, or other groups targeted in various ways by the Nazis. While that disparity might indicate the difficulty in mustering Christian theological arguments in support of racial attacks against those groups, in contrast to Jews, most importantly it demonstrates that the German Christians' enthusiasm for Nazism did not bring them to racism in general; rather, their theological anti-Judaism brought them to support National Socialism because of its antisemitism.

The Faculty of Theology at the University of Jena

AUTHORSHIP OF THE *Twenty-Eight Theses* had catapulted Grundmann into a national figure within the German Christian movement, even as his base within Saxony began to deteriorate. Coch was demoted in the fall of 1935 and the church of Saxony underwent a reorganization. In order to find a new institutional base for his activities, Grundmann entered into negotiations to unite the German Christians of Saxony and Thuringia. The Thuringian German Christians, known as the Kirchenbewegung Deutsche Christen (KDC), had been founded as an organization of pastors and teachers by Leffler and Leutheuser when they settled in the Werra Valley of rural western Thuringia. Negotiations between Grundmann and the KDC led to an alliance at the end of June 1936, and Grundmann brought 30,000 members of Saxony's German Christian movement into coalition with the KDC under the leadership of Leffler and Leutheuser.[1] Leffler, who held a position in the Thuringian Ministry of Education, enhanced Grundmann's stature by facilitating his appointment in 1936 as an instructor in theology at the prestigious and historic University of Jena, a self-proclaimed bastion of National Socialism. There he joined two other professors, also Nazi Party members, who became active members of the Institute. Together they transformed the curriculum according to Institute ideology, encouraging students to join the Institute and present their "research" at Institute conferences.

As professor in the University of Jena's theological faculty, Grundmann was able to forge an alliance between the Institute and the larger world of academic scholarship in the field of theology. Several members of the Institute were able to receive doctorates at Jena, and the Institute offered significant assistance by publishing many of the dissertations by Jena students and offering them an opportunity to present their research at Institute conferences. Grundmann's professorship was essential to giving academic legitimacy to the Institute and its dejudaization of Christianity, which was presented not as theological propaganda, but as the necessary conclusion of theological scholarship. Together with two of his faculty colleagues at Jena, Wolf Meyer-Erlach, professor

[1] Meier, *Die Deutschen Christen*, 153ff.

of practical theology, and Heinz Eisenhuth, professor of systematic theology, who became active collaborators in the Institute, Grundmann also reconfigured the theological faculty along Institute principles. The curriculum of courses and the topics of students' doctoral dissertations reflected the anti-doctrinal History of Religions methods, permeated with racial, antisemitic premises that Grundmann and many of his Institute colleagues promoted. History of Religions, in contrast to theology, was a discipline uninterested in the normative Christian doctrine of canonical texts, sanctioned by church authorities, instead viewing all data of an era, textual and otherwise, as historical evidence.

Thus, History of Religions opened the possibility of a radically revised interpretation of Jesus's message that would see it not as fulfilling God's promises, as contained in the (Jewish) Old Testament, but reflecting ancient Near Eastern and Asian ideas, some of which were then claimed to be Aryan in origin. The transformed theological faculty at Jena became the German Christians' model for a revised theological curriculum that they attempted to implement Reich-wide. The new curriculum's impact was carried beyond the Third Reich to the postwar years as Nazi-era students became pastors, teachers, scholars, and popular writers in the divided Germanys after 1945. The professors and students at Jena thus joined with other German academics to become, as the historian Dirk Rupnow writes, "less prophesiers of genocide than profiteers of genocidal politics."[2]

The success of the theological faculty in becoming a self-proclaimed bastion of National Socialism was similar to that of other nazified faculties of the Friedrich Schiller University at Jena and marked one of the Institute's central goals: a reconfiguration of the theological curriculum and scholarship.[3] Although the Institute was not able to establish its offices at the university, as Grundmann had wished, he had the support of his professorial colleagues at Jena as well as his German Christian colleagues who held powerful positions in the Thuringian Education Ministry and the church hierarchy. The Institute's anti-Jewish goals were translated into the Jena theological curriculum: Hebrew was no longer required of students; History of Religions methods were substituted for theology; and racial theory was made an essential tool of interpretation. Meyer-Erlach insisted that prior to their examinations, students had to have read *Mein Kampf*

---

[2] Rupnow, "Judenforschung als Musealisierungsstrategie," paper delivered at the German Studies Association meeting in New Orleans, October 2003.

[3] On the university during the Third Reich, see Gottwald and Steinbach, eds., *Zwischen Wissenschaft und Politik*, and Hossfeld et al., eds., *Kämpferische Wissenschaft*.

and the writings of Alfred Rosenberg.[4] Theological doctrine was replaced by a History of Religions approach that allowed principles of Volk and race to be the hermeneutical tools for distinguishing between acceptable sources of Germanic religiosity and those to be discarded as non-Aryan. Systematic theology was to investigate the power of the gospels in shaping pious German life within the völkisch orders of creation, rather than elaborate points of doctrine, and church history became the history of the faith of Germans rather than the history of Christianity. The transformation at Jena occurred largely through the unstinting efforts of Grundmann, Eisenhuth, and Meyer-Erlach, but their power was assured thanks to the cooperation of a fourth, Karl Heussi, whose ostensible "neutrality" facilitated their empowerment.

Jena in German Intellectual History

That the theological faculty at Jena was nazified so easily is due, in part, to its intellectual heritage as a site of avant-garde liberal scholarship, which is how the Institute, too, presented its work. Indeed, while the theological faculty at Jena was quite small, it had a distinguished scholarly heritage and had long been considered one of the centers of liberal theological scholarship in Germany. Jena had been one of Germany's most prominent and influential universities in the eighteenth and early-nineteenth centuries for its freedom of thought, and it retained that reputation in the twentieth.[5] When Heinrich Steffens, later a noted philosopher, first arrived at the University of Jena in the summer of 1798, he felt he had arrived at "the real centre of intellectual life in Germany."[6] During the six months he was there, Steffens came to know Schiller, Goethe, Fichte, and August Schlegel, and wrote that "[w]hat made those times so delightful at Jena was the unity which prevailed among all those founders of a new school of literature. . . . They all felt that they had a common work to do, and that they could do it together."[7]

The sense of being at the intellectual vanguard prevailed in the theological faculty from the nineteenth century to the 1930s. From 1829 to 1890, theological studies at Jena were shaped by one of the great scholars of historical theology in his day, New Testament scholar and historian of Christianity Karl

---

[4] See the report of the head of the Reich Security Service, dated October 1, 1942, to the German Foreign Office, including an undated and unsigned "Report on Prof. Dr. Meyer-Erlach" (Politisches Archiv des Auswärtigen Amts, Berlin, Inland I D, R 98796, 1949).

[5] Howard, *Religion and the Rise of Historicism*, 27.

[6] Steffens, *The Story of My Career as Student and Professor*, 24.

[7] Ibid., 53.

von Hase (1800–1890).[8] At the outset of his professional life, in the 1830s, he was perceived as a maverick, though by the end he had become an old-fashioned figure who hindered the careers of younger, avant-garde scholars. His role in blocking the professorship of the renowned historian of religion Adolf Hilgenfeld (1823–1907) is a case in point. Hilgenfeld, one of the first to apply History of Religions methods to the study of Christian origins, was forced to remain an instructor until von Hase's death, when he was finally accorded a professorship in 1890, at age 67, more than thirty years after the publication of his first important book, *Die jüdische Apokalyptik*, in 1857.[9]

The university's theology faculty was the smallest of the seventeen Protestant theological faculties in Germany and never as prestigious as those of Berlin or Tübingen. Yet its size was a positive factor in attracting students who wanted the opportunity to have informal exchange with faculty.[10] Jena had only five tenured professorships in theology, out of a total in Germany of more than a hundred (126 in 1931, 103 in 1938).

After the number of theology students reached its high point in 1885 at Jena, with 148 students, it declined sharply to 37 in 1897, growing slowly to 57 in 1906.[11] Giving a boost to the faculty, the Protestant church of Thuringia began to require its candidates for the ministry to study at Jena in the 1930s. The transformation of the faculty, and the university more broadly, into a Nazi stronghold occurred early and forcefully, facilitated by a smooth collaboration with state government officials and with church authorities, and, no doubt, influenced by the temper of the region.[12]

NAZIFICATION OF THE FACULTY

As early as the mid-1920s, students had taken the lead in promoting Jena's nazification, as they had on so many other university campuses. By 1926, the University of Jena's Nazi student organization was stronger and more

---

[8] Von Hase was involved in founding and editing the journal *Protestantische Kirchenzeitung für das evangelische Deutschland*, 1854–96, which became the major organ of theological liberalism.

[9] Heussi, *Geschichte der theologischen Fakultät zu Jena*, 294 fn 558: "Within the faculty it was above all Hase who, until his death in 1890, prevented Hilgenfeld's tenured professorship. The reason for this position was—according to a very reliable orally transmitted tradition—essentially aesthetic: Hase wanted to prevent Hilgenfeld from being appointed rector. So he [Hilgenfeld] was not appointed full professor until he was 67 years old and then naturally could no longer become rector."

[10] Private interview with Hans-Joachim Thilo in Lübeck, Germany, July 20, 1995.

[11] Heussi, *Geschichte der theologischen Fakultät zu Jena*, 403.

[12] Werner, *Moderne in der Provinz*.

representative of the student body than at any other major German university.[13] During the Third Reich, students at Jena, as at other universities, were in the forefront of promoting racial theory, and the theology students at Jena were no less engaged in this endeavor than their counterparts in the science and social science disciplines.[14] Not coincidentally, Jena also had fewer Jewish students, both in numbers and as a percentage of its student body, than most other major German universities. In 1928, Jewish students constituted less than four percent of the German university student body, but at Jena they were less than one half of one percent of the total student body.[15]

Jena's theology students, in particular, were enthusiastic Nazi supporters, consistent with patterns across the country. Throughout Germany, students of theology were disproportionately represented in Nazi student groups by 1930, especially at north German universities.[16] By the summer of 1934, twenty percent of Germany's theology students were members of the NSDAP, compared to twenty-five percent of students in law and medicine.[17] But in 1935, the SS closed its membership to theology students and pastors, and the SA, Hitler Youth, and other organizations followed suit in 1937, which affected the ability of theology students to receive educational stipends.[18] Jena students of theology, however, retained their devotion to Nazism; while only a minority of theology students throughout the Reich became members of the German Christian movement, most of Jena's theology students were.[19] Nazi students attacked professors who were Jews, communists, or socialists, but since there were no Jewish or communist professors of theology, and few with open socialist commitments, the conflict in the theological faculties focused on whether Christianity could coexist with National Socialism.

The German professoriate, for its part, was won over to the Nazi cause more slowly. It was unusual to find a German professor prior to the March 1933 Reichstag election holding membership in the NSDAP, let alone publicizing

---

[13] Zimmermann, *Die medizinische Fakultät der Universität Jena*, 71. For a more general overview of German students and the Nazi Party, see Giles, *Students and National Socialism in Germany*.

[14] Noakes, "The Ivory Tower under Siege," 371.

[15] Zimmermann, *Die medizinische Fakultät*, 79f. Grüttner gives the figure at 0.6%, p. 495. Jena, Münster, and Tübingen were the universities with the lowest percentages of Jewish students, while the highest percentages were found at Berlin, Frankfurt, and Heidelberg. See Grüttner, *Studenten im Dritten Reich*, 495.

[16] Grüttner, *Studenten*, 53. Grüttner notes that within the membership of the NSDStB, a Nazi student organization, Protestant theologians were disproportionately represented. See Kater, *Studentenschaft und Rechtsradikalismus*, 122f and 212f.

[17] Zimmermann, *Die medizinische Fakultät*, 80.

[18] Grüttner, *Studenten*, 442

[19] Grüttner, *Studenten*, 436.

that fact.[20] That, in turn, reflected a long-standing aloofness of the German professoriate toward the public sphere and politics. After March 1933, the political situation of the professoriate changed dramatically. A large number of German academics emigrated—3,120, of whom 756 were full professors—between 1933 and 1938,[21] and since most held dissident views, their migration made nazification simpler. At Jena there were few Jews on the faculty; with the passage of the Reich's "Law for the Reinstatement of the Professional Civil Service" in April 1933, the so-called "non-Aryan" professors at Jena lost their positions, even as a series of racial theorists were appointed.[22]

Theology was affected far less than other fields by emigration, since none of its professors and instructors were Jews and few were labeled non-Aryan.[23] While national figures of Nazi Party membership for faculty members in theology are not available, the numbers are startling at the University of Berlin, where over seventy percent of the tenured theology professoriate were party members, compared to only twenty-eight percent of those in medicine and sixty percent of those in law.[24] Party membership among theologians was at least comparable to other faculties, if not higher.[25] Most faculty appointments after 1936 required Nazi Party membership. Both the Enabling Act and the Aryan Paragraph stimulated public declarations of support for the NSDAP by German university professors, who participated in the ongoing Nazi process of coordinating German institutions and culture with the National Socialist state "from below, from above, and from inside the faculty" starting in May of 1933.[26] Almost immediately, professors established research institutes at their universities with Nazi-related themes; Jena became a center for such research, with institutes of racial theory in several academic departments.[27] The curriculum

---

[20] Faust, "Professoren für die NSDAP," 31–49, cited by Muller, *The Other God That Failed*, 230 fn 27.

[21] Noakes, The *Ivory Tower under Siege*, 379.

[22] Hoßfeld, John, and Stutz, "Weaving Networks."

[23] For a list of the names of non-Aryans expelled from the University of Jena, see Schmidt, ed., *Alma mater Jenensis*, 287–88.

[24] Hellmut Seier, "Die Hochschullehrerschaft," 247–95.

[25] Wolgast, "Nationalsozialistische Hochschulpolitik," 78.

[26] Muller, *The Other God That Failed*, 227, 231.

[27] For example, Konrad Meyer, a specialist in Nazi agriculture directed Jena's Ackerbau- und Pflanzenbauinstitut starting in 1934; Richard Lange, an expert in criminal law who wrote a commentary on the Nuremberg Race laws, joined the faculty in 1938; Werner Gerlach, a pathologist at the University's medical faculty, served on Himmler's personal staff. Falk Ruttke was appointed in 1940 as a specialist in "Rasse und Recht," becoming director in 1942 of the Institut für Rasse und Recht; and Bernhard Kummer became director in 1942 of the Nordisches Seminar. Schmidt, ed.,

Figure 5.1. Hitler with Hans F. K. Günther at the University of Jena in 1930.

throughout the faculties at Jena was impregnated with racist concepts.[28] All this was encouraged by the presence on the faculty of one of Germany's most notorious racial theorists, Hans F. K. Günther, appointed at Hitler's orders to a professorship in social anthropology at Jena in 1930, which he held until 1935, when he moved to Berlin.

Günther's professorship initially was not welcomed by most of the Jena faculty and occasioned protest from the German League for Human Rights, which included thirty-one professors as members.[29] The rector at the time was Heussi, who protested that the faculty senate had not been asked to vote on

---

Alma mater Jenensis, 291–92. Members of the medical faculty were able to work at Buchenwald concentration camp. See Bruhn and Böttner, "Studieren in Jena 1933 bis 1945," 107–22.

[28] The Law Faculty, for example, offered courses on "Volk und Rasse," "politische Volkskunde," and "Bevölkerungspolitik." The Institute for Biology turned itself almost entirely into a race faculty, offering studies in "Menschliche Züchtungslehre" and "Vererbungsforschung," taught above all by Karl Astel, who was appointed rector of the university in 1936.

[29] Saller, *Die Rassenlehre des Nationalsozialismus*, 27.

Günther's appointment. Günther was criticized for lacking a habilitation, for being trained in philology and not anthropology or racial science, for lacking scholarly originality in his writings—but not for his racism. The mathematical–natural science faculty as a whole concluded that he lacked the credentials for the appointment.[30] He also had defenders on the faculty, such as Ludwig Plate, professor of zoology, who noted Günther's success in "opening the eyes of thousands to racial difference."[31] Remarkably, these faculty debates never addressed the question of whether a professorship in racial hygiene or the ideological direction of Günther's work was appropriate for a university professorship.[32] Instead, the faculty was preoccupied with its usual concerns—the scholarly qualifications of the candidate, and protecting its prerogatives against state intervention in faculty appointments.

Despite the protests, Günther was appointed as tenured professor of social anthropology on October 1, 1930, just as his book, *Rassenkunde des jüdischen Volkes* (*Race Studies of the Jewish Volk*), was published. Six weeks later, amidst great fanfare, he delivered his inaugural lecture. At Jena, as at other German universities, inaugural lectures were formal events which traditionally reflected on the state of the academy, on the nature of the university and scholarship. Günther's inaugural lecture, delivered on November 15, 1930, discussed "The Causes of the Racial Deterioration of the German Volk since the Period of Migration of Volks." In attendance were Hitler, Hermann Göring, Wilhelm Frick (Minister of the Interior for Thuringia), Fritz Sauckel (Nazi Party district leader for Thuringia and Nazi deputy in the Thuringia Diet) and other Nazi leaders. It was the first and last time Hitler visited a university.[33] There were large demonstrations by students in support of Günther the night before his lecture, with fifteen hundred marching through the streets of Jena carrying Nazi flags.[34] Günther's presence as professor at the university made a clear statement about the direction faculty research was now expected to proceed.[35]

[30] Zimmermann, *Die medizinische Fakultät*, 17.

[31] Ibid., 16.

[32] Ibid., 17.

[33] Heiber, *Universität unterm Hakenkreuz*, 396 and 583; Schüfer, "Die theologische Fakultät der Friedrich-Schiller-Universität Jena," 2. For details concerning Günther's appointment by Frick, see Lutzhöft, *Der nordische Gedanke*, 36–41.

[34] Stutz, "Die NSDAP in Jena."

[35] In addition to Günther, two other notorious antisemitic writers were also appointed to professorships at Jena in 1930, Paul Schultz-Naumburg and Hans-Severus Ziegler. Steinweis, *Studying the Jew*.

The study of race undertaken by faculty at the university was not simply theoretical; professors played central roles in the racial programs undertaken by the state of Thuringia. In July 1933 Sauckel, the NSDAP's governor of Thuringia,[36] established a Thuringian State Agency for Racial Measures, whose president was Karl Astel, professor of medicine at the University of Jena and its rector from 1939 to 1945.[37] The purpose of the agency was to register the hereditary records of all the citizens of Thuringia. In response to a 1933 Law for the Protection of Congenitally Diseased Offspring, the agency collected names of persons suspected of inherited illnesses; by December 1934, 330,000 names had been collected.[38] Astel secured his power not only through his friendly relations with Sauckel and Himmler, but also through his power as university rector. At the agency, he granted proof of Aryan or non-Aryan identity to Germans, new immigrants, and even babies who were candidates for adoption.[39] Astel used his political position to secure research funds. For example, he proposed to Himmler in 1937 a program to exterminate criminals, hoping thereby to secure funds for a research project in eugenics at the university that involved 4,600 prisoners in Thuringia.[40] Thuringia's Race Agency was part of a larger effort by Nazi officials to alter the nature of the Rhine valley population of Hessen and Thuringia through racial measures; 14,000 citizens of Thuringia were sterilized from 1933 to 1943.[41] Similarly, when the euthanasia program was initiated by the Reich in the fall of 1939, another University of Jena faculty member, Berthold Kihn, a professor of pediatrics, was appointed director of a children's euthanasia center in Stadtroda, a town near Jena.[42]

[36] Sauckel joined the NSDAP in 1923. In 1925 he was made district manager of the Nazi Party in Thuringia and two years later he was appointed district leader From 1927 to 1933 he was an NSDAP deputy in the Thuringian diet and the leader of its legislative faction after 1930. Appointed Thuringian Minister of the Interior in August 1932 and Governor in May 1933, Sauckel was elected to represent the district in the Reichstag in November 1933. An honorary SA General and SS General without function, Sauckel was responsible during the Third Reich for mobilizing German and foreign workers for the Wehrmacht war machine. He was convicted of war crimes at Nuremburg and hanged in 1946.

[37] Astel had held a chair in the medical faculty in "human breeding and hereditary research" since 1934. He joined the NSDAP in July 1930, was an SS-Hauptsturmführer. See Aly, Chroust, and Pross, *Cleansing the Fatherland*. See also Hohmann, *Landvolk unterm Hakenkreuz*.

[38] Peter, "Landesamt für Rassewesen," 323.

[39] Ibid., 325.

[40] Aly, Chroust, and Pross, *Cleansing the Fatherland*, 70–71. See also Hohmann, *Landvolk unterm Hakenkreuz*.

[41] Hohmann, *Landvolk unterm Hakenkreuz*.

[42] Hoßfeld, John, and Stutz, "Weaving Networks," 202.

THEOLOGICAL FACULTY

Theology students and faculty were not actively involved in sterilization or euthanasia efforts, and their racism targeted the traditional enemy of the church, the Jews, not Aryans labeled handicapped or genetically impaired. Their absence from the biopolitics of National Socialism is surprising, given the widespread engagement with those efforts by other members of the university faculty, but it should not be interpreted as the theologians' lack of enthusiasm for Nazism. Rather, they found the fulcrum at which Nazism and Christianity met: antisemitism.

At Jena, the first major confrontation between the theological faculty and the Nazis occurred in 1931. Eric Fascher had just arrived at Jena as a tenured professor of New Testament in 1930, and was a member of the German Christian movement. During the summer semester of 1931, he delivered a series of lectures on "Race and Religion in Biblical Elucidation," during which he criticized Alfred Rosenberg's claim that Christianity was incompatible with Nazism. A student, Wolfgang Geibel, filed accusations against him with the Thuringian Education Minister, Stier, accusing Fascher of insulting Nazi theology students.[43] A student protest flyer accused Fascher of insulting the German and Christian values of millions of Germans. Geibel's protests led the theological faculty to issue a statement of support for Fascher that was adopted by the faculty senate on July 18, 1931.[44] Geibel then wrote an article in the student newspaper, presenting himself as the victim of Fascher's sarcasm.[45] Geibel was given a warning, but not expelled from the university, and in publishing his article, he brought the conflict into public view. The case is not unique to Jena or the field of theology, and illustrates the "street power" of students to disrupt classes and threaten the careers of established professors. Fascher was protected for the moment, but his situation changed within a few years.

While the first three years of the Nazi regime saw a striking activism on the part of university students, reflected in Jena's theological faculty as well, students who entered the university after 1935 tended to be less politically active on campus.[46] Student life at Jena changed: more women enrolled, while the number of male students dropped; the economic conditions for students wors-

---

[43] Letter from Geibel to Stier, undated (UAJ: Theologische Fakultät. Disziplinarfälle von Studenten betr. 1927–37 J 289).

[44] UAJ J 289.

[45] *Nachrichtenblatt für die Studentenschaft der Universität Jena*, dated July 18, 1931 (UAJ J 289), 50.

[46] Bruhn and Böttner, "Studieren in Jena 1933 bis 1945," 108.

ened; soldiers took courses through correspondence; starting in 1942, students were required to undertake volunteer work during vacations, though they did so reluctantly.[47] The war and its draft also resulted in lower student enrollment, and the general militaristic mood, as well as a cultural contempt for the churches, further contributed to a drop in the number of students in theology.

The nazification of the theological professoriate at Jena was made possible by a three-way institutional collaboration between Thuringian church officials, state government officials, and Jena's students and theology faculty members. The Thuringian branch of the German Christian movement, led by two pastors, Julius Leutheuser and Siegfried Leffler, who subsequently became pivotal in establishing the Institute, ensured that Jena's theology faculty would be quickly nazified. Leffler, as an official in the Thuringian Ministry of Education, wanted to replace all theology professors with scholars who had German Christian sympathies.[48] His first major interference in the theology faculty at Jena involved the demotion of Waldemar Macholz from tenured professor of practical theology to an untenured professor of "Study of Beliefs and Related Disciplines" ("Konfessionskunde und verwandte Fächer"), and his replacement in the tenured post with Leffler's old friend, Wolf Meyer-Erlach, a Bavarian pastor, in November 1933.[49] Leffler had a long-standing personal conflict with Macholz, stemming from a failing grade Macholz had given him in his second theological examination years earlier.[50] Similar action was taken against Paul Glaue, whose nontenured position in practical theology was redefined, as of the winter semester of 1933–34, as " Religious Volk Studies, Thuringian Church History, Missiology, and History of Church Music." Neither Macholz nor Glaue held positions in Nazi organizations.

Meyer-Erlach was little more than a Nazi propagandist and had no academic qualifications. He had written neither a doctoral dissertation nor a habilitation thesis, but he was an enthusiastic Nazi who joined the party in 1933.[51] Born in 1891 in Bavaria, he studied theology at Erlangen and then

---

[47] Ibid., 108–10.

[48] "We demand that teaching positions that are open and going to become open in the coming years should be filled with theologians of our direction until only German Christians will be active." Statement in the journal *Evangelium in Dritten Reich*, May 7, 1933, cited by Meier, *Die theologischen Fakultäten*, 150.

[49] The opening was not announced, nor were other candidates considered. Macholz's demotion lasted until the winter of 1939, when he was severed from the university. Raschzok, "Wolf Meyer-Erlach und Hans Asmussen," 174.

[50] Schäfer, "Die Theologische Fakultät Jena," 95.

[51] Meyer-Erlach joined the NSDAP, on May 1, 1933, receiving membership number 3135571, and retained that membership until March 20, 1945; on February 2, 1934, he joined the NSLB;

Tübingen, becoming a pastor in 1911, and served in the military from 1914 to 1916, when he was wounded. After World War I he became involved in a variety of right-wing activities. In 1916 his pastor's residence in Bavaria served as a munitions depot for the Freikorps, a paramilitary group of World War I veterans with right-wing and antisemitic tendencies that agitated against the French occupation of the Ruhr and the "betrayal" of Germany represented by the democratic Weimar Republic. He became involved with Hitler at the end of 1922 as a propagandist—where his true talent lay—while continuing his work as pastor in Heidingsfeld. He was a regular preacher on Bavarian radio, starting in June 1931, proclaiming a völkisch message filled with rage and threats of violence that were also conveyed in radio plays that he wrote during the 1920s. *Das deutsche Leid* of 1923 is a violent and racially and sexually charged play about the rape of a German woman by a black French soldier, a story presented as an allegory for Germany and its need to take revenge: The woman announces to her father, "But if I now think that out of this disgrace a child will come, then my heart turns into flames of hell. I yank it out of my wounded body and when it smiles at me, when it looks at me like a holy angel, then I take it by the legs and smash its head against the wall. Its first cry should also be its last."[52] Such were Meyer-Erlach's publications prior to receiving a professorship at the University of Jena.[53] His Nazi politics and German Christian activities were sufficient to solidify his credentials with Leffler, Leutheuser, and university officials in the absence of academic qualifications; his faculty colleagues were not consulted.

Appointed to the professorship in practical theology, Meyer-Erlach's duties included serving as university preacher. At his inaugural lecture, he proclaimed himself the Hitler of the churches and declared: "I would rather go with my Volk to hell than without my Volk to your heaven."[54]

---

the NSV on September 1, 1934; the German Christians from June 1933 to 1943 (BDC, Meyer-Erlach materials); his wife joined the party in 1937. In 1933, he also joined the NS-Dozentenbund and the NSKOV (UAJ D 2031). He also held Honorary Cross for Front-Line Soldiers. On May 11, 1935, in Weimar, he changed his name from Meyer to Meyer-Erlach, to distract from the Jewish-sounding Meyer (BDC, Meyer-Erlach materials).

[52] Meyer-Erlach, *Das deutsche Leid* (1923) (BDC, Meyer-Erlach materials, Persolanakte R577), 15. Another of his plays is *Anno 1634* (1924), about the siege of Augsburg by Catholic troops that led thousands to die of hunger and disease.

[53] In 1927 he published a series of pamphlets on Dante, Cromwell, Carlyle, Dürer, and Shakespeare that appeared under the heading, "Nordische Seher und Helden."

[54] His talk, held on May 12, 1934, was published as *Das neue Deutschland und die christliche Verkündigung*, 9.

Figure 5.2. Wolf Meyer-Erlach.

Within a few months, Meyer-Erlach was appointed dean of the theology faculty, replacing Macholz,[55] and in April 1935 the Reich Ministry of Education in Berlin appointed him Rector of the university, against the vote of the faculty.[56] His rector's address, "The Friedrich Schiller University in the Spiritual Struggle of the Century," was a political statement in which he proclaimed himself a "soldier of the Führer" and called for the creation of a "political university."[57] Indeed, he removed the inscription "Verbum dei manet in aeternum" ("The Word of God Remains Eternal") from the university's main lecture hall. His rectorate was markedly anti-intellectual and aroused the contempt of the older faculty,[58] but he now presided over a new generation of students who had already been exposed to Nazi indoctrination in high school, in the Hitler Youth, and in military or work service.[59] His political devotion to Hitler was not sufficient to overcome his buffoonery, and a year later he was replaced as rector by Astel.

The next professor appointed in the theology faculty was Gerhard von Rad, in Old Testament, replacing Willy Staerk, who retired in 1934.[60] Born in Nuremberg in 1901, von Rad had already published significant work on Deuteronomy and the Hexateuch when he came to Jena from Leipzig in 1934.[61] Leffler and Meyer-Erlach may have assumed that von Rad was sympathetic toward the German Christian movement because of his membership in the SA, and perhaps because he was also one of the contributors to Gerhard Kittel's *Theological Dictionary of the New Testament*, among whom were numerous

[55] He became dean in October 1934. He first served as advisor to the rector of the University of Erlangen, Fritz Specht. See Elert, "Bericht über das Dekanat," 275; Loewenich, *Erlebte Theologie*, 181, cited by Raschzok, 182.

[56] On the variety of rectorats held in Jena during the Third Reich, and the relationships between rectors and Thuringian party officials, see Stutz, "Wissenschaft als 'Dienst an Volk und Vaterland,'" 123–54.

[57] Meyer-Erlach, *Universität und Volk*, 21.

[58] Stutz, "Wissenschaft als 'Dienst an Volk und Vaterland,'" 139 and 152 fn 63.

[59] Bruhn and Böttner, "Studieren in Jena 1933 bis 1945," 108. See also Grüttner, *Studenten im Dritten Reich*.

[60] Staerk's opposition to Nazism is discussed by Uriel Tal as an example of antisemitic anti-Nazism; Staerk compared Nazism to Judaism; in contrast to Christianity, a spiritual religion, both were rooted in blood, flesh, and soil. Staerk, *Das religiöse Leen der westeuropaeischen Judenheit*, cited by Tal, ed., *Religion, Politics and Ideology in the Third Reich*, 193–94.

[61] For a biographical sketch, see Andrew, "Gerhard von Rad: A Personal Memoir," 296–300. Andrew mentions that von Rad knew Dietrich Bonhoeffer during the year their studies overlapped at Tübingen, 1923–24. See also Smend, *Deutsche Alttestamentler in drei Jahrhunderten*; Rabenau, "Als Student bei Gerhard von Rad," 7–12. For a study of von Rad's scholarship on Deuteronomy, see Levinson and Dance, "The Metamorphosis of Law into Gospel."

Figure 5.3. Gerhard von Rad.

German Christian members;[62] von Rad, however, subsequently became affiliated with the Confessing Church. Both Meyer-Erlach and Leffler soon came to regret their choice, however, for von Rad proved to be a political disappointment. After a few years at Jena, von Rad was confronted with the efforts of his colleagues and students to eliminate the Hebrew language requirement and minimize the study of the Old Testament, which rendered von Rad's own scholarship marginal and left him with few students. Such actions undoubtedly encouraged von Rad's involvement with the Confessing Church, which served as a buttress against German Christian denigrations of the Old Testament and insisted on the inviolability of the Christian Bible. A report by the dean in 1938 criticized von Rad for insisting on the value of the Old Testament for Christians and for failing to integrate racial historiography into his theology.[63]

Like other members of the Confessing Church, von Rad came to defend the significance of the Old Testament for Christians. He did so by rejecting its Jewishness: Deuteronomy, the major focus of his scholarship, was a proto-gospel, a kerygma, and not a law book, he argued.[64] Yet that redefinition demonstrates not von Rad's opposition to the German Christian Movement, as Bernard Levinson has argued, but a more fundamental methodological affinity with the German Christians regarding the unacceptability of Jewishness within Christianity. Just as the German Christians transformed Jesus from Jew to Aryan in order to retain him in a Germanic Christianity, von Rad transformed Deuteronomy from a stigmatized "Jewish" book of law into a Christian text of kerygma. Despite his redefinition, von Rad continued to view the Old Testament as inferior to the New Testament.[65] His efforts were insufficient to win

[62] While in Leipzig, von Rad became a member of the SA in 1933; he withdrew in 1936 while in Jena. He was a member of the NSV until 1945, though he apparently never held membership in the NSDAP. Gerhard von Rad, Questionnaire (ThHStA 3426, 23). His views of the Nazi regime are not clear, but he signed his letters "Heil Hitler" through the Nazi era (ThHStA 3425, 122). Von Rad had joined Albrecht Alt and Joachim Begrich in a lecture series at the University of Leipzig in 1934, published as *Führung zum Christentum durch das Alte Testament: Drei Vorträge von Albrecht Alt, Joachim Begrich, Gerhard von Rad* (Leipzig: 1934). The lectures sought to defend the Old Testament against the charges of antisemites, particularly by Theodor Fritsch. Begrich was active in the Confessing Church. See Begrich, *Antisemitisches im Alten Testament*, and Fritsch, *Der falsche Gott*.

[63] Report by Heinz Eisenhuth, dean of the theological faculty (UAJ J, BB 87, 115).

[64] The redefinition of the Old Testament as kerygma is argued by Bernard M. Levinson as evidence of von Rad's opposition to the German Christians. Levinson and Dance, "The Metamorphosis of Law into Gospel."

[65] Luise von Rad writes that her husband told her that he had "again noticed that the New Testament truly was more than the Old." In "Nachwort," von Rad, *Erinnerungen aus der Kriegsgefangenschaft*, 45.

support from his German colleagues, who repudiated the Old Testament and insisted on racially informed methods of scholarship. Increasingly isolated by his colleagues at Jena, and with few students, his was generally the only voice of opposition to the changes that were brought about to nazify the curriculum.

Meyer-Erlach was more successful politically with his next two appointments: those of Eisenhuth and Grundmann. Eisenhuth's appointment was made possible by the sudden death, in the fall of 1936, of Heinrich Weinel, who had held the professorship, since 1925, in systematic theology. Meyer-Erlach and Heussi, as rector and dean, invited Eisenhuth, then an instructor at the University of Leipzig, to lecture during the winter semester, 1936–37. Faculty deliberations over Weinel's replacement began in January 1937. Macholz, then near retirement, and von Rad proposed several names, including Helmut Thielicke, who had completed a doctorate under Paul Althaus at the University of Erlangen and was affiliated with the Confessing Church but was not a Nazi Party member. After some debate the majority voted for Eisenhuth, who had joined the Nazi Party in May 1933 and who, according to a 1937 report of the NSDAP national leadership to Jena, was "a quiet, dignified person who has always campaigned for National Socialism willingly and assiduously."[66] Eisenhuth had bona fide academic credentials as well as a Nazi orientation: he had earned a doctorate in theology at Berlin and in philosophy at Frankfurt, and completed a habilitation at Leipzig, where he was teaching as an instructor[67] and had already published several books.[68] However, the

---

[66] Report on Eisenhuth from NSDAP Reichsleitung, Munich, September 22, 1937 (UAJ D 608.)

[67] Eisenhuth earned his doctorate in theology with a dissertation on Karl Heim (published as *Das Problem der Gewissensfreiheit bei Karl Heim*, Göttingen: Vandenhoeck & Ruprecht, 1928), and a doctorate in philosophy with a dissertation under Hans Cornelius and Paul Tillich on "Philosophical Studies on the Concept of the Irrational in Connection with Present-Day Theology." He joined the NSDAP on May 1, 1933 (number 2933000; Bundesarchiv [former BDC], Nazi membership files), and the SA in July 1933, and was a member of the Nazi Party's Teacher's Organization (NSLB) (see Report on Eisenhuth from NSDAP Reichsleitung, Munich, September 22, 1937, UAJ, D 603). He was a leader within the German Christian movement, lecturing at its meetings, starting in the fall of 1934 in Berlin. In a 1937 report sent by the NSDAP Reichsleitung to Jena, Eisenhuth was called "a calm, solid man who is always willing and eager to stand up for National Socialism." His politics and scholarship were united; at Leipzig he had offered a seminar on "Nordic Faith."

[68] Eisenhuth's publications included *Ontologie und Theologie* (1933), dedicated to Martin Heidegger; *Die Idee der nationalen Kirche bei Paul de Lagarde* (1934); *Der Begriff des Irrationalen als philosophisches Problem: Ein Beitrag zur existenzialen Religions-Begründung* (1931); *Christus und das deutsche Leben* (1938); and *Glaube und Sein* (1937).

Figure 5.4. Heinrich Weinel.

quality of his scholarship and scholarly output were not mentioned in the minutes of the faculty meeting regarding his appointment.

In his letter of March 6, 1937, to the Thuringian Ministry of Education, Rector Meyer-Erlach justified Eisenhuth's appointment on political grounds:

Eisenhuth . . . is an unconditionally reliable member of the Party who is loyal to the Führer and the movement from his innermost convictions. He works with great earnestness to promote the essential insights of National Socialism in his discipline. Precisely because the University of Jena consciously wants to become a bastion of National Socialism, I consider it of utmost importance that in addition to the academic qualification new appointments consider National Socialist reliability in the first place. Given the sad state of most faculties of theology in Germany, which to a large extent have not yet found the way to an inward relationship with National Socialism, the theology faculty in Jena must be built up in such a way that, in contrast to most faculties, it consciously supports National Socialism.[69]

Eisenhuth's appointment to a tenured full professorship on December 17, 1937, was signed by Hitler; he was appointed dean of the theological faculty in the summer semester, 1938. He became active in the Institute and served as its director for six months in 1943 before he was conscripted to military service.

Grundmann's own appointment at Jena was made possible by the fall from grace and eventual removal of New Testament scholar Fascher. Whereas in the autumn of 1935, while serving as dean of the theological faculty at Jena, Fascher gave a speech at the university calling for an integration of Christianity with race, along the lines of German Christian ideology,[70] in June of 1936 he delivered an address at a German Christian meeting in Weimar that outraged its leaders because he emphasized freedom of conscience. German Christian leader Julius Leutheuser, who was present at the talk, accused Fascher of having secretly worked against National Socialism since 1933, and shouted at him after the speech, "You are a scoundrel!"[71] Although Fascher protested his loyalty to the Nazi movement, he was expelled from the Thuringian branch of the German Christian movement the very next day, and at a faculty meeting was pressured to give up his deanship of the theological faculty, which he did

[69] UAJ 603.

[70] Fascher's speech was published as "Die Christus bekennende Reichskirche" (Bremen: DC Verlag, 1935); cited by Schenk, "Der Jenaer Jesus," 191 fn 117.

[71] Letter from Leffler to Erlach, dated June 23, 1936, reporting on Fascher's talk and the debate that followed (ThHStA, Akte Thüringisches Volksbildungsministerium in Weimar über die theologischen Fakultät 3425, pp. 81–87).

Figure 5.5. Heinz Eisenhuth.

on July 15, 1936.[72] In a jointly composed letter to the Thuringian Ministry of Education sent that day, Heussi and Meyer-Erlach demanded that Fascher be relieved of his professorship; he was.[73] The incident reveals the power achieved by the German Christians by positioning Leffler in the Thuringian Ministry of Education and Leutheuser in church headquarters. Even more significant, the case of Fascher indicates the willingness of Heussi to support German Christian decisions and assist in the marginalization and eventual removal of a tenured faculty colleague, a noted scholar, on political grounds and ultimately replace him with a known Nazi theologian with far lesser scholarly qualifications.

Fascher took an immediate leave of absence from Jena that summer and began teaching in Halle, creating an opening for Grundmann. On September 22, 1936, Heussi wrote to the Reich Ministry of Education suggesting the appointment of Walter Grundmann to a temporary teaching assignment in "Völkisch Theology and New Testament" during Fascher's absence. In his letter Heussi states that he has read Grundmann's work, has gotten to know him personally, and has discussed the matter with the rector, Meyer-Erlach.[74] Heussi's suggestion was accepted; a letter sent by the Reich Ministry of Education to the Thuringian Ministry of Education, dated October 13, 1936, proposed inviting Grundmann to lecture during the winter semester, 1936–37.[75] In January 1936, despite the fact that he had never written a habilitation thesis, Grundmann received the appointment and moved with his family to Jena.

Since Fascher was officially on leave of absence and had not yet resigned from Jena, Grundmann's appointment was at first temporary. But on October 13, 1937, the Thuringian Ministry of Education notified the rector of Jena that Fascher had been offered a tenured professorship at the University of Halle and that his professorship in Jena was now free.[76] Jena's theology faculty quickly began the pretense of a search to fill the position in New Testament. Two candidates in addition to Grundmann were considered, Günther Bornkamm and Carl Schneider, both of whom presented far better academic credentials. The New Testament scholar Bornkamm, who had been an instructor in Königsberg, was disqualified because of his known sympathies for the Confessing Church, while Schneider, who held a professorship in Königsberg and had taught in Riga and Leipzig, fell under suspicion because he had

---

[72] UAJ: Die Anstellung ordentlicher Professoren, 1936–38 vol. VII; 910.
[73] *Briefe an die Deutsche Christen* 5: 14 (July 15, 1936), 160; 5:16 (August 15, 1936), 183.
[74] UAJ BA 909.
[75] UAJ 910.
[76] UAJ 910.

Figure 5.6. Karl Heussi.

taught for several years as a professor outside Germany, at a seminary in Springfield, Ohio.[77]

Faculty voting on the new appointment took place even before Bornkamm's list of publications arrived, prompting von Rad to write a letter of complaint to the Thuringian Ministry of Education.[78] Meyer-Erlach, Eisenhuth, and Weinrich supported hiring either Grundmann or Schneider, whereas Macholz and von Rad voted for Bornkamm. Heussi was out of town. As rector, Meyer-Erlach wrote to officials at the Reich Ministry of Education to inform them that the theological faculty supported Grundmann's appointment. Further support came from Leffler at the state level. In addition, the bishop of Thuringia, Martin Sasse, urged his appointment, writing that Grundmann could "liberate young students from narrow dogmatic paralysis."[79]

Grundmann's publications were limited to his doctoral dissertation, some articles in Kittel's *Dictionary* and other reference works, and a large number of political pamphlets lending theological support to National Socialism.[80] He did, however, have the right political credentials, as Meyer-Erlach wrote in his letter to the Reich Ministry of Education nominating Grundman:

> Dr. Grundmann is an old party comrade. He joined the party in Tübingen in 1930 and proved himself as a party member in the period of struggle. Above all he remained true to the Führer and the NS movement as a member of the Saxonian church council during the most difficult period of church-political struggle. . . . While other theologians, novices in the party, genuflect to the anti-Nazi church governing councils, Dr. Grundmann took up in the fiercest way a struggle against the reactionary church administration. Thanks in greatest measure to his dedication and his loyalty, the Reich church ministry now can remove the subversive church council in Saxony from power.[81]

Meyer-Erlach concluded his letter with an evaluation of the National Socialist quality of Grundmann's scholarship, and the reasons for rejecting the other two candidates:

---

[77] UAJ 910.

[78] UAJ 910.

[79] Schüfer, "Die Theologische Fakultät Jena," 106.

[80] Other reference works to which Grundmann contributed articles include the *Reallexikon für Antike und Christentum*, ed. Franz Joseph Doelger and Hans Litzmann (Stuttgart: A. Hiersemann, 1950), and the *Meyers Konversations Lexikon* (Leipzig, Bibliographisches Institut, 1936–42). Letter from Meyer-Erlach to the Reich Ministry of Education, dated October 23, 1937 (UAJ 910).

[81] UAJ 910.

Dr. Grundmann proved himself as a loyal National Socialist not only in the realm of church politics, but also in the difficult realm of theology, and this long before the National Socialist assumption of power. In his first publications he took such a strong position for National Socialism that Reich Leader [Alfred] Rosenberg, appointed by the Führer to be in charge of surveillance of the National Socialist position, spoke very positively in his book *Protestant Pilgrims to Rome* [*Protestantische Rompilge*] about Grundmann's publication, *Gott und Nation*. Dr. Grundmann is one of the few theologians who, with complete self-consciousness, makes National Socialism the foundation of his scholarship.

The Friedrich Schiller University, as the Thuringian state university, has to propel the development of clear-cut National Socialist work. All the faculties have to build themselves on the viewpoint of the party. Dr. Grundmann fulfills this challenge both politically and scientifically in full measure. He is one of the main representatives within the church of a movement unconditionally devoted to the Führer and his goals. . . .

Prof. Dr. Carl Schneider, Königsberg, would be more appropriate at the border university of Königsberg, because of his rich foreign experiences, than here at Jena.

The instructor Günther Bornkamm is out of the question at Jena. The theological school at Bethel is so clearly oriented to the Confessing Church front that offering him the appointment at Jena would mark a break with the entire position of the university. He was named only by the two faculty members who themselves are inclined toward the Confessing Church.

For all of these reasons I request that you only appoint Dr. Grundmann.

Not surprisingly, the Reich Education Ministry approved Grundmann's appointment as professor of New Testament and völkische theology, which was publicly announced, along with Eisenhuth's, on October 5, 1938. The appointments were presented as coming from Hitler himself, and were reported as such in the newspapers.[82] Congratulatory letters flowed for the honor of being Hitler's own choice for the professorship. Grundmann's inaugural address, delivered on February 11, 1939, just three months before the Institute was opened, argued that the Sermon on the Plain in the Gospel of Luke was the authentic speech of Jesus, not the more Jewish version in the Gospel of Matthew, the Sermon on the Mount.[83] It was a foretaste of his theological and

---

[82] UAJ D, 986; the order, signed by Hitler and dated October 5, 1938, was sent by Zschintzsch from the Reich Ministry of Education.

[83] The speech, " The Question of the Oldest Form and Original Meaning of Jesus's Sermon on the Mount," was delivered at noon in the main auditorium of the university to a packed audience.

ecclesial program: identifying and purging any and all Jewishness from Christianity, including the gospels.

Salaries paid to the theological faculty at Jena reflected neither political commitments nor quality of scholarship. Heussi and Macholz were the highest paid, both receiving 11,600 RM. Von Rad received 8,700 RM when he was appointed in 1934, and was receiving 10,500 RM in 1944. By contrast, Eisenhuth was paid only 7,700 RM in 1943, and Grundmann received 9,000 RM in 1942, in comparison with Meyer-Erlach's salary of 11,100 RM in 1943.[84]

Nazification of the Curriculum

With Grundmann's appointment, the theological faculty was secured in German Christian hands and well under the control of the Institute. Its principle of dejudaization became central to the changes in the Jena curriculum, which it sought to export to other Reich universities. Race was central, and History of Religions methods were championed as the way to recognize the unique religious message appropriate to the German race—and eliminate Jewish influences that had distorted it. The German Christian leader Friedrich Wieneke, for example, argued that since each Volk received the message of God in a distinctive way, religious texts such as the Old Testament could not be studied "theologically," that is, as the unmediated word of God with a message for all peoples.[85] Reich education officials, while closing some university departments of theology, encouraged the establishment of History of Religions professorships. Indeed, in the fall of 1942, a seminar was organized at Alfred Rosenberg's teacher training school to train instructors in History of Religions. Among the instructors were several noted scholars, including Anton Jirku, Gerhard Kittel, Hans Lietzmann, and Karl Georg Kuhn.[86]

Over time History of Religions became identified with the German Christian movement, which used it as cover to overturn church doctrine and discipline. German Christian–affiliated scholars championed its putatively objective approach to religion and sought to imbue it with racial theory. At a German Christian conference in 1935, Cajus Fabricius, professor of Old

---

[84] BA Potsdam, File 49.01: Reichsministerium für Wissenschaft, section 1175: Verzeichnis der ordentlichen, Honorar-, ausserordentlichen und von den amtlichen Pflichten entbundenen Professoren der Universitäten, Jena, 1940–1944/45.

[85] Wieneke, "Theologie und Hochschule," in Schriftenreihe der "Deutschen Christen," ed. Joachim Hossenfelder, vol. 4 (Berlin 1933), 13, cited by Meisiek, Evangelisches Theologiestudium, 208 fn 789.

[86] BA Potsdam, 62Di1, 56/4.

Testament at the University of Berlin, called for shrinking the number of Old Testament professorships, and tranforming the study of the Old Testament into a larger study of the history of Judaism under the rubric of the "Aryan question."[87] Ethelbert Stauffer, professor of New Testament at the University of Bonn, spoke of a relationship of trust between state and church that was guaranteed by the theological faculties, who are responsible to both institutions.[88] He called on the theological faculties not to engage in politics, but to strengthen, through their theological work, the "political resiliency" of the German Volk; the unity of the German Volk could not exist without Jesus Christ.[89] At the same time, Stauffer wrote, theological education required not only political and intellectual training, but physical training as well; practical theology should include training in sports as well as homiletics, to train body and soul.[90] Jena's rector, Astel, declared in a speech on "The Task of the University of Jena," delivered in November 1936, that the university must appoint professors to serve both the army and the economy of the Nazi Reich in practical ways, not merely lending their ideological support. Even the field of theology, Astel stated, "must, if it is to have a fair claim to be represented as scholarship at the university, pay tribute to the new value system. It has to make an honest effort to undertake comparative study of religion exclusively with the perspective of what best serves the German Volk on the basis of its racial quality: that is the essence of its view of God and piety."[91]

Once installed in tenured positions at Jena, Grundmann and Eisenhuth were at the forefront of efforts not only to remake the theology curriculum at Jena in conformity with this "new value system" but also to alter theological education nationwide in the same manner. Their aspirations for reform were, of course, bound up with their plans for the Institute. In a paper coauthored in the summer of 1937, Grundmann and Eisenhuth proposed the eradication of Jewish elements from church teachings, liturgical practices, and the interpretation of Scripture, and from the educational training given to pastors—an agenda that anticipated the work of the Institute.[92] The document included a list of eighteen theology professors whose viewpoints were called unreliable

[87] Meisiek, *Evangelisches Theologiestudium*, 209. See also Wolgast, Nationalsozialistische Hochschulpolitik und die evangelisch-theologischen Fakultäten," 63.

[88] Stauffer, *Theologisches Lehramt in Kirche und Reich*, 18.

[89] Ibid., 24.

[90] Ibid., 38f.

[91] In Karl Astel, *Jenaer Akademische Reden: Die Aufgabe* (1937), 16; cited in Schüfer, "Die theologische Fakultät . . . Einige Forschungserträge" (unpublished student paper), 16.

[92] The document is in the private possession of Tobias Schüfer and is quoted in his paper, "Die Theologische Fakultät," 15.

for a National Socialist university, and a list of those whose National Socialist convictions were above suspicion.

Grundmann and Eisenhuth also initiated a series of national meetings of theology professors affiliated with the German Christian movement and church representatives to discuss reforms of theological education.[93] In April 1938, a formal conference of representatives of each of the Protestant theological faculties, the Evangelische Fakultätentag, was held in Halle to discuss a memorandum prepared by Eisenhuth outlining a thorough reform of theological education.[94] Its interpretive principles would be rooted in the "laws of race and species." Through that lens, Eisenhuth proposed significant changes in each of the subfields of theology to racialize the history on which Protestant theology was based. The professorship in Old Testament would be replaced by a chair in the "History of Religions of the Near East," whose goal would be to examine the ancient Orient with particular attention to Semitic elements. Latin and Greek would be required, but Hebrew would be optional, offered as one of many old Oriental languages. New Testament would be replaced by "Study of the Gospels and the Origins of Christianity," Jesus would be studied in the context of his religious and völkish environment. The synoptic gospels and other New Testament writings would be placed in the context of Hellenism and early Christianity. Church history would be the history of Germanic piety, and religions of the East would be examined to find their "Aryan religious element." Systematic theology would be taught as "reflection on the effective powers of the gospel for pious German life." The proposal reversed traditional systematic theology by making present-day experience the hermeneutical key to truth.

The goal was no longer to find the word of God, but the consciousness of the German Volk. As historian Cornelius Meisik argues, "The Christian was dissolved in the deification of Germanness."[95] Historical method would uncover the religious consciousness of the Germans; Eisenhuth wrote, "the goal, to give to the German Volk people who, in complete National Socialist reliability and national political responsibility, with inner piety and objective knowledge, are prepared to carry and shape the religious life of the German

[93] Among those present at the first meeting in Berlin on February 4, 1938 were Grundmann, Theodor Odenwald, Herbert Preisker, Martin Redeker, Hans Schmidt, Erich Seeberg, Robert Winkler, and Georg Wobbermin.

[94] Heinz Eisenhuth, "Denkschrift zu den Fragen der Studienreform und Fakultätsreform der theologischen Fakultäten" (UAB Akten der Ev. theol. Fakultät, vol. 35). The document is printed in Merk, "Paul Anton De Lagarde," and discussed by Meisiek, Evangelisches Theologiestudium, 212 fn 805. Merk notes that the document was included in the minutes of the theological faculties at the universities of Erlangen and Jena in the spring and summer of 1938.

[95] Meisiek, Evangelisches Theologiestudium, 215.

Volk, in order that the German Volk in its religious life achieves communion with God and clarity about itself."[96] That in turn, would assist Germans in understanding their own national identity, as Ernst Stricke, professor of church history at Tübingen, wrote in a letter to his friend Theodor Odenwald, a church historian at Heidelberg and member of the Institute.[97]

A major question concerned the requirements in Hebrew language and Old Testament for pastors' education. Few theology students entered university with background in Hebrew, and some had no prior preparation in Greek and Latin, which were deemed even more important for theological education. Students were also facing two and a half years of mandated military or work service, leaving little time to acquire proficiency in three languages. Given the plummeting status of the Old Testament, elimination of the Hebrew requirement was proposed, though controversial even among German Christian faculty, especially professors of Old Testament, concerned to protect the status of their field. Hans Schmidt, professor of Old Testament at the University of Halle and an active German Christian, emphasized the necessity of sound Hebrew knowledge for theological studies. Anton Jirku, professor of Old Testament at the University of Bonn, insisted that elimination of Hebrew study would be a return to the Dark Ages: "The question of Hebrew study has to be considered only as a scholarly one, but never considered as a matter of world view or ethos (one is hardly a Bolshevik if one learns Russian)."[98] No final decision regarding study of the Hebrew language was taken, nor could all the theological faculties of the Reich be mandated to eliminate the Hebrew requirement, since each regional church set its own requirements for ordination to the ministry. At Halle, Bonn, and Tübingen, for example, the Hebrew requirement was retained.[99] The study of Hebrew, like the study of Judaism more generally, could be transformed by German Christians into the study of a pathology that had infected Christianity, necessitating its dejudaization. After all, most of the Institute's attention was given to delineating the pathology of Judaism and its nefarious influence on Christianity.

Discussions about transformation of the curriculum began in earnest among the Jena theology faculty during the academic year 1937–38. Elimination of instruction in Hebrew language and the transformation of Old Testament studies into History of Religions rubrics were urged by Grundmann, Meyer-Erlach,

---

[96] "Denkschrift," cited in Meisiek, *Evangelisches Theologiestudium*, 212 fn 805.

[97] Cited by Meisiek, *Evangelisches Theologiestudium*, 215.

[98] Two-page memorandum by Anton Jirku, "Thesen zur Reform des theologischen Studiums," dated April 1938 (LKA Eisenach).

[99] Eisenhuth, "Denkschrift," 5, cited in Meisiek, *Evangelisches Theologiestudium*, 215.

and Eisenhuth, who formed a voting block. Their position was backed by Leffler and the Thuringian Ministry of Education as well as by the church of Thuringia. Von Rad constituted the opposition, and Heussi wavered between the two. Von Rad considered the position of Leffler and the ministry an attack on Christianity and wanted a statement of opposition to be issued by the faculty; he was opposed by all of his colleagues.[100] Grundmann supported Leffler because, he argued, the early Christians had read the Greek Bible and because the Greek text of the Old Testament is older than the extant Hebrew manuscripts. Friedrich Weinrich and Grundmann agreed with the ministry's position, and joined with the dean in support of the decision.

The rejection of Hebrew and Old Testament study received a boost from the Thuringian church, which decided on November 15, 1938, days after Kristallnacht, to end the Hebrew requirement for pastoral ordination,[101] and notified the Jena faculty, which voted on December 12 to make Hebrew study optional for ministerial students.[102] Heussi joined von Rad in objecting, on the grounds that eliminating the Hebrew requirement would undermine the scholarly training of pastors.[103] Eisenhuth rebutted their stance in a letter to the university Rrector in April 1939, in which he claimed that Heussi and von Rad failed to recognize "the antithetical character of the Old Testament to Christianity."[104] Hebrew was no longer required at Jena, and the Hebrew instructor, Arno Heerdegen, a Nazi Party member who was also involved with pro-Nazi Christian

---

[100] Von Rad did not hesitate to proclaim in public his view of the religious sanctity of the Old Testament. In a lecture to the pastors of Bavaria on June 13, 1944, "The Christian Understanding of the Old Testament," von Rad stated:

> It seems paradoxical: Perhaps there was never a time when the attentiveness to the message of the Old Testament was as urgent as ours. The Old Testament stands as the most faithful guard to the doors of the New Testament, and it assures us of the breadth and fullness of the message of Christ . . . The exclusion of the Old Testament has inevitably as its consequence a distortion and curtailment of the New Testament message of Christ . . . There are certainly many ways into the New Testament. But the era seems to be past in which each could see his honor, could have found his own private way. There is only one way that leads into the holy of holies of the New Testament, and that is the way over and through the Old Testament.

LAN KKU 12/VII: Umdruck der Landeskirchenrat an die Geistlichen vom 17.7.1944, cited by Baier, *Kirche in Not*, 235.

[101] UAJ, J 280. See also Stegmann, *Der Kirchenkampf in der Thüringer Evangelischen Kirche*, 105.

[102] Memorandum dated December 12, 1938 (UAJ, J 280).

[103] Letter from Heussi and von Rad to Bernhard Rust, Reich Ministry of Education, dated December 14, 1938 (UAJ, Bestand C, no. 358), cited by Böhm, "Gerhard von Rad und der Streit um das Alte Testament," 32.

[104] UAJ, Bestand BB, No. 87, Bl. 115, letter from Eisenhuth to the Rector, Karl Astel, dated April 24, 1939, cited by Böhm, "Gerhard von Rad."

groups, was summarily dismissed from his instructorship by the Thuringian education ministry in January 1939.[105] As dean, Eisenhuth ruled that Hebrew would henceforth be optional, but History of Religions methods would be required and would replace Hebrew in the required oral examinations.[106]

The Institute's call for dejudaizing Christianity became the model for the Jena theology curriculum and may have spared the Jena faculty from a series of closures and consolidations of theology faculties announced by the Reich Ministry of Education in 1939.[107] Jena was spared because of the regime's confidence in its National Socialist sympathies, and serves as a model of what all theological education would have become had the Reich survived. As Martin Bormann, head of the Party chancellery, reported at the time, "for the time being, I would like to leave the small Jena faculty—which is oriented in an extremely German Christian direction—alone, as it holds its ground in the intellectual exchanges of the future. The theology faculty in Jena should be retained as such for the time being."[108] The policy was approved by Meyer-Erlach as a tactic to impose political discipline on the field. As he subsequently wrote to the Reich Ministry of Education: "I beg you to occasionally take our work into consideration. Having become awakened by the fundamental insights of National Socialism, we work steadfastly to dissolve the morbid crust that the confessional churches have placed around the religious life of our Volk. . . . The state cannot retain theological faculties that reflect the overbearing self-cannibalism of the German people. But it will always need men who, out of passion and devotion to the Reich, speak of the great God who sent the Führer to liberate us from their dull narrowness, their hypocrisy, [their] satanic delusion that makes them murderers of each other, and liberate [Germans] to [become] a great community in which one serves the other."[109]

Additional changes to the composition of the theological professoriate occurred in 1938. Macholz reached the age of 62, and asked to be released from his position, and Glaue turned 65, the age of retirement. Within the faculty,

---

[105] Heerdegen, speech to Bund DK, March 5, 1930 (UAJ J 280).

[106] Memorandum by Eisenhuth, dated April 4,1939 (LKA Eisenach: Akten betreff. DC: Hochschulangelegenheiten, 1937–40).

[107] Left open by the fall of 1939 and the onset of the war were the theology faculties of Berlin, Jena, Vienna, Breslau, Halle, Erlangen, Königsberg, and Göttingen. Theology faculties closed by this time were those of Bonn, Giessen, Greifswald, Heidelberg, Kiel, Leipzig, Marburg, Münster, Rostock, and Tübingen. Cf. Meisiek, *Evangelisches Theologiestudium*, 341.

[108] BA Potsdam 62Di1, 56/4: Dienstellen Reichsleiter Rosenberg: Reorganization of theological faculties.

[109] Letter from Meyer-Erlach to State Secretary Zintzsch, January 1, 1941 (BDC, Meyer-Erlach materials, Research WI 2003).

Figure 5.7. Wolf Meyer-Erlach, second from right, at an athletic event, University of Jena, 1935.

scholarship continued. Von Rad published his important work on the Hexa-teuch in 1938 and began his studies of Deuteronomy, which appeared in 1947.[110] Heussi published "The Germanization of Christianity as a Historical Problem" in 1934, and an important study of the origins of monasticism in 1936, among other work.[111] Meyer-Erlach was given an honorary doctorate in 1937 by the University of Athens, and returned to Athens the following year for a series of lectures, including a talk about the University of Jena as a stronghold of classical idealism. He was nonetheless an object of mockery by local Nazi Party officials. In October 1940, Astel received a letter from the Nazi Party district leader of Thuringia, opposing Meyer-Erlach's efforts to es-tablish a working relationship with Orthodox churches in the Balkans.[112] The letter went on to mock Meyer-Erlach's honorary doctorate as well as his Nazi commitments.[113] As evidence, the letter included a short newspaper clipping from the *Würzburger Anzeiger* of 1929, reporting Meyer-Erlach's presence at a synagogue dedication in Heidingsfeld, at which he spoke as representative of the church.[114] Astel himself was annoyed with Meyer-Erlach and unimpressed by his devotion to the Nazi cause; in 1942, for example, he complained to the Reich Ministry of Education in Berlin that Meyer-Erlach went on a lecture tour on the Eastern Front at the beginning of the semester without his knowledge or permission.[115]

SOME NOTABLE STUDENTS AND THEIR DISSERTATIONS

Even as the number of students studying theology in Germany, went into slow decline during the Nazi years—a decline accelerated by the onset of the war[116]—Jena remained a viable site for theological study under the Nazis. In

---

[110] Rad, *Das formgeschichtliche Problem des Hexateuchs*, and *Deuteronomium Studien*.

[111] "Die Germanisierung des Christentums als historisches Problem"; see also Heussi, *Der Ur-sprung des Mönchtums*.

[112] Letter from Hahland, NSDAP district leader in Thuringia, to Astel, dated 30 Oktober 1940 (BA Potsdam, Reichsministerium für Wissenschaft, Erziehung, etc.: 2966).

[113] Meyer-Erlach was invited again to Athens in April–May 1938, by Professor N. I. Louvaris, to deliver a series of lectures at the university, the literary society Parnassos, and the German-Greek Society of Athens. UAJ, D 2031.

[114] "Die Einweihung der wiederhegestellten Synagoge in Heidingsfeld" (*Würzburger Anzeiger*, September 27, 1929).

[115] Letter dated June 20, 1942 (BA Potsdam: Reichsministerium für Wissenschaft, Erziehung, etc.: 2966).

[116] While 209 students had studied theology at Jena in 1932, there were 98 students in the summer of 1936, 67 the following year, 54 in summer, 1938, and 31 in summer, 1939. Report

Figure 5.8. The University of Jena building that housed the theological faculty during the Third Reich.

addition to those candidates for the ministry in the Thuringian church who were required to enroll at Jena, the faculty attracted students for ideological reasons. Institute members came to Jena to earn a doctorate, and Institute publications included many of their dissertations. Heinz Hunger, business manager of the Institute and one of the editors of its dejudaized New Testament, studied at Jena, and the Institute published his habilitation thesis, "Essence and Method of a Racial History of Religion."[117] Already the author of several works of political propaganda, Hunger later wrote on the difference between "Jewish psychoanalysis" and "German psychotherapy," the latter concerned with the soul and hence the basis for pastoral counseling, in an article published by the Institute.[118]

---

from Heussi dated October 21, 1946 (UAJ). Besier, "Zur Geschichte der kirchlichen Hochschulen," appendix IV, 275.

[117] The thesis was delayed at Jena and finally approved at the University of Vienna in 1942 (UAJ J 92). It was published in an Institute-sponsored volume: Heinz Hunger, "Wesen und Methode einer rassekundlichen Religionsgeschichte."

[118] Hunger, *Geschändete Neutralität*; Hunger, "Jüdische Psychoanalyse und deutsche Seelsorge."

Faculty evaluations of doctoral dissertations in theology were also politicized. Students were expected to adhere to principles of racial theory. While some dissertations were rejected for poor quality of scholarship, others were rejected because they did not champion Nazi racial theory. Students could not cite the work of Jewish authors favorably, nor could they write sympathetically about Jesus's connections to the Old Testament. Identification of theological anti-Judaism had to be reinforced by recognition of racial antisemitism. Opposition to those evaluations was sometimes expressed by von Rad and Heussi, but Heussi at times sided with the Grundmann faction, and Heussi tended to prevail. Students were asked to revise and resubmit theses, which was at times not possible due to their military service during the war years. Of the forty-five doctoral dissertations in theology submitted by students between 1933 and 1945, thirty-five of which were successful,[119] Heussi was the primary advisor of thirteen, while the remaining twenty-four were split among Grundmann, Eisenhuth, and Meyer-Erlach; von Rad was primary advisor of only one dissertation, secondary reader of four.[120] Six of the dissertations were written under Grundmann's primary supervision, and several students were Institute members.

Students were sympathetic to their professors' theological politics and enjoyed close relationships with them. Professors often invited students to dinner, and there were group outings on the weekends, something that did not take place at the larger universities such as Halle or Leipzig. Some Catholic students also studied at Jena, including priests from the Münster area, because the Thuringian German Christians wanted to establish a church uniting Protestants and Catholics. Given the atmosphere of the Jena theological faculty, it was attractive to Nazi Party members. Most of its theology students were members of the German Christian movement or sympathizers and found kindred spirits on the faculty. Many students were also Nazi Party members and attended classes dressed in their SA uniforms.[121]

Indeed, the German Christian dominance of the faculty was the reason a group of theology students from Scandinavia arrived in Jena in 1942. Thanks

[119] The University of Jena archives are missing some documents regarding doctoral dissertations in theology (UAJ, J). My thanks to the archivist, Margit Hartleb, for her efforts to gather information about dissertations in theology during the Third Reich. She has indicated to me that faculty decisions regarding two dissertations are not recorded, and that the files of two students who entered the doctoral program are not extant (private communication, April 30, 1992).

[120] Von Rad is listed as the primary advisor of a thesis by Kurt Möbius, "The Timeliness of Eschatology in the Old Testament Prophets," completed in November 1940 (UAJ J 88).

[121] Herbert von Hinzenstern, quoted by Schüfer, "Die theologische Fakultät," 102.

to the Institute, a close working relationship had developed between Meyer-Erlach, Grundmann, and Hugo Odeberg, professor in Lund and a distinguished scholar of rabbinic Judaism who had worked with Kittel to produce critical editions of rabbinic texts. In 1941 Odeberg joined Grundmann and Meyer-Erlach in forming a working group, Germanentum und Christentum, which brought Scandinavian theologians and writers to participate in Institute-sponsored conferences in Germany.[122] Odeberg took the initiative among the Scandinavians, inviting thirty academics, students, and writers from Sweden, Norway, and Denmark to lecture at the conferences, which were held in Weissenfels and in Eisenach. Impressed by the high quality of scholarship practiced by Institute members, Odeberg sent seven Swedish students to Jena to write doctoral dissertations under Grundmann.[123] One of them, Erik Douglas Edenholm, a pastor, was active in a pro-Nazi Christian group in Sweden and had published on the Aryan Jesus; his dissertation argued that Germanic religiosity formed the basis for Swedish piety.[124]

As at the Institute, the intellectual atmosphere at Jena was mixed. Heussi was an outstanding scholar of church history; and, according to a former theology student at Jena, Hans-Joachim Thilo, the consensus among Jena's theology students was that Grundmann and Eisenhuth were also serious intellectuals. Eisenhuth was an old-fashioned, somewhat distant, reserved teacher, but "encyclopedically knowledgable." His seminars treated topics in ethics, such as just war and sexual issues. Grundmann—again, according to Thilo—was an exciting teacher, and his lectures were the best attended by students, who were "thrilled" by him. His seminars were packed, and heated discussions ensued. Conferences run by Grundmann and Eisenhuth's Institute were attended by many students, who were stimulated by the level of discussion. Meyer-Erlach, by contrast, was considered a lightweight. His lectures were intellectually low-level ("kleine Brötchen backen") and were "nothing more than rants

---

[122] AA Inland I-D 3/4, R98796: Überwachung von Arbeitstagungen der Arbeitsgemeinschaft "Germanentum und Christentum" und ihrer Leiter Professor Wolf Meyer-Erlach und Professor Grundmann, Verweigerung von Reisesichtvermerken, 1942–44.

[123] Only one of those Swedish students, Erik Douglas Edenholm, completed his dissertation at Jena. A second foreign student to complete a dissertation at Jena was Veselin Sarenac, from Belgrade, who wrote under Heussi and Eisenhuth.

[124] Edenholm's dissertation was published by the Institute: Edenholm, "Das germanische Erbe in der schwedischen Frömmigkeit." Edenholm was active in a reform movement within the Swedish Protestant church that was allied with the German Christian movement and led by Emanuel Linderholm, professor of church history at the University of Uppsala. See Gerdmar, "Ein germanischer Jesus auf schwedischem Boden."

[Schimpfereien]," and he himself was an especially outspoken and vulgar antisemite who praised the burning of the synagogues on Kristallnacht, while other German Christian members of the faculty simply remained silent.[125] (An unsigned document in Meyer-Erlach's file in the university archives supports Thilo's recollections, describing him as an "imposter and actor by nature with strong hysterical admixtures. Very strong need for prestige."[126])

Since three of the five full professors were members of the Institute, students' dissertations underwent as much antisemitic scrutiny as the curriculum of the faculty, expressed in faculty evaluations of doctoral dissertations. Of thirty-seven dissertations in theology submitted by students between 1933 and 1945, ten were rejected by the faculty or withdrawn by the students for reasons ranging from poor quality of scholarship to failure to champion Nazi racial theory. Students were also provided opportunities to present their research at Institute-sponsored conferences, and the Institute paid for publication of ideologically sympathetic dissertations as well.

Thilo's dissertation, "The Influence of Völkisch Awakening on German Religious Life," made extensive use of Nazi theory and urged the church to recognize the usefulness of racial politics for religion. Thilo, who was a member of the Nazi Party, the German Christians, and the SS, served as Grundmann's research assistant and was an active member of the Institute before military service on the Eastern Front, where he witnessed the murder of the Jews in Minsk.[127]

Herbert von Hintzenstern was one of the more successful graduate students at Jena, thanks to his close relationship with Grundmann and his membership in the Institute. Active as a leader in the Hitler Youth between 1934 and 1936, Hintzenstern was excused from military service because of a knee injury in the summer of 1939. In October of that year he joined the Institute and began his studies at Jena. His dissertation, "[Houston Stewart] Chamberlain's Portrayal of Early Christianity," was written under both Grundmann and Heussi and was submitted July 8, 1940. The thesis emphasized the influences of Richard Wagner and Hans von Wolzogen on Chamberlain's theories of the Aryan origins of Christianity. Both advisors judged the work to be magna cum laude

---

[125] Interview with Hans-Joachim Thilo, Lübeck, July 20, 1995.

[126] UAJ Personalakten Meyer-Erlach.

[127] Thilo claimed that he spent the war in the cavalry, transporting weapons. He was in Belarus and witnessed the murder of Jews in Minsk. Taken prisoner by the British in 1944 in Normandy, he did not return home until 1948. Thilo related this to me in a private conversation at his home in Lübeck on July 20, 1995.

and deserving a prize, and Eisenhuth agreed.[128] The work was presented at an Institute conference and published as an article in a book edited by Grundmann.[129]

Another Jena graduate student during the Nazi era, Wilhelm Richter, was not as favored by the faculty. Although a member of the NSDAP since 1931, he argued in his dissertation that Jesus' s ideas must be understood within an Old Testament context. His work was rejected, even after a revision. As Meyer-Erlach explained, "The theologian lacks the necessary understanding of National Socialism, that the racial question is the foundational question for everything. . . . Of the importance of the racial question the man, who has been a party member since 1931, has no idea. A theological faculty that is avowedly National Socialist must disavow the possibility of a positive evaluation of the work."[130]

One dissertation that was a cause of some embarrassment for the faculty was prepared by Karl-Erich Wilken, a member of the Nazi Party and the German Christian movement who had served as a pastor in Magdeburg when he enrolled at Jena.[131] In 1926 he had received a stipend to spend several months in Palestine, where he claimed to have studied at the Hebrew University of Jerusalem. Wilken's doctoral dissertation, a study of the gospel parable of the rich man and poor Lazarus in connection with antique Judaism's views of sin and punishment, was presented to the Jena faculty in March of 1938. Grundmann praised the work for demonstrating the opposition between Jewish and New Testament texts, and recommended honors.[132] Von Rad, by contrast, was highly critical. One month later, Wilken sent a letter to Eisenhuth, admitting that he had erred in identifying certain documents in his dissertation as stemming from antiquity when they had actually been published in 1800. His thesis was quickly withdrawn. With undeterred ambition, however, Wilken presented a sinister proposal to the Reich's intelligence office in September of 1939, offering to lead a team of German experts to evaluate Jewish libraries in occupied Poland for Nazi confiscation, proclaiming his expertise in Judaism and, in particular, Hebrew magical texts. In a letter of support for Wilken's proposal, the intelligence office in Magdeburg explained that Hebrew magical texts contain the Jews' political objectives that remain in effect to the present

---

[128] UAJ J 90: Promotionsakten der Theologischen Fakultät, 1939–41.

[129] "Das religiöse Problem in Bayreuther Kreis," in Grundmann, ed., *Christentum und Judentum*, vol. 1.

[130] Wilhelm Richter, "Notwendiger Christ" (UAJ J 90).

[131] He was pastor of the Martinsgemeinde in Magdeburg. Margrit Müller, archivist of the Protestant Church of Saxony, personal communication, October 15, 2002.

[132] UAJ J 89.

day and would be useful for Nazi political propaganda.[133] It is not known if Wilken's request was granted.

Another doctoral student at Jena whose dissertation ran into trouble was Fritz Schmidt-Clausing, a Protestant pastor who had converted from Catholicism as a young man. Active in the German Christian movement since 1935, he joined the Institute and was especially interested in questions of Catholicism and antisemitism. His dissertation, submitted in the fall of 1941, was entitled, "The Metamorphosis of the Catholic Church in Its Position regarding the Jewish Question since the French Revolution." He argued that the Catholic Church, prior to the Protestant Reformation, was opposed to Judaism, but that later Catholicism fell victim to the poisonous influence of Judaism.[134]

The dissertation, despite its apparent ideological conformity to Nazism, was not well received; it was nothing more than a compilation of citations from secondary literature. Heussi criticized the misuse of sources, and also questioned the inclusion of a discussion of Luther in a dissertation on Catholicism as well as the student's failure to discuss Jewish influences on Catholicism. The work relied too heavily, Heussi argued, on other authors—almost to the point of plagiarism—and discussed views of Church Fathers on Judaism out of their religious, racial, and historical context. The dissertation might be revised as a propaganda pamphlet, Heussi concluded, but it was not a work of scholarship.[135]

Writing in qualified defense of the dissertation, Grundmann observed that it should be seen not within the genre of church history but rather as a "religious-political work" with a contribution to practical theology. Its purpose was to provide evidence of anti-Jewish Catholic theologians, and to demonstrate that within official Catholic theology—which was barely attentive (wrote Grundmann) to the Jewish question—there was an anti-Jewish stream. Yet Grundmann ultimately rejected Schmidt-Clausing's thesis as too sympathetic to Catholicism, as evidenced by the dissertation's claim that the racial laws of the Third Reich were nothing more than a continuation of Catholic anti-Jewish laws. A year later, Schmidt-Clausing submitted a heavily revised dissertation.

---

[133] The two-page letter, dated September 18, 1939, was sent by the Sicherheitsdienst (SD) of Magdeburg-Anhalt to SD headquarters in Berlin. A copy of Wilken's letter to the SD was kindly forwarded to me by Rabbi Efrayim Grossberger, Brooklyn, New York. After the war, Wilken published several popular books, including *Denen, die Gott lieben* (the 1989 fourth edition indicates that the book had sold over 20,000 copies). In 1946 he visited Palestine in search of Christian places of interest and wrote about his experiences in *Der Stein des Pilatus*. The date of his trip to Israel is not stated in the book.

[134] Kühl-Freudenstein and Wagener, "Kirchenkreis Potsdam I," 565–73.

[135] UAJ J 92, 14–15.

This time, Heussi and Grundmann approved it, and despite von Rad's objections, the student was awarded his doctorate magna cum laude.

Dissertations were expected to arrive at antisemitic conclusions. For example, a thesis on preexistence and immortality, by Eberhard Zetzel, written under Grundmann, von Rad, and Hermann Johannsen of the philosophical faculty, was rejected by Grundmann, who wrote: "The author correctly observes that Judaism takes over its understanding of preexistence and afterlife of the soul from other religions. This does not lead it, however, to the fundamental conclusion of the spiritual unproductivity of Judaism." Zetzel was required to make revisions in his thesis, but he never replied to that demand.[136]

The faculty attracted students with strong involvement in Nazi activities although not all of them worked with the Nazis on the faculty. Kurt Möbius, who had been a propagandist for the NSDAP since 1930, then served as director of the Office of Social Welfare after 1933, and joined the SS early in 1933. He enlisted in military service in 1934. He was awarded a prize for a paper critical of Max Weber's work on ancient Israel, but encountered difficulties with his thesis, "The View of His Epoch in Proto-Isaiah (Chapters 1–39)." Heussi criticized Möbius sharply for citing Martin Buber and Paul Tillich, a Jew and an anti-Nazi, and Möbius did not pass his oral examinations, which he took on December 7, 1937. Ultimately, he wrote his dissertation on a new topic, under von Rad, that was resubmitted and accepted as "satisfactory" in May of 1940.

Max-Adolf Wagenführer came to study at Jena in 1937 and served as Grundmann's research assistant, writing his dissertation on the Epistles to Colossians and Ephesians under Grundmann, whom he regarded as an outstanding exegete of Scripture. Wagenführer was also hired by the Thuringian church to work as a research assistant at the Institute, helping to prepare its publications, and was one of the editors of its hymnal and catechism. In 1938 he joined the Nazi Party. Wagenführer was among the most active members of the Institute, lecturing at its conferences and contributing to its publications.[137]

Several students came from Scandinavia to study at Jena; one wrote on "Germanic Elements in Christianity," another on "The Germanic Heritage of

---

[136] UAJ J 91, Promotionsakten der Theologischen Fakultät, 1940 and 1941).

[137] His dissertation was published as *Die Bedeutung Christi für Welt und Kirche: Studien zum Koloser- und Epheserbrief* (Leipzig: Otto Wigand, 1941). Wagenführer described his studies at Jena in two personal letters to me, dated July 7, 2005, and February 23, 2006, in my private possession.

Swedish Piety." According to Meyer-Erlach, writing in January of 1944, such work would promote History of Religions methods in Sweden and encourage recognition of the centrality of race to National Socialism.[138]

As the total number of students of theology in Germany fell, from over 3,000 in 1936 to 400 in 1940, the number at Jena also shrank. In 1938–39 there were thirty, but by the winter term of 1941–42 there were only four students, two of whom had been sent to Jena by the Confessing Church in order to make certain that von Rad had an audience at his lectures.[139] By the winter of 1944–45 only one student was enrolled. When the university was reopened at the end of 1945, fourteen students enrolled in theology; in the summer of 1946 there were twenty-three, and in the winter of 1946–47, twenty-seven.

Conclusion

Its alliance with the theological faculty at the University of Jena was one of the great advantages of the Institute. Three of its leaders were given academic positions that they used to implement their ideology within the curriculum and grant Institute members university degrees. Affiliation with the Institute was a further boon to newly minted doctoral students, who were given the opportunity to present their work at an Institute conference or gather with senior professors in one of the Institute's working groups.

Nazification of the theological faculty at Jena was as thorough as the most extreme cases, medicine and law. No significant internal brakes were applied, despite the presence of von Rad and Macholz, primarily because Heussi refused to ally himself firmly with them. Nor were brakes applied from the church and state government, both of which were dominated by members of the German Christian movement and the Institute. The person on the faculty who facilitated the transformation during the Nazi period, and who enabled former Nazis to receive positions after 1945, was Heussi. With no evidence for his membership in the NSDAP, the SA, or other Nazi organizations, nor involvement with the German Christian movement in any overt way, Heussi epitomizes the power of the politically "neutral" figure. It was precisely the appearance of neutrality that allowed him, behind the scenes, both to facilitate

[138] Five-page letter from Meyer-Erlach to the Reich Foreign Ministry, dated January 17, 1944 (AA I-D, 3/4, R 98796).

[139] Besier, "Zur Geschichte der kirchlichen Hochschulen," appendix IV, 275; on von Rad, see Schüfer, "Die theologische Fakultät Jena," 104.

the faculty's nazification after 1933 and to prevent its thorough denazification after 1945, and that won him great accolades from his colleagues.[140]

Theodor Adorno has written, "Even the man spared the ignominy of direct co-ordination bears, as his special mark, this very exemption, an illusory, unreal existence in the life-process of society."[141] There is, indeed, no neutrality; the "inviolable isolation" that Adorno describes is never possible because it is always structured by the dominant order. The transformation of Jena into a stronghold of National Socialism eroded the university's moral and scholarly integrity, and within the theological faculty, the language of Christianity was used to promote opportunism under the Nazi regime. After the collapse, it was easy to retain that Christian language and pretend that Christianity had overriden the corruption of the regime. Deference to Nazism was undertaken and postwar self-legitimations proclaimed, both in defense of the church. A figure such as Heussi, whose dry histories of the patristic and medieval periods did not proclaim a synthesis with National Socialist ideology, could convince others (and perhaps himself as well) that hiring Nazis and transforming the curriculum were in the best interest of the church because they succeeded in maintaining the theological faculty at Jena during an era that saw the closure of other faculties. Christian loyalties, not opportunism, could be invoked to justify collaboration with the Third Reich.[142]

[140] Heussi was remembered as an anti-Nazi hero in later years. His action as rector in 1930, around the appointment of Hans F. K. Günther, was subsequently praised as a stance "for law and legality and resisted the illegality and untruth which he encountered in Nazi ideology and demagoguery," in the words of Eberhard Pältz, professor of systematic theology at Jena. Hannah Jursch, in a tribute on Heussi's seventieth birthday in 1947, described his courage in 1930 in preserving Christian values during a time of the persecution of Christianity. See Pältz, "Geschichte als Selbstorientierung in der Zeit," and Jursch, "Zum 70. Geburtstag von Karl Heussi."

[141] Adorno, *Minima Moralia*, trans. E.F.N. Jephcott, aphorism number 13.

[142] Compare with Ellen W. Schrecker's study of McCarthyism and American universities in the 1950s, in which she concludes, "Opportunism and dishonesty existed, of course, but most of the men and women who participated in or condoned the firing of their controversial colleagues did so because they sincerely believed that what they were doing was in the nation's interest. Patriotism, not expedience, sustained the academic community's willingness to collaborate with McCarthyism." *No Ivory Tower: McCarthyism and the Universities* (New York: Oxford University Press, 1986), 340.

The Postwar Years

AMERICAN TROOPS UNDER the command of General George Patton arrived in Thuringia on Easter Sunday, April 1, 1945, encountering almost no resistance. Eisenach fell easily on April 7, and on April 11 the Americans liberated the Buchenwald concentration camp, located on a hill above the town of Weimar. Within days, the concentration camp was opened and residents of the region were forced on tours of its horrors. The Americans continued east to Jena on April 13, making it the first university city under allied occupation. Their arrival came after two months of bombings that had destroyed much of Jena's town center and killed many residents, including members of the university community. By early May Soviet troops had arrived in the region, and on July 3 authority for Thuringia was transferred from American to Soviet military authorities.

Georg Bertram, who was appointed Institute director following the military conscription of first Grundmann and then Eisenhuth, left Giessen and moved to Eisenach in the last months of the war. He tried to preserve the Institute even as the Nazi Reich collapsed around him. On May 6, 1945, he appealed to the Thuringian church for continued financial support for the Institute's activities. While he saw that the German Christians' control of the church had ended with the collapse of the Nazi regime, he was no doubt aware that members of the Confessing Church, poised to assume power, were just as sympathetic to antisemitism, particularly to charges against Jews of deicide. The Institute, Bertram wrote, had sought to defend Christianity against claims by Alfred Rosenberg that Christianity was nothing more than Jewish propaganda; the Institute had shown that Jesus "took up the fight against the Jews with great severity and fell as a sacrifice to it . . . it was the Jews who brought Jesus to the cross." Future Institute work would include training pastors in philology (only Greek and Latin; he did not mention Hebrew) and the history of Germanic piety, and creating new liturgical materials. The Institute, as he presented it, was an apolitical research center on behalf of the church, whose purpose was demonstrating that "there is no Germanness without Christianity."[1] Its name would henceforth be the "Theo-

---

[1] Georg Bertram, memorandum concerning the work of a theological research institute in Eisen-

logical Research Institute of Eisenach," and he proposed to serve as scholarly director until Grundmann's return from military service.

The church council of Thuringia met with Bertram two weeks later to consider his request.[2] Members expressed concern about the financial costs of retaining the Institute and considered moving it to the University of Jena's theological faculty or to the Lutheran Academy in Sondershausen.[3] A week later, the council decided not to continue support of the Institute.[4] Moritz Mitzenheim, who was appointed head of the governing council of the Thuringian church after the war, thanked Bertram for his work "in the service of the gospel." Members of the Institute were asked to vacate their offices in the Predigerseminar (pastors' training seminary), but the Institute's library was retained in the spacious rooms of the Predigerseminar and became the property of the church.[5]

None of the occupying powers knew quite what to do with Germany's nazified universities and churches. The emerging policies contained conflicting aims: the urgent need to eradicate all Nazi remnants was matched by a desire to make use of Germany's spiritual and intellectual elites in the reconstruction of the country.[6] The influential postwar rector at Heidelberg, Karl Heinrich Bauer, for example, presented the universities and the churches as two intact institutions at the disposal of the allies for building a new spiritual leadership in Germany.[7] This line of thinking, widely adopted in the early postwar years, worked against a thoroughgoing denazification of these institutions and also served as a screen to protect individuals, such as Bauer himself, from investigation of Nazi involvements.[8] The churches were left to carry out their own denazification

ach, May 6, 1945 (LKA Eisenach A 921), 2. Nothing was mentioned in Bertram's report about dejudaization, nor about the prior publications of the Institute, particularly its liturgical works. Bertram asserted that the Institute would avoid any appearance of theological partiality; it would be a neutral eccliastical effort.

[2] The meeting was held on May 17, 1945 (minutes at LKA Eisenach A 122).

[3] Moritz Mitzenheim, soon to become bishop of Thuringia, urged dissolution of the Institute, but retention of its property. Senior church councillor Gerhard Phieler wanted the Institute retained, but with its goals changed to a historical study of the Luther Bible and its effects on German culture and the Protestant people.

[4] Letter from Bertram to the church council of Thuringia, dated June 8, 1945 (LKA Eisenach A 921).

[5] Letter from Ermisch to the regional church council, dated July 12, 1945 (LKA Eisenach A 921).

[6] John, "Die Jenaer Universität im Jahre 1945," 20. See also Ash, "Verordnete Umbrüche," 903–24, esp. fns 18, 20, 65.

[7] On the University of Heidelberg after the war, see Remy, The Heidelberg Myth.

[8] Heinonen, Anpassung und Identität, 181. On Bauer, a surgeon who published a book on racial hygiene in 1942, see Remy, The Heidelberg Myth, 88–90 and passim.

procedures, unsupervised by the Allies. Church leaders, in turn, protested the denazification investigations and the trials of Germans accused of war crimes on the grounds that they were vindictive and violated Christian precepts of compassion and mercy.[9]

Within the universities, those who had joined the NSDAP prior to 1933 were dismissed from their professorships by state authorities, while many others who had been active Nazi supporters retained their professorships. To be convicted and penalized required—according to the denazification rules established by the Allies—evidence that a particular faculty member had engaged in Nazi activities, for which membership in the Nazi Party or affiliated organization offered only limited proof. Greater proof could come from actual publications in which enthusiasm for Hitler was expressed. But the legitimacy of these publications was challenged in denazification hearings on the grounds that Nazi-era documents were tainted and unobjective.[10] Far more reliable, argued attorneys representing the accused in denazification hearings, were postwar reflections and letters of recommendation from friends and colleagues of the accused, since they were produced in a setting shorn of Nazi pressures and threats. In numerous cases, these reflections and recommendation letters—often self-exculpatory, disingenuous, and dishonest about the accused's activities and convictions during the Third Reich—won exoneration for former Nazis and Nazi sympathizers.

Denazification was a failure not only because the process assumed that those under investigation would respond openly and truthfully about their past during the Third Reich; it also foundered on the lack of consensus over what constituted Nazi activity or conviction. This allowed many German theologians in university theology faculties, in particular, to escape the process unscathed. Clear evidence of antisemitism in published scholarly writing could be attributed to classic motifs of Christian theological anti-Judaism, rather than taken as evidence of Nazi sympathy. Facing denazification investigations, theology academics and pastors with demonstrable ties to the German Christian movement did not necessarily need to resort to lies about their German Christian theology to save their careers.

In many cases they simply claimed that they had acted solely out of ecclesial motives. One self-exculpatory line often adopted was that their efforts during the Nazi era were aimed at defending the German church, both against the propaganda of the neo-pagans, and against the Nazi Party itself. They con-

[9] Frei, *Adenauer's Germany*, 99.
[10] See Remy, *The Heidelberg Myth*, 146–76.

stituted—so the story typically went—a church-based resistance to Hitler. As "proof" of such claims, theologians would point, for example, to excision of the Old Testament as a conciliatory effort to keep anti-Christian Nazis from attacking the church as "Jewish," or to their Nazi-era support for retaining the Old Testament as evidence of their alleged anti-Nazi stance. Those who joined the NSDAP prior to 1933 and hence were in a more difficult position—the denazification tribunals tended to see pre-1933 party membership as evidence of heartfelt adherence to Nazi ideology—claimed that they joined the party when it seemed sincere in its promise to combat anti-Christian and anti-church tendencies in Germany. In such cases theologians and other academics who were former party members and Nazi sympathizers drew on the German tradition of apolitical Wissenschaft to claim that their immersion in scholarship was itself sufficient evidence of their abstinence from political involvement.

THE POSTWAR CHURCH IN THURINGIA

Denazification of the Thuringian church, which had housed the Institute, followed patterns common to other regional churches.[11] First, occupation authorities proclaimed a set of laws and procedures that classified levels of Nazi involvement and their consequences for further state employment. Then the churches established categories of pastors based on their membership in Nazi-related organizations and ideological commitments to National Socialism. Following the denazification laws issued by the state of Thuringia on July 23, 1945, the Thuringian church synod declared that pastors and other employees or retired employees of the church would be discharged if they had "through their political or church-political behavior grossly violated the duties of their office and injured the church." Church officials implicated in the law included those who had joined the NSDAP or the German Christian movement prior to April 1, 1933, or who had joined later and had taken leadership positions in the German Christian movement, the party, the SS, SA, or other affiliated organizations. Also implicated were those who had not been members of these organizations but who "vigorously put their goals into action."[12]

[11] Vollnhals, *Evangelische Kirche und Entnazifizierung.* Vollnhals's study concentrates on the churches of Bavaria, Württemberg, Hessen, and Bremen, and offers a good point of comparison to Thuringia.

[12] Denazification rules of the Thuringian church of December 12, 1945, cited in Vollnhals, *Entnazifizierung und Selbstreinigung,* 91.

Those who had left or been expelled from the German Christians or Nazi organizations or who could demonstrate their opposition to or even persecution by the Nazi Party or the German Christian movement would not be discharged but might be moved to a different position within the church or to a different community.[13]

The Thuringian church—despite an impressive set of declarations announced after the war—carried out a notably mild and superficial process of denazification, given the particularly compromised nature of the Thuringian pastorate. Of the approximately 800 pastors in Thuringia, close to half had been members of the German Christian movement, and it is likely that many of the rest had been sympathizers.[14] Had all the pastors sympathetic to the German Christian movement been fired, the Thuringian church would have collapsed for lack of personnel. However, an eradication of Nazi sympathizers from the ranks of the clergy was never even considered. Many of those who assumed power in the church after the war had been members of the Confessing Church, putative opponents of the German Christians, yet their postwar leniency toward their former antagonists is a striking illustration of the combination of memory and forgetfulness that, Tony Judt has argued, characterized postwar Europe.[15] On the one hand, the collaboration of the former German Christian pastors with the Nazis was remembered in order to justify the appropriation of power by theologically conservative clergy, but on the other hand, the collaboration was conveniently "forgotten" in order to keep those tarnished pastors working within the church. Fear of exposure of their Nazi past also meant that former German Christians could be easily controlled and disciplined. Thus, retaining the former German Christians gave added power to those now in control of the postwar church, which is precisely what happened in Thuringia.

The percentage of Thuringian congregations that had been governed by German Christian principles in their liturgies, religious instruction, and theologies is not precisely known, but the immediate postwar challenge was considerable: churchgoing Christians had to be persuaded that the German Christian theology they had been taught for the past twelve years was no longer acceptable, an overwhelming task for the new church leaders. Most important, these former Confessing Church pastors, while repudiating the work of the

---

[13] Other options included early retirement, curtailment of salary, and loss of "Dienstbezeichnung," designation of employment status.

[14] Seidel, ". . . Im Sturm und Gericht der Gegenwart," 174–75.

[15] Judt, *Postwar*.

Institute, often shared the German Christians' negative theological views of Judaism. As a result, the postwar church was anxious to restore doctrinal discipline but did not address the antisemitism that had flourished during the Third Reich.

An example is Moritz Mitzenheim, who was elected bishop of the Thuringian church in December 1945, a position he held until 1970. Within weeks of his installation, Mitzenheim had organized dozens of meetings of pastors, and officially restored the use of the prewar hymnal and catechism.[16] But he expelled few pastors from the church, and he never confronted the church's involvement in Nazi politics nor addressed the antisemitic teachings that had been so rampant within the Thuringian church prior to 1945.

The exact number of Thuringian pastors released from the church or reassigned after the war is unknown, due to German privacy laws regulating the archives, and to the fact that many documents went "missing," purged at the end of the war by church officials.[17] A 1948 article in the Thuringian church newspaper, *Glaube und Heimat*, claimed that 84 pastors were released from church service, out of a total of 800, and that all superintendents with Nazi Party membership stepped down.[18] But the pastors were eventually reinstated or found positions elsewhere; as a Thuringian official noted in 1950, "Bishop Mitzenheim and his church council did not denazify the pastorate and church leadership after 1945."[19] Mitzenheim believed he could reeducate nearly all the pastors and "exclude the uneducable and the compromised."[20] Who precisely constituted "uneducable and compromised" in Mitzenheim's eyes remains unclear, given his willingness to retain even the most egregious Nazis and leaders of the German Christian movement, such as (as we shall see) Grundmann and Eisenhuth. Thuringian state officials, for their part, had no illusions, and expressed their concerns in official reports about the religious education in the public schools that would be provided by former German Christian members: "Here sat pastors . . . two repulsive servants of Hitler and nasty and dangerous war enthusiasts, both orally and in writing . . . [T]he Nazi pastorate remained utterly intact, not only in its personnel but also in its organizational structure."[21] As one state official bluntly observed, "a purification

[16] Freudenberg, "Bemerkungen zur kirchlichen Lage in Deutschland, Juli 1945," 17.

[17] Seidel, "In Sturm und Gericht der Gegenwart," 172, and 176 fn 44.

[18] Erich Hertzsch, "Wie steht es um die Thüringer evangelische Kirche?" *Glaube und Heimat* 3 (1948), p. 8; cited by Seidel, "In Sturm und Gericht der Gegenwart," 176 fn 44.

[19] ThHStA Büro MP 868; cited by Seidel, "In Sturm und Gerich der Gegenwart," 171.

[20] Freudenberg, "Bemerkungen zur kirchlichen Lage in Deutschland," 17.

[21] ThHStA, 3426, 39.

of the pastorate has not been successful. Not once was the law of July 23 applied to the pastorate."[22] Clearly Mitzenheim was not interested in initiating a thorough theological cleansing of the church. Under his leadership, critical public discussion of Grundmann's Institute and of the activities of the German Christian movement within Thuringia was taboo—and indeed remained so for the next half-century.

Not only in Thuringia, but throughout Germany, former German Christians reorganized after the war. Regional churches reassigned the more notorious German Christian pastors to remote villages or institutional chaplaincies.[23] Some who remained within the Protestant church established private theological discussion groups, while others left the church and reappeared in the so-called "free churches," Protestant churches that were unaffiliated with the state; former German Christian members, together with former members of the neo-Teutonic Deutsche Glaubensbewegung, created the Deutsche Unitarier Religionsgemeinschaft and the Freie Akademie, two independent religious and cultural organizations.[24] Within Thuringia in the 1950s a circle of former German Christian pastors took shape in Weimar, led by Herbert von Hintzenstern, who had studied under Grundmann at Jena and had been active in the Institute. Von Hintzenstern held a prestigious position in the Thuringian church after the war, serving as editor of the church newspaper, *Glaube und Heimat*.[25] Similar circles of ex-German Christians formed elsewhere.[26]

The most notorious postwar rehabilitation was that of Leffler, who had served as an official in the Thuringian Ministry of Education and as nominal head of the Institute. He was arrested and imprisoned in Ludwigsburg in July 1947 and classified as guilty ("Belasteter"), level two, and given a punishment of one year in a work camp, a 2,000 RM fine, and a five-year suspension from his profession. Immediately, Leffler issued a public declaration of repentance,

---

[22] Ibid.

[23] Barnett, *For the Soul of the People*, 250.

[24] Peter Kratz, "Deutsche Unitarier: Völkisch rassistische Sekte aus Wohlfahrtsmarken finanziert," *Der rechte Rand* 6 (April 1990), 14–15, cited by von Schnurbein, *Religion als Kulturkritik*, 123. See also Nanko, "Von 'Deutsch' nach 'Frei' und zurück?," 214–33.

[25] Böhm "Die ersten zehn Jahre der Evangelische Akademie Thüringen,"195. Rainer Lächele reports that in Thuringia in 1946, a retired German Christian pastor conducted a confirmation service "in the German Christian sense." Lächele, "Religionsfreiheit,"150.

[26] One of the major leaders of the national German Christian movement, Eduard Le Seur, founded the "Einung Christliche Volkskirche" at a June 1946 gathering of former German Christian pastors in Stuttgart. Lächele, "Religionsfreiheit," 146–48; see also Lächele, *Ein Volk, ein Reich, ein Glaube*, passim.

and solicited support for his case from a variety of prominent church figures. As Bergen notes, Leffler's repentance was joined to an insistence that he was not responsible for atrocities against the Jews, since he had always believed in "genuine tolerance and reconciliation."[27] Leffler's prostration as atoning sinner combined with insistence that he was not responsible for the Reich's crimes was a perfect combination in the eyes of German Protestants, who presented his case sympathetically in church newspapers.[28] Leffler's self-effeminization, confessing sin while asserting powerlessness, became classic for Christians in postwar Germany and was reflected in the new image of Jesus that was promoted during that era: suffering and empathic yet powerless against his enemies.[29] In less than a year Leffler was released from the work camp, and by 1949 he was employed again as a pastor for the church of Bavaria; he retired in 1970 and died in 1983.[30]

THE POSTWAR REHABILITATION OF WALTER GRUNDMANN

Grundmann experienced an even easier rehabilitation. He had been drafted into military service in August of 1943 and sent to Riga, then to the Soviet Union.[31] He claimed that he was assigned by the army to work as a radio operator, reporting on troop movements on the Eastern Front. At the end of the war, he was taken prisoner by the Americans near Prague and brought to a Soviet prisoner of war camp at Focsani, in southern Transylvania. He was released from the POW camp on medical grounds at the end of October 1945, among the first German soldiers to return home.

When he first returned from the POW camp, Grundmann lived in Jena, where he became active in diaconate work. He was one of forty-five Thuringian pastors who were former members of the Nazi Party temporarily suspended

[27] Bergen, *Twisted Cross*, 223. See also Vollnhals, *Evangelische Kirche und Entnazifizierung*, 287.

[28] This is documented by Bergen, *Twisted Cross*, 223.

[29] For example, wives of imprisoned Nazis were urged to follow the example of a Jesus imagined in those terms; see Kellenbach, "God's Love and Women's Love."

[30] Leffler's postwar years are described in Rinnen, *Kirchenmann und Nationalsozialist*.

[31] In response to a telegram, asking which professors and instructors should be drafted, the rector, Karl Astel, replied on January 30, 1942, to the Ministry of Education in Berlin stating that professors could not be drafted because they were irreplaceable as experts in their fields, directors of independent institutes or clinics, or already engaged in war-related work (UAJ BA 2138).

Grundmann accused Astel of arranging to have him drafted; see his post-1950 curriculum vitae (LKA Eisenach) and in his unpublished 1969 memoir, *Erkenntnis und Wahrheit*. The accusation was part of his postwar claim of having been persecuted during the Third Reich.

from their duties until their cases could be reviewed by church officials. In the interim, they were assigned to work as adjunct preachers and church administrators; only a few were let go. As of September 1945, Grundmann had been officially released from his Jena professorship on the grounds that he had entered the NSDAP prior to April 1, 1933.[32] Grundmann protested these decisions and launched an energetic and well-coordinated campaign for his reinstatement in the Thuringian church. Although he was unable to save the Institute—which was dissolved by the church in late 1945—in all other respects Grundmann's campaign was a stunning success.

Grundmann's appeal for a position as pastor was rejected by Thuringian church officials just two weeks after he returned from a POW camp, and he was urged to return to his home church of Saxony, a decision he appealed with passion. He defended himself to Mitzenheim by hiding under the skirts of Christian theology: "I ask myself, what exactly I am guilty of. . . . For what was my life until now? I can affirm with a good conscience: dedication to Christianity."[33] Indeed, he continued, had the state and the church listened to him, Germany's fate would have been different—though he does not spell out any specifics. But those around Grundmann disputed that view. Heussi, for example, wrote to Mitzenheim that Grundmann had devoted all his talents to supporting the theology of the German Christians.[34] Neither his academic nor his church colleagues ever linked Grundmann to Nazi crimes nor labeled his views antisemitic. Grundmann's defense was that his efforts during the Third Reich had the sole purpose of defending the church against its putative enemies within the Nazi Party, particularly Alfred Rosenberg.

As with other cases of postwar rehabilitation of Nazis and Nazi sympathizers, Grundmann's campaign rested largely on the solicitation of letters of personal testimony from former colleagues. The first wave of letters was aimed at Thuringian state officials. Once they granted him state clearance, Grundmann adroitly used their decision to pressure the Thuringian church for full reinstatement.

One of the first letters on Grundmann's behalf came from Waldemar Macholz, who had come out of retirement as professor at the University of Jena to serve temporarily as dean of the faculty of theology. In a statement dated January 11, 1946, Macholz wrote that while Grundmann had been a member

[32] Letter from Thuringian State Office for Education, September 13, 1945, signed Wolf, director: "We are firing you according to Regulation #2 of the Regulations for the Purification of Public Office of Nazi Elements with Immediate Impact on Public Service (LKA Eisenach, III, 2).

[33] Letter from Grundmann to Mitzenheim, dated December 13, 1945 (LKA Eisenach, PA Grundmann G 2402/I, 5).

[34] Heussi to Mitzenheim, April 4, 1949 (LKA Eisenach, Grundmann G 2402.I, 44).

of the NSDAP, he had not been an "activist." He neither held party office nor was given any assignments on behalf of the party. Further, Macholz wrote, "There can be no doubt that Herr Dr. Grundmann as a professor spoke up for Protestant Christianity through sermons, through witness and intervention of many kinds, and served the church." His devotion to Christianity, claimed Macholz, had brought Grundmann into conflict with the rector of the university, Astel, and with other representatives of the NSDAP, causing him great troubles. Finally, Macholz attested to Grundmann's importance as a scholar.[35]

Meyer-Erlach, who was also seeking a favorable verdict from denazification officials in 1946 after his dismissal from his professorship, added his voice on behalf of Grundmann. In a letter written in January of 1946, he claimed, without evidence, that the office of Nazi ideologue and party official Alfred Rosenberg had lobbied against the appointment of Grundmann as professor of New Testament at Jena. As a result, he claimed, Grundmann's professorship was delayed from October 1936 to November 1938. The opposition arose, in his view, as a result of Grundmann's published views on the "centuries-old synthesis of Christianity and the German spiritual life." Meyer-Erlach reminded the denazification officials of Rosenberg's antagonism toward Christianity and his view that Nazism could be established only by bringing an end to Christianity. In this same letter Meyer-Erlach claimed that Rosenberg's opposition to Grundmann intensified during the war.[36] In fact, Grundmann's appointment as tenured professor at Jena was delayed until 1938 solely because the university was waiting to learn if his predecessor, Erich Fascher, would resign and accept a position at the University of Halle. Moreover, Grundmann expressed his gratitude to Rosenberg in the introduction to one of his books.[37]

Others prepared to write on Grundmann's behalf included Fritz Schmidt-Clausing, who had earned a doctorate at Jena under Grundmann. In his letter he insisted that Grundmann had rejected the NSDAP in 1942, that his work with the Thuringian German Christian movement was on behalf of his "faith in Christ" ("Christusbekenntnis"); and that he had struggled against the neo-pagan movement even harder than had the leaders of the rival Confessing Church.[38] Written support also came from another former Jena theology student, Hans Mieskes, who by early 1946 had become assistant to the dean of

---

[35] ThHStA, Walter Grundmann Personalakten (PA), 104.

[36] ThHStA, Grundmann PA, 108.

[37] See the introduction to Grundmann and Euler, *Das religiöse Gesicht*.

[38] Letter from Schmidt-Clausing to Grundmann, dated January 3, 1946 (ThHStA, Grundmann PA, 110). He refers in the letter to a member of his congregation, Walther Körber, who worked at the propaganda ministry, despite being a devout Christian, and informed Schmidt-Clausing of the ministry's dislike of Grundmann.

the social pedagogy faculty at Jena. Mieskes wrote that Grundmann's position on race and Judaism placed him in hidden opposition to Nazi ideology.[39]

From within the Thuringian church came letters from church officials Theodor Elle and Reinhold Jauernig, who both claimed that university rector Astel considered Grundmann's work contrary to Nazism. Jauernig testified that in 1943 Astel had attempted to force all professors of theology, including the 66-year-old Heussi, into military service, on the grounds that they were "saboteurs" working against National Socialism.[40] The völkisch writer Lulu von Strauss und Torney-Diederichs also wrote on Grundmann's behalf.[41] In a letter to him, she wrote that she "still think[s] happily of the many evening conversations that concerned the deepest religious and ecclesiastical concerns and questions. Even in those discussions I did not have the impression that you were a fanatical disciple of National Socialism, but rather a scholar dedicated to the German spirit and faith."[42] And Rudolf Volkmann, who served in the 1920s and '30s as music director of at the University of Jena, and who subsequently became renowned as a choral director, organist, and pianist, wrote that as far as he was concerned Grundmann had joined the NSDAP for social reasons and did not withdraw out of concern for his family.[43]

Even as he applied for denazification, Grundmann laundered the work of the Institute by denying its racism. In a December 1945 report to Thuringian church officials, he described the Institute's work as an effort to counter Nazi charges that Christianity was "Judaism for Aryans and has to be destroyed. As a spiritual Judaism it poisons the German soul." He defined *Die Botschaft Gottes* as a reworking of the New Testament whose goal was opening the divine truth of the New Testament to contemporary Germans, not creating a "Jew-free New Testament." Rather, the concern was "a deeper question" concerning the "historical conditioning and eternal content" of the gospels. He acknowledged that the relation of religion and race was the basis of the Institute's work: "Religion is a matter of the character of a Volk. In the Volk, race, landscape, and historical fate are operating," a recognition Grundmann attributed to the philosopher Wilhelm Wundt, not to Nazi theorists. Since non-German scholars

---

[39] Letter from Hans Mieskes, January 22, 1946 (ThHStA, Grundmann PA, 109).

[40] Letter from Theodor Elle, January 21, 1946 (ThHStA, Grundmann PA, 105); letter from Reinhold Jauernig, January 19, 1946 (ThHStA, Grundmann PA, 106).

[41] Lulu was married to the völkisch publisher Eugen Diederichs. See Horn, "Lulu von Strauß und Torney-Diederichs," 311–25.

[42] Letter from Strauss and Torney-Diederichs to Grundmann, dated January 12, 1946 (ThHStA, Grundmann PA, 111).

[43] Letter from Volkmann to Grundmann, January 12, 1946 (ThHStA, Grundmann PA, 8807, 112).

had also concluded that Jesus has stood in opposition to Judaism, the Institute should not be viewed as politically motivated, he wrote. Grundmann presented himself as an objective scholar who had fallen victim to Nazi attacks as a result of his efforts on behalf of Christianity and his scholarship.[44] He continued presenting himself as a victim in subsequent communications with the church, arguing that he had undertaken an active resistance against leading figures of the Nazi Party, including the University of Jena's rector, Karl Astel, and had consequently been persecuted by them.[45]

Indeed, Grundmann argued that the cause of the German Christian movement, for all its errors, was not yet over, because the church still needed renewal.[46] Erich Hertzsch, a member of the governing board of the Thuringian church who shortly thereafter was appointed to the professorship in practical theology at the University of Jena once held by Meyer-Erlach, wrote back that he regretted the curtailment of Grundmann's scholarship, which he respected, but that the church could not retain the Institute, and Grundmann was urged to return to the church of Saxony.[47]

In January 1946 letters on behalf of Grundmann were submitted to the Thuringian Ministry of Education to win support for his reinstatement within the church.[48] Meanwhile, Grundmann was appealing directly to the church, now in the hands of his former opponents of the Confessing Church. His appeal was immediately rejected by state officials. The response of the church was similarly negative at first. Mitzenheim, aware that the denazification proceedings of the Thuringian church were under scrutiny, suggested that Grundmann return to his home church of Saxony,[49] and he also tried unsuccessfully to secure a position for Grundmann in Braunschweig. Over the next months, however, the mood of the church changed. Heinz Eisenhuth, for example, was reinstated by the Thuringian church with almost no objection and given a pastoral position in Jena in January 1946; in 1952 he was elevated to church superintendent in Eisenach, a position he retained for the remainder of his life. He died in 1983.

[44] Letter from Grundmann to the LKR, dated December 12, 1945 (LKA Eisenach A 921).

[45] Letter from Grundmann to Mitzenheim, January 29, 1946 (LKA Eisenach, PA Grundmann G 2402/I, 10).

[46] This argument appears in a text Grundmann wrote in the summer of 1946, *Sinn, Irrtum und Schuld der DC* (LKA Eisenach PA Grundmann G 2402/I), 51.

[47] Hertzsch to Grundmann January 14, 1946 (LKA Eisenach, Akten betr. Institut).

[48] Letter from Grundmann to government official Lindemann, January 24, 1946 (ThHStA Grundmann PA, 121). The response from Lindemann, dated the very next day, was negative: "After examining the documents I gain the impression that you can hardly be granted the administrative approval that you desire."

[49] Letter from Hertzsch to Grundmann January 14, 1946 (LKA Eisenach A921).

Grundmann's breakthrough came when Thuringian state officials, in the fall of 1946, urged the church to reinstate him on the grounds that he had waged a "manly struggle" ("mannhaften Kampf ") *against* National Socialist ideology. His early membership in the NSDAP was dismissed as the naïve mistake of a head-in-the-clouds theologian who realized his error soon after 1933. His value as an internationally recognized scholar was cited by pointing to his membership in the distinguished Society of New Testament Studies (SNTS), which had offered him membership in 1938.[50]

The state's verdict forced the Thuringian church to accept Grundmann. In September 1946, Mitzenheim concluded, based on testimony from Grundmann and his supporters, that Grundmann had distanced himself coura- geously from the Nazi Party shortly after Hitler came to power, and that "he stood in a struggle against the Nazi Party, as only a few other courageous peo- ple within the party did."[51] That this was a falsehood was known to members of the Thuringian church council.[52]

Before assigning Grundmann to new duties, however, he was asked to a se- ries of meetings in late 1946 and 1947 with church leaders to discuss his theological views. At those discussions he reluctantly affirmed the supremacy of Christ over political leaders, as had been asserted by the Confessing Church in its Barmen Declaration of 1934, and defended his behavior during the Third Reich. He had joined the Nazis as a Christian, he claimed, and had criti- cized Alfred Rosenberg's attacks on Christianity as anti-Nazi. His views on Ju- daism were not antisemitic, but affirmed his belief that Christ takes a unique shape for each "Volk."[53] What was not a part of these meetings was a discus- sion of Jews, antisemitism, and the Nazi murder of the Jews. Nor was Grund- mann challenged on the question of Jesus's Jewishness. Indeed, a private cor- respondence gives evidence that he did not renounce his previous position after the war; in 1949, Grundmann, responding to a private query from a fellow

[50] Letter from senior privy councillor Erle, president of the state of Thuringia, to the regional church council, dated September 10, 1946 (LKA Eisenach, Personalakten Grundmann; ThHStA, Grundmann PA).

[51] LKA Eisenach G 2402, no. 25.

[52] A sole dissenting voice was church councillor Gerhard Lotz, in September 1946, who strongly disagreed that Grundmann could be seen as a nominal Nazi Party member. "As director of the de- judaization Institute he strengthened, built up, and scientifically strengthened racism within the church." Lotz was appalled to see scholars with minimal Nazi involvements lose their professor- ships and livelihoods, while an old party member such as Grundmann was given employment by the church. Report by Lotz about Grundmann, September 10, 1946 (LKA Eisenach G 2402 no. 29).

[53] Minutes of the meetings (LKA EisenachG 2402).

pastor, Gerhard Kropatscheck, who had been a member of the Confessing Church in Saxony, wrote that the question of Jesus's "racial blood" remained an open historical question. He had never asserted that Jesus was an Aryan, Grundmann wrote, simply that his Jewishness could not be proven.[54] Somehow that reassured Kropatscheck that Grundmann qualified for church denazification, and he wrote to Mitzenheim that Grundmann recognized his guilt and should be given a position as pastor.[55]

By the summer of 1948, Grundmann conceded in a letter to church officials that he had recognized the errors of the German Christian movement, and again requested reinstatement as a pastor.[56] The reinstatement took another two years to achieve. Gerhard Gloege, a former Confessing Church pastor who became professor of practical theology at the University of Jena after the war, found Grundmann's repentance insincere—"He tries to vindicate himself and to emphasize the theological legitimacy of his prior actions"—yet recommended his reinstatement as pastor so that the church might control him: "One never knows with Grundmann where his sharp intellect will turn, if someone does not lead him in the right direction and take him under their wing."[57] That concern, as Thomas Seidel has pointed out, had already been voiced by the Nazi bishop Martin Sasse in 1936 when Grundmann was under consideration for the professorship in Jena: "Be careful with Grundmann!"[58] The church of Thuringia did indeed retain Grundmann, granted him forgiveness, and gave him a pulpit. Thus in July 1950, Grundmann found himself pastor in the remote rural village of Waltershausen, the kind of penance assigned by the church to pastors who had erred.[59] He remained there for three years, and in 1952 began delivering weekly lectures in New Testament at a seminary in Saxony that trained teachers of religion.

From exile to crown jewel: In 1954 Grundmann was offered a full-time faculty position in Naumburg, Saxony, but instead he took a position as rector of

[54] Letter from Kropatscheck to Grundmann, March 29, 1949 (LKA Eisenach A 920, G 2402); letter from Grundmann to Kropatscheck, April 2, 1949 (LKA Eisenach, PA Grundmann G 2402/I, Bl. 50); both cited by Seidel, "Die 'Entnazifizierungs-Akte Grundmanns,'" 26–27.

[55] Letter from Kropatscheck to Mitzenheim, June 14, 1949 (LKA Eisenach, PA Grundmann G 2404); cited by Seidel, "Die 'Entnazifizierungs-Akte Grundmanns,'" 367–68.

[56] Grundmann, application for reinstatement to the Thuringian church, August 1, 1948 (LKA Eisenach, PA Grundmann G 2402, 33).

[57] Letter from Gloege to Mitzenheim, July 15, 1949 (LKA Eisenach PA Grundmann G 2402, 54).

[58] Seidel, "Die "Entnazifizierungs-Akte Grundmanns," 349.

[59] For a description of his work in Waltershausen, see Grundmann, *Erkenntnis und Wahrheit*, 80. He devoted particular attention to working with youth groups, often taking them on hiking trips.

the Thuringian seminary in Eisenach that trained religion teachers and church musicians. The appointment of a former Nazi as rector was not unusual at the time; John Connelly has found that sixty percent of the rectors appointed to East German institutions of higher education between 1954 and 1962 were former Nazi Party members. While he has not uncovered evidence of a concerted effort by the communist bureaucracy to steer old Nazis to positions of power, Connelly argues that having former Nazis in influential positions was purposeful because they were easier to control, at the very least through blackmail, than Christians or other nonsocialist antifascists, who were likely to be anticommunist as well.[60] Grundmann moved into a large apartment in the seminary's villa at the top of the Hainstein hills overlooking the city of Eisenach in 1954. He also taught occasional classes in church history and New Testament at a women's seminary, and lectured at seminaries in Naumburg and Leipzig. During the 1950s and '60s, Grundmann was remarkably prolific, publishing a vast number of popular and professional studies of the New Testament, including three massive commentaries to the synoptic gospels. He also lectured to the ministers-in-training at the Thuringian Predigerseminar, with the encouragement of Walter Saft, its rector from 1964 to 1976.[61] After 1967, Grundmann was invited to teach courses training pastoral assistants and vicars who were preparing for their second theological examinations. Shortly before his death in 1976 he was appointed church councillor of Thuringia, an honorific position that indicates the esteem with which he was regarded by the postwar church in East Germany.[62]

Grundmann's Involvement with the East German State

Despite this impressive rehabilitation, Grundmann nursed an abiding resentment toward Thuringian church officials, who were former members of the Confessing Church, his one-time adversaries. His resentment laid the foundation for his second, flourishing postwar career as a secret informer to the Stasi,

---

[60] One example is Hans Beyer, a chemist who had been a member of the SA and the NSDAP, who was appointed rector of the University of Greifswald. Connelly, *Captive University*, and Connelly and Grüttner, *Zwischen Autonomie und Anpassung*.

[61] Private interview with Hermann Lins, rector of the Predigerseminar from 1976 to 1992, February 1993.

[62] A report on the funeral service was written by his former student, Herbert von Hintzenstern, "Abschied von Kirchenrat Dr. theol. Walter Grundmann," *Glaube und Heimat* 37:12 (1976), 9. The last essay written by Grundmann, "Vom Sinn des Lebens," appeared in *Glaube und Heimat* 43 (1976), 5.

the East German communist regime's pervasive and powerful secret police. Grundmann's Nazi past was no impediment to collaboration with the communist state. Indeed, he abandoned his passion for Nazism quite easily, but his abiding belief that theology should suit the interests of the state would place him during the 1950s and '60s in the same position he had held in the 1930s and '40s. That there was, of course, no significant number of Jews remaining in East Germany alleviated the immediacy of his passionate antisemitism and with it his commitment to Nazi ideology. Such easy transfers of political loyalties from fascism to communism were all too common. Once Nazism's function as a political legitimator of antisemitism was accomplished with the elimination of the Jews, Institute members became involved in whatever political movement was in the ascendancy. In West Germany, Redeker became a representative of the conservative Christian Democratic Union (CDU), serving from 1954 to 1967 in the state parliament of Schleswig-Holstein, and Meyer-Erlach became a vocal anticommunist in Lower Franconia, while Leipoldt represented the CDU from 1953 to1963 in the East German parliament.

Grundmann's Nazi-era activities were known to East German officials. As late as 1990 a Stasi document lists his name among other Nazi supporters and war criminals who had eluded responsibility by receiving a church position.[63] When he was first recruited, in 1956, a Stasi report about his scholarship cited some of his most notorious antisemitic prewar and wartime publications and drew upon information from two anonymous informers, code-named "Karl" and "Maier," in its discussion of Grundmann's Nazi Party membership and directorship of the Institute. [64]

According to a Stasi report of Grundmann's first meeting with officials of the Stasi in April of 1956, "Grundmann . . . said that he welcomed being able to have a conversation with us and that he had anticipated such a discussion because of his past." In discussing his own background, Grundmann told them that the Institute had been founded on the initiative of several church leaders and that he had been given the assignment of its leadership. Its goal was to study what influence Judaism had exerted on Christianity, "and not, as today is falsely assumed, to prove that this influence was necessarily present." He claimed that a controversy over a 1943 journal article led to his military draft,

[63] Besier and Wolf, eds., "*Pfarrer, Christen und Katholiken*," document 133, 653.

[64] Stasi file dated April 30, 1956, unsigned. Grundmann himself was known to the Stasi variously as "Walter," "Berg," or "Burg," and his meetings were held at the Thuringer Hof hotel in Eisenach, at a pub in Erfurt, or in Berlin. I would like to express my gratitude to Prof. Gerhard Besier, University of Dresden, and editor of the journal *Kirchliche Zeitgeschichte*, for providing me with a copy of Grundmann's Stasi file.

and by that time he had reconsidered his "1933" [sic] membership in the Nazi Party.[65] The Stasi's report notes Grundmann's hatred of East German church leaders, and of former members of the Confessing Church who were now in positions of authority, and suggested that Grundmann could be used to reveal conflicts among church leaders. Grundmann himself reported his intensive study of Marxist literature, and his belief that the future belonged to socialism. He promised to keep his meetings with the Stasi secret, and to provide church-related material.

Through the 1950s and '60s, he met every few months with the Stasi, often taking the initiative to arrange a meeting.[66] His handlers found him more eager than they to meet. By September of 1956, he was ready to provide names and details about the church's activities.[67] He reported to the Stasi on private discussions he held with the bishop of Thuringia, and the contents of private letters sent by Mitzenheim to his pastors; he claimed that church leaders judged East Germany to be a "necessary evil," and he wrote a Christian justification of the socialist state, just as he had done in the Third Reich and using almost identical language.[68] His Stasi handlers were not impressed; he was said to be a typical academic: desperate for admiration and with an inclination to intrigue.[69]

Whether his cooperation with the Stasi was undertaken with the intention of advancing his career, taking revenge on his enemies within the church, or mitigating his Nazi past, it clearly achieved all three goals for him. His Stasi connections allowed him to attend international theological colloquia—in West Germany, Austria, England, and Prague—and he supplied secret reports

[65] In an undated report in Grundmann's Stasi file, signed by "Maxim," Grundmann urged that his meetings with the Stasi be kept a secret because "he would not like it if it would be told about him that he had previously worked with the Nazis and now with the Stasi" (Stasi report, December 3, 1956).

[66] For example on October 9, 1958, "Walter" telephoned and made an appointment for October 11, 1958, to report on a church meeting that had occurred in West Berlin on the question of atomic weapons.

[67] Grundmann informed the Stasi, for example, that a reactionary church circle had developed in Magdeburg, with followers in Eisenach, and gave the names of church officials in the West who, he alleged, were trying to rehabilitate the German Christians (Grundmann's Stasi file, September 24, 1956).

[68] He also offered to compose a formal set of theses for GDR pastors that would synthesize Christianity and socialism, just as he had composed the Twenty-Eight Theses of the German Christians in 1933. And he requested funding from the Stasi to found a journal for his former German Christian comrades who had formed a theological circle in Weimar (Grundmann's Stasi file, April 4, 1960).

[69] Report signed by "Ludwig" (Grundmann's Stasi file, May 11, 1960).

when he returned. He was given money to spy on former German Christian leaders in Kiel,[70] and received assistance to attend a meeting of the Society for New Testament Studies (SNTS) in England, of which he was one of only thirty-eight international members, elected by their peers to membership in the organization, the most prestigious in the field of New Testament scholarship; Leipoldt was the only other member from East Germany.[71]

Grundmann's political intrigues in East Germany were similar to those he undertook during the Third Reich, and he used the same tactics to achieve power in the two ideologically opposed states. In both regimes he used his position within the church as a base for political influence within the state, and exploited his reputation as a respected figure within the state to achieve power within the church. In his meetings with the Stasi, he presented the church as a powerful force within East German society, and himself as one of its most important leaders. His influence within the church, he implied, would be of enormous usefulness to the state. And his Stasi handlers believed him: Grundmann was of value to the communist state in transmitting materials from the Nazi era that compromised postwar church figures.[72]

GRUNDMANN AND POSTWAR GERMAN THEOLOGY

Most remarkable about Grundmann's postwar career is his extraordinary literary productivity. He published extensively, though much of what he wrote repeated itself. As he did during the Third Reich, Grundmann continued to write for a wide range of audiences, from popular lay Christians to ordained clergy to international scholars. Some of his publications were commissioned by the church, some were solicited by other scholars. In these postwar publications, as with his pre-1945 writings, he remained a synthesizer rather than a breaker of new ground. His books were priced reasonably, from the several versions of the lives of Jesus, geared to a popular readership, to the beautifully printed three-volume *Umwelt des Urchristentums* (*The World of Early Christianity*), coedited with Leipoldt. Other studies of Jesus also appeared, including a large, 400-page life of Jesus, *Die Geschichte Jesu Christi*, published in 1956, and

---

[70] Grundmann's Stasi file, November 27, 1956. He also reported that former German Christian members living in West Germany were planning to issue a journal, and expressed resentment that they were hindered in their careers by the West German church (Grundmann's Stasi file, September 24, 1956).

[71] Grundmann's Stasi file, May 22, 1956. Grundmann was officially registered as a secret informant on December 3, 1956.

[72] Report signed by "Ludwig" (Grundmann's Stasi file, May 11, 1960).

a shorter volume in 1975, *Jesus von Nazareth: Bürge zwischen Gott und Mensch*, in which he speaks of Jesus's "contemporaries" ("Zeitgenossen") rather than his fellow Jews.[73]

The sheer size and scope of Grundmann's postwar literary production is impressive. He coedited a volume of biblical stories and commentary on the Ten Commandments, geared to Christian families, in 1963,[74] and, at the behest of the church, wrote a study of biblical history in religious instruction,[75] a small pamphlet of catechism,[76] an interpretation of religious art,[77] and a religious guide for adults.[78] In addition, his individual commentaries on the three synoptic gospels, which first began to appear in 1959 in the prestigious scholarly series, *Theologischer Handkommentar zum Neuen Testament*,[79] sold well and influenced the postwar generation of theology students and pastors, appearing as late as the 1990s as recommended reading in preparation for theological examinations that were required for ordination to the ministry in Protestant churches in Germany. The commentary volumes were large and substantial, reviewing the scholarship, analyzing the Greek, and offering synthetic interpretations of each pericope that could be easily transformed into a sermon.[80] Their low price made them accessible to a wide audience in both East and West Germany.

In Grundmann's postwar scholarship, there is a shift from efforts to reconstruct the historical figure of Jesus to describing the portrayal of Jesus in the gospel texts. In that way, Grundmann sought both to distance himself from claims about Jesus's historicity and to adopt a more sophisticated, form-critical approach to the historical evidence. Much of his Nazi-era vocabulary disappeared, and Jesus was no longer termed an "Aryan," but Grundmann's descriptions of the degeneracy of Judaism in antiquity remained intact, and he

---

[73] A partial list of Grundmann's numerous postwar publications is included in the Bibliography.

[74] Grundmann, and Kramer, *Auf dass ich sein Eigen sei.*

[75] "Die biblische Geschichte im kirchlichen Unterricht."

[76] *Du gehörst Gott: Handbuch für den Katechismusunterricht* (with Helmut Kramer).

[77] *Die Sprache des Altars.*

[78] *Dem Ursprung neu verbunden.*

[79] The commentary series was edited after the war by Erich Fascher, professor of New Testament at the University of Halle and Grundmann's predecessor in the chair of New Testament at Jena.

[80] The commentary on Mark (347 pages) appeared in 1959; Luke (418 pages) appeared in 1961; Matthew (580 pages) appeared in 1968. The commentaries on Mark and Luke were reprinted in the late 1980s. Although Wolfgang Wiefel published new commentaries on Luke (1988) and Matthew (1998) for the *Theologische Handkommentar* series, there has thus far been no new commentary on Mark in the series. Grundmann's commentaries remain in print today.

Figure 6.1. Walter Grundmann.

continued to emphasize the non-Jewish milieu of early Christianity. In his postwar writings the Hasmoneans remain dangerous and violent, and Galilee remains essentially Gentile. As in Third Reich publications, Grundmann presents Jesus in opposition to the Pharisees and in solidarity with those whom the Pharisees held in contempt. Jesus is opposed to Sabbath observance, cultic purity, and oral law, and for that opposition, the Jews had him crucified.[81] In his commentaries, Grundmann argues that particular New Testament texts emerged in entirely Gentile contexts; 2 Peter, he claims, originated in Rome, and Jude in Galilee, both without Jewish influence.[82] He claims that Jesus's opposition to Judaism was not originally part of his teachings, which were intended for a universal audience, but had developed in response to the Pharisees' hostility toward Jesus and those to whom he preached. Echoing the language of the Godesberg Declaration of 1939, which proclaimed an "unbridgeable opposition" between Judaism and Jesus, Grundmann describes the opposition between Jesus's message and that of the Pharisees: "A decision must be made between brotherliness and selfish fear of being placed at a disadvantage, between joy in sonship and brotherhood and harsh, joyless service."[83]

Particularly striking is Grundmann's continued portrayal of Jews as violent: "The demons of a fanatical nationalism pushed Israel into the abyss; in the Jewish war this word was fulfilled in terrible ways."[84] Another motif Grundmann reiterated frequently is that women were treated terribly in the ancient Jewish community, as property rather than human beings, whose fathers could beat them or marry them off with impunity and without regard for their wishes.[85] Jesus, Grundmann writes, was the first man within the "Jewish realm" whose relationships with women gave them full personal and religious worth.[86] Jesus himself did not begin with an opposition to the Pharisees; rather, they rejected him. By exaggerating the conflict between Jesus and his Jewish opponents, Grundmann attests the "evidence" that "cost him his life."[87] "What Jesus suffered from and what alienated him from his generation, is his

[81] Grundmann, *Die Gotteskindschaft in der Geschichte Jesu*, 109, 127.

[82] Grundmann, *Der Brief des Judas und der zweite Brief des Petrus*. Grundmann had initially begun those commentaries in his student days at the request of Kittel; they were published as a single volume in 1974. His commentary on 2 Peter was judged in 1989 by Birger Pearson, an American New Testament scholar, as the best currently available, and Jude as one of the most important; see Pearson, "James 1–2 Peter, Jude," 384 and 386.

[83] *Die Geschichte Jesu Christi*, 112.

[84] Ibid., 160–61.

[85] *Die Entscheidung Jesu*, 23–24.

[86] Leipoldt and Grundmann, eds., *Umwelt des Urchristentums*, 1:180.

[87] Ibid., 1:439.

generation's inability to have faith."[88] In a postwar book about the altar carvings of the sixteenth-century artist Hans Witten, found in churches in Chemnitz and rural Thuringia, Grundmann describes the scourging of Jesus as undertaken with a "determined hatred" that sought Jesus's "extermination" ("Vernichtung"); that it was the Romans, not the Jews, who carried out the death penalty is left unsaid.[89] Matthias Grünewald's Isenheim altar, long an object of identification for Germans as a martyred people, also occupied Grundmann's postwar attention.[90]

In her study of German theological anti-Judaism, Charlotte Klein has noted Grundmann's claim that Judaism has no morality.[91] Jewish law, Grundmann wrote in 1957, leads only "to unbrotherliness, to contempt and hatred for the other person."[92] Ten years later, in *Umwelt des Urchristentums*, he and Leipoldt wrote that for the Jews, "God is frequently seen in the metaphor of a tradesman with his bookkeeping and accounting: a metaphor which occurs also in Jesus's parables—there, however, in order to be transcended. Every fulfillment of the law is entered on the credit side, every transgression on the debit side."[93] Defining Judaism as a business transaction with God denies its religiosity.

Grundmann's contemporaries in the field of New Testament, however, regarded him with respect and often defended him. The SNTS did not ask him to withdraw his membership after the war, when his Institute activities became known.[94] He was invited to contribute to edited volumes honoring colleagues in the field of theology, and he wrote reviews for major journals of new and important scholarship.[95] He also gave papers at conferences in the emerging

---

[88] *Die Geschichte Jesu Christi*, 161.

[89] Grundmann, *Der Meister H.W.*, 25–26. In 1942 an exhibit took place in Chemnitz that included the work of Hans Witten.

[90] Grundmann, *Die Sprache des Altars.* On German identification with the Christ figure of the Isenheim altar, see Stieglitz, "The Reproduction of Agony."

[91] Klein, *Theologie und Anti-Judaismus*; published in English as *Anti-Judaism in Christian Theology*.

[92] *Geschichte Jesu Christi*, 124.

[93] Leipoldt and Grundmann, eds., *Umwelt des Urchristentums*, 1:274. It might be noted that the work of Jewish scholars is not cited in *Umwelt des Urchristentums*, a remarkable omission for the late 1960s.

[94] On Grundmann's membership in the SNTS, which was accorded him in 1938 and never withdrawn, see Head, "The Nazi Quest for an Aryan Jesus," 55–89.

[95] Grundmann, "Das Angebot der eröffneten Freiheit," (*Catholica* 28 [1974]); Grundmann, ed., *Anschaulichkeit als katechetisches Problem* (1966); Grundmann, "Die Frage nach der Gottessohnschaft des Messias im Lichte von Qumran" (in *Bibel und Qumran: Beiträge zur Erforschung der Beziehung zwischen Bibel und Qumranwissenschaft*, 1968).

field of Dead Sea Scroll studies.[96] Scholars assumed that the scrolls had been composed by a religious community of Essenes, a Jewish sectarian group, who were marginal to what was thought of as the "normative" Jewish community of Pharisees and priests. Some identified Jesus or John the Baptist as an Essene. Grundmann insisted that Jesus was not to be classified with the Essenes, nor with any other Jewish group of his day. Given the prewar history of German scholars arguing that the Essenes had been influenced by religious ideas from Iran, and the identification of Iran as Aryan, scholarship on the scrolls, not surprisingly, attracted former German Christian members in the postwar years, including Grundmann, Karl Georg Kuhn, and Leipoldt, among others.

With all of these motifs—the misogyny of ancient Judaism, its lack of morality, its violence—Grundmann recapitulated themes central to German Christian theology and transmitted them to a postwar generation of German theologians, academic and popular.[97] Indeed, he and his comrades from the Nazi era collaborated after the war by praising each other's work. In 1958, for example, Grundmann published a very positive review in the prestigious journal, *Theologische Literaturzeitung*, of a new book on Jesus by his former German Christian colleague Ethelbert Stauffer, *Jesus: Gestalt und Geschichte*. Basing his argument on the Gospel of John, which had been favored by the German Christians for its hostility to Jews, Stauffer reiterated the German Christian view of Jesus as a lonely fighter against the Jewish legalistic pseudo-piety he opposed. Although Stauffer cited rabbinic texts extensively, he used them not to contextualize Jesus's teachings nor to demonstrate his Jewishness, but to present a contrasting, negative picture of the Jewish background against which Jesus fought; he writes that "Jesus is far less a child of his era and his [Jewish] Volk than one has until now supposed."[98] Stauffer argued in a 1959 book, *Die Botschaft Jesu*, that obedience to commands had led Christians to commit murder through the centuries. Jesus, according to Stauffer, tried to liberate his fol-

---

[96] Grundmann, "Stehen und Fallen im qumranischen und neutestamentlichen Schrifttum"; "Der Lehrer der Gerechtigkeit von Qumran" (published in English as "The Teacher of Righteousness of Qumran").

[97] Some of the best-selling books on Jesus that appeared in Germany in the 1980s and '90s repeated themes central to German Christian theology: Gerda Weiler, in *Ich Verwerfe im Lande die Kriege*, describes the violence and militarism of Jews and the Old Testament; Christa Mulack draws an analogy between Jewish morality and the Holocaust, in *Am Anfang war die Weisheit*; Elisabeth Moltmann-Wendel (*Freiheit, Gleichheit, Schwesterlichkeit*) depicts Jewish women's treatment by the rabbis using examples nearly identical to those offered by Leipoldt and Grundmann in their *Umwelt des Urchristentums*.

[98] Stauffer, *Jesus: Gestalt und Geschichte*, 11.

lowers from moral duties of the Old Testament, advocating instead a "free conscience," an argument close to Grundmann's.[99] Indeed, even the leading racial theorist of the Nazi era, Hans F. K. Günther, was struck by the parallels between Stauffer's postwar Jesus and the Aryan Jesus of the Nazi era.[100] Günther, who had written about Germanic religion and religiosity in 1934,[101] turned to Christian theology after the war, publishing—under the pseudonym Heinrich Ackermann—two major scholarly studies of the representations of Jesus in modern theology.[102]

Grundmann never discussed his Nazi-era writings apart from an allusion in the preface of a 1957 book, *Die Geschichte Jesu Christi*: "Whoever knows the earlier work of the author will notice what kinds of approaches have turned out to be fruitful and therefore been pursued further, where errors have been overcome and false perspectives have been corrected."[103] That refers solely to the depiction of Jesus, not of Judaism, which he continued to describe in denigrating language. For example, Grundmann asserts falsely that Jewish (Pharisaic) law prohibits healing the sick on the Sabbath but permits "ambushing" ("auflauern"), which leads to "killing the messenger of the Kingdom of God."[104]

Grundmann's Nazi involvements were known but rarely mentioned by his academic colleagues. An exception is the New Testament scholar Ernst Bammel, who formulated this defense of Grundmann in the 1980s:

> The first world war, which altered the theological scene so decisively in a general way, brought about certain new accents in the portraits of Jesus. The "militant Christ" was only a slogan and of ephemeral importance. . . . The "heroic Jesus"—heroic rather in action than in suffering—became the watchword that characterised the attempts of Chamberlain and of other German nationalists to conceive of a Jesus who was congenial to them. Tinges of social colour in the characterisations of Jesus retreated into the background in this period apart from J. Leipoldt and his pupil W. Grundmann and a few Marxist sketches.[105]

[99] *Die Botschaft Jesu*, 25.

[100] "Heinrich Ackermann" (pseudonym for Günther), *Entstellung und Klärung der Botschaft Jesu*, 326. Günther compares Stauffer to Karl von Hase, writing a life of Jesus in 1829 even though he realizes that John's gospel has been discredited as a historical source.

[101] Günther, *Frömmigkeit nordischer Artung*.

[102] Günther also published under the pseudonym Ludwig Winter after the war. See Lutzhöft, *Der nordische Gedanke*, 46 fn 113.

[103] Grundmann, *Die Geschichte Jesu Christi*, 5.

[104] Ibid., 141.

[105] Bammel and Moule, eds., *Jesus and the Politics of His Day*, 31.

Bammel's linkage of Leipoldt and Grundmann, who were Nazis, with un-named Marxists, and his transformation of the "Aryan Christ" of Chamberlain and Grundmann into a "heroic Christ" effectively concealed the true nature of Grundmann's work. Bammel's comments introduced a collection of scholarly essays that included an article by Grundmann.[106] Similarly, Werner Kümmel, a noted historian of New Testament scholarship, also championed Grundma-nn's writings of the Third Reich, particularly his work on the divine sonship of Jesus.[107] By contrast, Sean Freyne more recently has written, "To water down the Jewishness of Galilee and thereby to deny the Jewishness of Jesus not only has the potential for anti-Semitism, as Walter Grundmann's 1940 book on Jesus the Galilean shows, it also involves a refusal to acknowledge that the Christian understanding of God is grounded in the Jewish religious experi-ence."[108] A repudiation of Grundmann came in a review of a book manuscript submitted posthumously by his wife to his regular publisher, the Evange-lisches Verlagsanstalt of East Berlin. The reviewer wrote that the book ex-pressed a "belated wrath of the German Christians for the Confessing Church!" and it was rejected by the press. The family eventually had it pri-vately printed.[109]

DENAZIFICATION OF INSTITUTE MEMBERS: STUDENTS

Members of the Institute who had been students, many with doctorates from the University of Jena, were unhampered in postwar careers within the church. Hans-Joachim Thilo, who had worked closely with Grundmann at Jena on his dissertation, "The Influence of Völkisch Awakening on German Religious Life," enjoyed a successful public career after the war. He served as pastor in Geneva from 1956 to 1964 and subsequently became one of the directors of the Evan-gelische Akademie at Bad Böll, a Protestant church conference center in

---

[106] Grundmann, "The Decision of the Supreme Court to Put Jesus to Death."

[107] Kümmel, "Das Urchristentum" IV (cont.), *Theologische Rundschau* new series 17, no. 2 (1948):103–42; reprinted in Kümmel, *Heilsgeschehen und Geschichte*, 1:475f.

[108] Freyne, "Galilean Questions," 91. See also Reed, "Galileans," 87 fn 1.

[109] *Weisheit im Horizont des Reiches Gottes: Erwägungen zur Christusbotschaft und zum Christusver-ständnis im Lichte der Weisheit in Israel* (Stuttgart/Eisenach, privately printed, 1988). The reader's report is found in the BA Potsdam, DR-1/2559 (Plan 1981): Report by Gerhard Bassarek dated May 5, 1980, cited by Bräuer and Vollnhals, *"In der DDR gibt es keine Zensur,* 110. I was given a copy of the book by Mrs. Annelise Grundmann. Thirty-five years after the war and six years after his death, Grundmann's membership in the German Christians finally cost him one posthumous publication.

Germany, where he was responsible for political issues. He trained at Oxford University to become a psychoanalyst, and practiced as a psychotherapist in Lübeck starting in 1968, and also taught practical theology at the University of Hamburg from 1972 to 1984. His many popular books on psychology sold well, and he remained a respected figure within the church, serving as a consultant to the bishop of Hamburg. In 1991 he became one of several Institute members awarded the highly prestigious National Medal of Merit (Bundesverdienstkreuz) from the Federal Republic of Germany.

The utter collapse of moral compass in the Third Reich required repair. Theologians who had spent the Third Reich interpreting Christianity as a justification for Nazism perforce had to turn to another field to reconstruct a moral base. Like Thilo, Heinz Hunger, who had served as business manager of the Institute and had written a dissertation at the University of Jena developing a racist approach to the study of religion, turned from theology to psychology after the war, writing on religion and sexuality and becoming a noted expert on the sex education of youth.[110] Another student who became active in the Institute, Max-Adolf Wagenführer, found employment for several years after the war as a pastor with the Luther church of Cologne whose pastor had been deported and murdered in 1942 as a "non-Aryan."[111] Once it was discovered that Wagenführer had not been ordained, he could not retain a position as pastor, but because he was one of the authors of the Institute's catechism, *Deutsche mit Gott*, and holder of a doctorate earned under Grundmann at the University of Jena, he was considered trained in religious pedagogy and was appointed as a schoolteacher of religion by the church of the Rhineland. After his retirement, Wagenführer moved to Bavaria, where he became a very popular speaker in church circles. He was still alive as of 2007, and in private correspondence wrote that Grundmann told him in 1942 that he was terribly disappointed that Hitler was tolerating the spread of lies that meant the certain downfall of the German Reich.[112] Like the others, Wagenführer has denied the Institute's antisemitic purposes and has not accepted public responsibility for his involvements in it.[113]

Rudolf Meyer had also served as Grundmann's assistant and member of the Institute; he was described in Institute publicity as "one of the best scholars of

---

[110] Herzog, *Sex after Fascism*, 22. See also Prolingheuer, "Der Lutherisch Deutsch-Christliche Weg."

[111] Prolingheuer, *Ausgetan aus dem Land der Lebendigen*; he is also mentioned in Seidel, *Im Übergang der Diktaturen*, 362.

[112] Personal correspondence from Wagenführer, dated February 23, 2006.

[113] On Wagenführer, see Prolingheuer, "Der Lutherisch Deutsch-Christliche Weg," 75–79, 83–84.

the Talmud among the younger theologians."[114] Meyer had studied in the early 1930s in Leipzig, including under the Russian Jewish scholar Lazar Gulkowitsch[115] and Leipoldt, and had contributed to Kittel's *Theological Dictionary of the New Testament*. Appointed an assistant in the Jewish Studies (Wissenschaft vom Judentum) division of the New Testament faculty at Leipzig in 1934, Meyer lost his position in 1938 and then came briefly to the University of Jena to work with Grundmann.[116] Both his dissertation and habilitation dealt with rabbinic literature; the latter was a critical edition and translation of the first chapter of the Tosefta Shabbat, based on three manuscripts.[117] Meyer entered military service in 1939, returning to Leipzig in 1946 as an assistant in Old Testament, then as an instructor in New Testament in 1947, before replacing von Rad in Jena as professor of Old Testament in 1947.

Another student at Jena, Fritz Schmidt-Clausing, managed to escape denazification sanctions by lying to church officials, telling them that he had distanced himself from the German Christians in 1938, although he was active in the Institute throughout the war years. He was believed, and won appointment from 1947 to 1962 as pastor of the important and prestigious Kaiser Friedrich Gedächtniskirche in Berlin, where he reconstituted the congregation after the war.[118] With his doctorate from Jena and his conversion from Catholicism to Protestantism, Schmidt-Clausing was regarded as a Protestant expert on the Roman Catholic Church and contributed articles on Catholicism and also the Reformation to the postwar edition of the prestigious reference work, *Religion in Geschichte und Gegenwart*, published in 1957.[119]

[114] ZAK 7/4166, document 8.

[115] Gulkowitsch taught Jewish religious history at Leipzig 1932–33 before being forced to emigrate to Tartu, Estonia, in 1933, where he was killed by the Nazis in 1941.

[116] The precise reasons for his dismissal remain unclear. The stated reason was the new Reich regulations of December 13, 1934, regarding doctoral studies; it is possible that the Jewish topics of Meyer's scholarship also played a role. The decision to dismiss Meyer was ultimately taken by the dean of the faculty on December 31, 1938. Meyer wrote to Hugo Odeberg on March 28, 1939, asking if employment might be available for him at a Swedish university; Odeberg's reply is unknown (UAL, Odeberg materials).

[117] Meyer published extensively as a young scholar, and was commissioned to prepare a critical edition of the Tosefta Shabbat and Eruvin for the series edited by Kittel and K. H. Rengstorf. His dissertation, published in 1940, was entitled *Der Prophet aus Galiläa*.

[118] Kühl-Freudenstein and Wagener, "Kirchenkreis Potsdam I," 565–73. Roman Herzog, president of Germany from 1994 to 1999, was one of Schmidt-Clausing's parishioners.

[119] In the postwar years, Schmidt-Clausing also published several academic and popular books on Zwingli, as well as a small guidebook to Potsdam and to the Hansaviertel. See Schmidt-Clausing, *Geschichte des Hansa-Viertels*.

After the war, Herbert von Hintzenstern, who had written a dissertation on Houston Stewart Chamberlain's theories of the Aryan origins of Christianity, remained a figure of importance within the Thuringian church, as editor of its weekly church newspaper, *Glaube und Heimat*, and author of several popular books, on church altars, figures of the Reformation, and Thuringian church history. He was selected to chair the Christliche Friedenskonferenz (Christian Peace Organization) of East Germany, and he received East Germany's Medal of Merit in 1975 and Fatherland Medal of Merit in 1986.[120] Never during his postwar career did he promote Christian consideration of the Holocaust or Jewish-Christian dialogue; and he mentioned Jews only twice in *Glaube und Heimat*, in 1978 and 1988, both times in connection with remembrances of Kristallnacht.[121]

DENAZIFICATION OF INSTITUTE MEMBERS: PROFESSORS AND PASTORS

The fate of the Jena theology professors is telling. Grundmann was fired as professor of New Testament at Jena, but was replaced by another Institute member whose views were equally nazified—Herbert Preisker. Heinz Eisenhuth lost his professorship, too, but was quickly rehabilitated by the Thuringian church. Meyer-Erlach wrote to the university on behalf of Eisenhuth, describing him as a defender of Christianity who had been persecuted as a consequence by Sauckel and Astel.[122] Other Institute members also fared well in Thuringia; Erhard Mauersberger, a member of the Institute, became director of the Thuringian church music school in 1950 and later, cantor at the prestigious Thomaskirche in Leipzig (Saxony) from 1961 to 1972.[123]

Equally dramatic was the case of Meyer-Erlach, who used his demagogic talents to launch an extraordinary protest of his innocence of Nazi involvement—extraordinary for its collection of lies regarding his activities during the period 1933–45, and extraordinary for the ease with which he fabricated biographical falsehoods in the company of his Nazi-era colleagues. Already in the winter of 1945 Meyer-Erlach was preparing his denazification case: he withdrew his NSDAP membership on March 20. In a letter written to the dean of the University of Jena, Heussi, on June 14, 1945, Meyer-Erlach described

---

[120] Seidel, *Gottlose Jahre?*, 78–79.

[121] Ostmeyer, *Zwischen Schuld und Sühne*, 100–103.

[122] Ratification signed by Meyer-Erlach, notorized by Heussi, dated January 11, 1946. (ThHStA, Personalakte aus dem Bereich des Volksbildungsministeriums, 5567,135).

[123] Seidel, *Im Übergang der Diktaturen*, 349.

Hitler as a German Cromwell and himself as defender of the church and fighter against National Socialism, persecuted by the Gestapo for his efforts. No one had hated National Socialism more than he had, he wrote, and his orientation had always been that of a religious socialist. He proclaimed himself a Jew-loving antifascist fighter. As proof, he claimed to have once consulted a physician who was a converted Jew, permitted a Jewish professor to operate on his two youngest children, had attended the dedication of a synagogue in Würzburg in 1929, and had been personally mocked for his Jewish sympathies as "Synagogenmeyer." His protests were of no avail; he was removed from his professorship on June 28, 1945.

Meyer-Erlach fled the German Democratic Republic in 1950 and, thanks to the assistance of Martin Niemöller, then head of the church of Hessen, he received a church position in the Taunus mountains just north of Frankfurt am Main, where he started a new career as anti-Soviet Christian propagandist.[124] Remarkably, on January 6, 1962, Meyer-Erlach was awarded the Bundesverdienstkreuz (Order of Merit) First Class by the Federal Republic of Germany. The award was given to him in recognition of his efforts to gather money and packages that he sent to families in East Germany, and for serving as director of an organization called Unteilbares Deutschland (Unified Germany), in the Lower Taunus. In 1952, he had founded a retreat center for school children (Landjugendheim) in Wörsdorf, which became part of a School for Gifted Ethnic German Girls (Förderschule für volksdeutsche Mädchen) in 1960, at which children of so-called "ethnic Germans" who had fled Eastern Europe after the war could be taught German and be integrated into the cultural life of the Federal Republic.[125]

Preisker came to Jena after leaving Breslau in October 1945. A bombing had destroyed most of his possessions, including his library, and he abandoned the rest, as he wrote to friends, including his wife.[126] On April 1, 1946, he was appointed to Jena as an tenured professor, serving as dean from April 1, 1950, to August 31, 1952. Preisker's appointment at Jena apparently remained controversial, and questions were raised about his Nazi affiliations even after he began teaching, delaying his official appointment to the professorship. In October 1946, Heussi wrote to Soviet occupying authorities to insist that Preisker never was a member of the Nazi Party, nor of any associ-

---

[124] Raschzok, "Wolf Meyer-Erlach und Hans Asmussen," 175.

[125] Documentation from the Office of the President of Germany, Bonn; letter dated April 5, 1995.

[126] Preisker's son went missing in the Soviet Union in 1941. See his letters of November 9, 1947 and March 1, 1948, ULA, Odeberg materials.

Figure 6.2. Heinz Eisenhuth.

ated organization. He required no rehabilitation, Heussi wrote, because "Professor Preisker is in no way tarnished and there is nothing to rehabilitate."[127] In 1951, Heussi again testified that Preisker's political position is "according to my observations irreproachably correct. He is outspokenly antifascist and exerts a definite positive influence on the students in terms of political viewpoint."[128] In 1952 Preisker left Jena for a professorship at Halle, where he had assumed the prestigious directorship of the Corpus Judaeo-Hellenisticum, a major research project on Hellenistic-era texts. He died there suddenly on December 24, 1952.

Other Institute members were equally protected by the church and their fellow academics, as well as by their own mendacity. Theodor Odenwald, who as dean of theology made his official seal a swastika and eagle, was removed from his professorship at Heidelberg in the fall of 1945 and judged by denazification officials as a "Class II" Nazi on the grounds of his membership in the NSDAP and the German Christian movement. Protesting, he defended the German Christians as another name for a liberal direction within the church and claimed he was supported in that contention by the noted church history Hans von Campenhausen.[129]

After the war, Carl Schneider left the University of Königsberg, where he was professor of New Testament, and was appointed by the church of the Palatinate to a prestigious position as director of its Evangelische Akademie, a conference center.[130] In 1954 he published a two-volume study of early Christianity that continued the History of Religions approach that governed his Nazi-era views, placing Jesus within the context of Hellenistic religions, and seeing early Christianity as an anti-Jewish movement.[131] Schneider died in 1977.

Johannes Hempel initially worked as a pastor after the war, but moved to Göttingen when he was named an honorary professor in 1955. He retained his editorship of the *Zeitschrift für alttestamentliche Wissenschaft* until 1959, though

---

[127] Letter from Heussi, Dean, to Deutsche Zentralverwaltung für Volksbildung in der Sowjetischen Besatzungszone, Berlin (UAJ D 986).

[128] Letter from Heussi to Berlin, dated September 30, 1951. For more on Preisker, see Hutter-Wolandt, "Spagat zwischen Wissenschaft," 275–318.

[129] Letter from the chairman of the denazification court to Odenwald, dated September 3, 1946 (Universität Heidelberg archives 180: Entnazifizierung). Odenwald's case is discussed in Remy, *The Heidelberg Myth*, 118, 133.

[130] Reichrath, "Die Evangelischen Sonntagsblätter der Pfalz," 51–64; Reichrath, "Die Judenfrage im Lichte der evangelischen Sonntagsblätter der Pfalz," 164–81.

[131] Schneider, *Geistesgeschichte des antiken Christentums*. See the highly critical review by Hermann Langerbeck, *Gnomon* 28 (1956), 481–501.

he was forced to share it after the war with a colleague, Otto Eissfeldt, to pacify his critics. The closest he came to apologizing for his 1942 editor's column was a statement that he would not have printed those words had he known "to what things antisemitism would lead with the intensification of the war."[132] That attempted apology was insufficient for many of his colleagues, who refused to publish in the *Zeitschrift* as long as it remained under his editorship, and in 1953 formed a new journal, *Vetus Testamentum*.[133] Hempel died in Göttingen in 1964.

Martin Redeker retained his professorship at the University of Kiel, despite letters of complaint sent to church officials. The bishop of Schleswig-Holstein, in a 1947 letter, explained that Redeker had denied any personal involvement in the Institute, claiming he had been sent by church officials simply to observe what was taking place.[134] The bishop explained that Redeker was hired as a professor by the state, and the church could not intervene. Volkmar Herntrich, a former Confessing Church pastor from Hamburg and later bishop, wrote to a colleague that he would not return to the faculty at Kiel until Redeker left; that did not occur, but Herntrich did accept a professorship in Old Testament.[135]

In the 1950s, Redeker became active in the Christian Democratic Union (CDU) party politics, elected four times between 1954 and 1967 to the Schleswig-Holstein parliament. His CDU involvements were primarily in the area of culture, but he also belonged to the Protestant working group of the CDU, eventually becoming a national figure within the CDU. On April 24, 1967, he was awarded the Große Verdienstkreuz der Bundesrepublik Deutschland, West Germany's highest civilian honor. In 1962, he was made dean of the theological faculty at Kiel, a position he retained until his death in 1970, despite the exposure by students in 1968 of his Nazi activities. In response to those charges, he wrote, "During the time of National Socialism I already distanced myself from the Nazi regime so clearly through public opposition to the Jewish politics [*e.g., Nazi antisemitism*] and the cult of the Führer that I did not need to repeat it after 1945." He falsely claimed to have protested against Grundmann's Institute, and stated that he had been named as a member without his knowledge.[136]

---

[132] ZAW 61 (1945–48), 231f.

[133] Smend, "Fünfzig Jahre International Organization," 4.

[134] NEK, Archives of the Confessing Church of Schleswig-Holstein, 72.

[135] A letter from Volkmar Herntrich, pastor and instructor in theology, to Pastor Otto Thedens, that he would not return to teach in the theological faculty at Kiel until Redeker was removed (NEK 72, 367).

[136] *Res Nostra* (student newspaper at the University of Kiel), no. 24, February 1968, 5, 7; cited by Buss, "Entjudung der Kirche," 185.

Institute members moved in a variety of political directions after the war. Like Redeker, Leipoldt became a CDU representative, serving from 1953 to 1963, but in the Volkskammer, the parliament of the German Democratic Republic. Leipoldt was regarded as a major scholar within the GDR and was honored with membership in the Saxon Academy of Scholarship. He moved to the University of Rostock in 1959, and died there in 1965.

Werner Petersmann, a pastor and Institute member from Breslau, retained his politics after the war. A member of the Hanoverian church, he stood as candidate for the German parliament in a neo-Nazi political party.[137] He also took his political theology elsewhere, using principles of German Christian theology to justify South African apartheid and racism.[138] The liberalism of the French Enlightenment had led to communism, and while Hitler "went too far" with his antisemitism, Petersmann wrote in 1975, Nazi racial principles were fundamentally correct, and he blamed "anti-Hitler hysteria" for Germans' failing to recognize that.[139] Petersmann died in 1988.

The leader of the Bund für deutsches Christentum, Herbert Propp, who helped organize regional German Christian church leaders into a formal body, and whose meetings set the groundwork for the Godesberg Declaration and subsequent establishment of the Institute, also had an active career after the war.[140] After the war, he departed from German Christian insistence on a "manly church," now writing in support of women's ordination.[141] He served as pastor for a German-speaking Lutheran church in Geneva from 1956 to 1964, then became one of the administrators of the Evangelical Academy in Bad Boll, Germany, 1964–68, before moving to Lübeck, where he served as a theological advisor to the bishop.

Some Institute members were not so fortunate. The Soviets, arriving in Thuringia, recognized leaders of the German Christian movement as Nazis and arrested them. Erwin Brauer, a pastor who served as one of the office managers of the Institute, was taken to Buchenwald by the Soviets and died there in December of 1946. Heinz Dungs, a pastor and Institute member who ran the German Christian publishing house (Verlag Deutsche Christen; later,

---

[137] The Nationaldemokratische Partei Deutschlands, which was founded in 1964. Osten-Sacken, "Der Nationalsozialistische Lutherforscher Theodor Pauls."

[138] Petersmann, *Die Deutschland-Frage in Ganzheits-Schau*; *Was ist des Deutschen Vaterland?*; *Auch die Kirche verrät die Nation?*; *Wider die "Irrlehre" des Weltkirchenrates.*

[139] Petersmann, *Wider die "Irrlehre" des Weltkirchenrates*, 18, 25.

[140] Propp seems to have written reports to the Gestapo on church officials. GSA Rep. 90 P/53: Kirchen- und Weltanschauungspolitik evangelisch, 1938–41 (vol. 4).

[141] Interview with Hans-Joachim Thilo in Lübeck, July 20, 1995. In calling for a "manly church," the German Christian movement was inclined to oppose women's ordination.

Der neue Dom) that published numerous works by Grundmann and other Institute members, was arrested by the Soviets in 1946 at the Weimar train station and was killed by them in 1949. By contrast, the pastor Wilhelm Bauer, who coedited the journal *Christenkreuz und Hakenkreuz* with Grundmann and Leffler, was fired by the Thuringian church for his Nazi activities in 1945, but then took a prestigious position as teacher at a gymnasium in 1950; he died in 1969.

Bertram eventually returned to Giessen, but the University of Giessen was among the universities closed briefly by American authorities at the end of the war, and in the course of its reopening, questions were renewed about the nature of the Institute and Bertram's involvement in it. An antisemitic article of his, published in 1943 by the Institute, was sent for clarification in early 1947 by Hessen investigators to church officials in Thuringia. In his response, senior church councillor Erich Hertzsch, a former Confessing Church member who earned a leadership position after the war in the Thuringian church, provided an exoneration. The article was typical of the work of the Institute, Hertzsch wrote, which attempted to provide a judgment of Judaism based on the research of Old Testament scholars and distanced itself from the rabble-rousing propaganda of other circles as well as from any attacks on Christianity and the church. The Institute's work was entirely scholarly and unpolitical, Hertzsch continued:

> The Christian church, for example Luther, sees in Judaism a danger, insofar as the rejection of Christian faith is the characteristic feature of the Jew. Admittedly the author failed to expand his critique with a positive evaluation of the church and of Christianity. Above all he allowed the impression to arise in his comments that he has nothing else in mind than giving the Nazis a good conscience. In that way correct and valuable scholarly conclusions are abused.[142]

Bertram was judged by the denazification court (Spruchkammer) of Giessen as a "Mitläufer" (fellow traveler) on March 25, 1949. As Steven Remy has argued, the court was nothing more than "a legal whitewash that facilitated the return of thousands of former Nazis to positions of influence in German public life."[143] Despite the verdict, the church gave Bertram teaching duties in Hebrew language and religion at Frankfurt high schools. However, he returned to Giessen in 1955 to teach Old Testament, and in 1956, at the age of 60, Bertram applied to the University of Frankfurt for a position that would give him

---

[142] Letter from Hertzsch, in response to a query from an anonymous former Institute member in Giessen, dated February 1, 1947 (LKA Eisenach A 921).

[143] Remy, *The Heidelberg Myth*, 243–44.

275

time for his scholarship, specifically his philological studies of the Greek Bible. With the departure of Georg Fohrer for a professorship at the University of Vienna, a position became available, and in the winter semester 1955–56 Bertram was appointed to an untenured teaching position in Old Testament at the University of Frankfurt, a position that was renewed annually and was expanded in 1959 to include biblical Hebrew.

The publication in 1965 of Rolf Seeliger's book, *Braune Universität*, which revealed the Nazi involvements of numerous prominent professors and sparked a widespread scandal in Germany, listed Bertram among the Nazi professors who had continued to teach at German universities after 1945. That same year, Bertram withdrew from his teaching position without a stated reason. The university rector, Walter Rüegg, wrote to Bertram in the name of the faculty senate after Seeliger's book appeared to reiterate the university's commitment to his continued teaching.[144] Bertram died in 1979.

Conclusion

The success of former Institute members after the war in retaining professorships and senior positions within the church was facilitated by a collaboration of allied officials and church leaders in concocting a fiction of Christianity's resistance to National Socialism. According to the fiction, the spiritual bulwark of faith had kept Christians from submitting to Nazism; at most, some theologians had compromised minor aspects of their religion in order to protect the church from destruction at the hands of the Nazi regime, which was always painted as anti-Christian. The portrayal of themselves as victims and resisters fell on sympathetic ears; the allies assumed that Germans who could demonstrate their involvement in the church during the Third Reich could not have been Nazis. Letters attesting to regular church attendance from pastors—some of whom had themselves been Nazis—helped win denazification. Such letters were often deliberate lies, and yet were organized at the highest level of the German Protestant church, as Robert Ericksen has shown.[145] Some bishops and pastors, most famously Martin Niemöller, felt the denzification investigations were demoralizing and were undertaken in a spirit of revenge against Germans who had already repented. Niemöller urged Christians not to participate in the denazification tribunals and forbade clergy from involvement.[146]

---

[144] Universitätsarchiv Frankfurt am Main, Archives of the Rector, Abt. 4, no. 33; and Abt. 134, no. 41, Personalakte Georg Bertram.

[145] Ericksen, "Hiding the Nazi Past."

[146] Spotts, The Churches and Politics in Germany, 105.

At the universities, professors similarly claimed they had resisted Nazi incursions and had retained the values of objectivity, autonomy, and academic freedom.[147] The result was a widespread exoneration of Nazi scholars who had "put their talents in the service of the regime." University administrators rarely participated in the denazification procedures; indeed, a resentment of those procedures was regnant.[148] Reinstatement of professors with training in Judaism, even the most notorious Nazi propagandists, was particularly easy because they were among the few left in postwar Germany with expertise in rabbinic texts, thus camouflaging their Nazi activities. Both universities and churches refused to consider antisemitic propaganda, such as that fomented by the German Christian movement, as a basis for disciplinary action.

Whereas the Allies regarded antisemitic propaganda as a potentially criminal offense, hanging Julius Streicher at Nuremberg, for instance, the churches had difficulty distinguishing the Nazis' antisemitism from what they considered legitimate expressions of Christian theological anti-Judaism. Connections between the two were dismissed out of hand, on the grounds that the antisemitism of the Nazis was rooted in a biologically based racism that had nothing to do with the Christian effort to win Jewish converts. Traditional theology had for so long presented negative depictions of Judaism that the antisemitism of the German Christian movement was not perceived as remarkable or as responsible for the crimes of the Third Reich against the Jews. Arguments about the inherently degenerate and violent nature of Judaism made by Institute members, among others, were ranked as theological scholarship, not antisemitic propaganda. Moreover, the postwar leaders of the churches, who were mostly former members of the Confessing Church, a movement with a conservative theological base, frequently shared with their former German Christian antagonists a sense that Judaism and even Jews were degenerate and posed a potential threat to the spiritual well-being of Germany.[149] When Grundmann and Eisenhuth were investigated after the war by Thuringian church officials, for example, they were asking nothing about their attitudes toward Jews, but whether they believed Christ reigned supreme over political leaders, as affirmed in the Barmen Declaration of 1934. The Holocaust was not—yet—a Christian theological issue nor even a moral issue within the Christian theological framework.

In the context of the German Democratic Republic, Grundmann's continued anti-Judaism in his publications performed a positive service to a church

---

[147] Remy, *The Heidelberg Myth*, 240.

[148] Ibid., 245.

[149] Christoph Raisig delineates the postwar attitudes of former Confessing Church members in *Wege der Erneuerung*.

reluctant to consider Christian responsibility for Nazi antisemitism and the Holocaust. The historian Irena Ostmeyer has shown that until the 1960s the Protestant church in the GDR was reluctant to accept any responsibility for the murder of the Jews.[150] Even in the later decades of the GDR, only minimal discussion of Jews and Judaism took place in public circles.[151] Grundmann's writings about Judaism's degeneracy lent support to the theological paradigm that the Holocaust was a divinely ordained punishment for the Jews' crucifixion of Jesus, so that his scholarship could be welcomed by factions within the church as exculpating Christians of responsibility.

The failure to root out antisemitic arguments in the postwar decades was due, in large measure, to the success of those arguments during the years of the Third Reich and, often, long before. The antisemitism of Christian theological literature was simply not recognized as antisemitic; it was more often seen as expressing historical or dogmatic truths about Jews and Judaism. Removing degrading comments about early Judaism, in particular, would undermine explanations for Jesus's alleged rejection of Judaism and the Jews' rejection of Jesus as messiah. On the political level, as Robert Ericksen has noted, postwar church leaders recognized that purging German society of Nazis would give added prominence to those who had not been Nazis—Jews and leftists—and who were viewed as enemies of the church.[152] Thus, even the modest and ineffectual denazification efforts undertaken by the Western allies, mitigated quickly by the Cold War, aroused a hostility from the church that was rooted in theological as well as political motivations.

[150] Ostmeyer, *Zwischen Schuld und Sühne*.

[151] While Jews living in the GDR could be included in the category of "victims of fascism" and be accorded the special privileges that accrued to those victims, Jewish cultural distinctiveness and the practice of Judaism as a religion were discouraged on socialist grounds. Zionism and the State of Israel were particularly maligned, especially after the 1967 war, which resulted in intensified propaganda by the GDR government against Israel. The publication of books about Jewish history during the last years of the GDR aroused some public interest, particularly the 1988 study of antisemitism by Rudolf Hirsch and Rosemary Schuder, two well-known writers. At the Protestant theological faculty of the Humboldt University in East Berlin, instruction in Judaism and Jewish theology was included in the curriculum, mandated by Heinrich Fink, professor of practical theology. See Hirsch and Schuder, *Der gelbe Fleck*.

[152] Ericksen, "Hiding the Nazi Past," 149–50.

Crucified or Resurrected

INSTITUTE THEOLOGY IN POSTWAR GERMANY

As THE AUDIENCE of the Oberammergau passion play of 1934 watched Jesus being hoisted on the cross, they saw a parable of the Third Reich: "There he is. That is our Führer, our Hitler!"[1] When the Third Reich came to an end and Nazism was defeated, no one in Germany was entirely certain if Germans had been crucified or resurrected, least of all the theologians. The warring factions of the Confessing Church and the German Christians now became united in their use of Old Testament images of the Israelites in exile to describe the "terrible plight" of Germans, who had been liberated from Hitler but conquered by the Allies; having murdered the Jews, the Germans could now take their identity. Wolf Meyer-Erlach wrote, "We are wandering through the wilderness like the Children of Israel. . . . We are like the generation of Israel that was in captivity in Babylon, who had to make bricks in Egypt and were in danger of perishing in the demoralizing service on the front."[2]

Such use of Old Testament images is ironic: Here was German Christian leader Meyer-Erlach, who a few years earlier had vigorously called for expunging the Old Testament from the Christian Bible, now comparing postwar Germans to the Children of Israel leaving Egypt. The Confessing Church pastor Werner Schmauch called the German civilian population "refugees," and compared them to Abraham being told by God to leave his fatherland.[3] Former rivals within the church, then, could identify themselves as biblical Jews—that is, as politically innocent figures following a divine plan of salvation. Invocations of the Old Testament by Christians in postwar Germany remained in place for some decades after the war and were put to good use in exculpating Christians of responsibility for the fate of the Jews by transferring Jewish identity from Jews to Christian Germans. Indeed, a major religious turning point

---

[1] Thompson, "Goodbye to Germany," 46. On the Oberammergau play, see Friedman, *The Oberammergau Passion Play*, and Shapiro, *Oberammergau*. See also Berghaus, "The Ritual Core of Fascist Theatre," 63.

[2] Letter to Schmidt-Clausing, May 26, 1947 (ULA, Odeberg materials).

[3] Schmauch, "Zur theologischen Frage des Flüchtlingsproblems," typescript (NEK, Repertorium des Archivs der Bekennnenden Kirche Schleswig-Holstein, Alte Signatur 76, Neue Nummer 393: Verschiedene kirchliche Angelegenheiten).

Figure C.1. Poster for the 300th anniversary of the Passion Play at Oberammergau, Germany, 1934. The caption reads: "Germany is calling you!"

for the Jewish theologian Richard L. Rubenstein resulted from his exposure to postwar German Protestant appropriations of the Old Testament to exonerate Christians from responsibility for the Holocaust. In 1961 Rubenstein met Heinrich Gruber, who, as a pastor in Berlin during the Third Reich, had provided assistance to non-Aryan Christians and Jews seeking help escaping the Reich, for which he was imprisoned in Sachsenhausen and Dachau concentration camps for three years. Gruber told Rubenstein that in his understanding of Old Testament theology, Germany had served as the instrument of God's wrath toward the Jews. As a consequence, Germans had been punished by Allied bombings and the division of Berlin into two sectors; according to Gruber, Germans were "now in the same situation as the Jews."[4] By becoming theological Jews, Christians in Germany could exonerate themselves from responsibility for the murder of the real European Jews. During those years, Nazism received little more than clerical scolding; Helmut Thielicke, like so many others, blamed it on lapsed religiosity: "National Socialism is the final and most terrible product of secularization."[5]

The first generation of postwar German church historians studying the role of the churches during the Third Reich also tended to exonerate theologians. The myth was carefully cultivated by Wilhelm Niemöller, among others, that the Confessing Church had sought to defend the church against Nazi hostilities toward Christianity. The German Christians were held up as the Nazis, the Confessing Church as the anti-Nazis.[6] Wolfgang Tilgner, writing in the 1960s, articulated the classic Confessing Church position that the German Christians had divinized the Volk and had failed to maintain a strong incarnational theology; for him, as for many others, the failures of the Nazi era were due to inadequate doctrinal discipline.[7] Memoirs by Confessing Church theologians who had been active during the Third Reich usually did not mention Jews, antisemitism, or the Holocaust, and German Christian theologians did not publish their memoirs to avoid exposing their erstwhile Nazi enthusiasm.[8] Other church historians changed their positions over time; Leonore Siegele-Wenschkewitz, who in 1980 published the first critical examination of any major Nazi theologian, Gerhard Kittel, initially defined the central problem of

---

[4] Rubenstein, *After Auschwitz*, 47–60.

[5] Report by Dr. Helmut Thielicke on the state of church (NEK, Alte Signatur 76, Neue Nummer 393).

[6] Ericksen, "Wilhelm Niemöller."

[7] Tilgner, *Volksnomostheologie*, 228.

[8] The absence of the Holocaust from the first generation of postwar memoirs by Christian theologians has been traced by Björn Krondorfer, *Mit Blick auf die Täter: Fragen an die deutsche Theologie nach 1945* (Gütersloh: Gütersloher Verlaghaus, 2006).

the Kirchenkampf as a conflict over the nature of the church, but in later pub-lications came to argue that the Jewish question was in fact central.[9]

Exposing and analyzing the activities of the Institute contributes to an on-going reassessment by historians of the Protestant church in Germany during the Third Reich. It reinforces Doris Bergen's argument that the German Christian movement did not disintegrate with the onset of the war, but actually reached a zenith of influence and power by carrying out its calls for dejudaizing the church and by engaging so many professors of theology in its pro-gram.[10] The pro-Nazi, antisemitic theological positions that Robert Ericksen delineated in his study of three professors of theology, Kittel, Althaus, and Hirsch, can now be recognized as having had much broader appeal, given the large number of theologians who joined the Institute. The combination of old völkisch antisemitism, nationalism, and racism with Christianity, and the Institute's emphasis after 1941 on bringing Teutonic elements into Christianity, broadened its appeal to Germans with a range of Christian commitments and theological understandings. The numerous conferences and publications gen-erated by the Institute show a remarkable number of theologians involved in its projects and the broad scope of its impact throughout the Reich. The pres-ence of three leading Institute members on the University of Jena's faculty demonstrates the ways theological education was brought into accord with German Christian principles. That German Christian theological notions man-aged to penetrate academic theological circles to such an extent is of particular importance, given earlier claims, for example by Trutz Rendtorff, that the Prot-estant theological faculties were immune to National Socialism thanks to the rigors of German theological methods.[11] Certainly the case of the University of Jena's theological faculty should put such claims to final rest. Able to use the church, its money, privilege, and voice of authority, the Institute exerted an influence far beyond its membership numbers.

The nature of Protestant church discourse in Thuringia may also contribute toward an answer to the question that has puzzled many a historian: what fa-cilitated the rapid transformation of a region that was "red" in the 1920s to "brown" in the 1930s?[12] Substantial credit for the transformations within Thuringia may well belong to the church. The rhetoric used by both the church and the Nazi Party, in their election campaigns, at their rallies, and in

[9] See Siegele-Wenschkewitz, *Neutestamentliche Wissenschaft vor der Judenfrage*. Compare with Siegele-Wenschkewitz, ed., *Christlicher Antijudaismus und Antisemitismus*.

[10] Bergen, *Twisted Cross*, 19–20.

[11] Rendtorff, "Das Wissenschaftsverständnis der protestantischen Universitätstheologie im Drit-ten Reich," 19–44.

[12] Walter, "Von der roten zur braunen Hochburg," 142–43.

their written and oral discourses, was remarkably similar. Moreover, the efforts of the two erstwhile Bavarian pastors, Leffler and Leutheuser, to found a branch both of the Nazi Party and of the German Christian movement in the Werra Valley of Thuringia in the late 1920s certainly were a factor. Such efforts by pastors were important not only organizationally but also ideologically, at the very least by reassuring doubters that Nazism and the church held shared values. As much as the pastors conveyed that the Nazi Party should be supported on Christian grounds, Nazi politics, in turn, made German Christian theology seem less radical, as if it were simply a strong religious affirmation of nationalism and the state.

The fusion of Protestantism and Germanism was read into Nazism by German Christians, and Jesus was viewed as prefiguring Hitler, who in turn was imagined as an avatar of Martin Luther; Leffler declared in 1935 that Hitler stood in a direct line with Luther. Both had brought about a national revival that Leffler interpreted as a part of religious history, and the two were conflated: "So we cannot think of Adolf Hitler without Martin Luther."[13] Through Nazism, Christianity could achieve its own revival; Leutheuser wrote in 1931:

> In Adolf Hitler we see the powers again awakening which were once given to the Savior. For the National Socialists there is the experience of joy that finally one can sacrifice his life for something that will remain. . . . Our way is rough, but one thing we know, that we shall as a result maintain a pure soul. Golgotha is followed by the resurrection. We are still standing on the way to Golgotha. Some will remain on it, but the soul, it cannot be stolen. Into your hands we commend our spirit, for Adolf Hitler we will gladly die.[14]

For the theologians such affirmations did not seem extraordinary. As a case in point, Grundmann's biography and career are notable for their lack of exceptionalism. Raised in a family that took religion and nation seriously, he came easily to a synthesis of Christianity and völkisch ideology. Nowhere did he encounter a challenge to his views, neither from the church nor from his professors at the university. On the contrary, he was given to feel that he was creating something new and valuable within the field of theology, standing at the pinnacle of German New Testament scholarship and ready to realize the principles that had been inchoate for several generations. If, as he believed, Jesus intended to bring an end to Judaism, and if the gospels had falsified his

---

[13] Leffler, *Christus im dritten Reich der Deutschen: Wesen, Weg und Ziel der Kirchenbewegung "Deutsche Christen"* (Weimar, no date; foreword dated 1935), 75.

[14] Leutheuser, *Peniger Tageblatt* of January 20, 1931; cited by Besier, "The Stance of German Protestant Churches," 152.

message in certain places, then it was incumbent upon him and his generation of superbly trained historical theologians, Grundmann believed, to emend the text and deliver the authentic version to Christian believers. The political need for such an authentication made the theological task all the more pressing, and it also enhanced for the theologians of the Institute a sense of their own significance.

Grundmann's scholarly writings operated both as interpretations of Christian origins and interpretations of contemporary Germany. In his 1938 book on the divine sonship of Jesus, he insisted that Jesus's teaching was an utter repudiation of Judaism.[15] Analogously, Germans were enacting a collective sonship of the Führer. Jesus's divine sonship meant he experienced an intimacy with God, understanding the Father's wishes and surpassing the need for laws and commands. Germans, too, would understand Hitler's wishes without needing explicit direction. Eradication of the Jews did not have to be proclaimed in order to be known as the goal. Moreover, just as the heart overrode the commandments in Jesus's teachings, Germans would know that certain commandments, such as the prohibition of murder, could be legitimately violated. Grundmann rejected Paul for misunderstanding Jesus's message due to his own Jewish background, and he elevated the anti-Jewish Gospel of John as the better interpretation of Jesus. Although Paul rejected the law, Grundmann could not accept Paul's definition of Christians as the "new Israel"; that smacked of an affirmation of Judaism. The Christian message that Grundmann identified led him to claim that all Christians are united as sons of God, freed from sin and fear of death, a theology better suited to a society at war. Most important, he argued, Jesus taught an eschatology not of a future era, but of a salvation within present history, opening the door to interpretations of Nazism as salvation and Hitler as savior.[16]

Grundmann's theological treatise in 1938 about Jesus's divine sonship reinforced Hitler's own identification of himself with Christ and his mission as the resurrection of Germany after its crucifixion in World War I. A newspaper reports that Hitler, in a speech delivered in 1922 in a Munich beer hall, declared, "I say my Christian feelings point me to my Lord and Savior as a fighter [tumultuous, prolonged applause]. They point me toward the man who, once lonely and surrounded by only a few followers, recognized these Jews and called for battle against them."[17] His words were echoed by German Christians;

---

[15] *Die Gotteskindschaft in der Geschichte Jesu.*

[16] Grundmann, *Aufnahme und Deutung der Botschaft Jesu*, 35.

[17] *Völkischer Beobachter* 13/4/22; cited by Steigmann-Gall, "Was National Socialism a Political Religion or a Religious Politics?," 403.

the Thuringian pastor Paul Dahinten wrote that the Nazis had revived the foundational belief of earliest Christianity in divine sonship through Hitler: "We only saw the incarnation of God in Christ, but not the divinization of man brought about by him. The movement of Adolf Hitler allowed us finally to understand again the nobility of spirit of the spiritual Creators of the Occident."[18] Although he did not respond to the many Institute efforts to win his attention and active support, Hitler, until the end of his life, spoke of the Aryan Jesus and the need to rid Christianity of the Jewish Paul.[19] His rants on the subject were not endorsements of the Institute's theology or of the Protestant church, but a continued effort at a Nazi supersession of Christianity grounded in antisemitism. National Socialism, in Hitler's mind, took up the antisemitism of Christianity but elevated it to a more intense level and transformed it from theory to action.

In 1943 anti-Jewish propaganda throughout the Reich became more intense and increasingly bitter, even as the Reich itself was being declared judenrein. From its early years to the last months of the war, Nazism defined itself in opposition to Judaism and claimed to be fighting a war of self-defense against the Jews for the life and survival of the German Volk. What persisted in the Third Reich was its unwavering definition of the enemy as Jewish. In the closing months of the war, as Jeffrey Herf demonstrates, antisemitism became even more virulent; the war was defined as the revenge of the Jews against Germany.[20] As much as Christianity may have been perceived as irrelevant by some Nazi theorists, and the church viewed as a potential source of opposition, the Institute helped promote Christian theology as a valuable ally in the fight against "the Jews." The Leipzig philosopher Alfred Bäumler, leader of the universities section in the office of Nazi party leader Alfred Rosenberg, defined the Jew in 1943 as "the demon who became visible and who is the primordial enemy of the German . . . hence this is a fight for life or death, it is either us or him [the Jew]. . . . The nation demands the whole person and thus reaches into the religious domain."[21] The Jew had come to represent not only Judaism, but monotheism, Western civilization, critical rationalism and humanism, and the destruction of the German people. However much Institute members

[18] Paul Dahinten, "Der Thüringer evangelische Pfarrerverein," unpublished manuscript dated 1964 (LKA Eisenach).

[19] Steigmann-Gall, "Was National Socialism a Political Religion or a Religious Politics?," 403–4. See also Friedländer, *The Years of Extermination*, 281.

[20] Herf, *The Jewish Enemy*, 254–56, 260, 264–67.

[21] See Bäumler, *Alfred Rosenberg und der Mythus des 20. Jahrhunderts*, 19f, cited by Tal, "Structures of German Political Theology in the Nazi Era," 45.

sought to alter Christian doctrine or adopt Teutonic ideas, they always placed antisemitism at the forefront of their agenda.

The sharp division made by most historians, theologians, church officials, and scholars of religion between Christian theological anti-Judaism and modern racial antisemitism has fostered the postwar myth that theologians did not contribute to the Nazi murder of the Jews, and also the widespread notion, common among Jewish theologians as well, that Nazism represented an anti-Christian pagan revival movement. As the texts discussed in this book indicate, however, the boundary between theology and race was highly porous. The affinities between theology and race were more than elective. Theologians gravitated toward racism as a tool to modernize Christianity and to demonstrate that its principles were in accord with those of racial theory. In addition, they considered racial theory a tool to grant scientific legitimation to religion: racial claims of an inherent societal hierarchy reinforced religious beliefs in God's creation of a natural order and a hierarchy of plants, animals, and humans within it. Racists, for their part, were not ultimately concerned with the biological or physical nature of human bodies, but with the levels of alleged degeneracy inherent in those bodies. What marks the distinction between Aryan and Jew, in the writings of Institute members, is not physical appearance but spiritual and moral qualities. When Grundmann argued that Jesus was most likely descended from racial non-Jews residing in Galilee who had been forcibly converted to Judaism, he was primarily concerned not with Jesus's genealogy, but with demonstrating the nature of his religiosity and his relationship to God; those were the markers of his racial identity. Racism itself can be seen as a form of incarnational theology, centrally concerned with moral and spiritual issues, but insisting that the spiritual is incarnate in the physical.

The ease with which Grundmann received denazification from Thuringian church officials and the warmth and honor he was accorded during the nearly thirty years of his postwar career reveals the lack of concern with antisemitism in theology and church politics. Grundmann's antisemitism reiterated and elaborated traditional tropes of Christian theological anti-Judaism, concealing his politics under the veneer of a Christian theologian. In the eyes of the postwar church, his "crime" of the Nazi years was not one against Jews but against church doctrine, discipline, and theological order, and his ecclesial denazification was achieved by his willingness to accept a theology of Christ's supremacy over earthly rulers. Moreover, the ease of his denazification within a church controlled after the war by former Confessing Church members calls attention to the elisions in this history: how antisemitism linked the competing German Christian movement and Confessing Church during the Third Reich, and facilitated an easy transition of power from one group to the other at the end of the war. The church made the denazification of Germany superficial, and facilitated the transformation of former Nazi leaders into respected members of postwar society without considering Christian responsibility for the fate of the Jews. Moreover, Christian theology, with its self-definition as a religion of forgiveness based on divine moral principles higher than those of a court of law or democratic political system, was used to oppose harsh judgments of Nazi criminals and suppress the sort of thoroughgoing investigation of Nazi affinities that might have brought the downfall of Institute members who instead enjoyed flourishing postwar careers.

The postwar church in Germany failed for several decades to come to grips with the responsibility of Christian theology for antisemitism and for the Nazis' disenfranchisement, deportation, and murder of the Jews. Both ideologically and practically, the church played a significant role in the Third Reich. As Gunter Lewy pointed out decades ago, the Nazi system of Aryan identification, heavily reliant on birth records supplied by the church, could have been obstructed had the church refused to cooperate with the regime, but that was never even debated.[22] Teachings about the moral degeneracy of Judaism and its alleged threat to Christians could have been repudiated once theologians saw how Nazi propagandists were using them; that, too, was never considered. On the contrary, it was theologians who often proposed actions against the Jews that were only implemented by the Reich years later, such as Grundmann's 1933 writings against miscegenation and Leffler's chilling comment in 1936 about murdering Jews.

Starting in 1980 with the Rhineland synod's declaration calling for major changes in Christian attitudes toward Jews, including a cessation of conversionary efforts, a remarkable number of German theologians have made concerted efforts not only to take responsibility for the church's role in the Holocaust, but to formulate new theologies and christologies that affirm Judaism. Indeed, some of the most creative theological efforts in the area of Christian-Jewish relations have emerged in Germany in the past thirty years.[23] Although encountering obstacles and resistance, theological education, pastoral training, biblical exegesis, and doctrinal formulations have all been reconsidered and often radically altered in light of the Nazi past. The Holocaust, in this view, was a wound in the heart of Christian theology and a profound challenge

[22] Lewy, *The Catholic Church and Nazi Germany*.

[23] Among the many important German Protestant theologians who have led the efforts for a positive Christian appreciation of Judaism are Berhold Klappert, Frank Crüsemann, Friedrich-Wilhelm Marquardt, Klaus Wengst, Peter von der Osten-Sacken, Ulrich Lutz, Johann-Michael Schmidt, Martin Leutch, Jürgen Ebach, and Leonore Siegele-Wenschkewitz. Among Catholic theologians, prominent are Johann-Baptist Metz, Hans-Hermann Henrix, and Rainer Kampling.

Figure C.2. Broken iron cross by Christoph Seidel at the Bonhoefferhaus in Essen, Germany.

to its moral authority. After the war, Wolfgang Gerlach, a pastor who had written on the silence of the Confessing Church in response to Nazi anti-Jewish measures, placed a sculpture in his church in Essen depicting a broken cross, a symbol of Christian brokenness as a result of what Christians had perpetrated.

Postwar New Testament scholarship shifted from Germany to the United States, but in both countries a new attention to Jewish sources predominated, although it was scholars in the United States who were the prime forces demanding a new and positive Jewish setting for Jesus and his teachings. The rejudaization of Jesus—and Paul—did not occur immediately, and mixed motives can still be found, as in the writings of Ethelbert Stauffer, but the postwar study of Christian origins created at least the opportunity for an affirmation of Christianity that did not denigrate Judaism, even as older methods persisted.[24]

Joseph Bendersky has commented that Carl Schmitt, the legal theorist, "could neither be nazified nor denazified."[25] Grundmann and his Institute colleagues operated similarly, in a supposedly "neutral" space of theological anti-Judaism that did not require Nazism to make its defamations of Judaism, nor lose its anti-Judaism in the postwar denazification program. Racism, however, was essential to their intellectual grounding as theologians, and Nazism was central to their careers as academics and pastors, providing them with a political arena to trumpet their views. Once the war had ended and the Jews were murdered, the theologians could retreat to the shelter of the church. Precisely the "neutrality" afforded them by Christian theology's long-standing defamations of Judaism meant that no prosecution of them would take place. Moreover, describing themselves after the war as Old Testament figures of suffering and victimization became a successful means to escape responsibility and claim a moral high ground. As the denazification investigations pursued them, the Christian antisemites of the Third Reich could present themselves as the true Jews who had been persecuted by the Nazis but remained loyal to their Christian faith and their church.

[24] There is a large literature on contemporary New Testament scholarship and its treatment of Judaism. See, for example, Arnal, *The Symbolic Jesus*; Borg, "Recent Developments in North American Jesus Scholarship"; Fredriksen, "What You See Is What You Get"; Kelley, *Racializing Jesus*; Levine, *The Misunderstood Jew*; Pearson, "The Gospel According to the Jesus Seminar"; Penner, "Die Judenfrage and the Construction of Ancient Judaism."

[25] Bendersky, *Carl Schmitt*, 274.

Bibliography

Abresch, Johannes. "Enfant Terrible im Altar: Albert Kalthoff (1850–1906)." *Geschichte in Wuppertal* 5 (1996): 18–51.

Adam, Karl. "Deutsches Volkstum und katholisches Christentum," *Theologische Quartalschrift* 114 (1933), 40–63.

———. "Jesus, der Christus, und wir Deutsche," parts 1–3. *Wissenschaft und Weisheit* 10 (1943): 73–103; 11 (1944): 10–23.

Adam, Karl-Peter. "Der theologische Werdegang Walter Grundmanns bis zum Erscheinen der 28 Thesen der Sächsischen Volkskirche zum inneren Aufbau der Deutschen Evangelischen Kirche Ende 1933." In Siegele-Wenschkewitz, ed., *Christlicher Antijudaismus und Antisemitismus.*

Adam, Uwe Dietrich. *Hochschule und Nationalsozialismus: Die Universität Tübingen im Dritten Reich.* Tübingen: J.C.B. Mohr, 1977.

Adorno, Theodor. *Minima Moralia: Reflections from Damaged Life*, trans. E.F.N. Jephcott. London, New York: Verso, 1978.

Alt, Albrecht. "Galiläische Probleme," *Palästinajahrbuch* 33 (1937), 52–88; 34 (1938), 80–93; 35 (1939), 64–82; 36 (1940), 78–92; reprinted in Alt, *Kleine Schriften zur Geschichte des Volkes Israel* (Munich: C. H. Beck'sche Verlagsbuchhandlung, 1959), II:363–435.

Alt, Albrecht, and Joachim Begrich. *Führung zum Christentum durch das Alte Testament: Drei Vorträge von Albrecht Alt, Joachim Begrich, Gerhard von Rad.* Leipzig: Dörffling & Franke, 1934.

Alwast, Jendris. "Die Theologische Fakultät unter der Herrschaft des Nationalsozialismus." In *Uni-Formierung des Geistes: Universität Kiel im Nationalsozialismus*, ed. Hans-Werner Prahl. (Kiel: Malik, 1995), 87–137.

Aly, Götz, Peter Chroust, and Christian Pross. *Cleansing the Fatherland*, trans. Belinda Cooper. Baltimore: Johns Hopkins University Press, 1994.

Andersen, Friedrich. *Das Alte Testament—Eine "heilige Schrift"?* Leipzig, Theodor Weicher, 1924.

———. *Anticlericus: Eine Laientheologie auf geschichtlicher Grundlage.* Schleswig: Julius Bergas 1907.

———. *Deutschchristentum auf rein-evangelischer Grundlage: 95 Leitsätze zum Reformationsfest.* Leipzig: Theodor Weicher, 1917.

Andrew, M. E. "Gerhard von Rad: A Personal Memoir." *Expository Times* 83 (1971–72): 296–300.

Applegate, Celia, and Pamela Maxine Potter. *Music and German National Identity.* Chicago: University of Chicago Press, 2002.

Arnal, William E. "The Cipher 'Judaism' in Contemporary Jesus Scholarship." In *Apocalypticism, Anti-Semitism and the Historical Jesus: Subtexts in Criticism*, ed. J. S. Kloppenborg and J. W. Marshall (London: T&T Clark, 2005), 24–54.

————. *The Symbolic Jesus: Historical Scholarship, Judaism, and the Construction of Contemporary Identity*. London: Equinox, 2005.

Arnhold, Oliver. "Dem Neuen Testament und dem Bekenntnis der Kirche in unerträglicher Weise entgegen: Zum theologischen Gutachten des Reichskirchenausschusses gegen die Thüringer 'Kirchenbewegung Deutsche Christen' vom Juli 1936." In *Theologische Wissenschaft im Dritten Reich: Ein oekumenisches Projekt*, ed. Georg Denzler and Leonore Siegele-Wenschkewitz (Frankfurt am Main: Haag and Herchen, 2000), 151–83.

Arvidsson, Stefan. *Aryan Idols: Indo-European Mythology as Ideology and Science*, trans. Sonia Wichmann. Chicago: University of Chicago Press, 2006.

Ash, Mitchell G. "Verordnete Umbrüche—konstruierte Kontinuitäten: Zur Entnazifizierung von Wissenschaftlern und Wissenschaften nach 1945." *Zeitschrift für Geschichtswissenschaft* 43 (1995): 903–23.

Baier, Helmut. *Die Deutschen Christen Bayerns im Rahmen des Bayerischen Kirchenkampfes*. Nuremberg: Verein für Bayerische Kirchengeschichte, 1968.

————. *Kirche in Not: Die Bayerische Landeskirche im Zweiten Weltkrieg*. Neustadt an der Aisch: Degener, 1979.

Bammel, Ernst, and C.F.D. Moule, eds. *Jesus and the Politics of His Day*. Cambridge, New York: Cambridge University Press, 1984.

Bankier, David. *The Germans and the Final Solution: Public Opinion under Nazism, Jewish Society and Culture*. Oxford: Blackwell, 1992.

Barnett, Victoria. *For the Soul of the People: Protestant Protest against Hitler*. New York: Oxford University Press, 1992.

Walter Bauer, "Jesus der Galiläer," in: *Festgabe für Adolf Jülicher* (Tübingen, 1927), 16–34; reprinted in Walter Bauer, *Aufsätze und kleine Schriften*, ed. Georg Strecker (Tübingen: J.C.B. Mohr, 1967), 91–108.

Bauer, Wilhelm. *Feierstunden Deutscher Christen*. Weimar: Verlag Deutsche Christen, 1935.

Baumgarten, Otto. *Kreuz und Hakenkreuz*. Gotha: L. Klotz, 1926.

Bäumler, Alfred. *Alfred Rosenberg und der Mythus des 20. Jahrhunderts*. Munich: Huheneichen Verlag, 1943.

Begrich, Joachim. *Antisemitisches im Alten Testament*. Jena: Frommannsche Buchhandlung, 1931.

Bendersky, Joseph. *Carl Schmitt: Theorist for the Reich*. Princeton: Princeton University Press, 1983.

Benes, Tuska. "From Indo-Germans to Aryans: Philology and the Racialization of Salvationist National Rhetoric, 1806–30." In *The German Invention of Race*, ed. Sara Eigen and Mark Larrimore (Albany: SUNY Press, 2006), 167–84.

Bergen, Doris L. "Hosanna or 'Hilf, O Herr Uns': National Identity, the German Christian Movement, and the 'Dejudaization.'" In Applegate and Potter, eds., *Music and German National Identity*, 140–54.

————. "The Nazi Concept of 'Volksdeutsche' and the Exacerbation of Antisemitism in Eastern Europe, 1939–1945." *Journal of Contemporary History* 29, no. 4 (1994): 569–82.

————. "One Reich, One People, One Church: The German Christian Movement and the People's Church, 1932–1945." Ph.D. dissertation, University of North Carolina, 1991.

————. *Twisted Cross: The German Christian Movement in the Third Reich.* Chapel Hill: University of North Carolina Press, 1996.

————. "'War Protestantism' in Germany, 1914–1945." In Gailus and Lehmann, eds., *Nationalprotestantische Mentalitäten,* 115–32.

Berghaus, Günter. "The Ritual Core of the Fascist Theatre: An Anthropological Perspective." In Berghaus, ed., *Fascism and Theatre,* 39–71.

Berghaus, Günter, ed. *Fascism and Theatre: Comparative Studies on the Aesthetics and Politics of Performance in Europe, 1925–1945.* Providence, Oxford: Berghahn Books, 1996.

Bergmann, Ernst. *Deutschland, das Bildungsland der neuen Menschheit: Eine nationalsozialistische Kulturphilosophie.* Breslau: F. Hirt, 1933.

Bernal, Martin. *Black Athena: The Afroasiatic Roots of Classical Civilization,* vol. I: *The Fabrication of Ancient Greece 1785–1985.* London: Free Association Books, 1987.

Bertheau, Martin. "Grosser Gott." *Theologische Blätter* 4, no. 21 (1942): 90–105.

Bertram, Georg. "Jesus und das Buch." In Grundmann, ed., *Germanentum, Christentum und Judentum,* 347–422.

————. *Die Leidensgeschichte Jesu und der Christuskult.* Göttingen: Vandenhoeck & Ruprecht, 1922.

Besier, Gerhard. "The Stance of the German Protestant Churches during the Agony of Weimar, 1930–1933." *Kyrkohistorisk Årsskrift* (1983): 151–63.

————. "Zur Geschichte der kirchlichen Hochschulen: Oder, der Kampf um den theologischen Nachwuchs." In Siegele-Wenschkewitz and Nicolaisen, *Theologische Fakultäten im Nationalsozialismus,* 251–75.

————. *Die Kirchen und das Dritte Reich: Spaltungen und Abwehrkämpfe, 1934–1937.* Berlin: Propyläen, 2001.

Besier, Gerhard, and Stephan Wolf. *"Pfarrer, Christen und Katholiken": Das Ministerium für Staatssicherheit der ehemaligen DDR und die Kirchen.* Neukirchen-Vluyn: Neukirchener, 1992.

Bialas, Wolfgang, and Anson Rabinbach, *The Humanities in Nazi Germany.* Oxford: One World Press, 2006.

Bierer, Dora. "Renan and His Interpreters: A Study in French Intellectual Warfare." *Journal of Modern History* 25, no. 4 (1953): 375–89.

Boberach, Heinz. *Berichte des SD und der Gestapo über Kirche und Kirchenvolk in Deutschland, 1934–1944.* Mainz: Matthias-Grünewald, 1971.

Böhm, Johann. *Gleichschaltung der Deutschen Volksgruppe in Rumänien und das "Dritte Reich" 1941–1944.* Frankfurt: Lang, 2003.

————. *Das Nationalsozialistische Deutschland und die Deutsche Volksgruppe in Rumänien 1936–1944: Das Verhältnis der Deutschen Volksgruppe zum Dritten Reich und zum Rumänischen Staat sowie der interne Widerstreit zwischen den politischen Gruppen.* Frankfurt am Main, New York: Lang, 1985.

Böhm, Susanne. "Die ersten zehn Jahre der Evangelischen Akademie Thüringen." In Seidel, ed., *Thüringer Gratwanderungen,* 189–208.

————. "Gerhard von Rad in Jena." In *Das Alte Testament—Ein Geschichtsbuch? Geschichtsschreibung oder Geschichtsüberlieferung im Antiken Israel*, ed. Uwe Becker and Jürgen van Oorschot, (Leipzig: Evangelische Verlagsanstalt, 2005), 203–40.

————. "Gerhard von Rad und der Streit um das Alte Testament—unter besonderer Berücksichtigung seiner Zeit in Jena." Master's thesis, University of Jena, 1996.

Bohn, Robert, ed. *Die deutsche Herrschaft in den "germanischen" Ländern 1940–1945*. Stuttgart: HMRG, 1997.

Bollmus, Reinhard. *Das Amt Rosenberg und seine Gegner*. Stuttgart: Deutsche Verlags-Anstalt, 1970.

Bonus, Artur. *Von der Germanisierung, Individualisierung und Nationalisierung der Religion*. 1898.

Borchert, D. Otto. *Das Volk und der Christ: Volk, Volkstum, Volkheit im Lichte der Wortes Gottes*. Braunschweig: Hallmuth Wollerman Verlagsbuchhandlung, 1934.

Borg, Daniel R. *The Old-Prussian Church and the Weimar Republic: A Study in Political Adjustment, 1917–1927*. Hanover, NH: University Press of New England, 1984.

Borg, Marcus J. "Recent Developments in North American Jesus Scholarship." *Qumran Chronicle* 5, no. 1 (1995): 63–73.

Bormann, Martin, ed., *Hitler's Secret Conversations 1941–1944*, with an introduction by H. R. Trevor-Roper. New York: Farrar, Straus and Young, 1953.

Börner, Robert. "Der Reichsparteitag." *Christenkreuz und Hakenkreuz* 9 (1936): 5–6.

Bousset, Wilhelm. *Jesu Predigt in ihrem Gegensatz zum Judentum: Ein religionsgeschichtlicher Vergleich*. Göttingen: Vandenhoeck & Ruprecht, 1892.

————. *Kyrios Christos: Geschichte des Christusglaubens von den Anfängen des Christentums bis Irenaeus*. Göttingen: Vandenhoeck & Ruprecht, 1913.

————. *Die Religion des Judentums im Neutestamentlichen Zeitalter*. Berlin: Reuther & Reichard, 1903.

Brakelmann, Günter, ed. *Kirche im Krieg: Der deutsche Protestantismus am Beginn des Zweiten Weltkriegs*. Munich: Christian Kaiser, 1979.

Bräuer, Siegfried, and Clemens Vollnhals, eds. *"In der DDR gibt es keine Zensur": Die Evangelische Verlagsanstalt und die Praxis der Druckgenehmigung, 1954–1989*. Leipzig: Evangelische Verlagsanstalt, 1995.

Braun, Christina von. *Der ewige Judenhass: Christlicher Antijudaismus, Deutschnationale Judenfeindlichkeit, Rassistischer Antisemitismus*. Berlin: Philo, 1990.

Broshi, Magen. "How to Recognize a Jew." *Israel Museum Journal* 2 (1993): 81–84.

Browning, Christopher, with Jürgen Matthäus. *The Origins of the Final Solution: The Evolution of Nazi Jewish Policy, September 1939–March 1942*. Yad Vashem Series. Lincoln: University of Nebraska Press, 2004.

Bruhn, Mike, and Heike Böttner. "Studieren in Jena 1933 bis 1945: Eine Fallstudie." In Gottwald and Steinbach, *Zwischen Wissenschaft und Politik*, 107–22.

Brunotte, Heinz, and Wolf, Ernst, eds. *Zur Geschichte des Kirchenkampfes: Gesammelte Aufsätze*. 2 vols. Göttingen: Vandenhoeck & Ruprecht, 1965–71.

Bryant, Edwin. *The Quest for the Origins of Vedic Culture: The Indo-Aryan Migration Debate*. Oxford, New York: Oxford University Press, 2001.

Buchheim, Hans. *Glaubenskrise Im Dritten Reich; Drei Kapitel Nationalsozialistischer Religionspolitik*. Stuttgart: Deutsche Verlags-Anstalt, 1953.

Büchsel, Friedrich. "Walter Grundmann, Jesus der Galiläer und das Judentum." *Theologische Literaturzeitung* 67 (1942): 91–94.

Buell, Denise Kimber. *Why This New Race: Ethnic Reasoning in Early Christianity*. New York: Columbia University Press, 2005.

Bunsen, Christian. *Outlines of the Philosophy of Universal History*. 2 vols. London: Longman, Brown, Green, and Longmans, 1845.

Burnouf, Emile. *The Science of Religions*, trans. Julie Liebe. London: S. Sonnenschein, Lowrey, 1888.

Buss, Hansjörg. *"Eine Chronik gemischter Gefühle": Bilanz der Wanderausstellung "Kirche, Christen, Juden in Nordelbien 1933–1945."* Bremen: Edition Temmen, 2005.

———. "'Entjudung der Kirche': Ein Kircheninstitut und die Schleswig-Holsteinische Landeskirche." In Linck, Göhres, and Liß-Walther, eds., *Als Jesus "arisch" wurde*, 162–86.

———. "Die nordelbischen Landeskirchen und das 'Institut zur Erforschung und Beseitigung des jüdischen Einflusses auf das deutsche kirchliche Leben' (1939–1945)." Christian-Albrechts-Universität, 2001.

Butler, E. M. *The Tyranny of Greece over Germany: A Study of the Influence Exercised by Greek Art and Poetry over the Great German Writers of the Eighteenth, Nineteenth and Twentieth Centuries*. Cambridge: [Cambridge] University Press, 1935.

Caplan, Jane. "Politics, Religion, and Ideology: A Comment on Wolfgang Hardtwig." *German Historical Institute Bulletin* 38 (2001): 28–36.

Caspari, Wilhelm. *Die Alttestamentliche Schicksalsfrage an die Deutschvölkskirchen*. Gütersloh: Bertelsmann, 1925.

———. "Über Alttestamentliche Bezugnahmen im Evangelischen Gesangbuch und ihre Beseitigung." *Monatsschrift für Gottesdienst und kirchliche Kunst* 7 (1933): 169–79.

Cehak, Karl, ed. *Jesus, der Künder und Kämpfer Gottes*. Hilfsbücher für die deutschen Religionslehrer. Breslau: F. Hirt, 1937.

Cesaire, Aimee. *Discourse on Colonialism*, trans. Joan Pinkham. New York: Monthly Review Press, 1972.

Chamberlain, Houston Stewart. *Briefe, 1882–1924, und Briefwechsel mit Kaiser Wilhelm II*. Munich: F. Bruckmann, 1928.

———. *Die Grundlagen des neunzehnten Jahrhunderts*. 2 vols. Munich: F. Bruckmann A.-G., 1899; in English, as *The Foundations of the Nineteenth Century*, trans. John Lees. 2 vols. New York: John Lane Co., 1910.

Chancey, Mark A. *The Myth of a Gentile Galilee*. Cambridge and New York: Cambridge University Press, 2002.

Chandler, Andrew, ed. *Brethren in Adversity: Bishop George Bell, the Church of England and the Crisis of German Protestantism, 1933–1939*. Woodbridge, Suffolk: Boydell Press, 1997.

———. "Wagnerismus in der Kaiserzeit." In *Handbuch zur "Völkischen Bewegung" 1871–1918*, ed. Uwe Puschner, Walter Schmitz, and Justus H. Ulbricht. Munich, New Providence: K.G. Saur, 1996.

Chroust, Peter. "Social Situation and Political Orientation: Students and Professors at Giessen University, 1918–1945." *Historische Sozialforschung* 2 (1986): 41–95.

———. *Gießener Universität und Faschismus: Studenten und Hochschullehrer, 1918–1945.* 2 vols.. Münster, New York: Waxmann, 1994.

Clark, Christopher M. *The Politics of Conversion: Missionary Protestantism and the Jews in Prussia, 1728–1941.* Oxford: Clarendon Press, 1995.

Connelly, John. *Captive University: The Sovietization of East German, Czech, and Polish Higher Education, 1945–1956.* Chapel Hill: University of North Carolina Press, 2000.

———. "Catholic Racism and Its Opponents." *Journal of Modern History* 79 (Dec. 2007): 813–47.

Connelly, John, and Michael Grüttner, eds. *Zwischen Autonomie und Anpassung: Universitäten in den Diktaturen des 20. Jahrhunderts.* Paderborn: Schöningh, 2003.

Conway, John S. *The Nazi Persecution of the Churches, 1933–45.* New York: Basic Books, 1968.

Crichton, Kevin. "'Preparing for Government?' Wilhelm Frick as Thuringia's Nazi Minister of the Interior and of Education, 23 January 1930–April 1931." PhD dissertation, University of St. Andrews, 2001.

Dalman, Gustaf. Die Worte Jesu mit Berücksichtigung des nachkanonischen jüdischen Schrifttums Leipzig: Hinrichs, 1898.

D'Angelo, Mary Rose. "Abba and 'Father': Imperial Theology and the Jesus Traditions." *Journal of Biblical Literature* 111, no. 4 (1992): 611–30.

Davies, Alan. "Racism and German Protestant Theology: A Prelude to the Holocaust." *Annals of the American Academy of Political and Social Science* 450 (1980): 20–34.

Deines, Roland. "Jesus der Galiläer: Traditionsgeschichte und Genese eines antisemitischen Konstrukts bei Walter Grundmann." In Deines, Leppin, and Niebuhr, eds., *Walter Grundmann,* 43–133.

Deines, Roland, Volker Leppin, and Karl-Wilhelm Niebuhr, eds. *Walter Grundmann.* Leipzig: Evangelische Verlagsanstalt, 2007.

Deleuze, Gilles. *A Thousand Plateaus,* trans. Brian Massumi. London: Athlone, 1988.

Delling, Gerhard. "Herbert Preisker in memoriam." *Theologische Literaturzeitung* 78 (1953): 181.

Denzler, Georg. "Antijudaismus und Antisemitismus in der Theologie unseres Jahrhunderts: Karl Adam, Michael Schmaus, und Anton Stonner." *Facta Universitatis, Series Law and Politics* 1, no. 1 (1997): 11–20.

Dickmann, Fritz. "Die Regierungsbildung in Thüringen als Modell der Machtergreifung: Ein Brief Hitlers aus dem Jahre 1930." *Vierteljahreshefte für Zeitgeschichte* 14, no. 4 (1966): 454–64.

Dierker, Wolfgang. *Himmlers Glaubenskrieger: Der Sicherheitsdienst der SS und seine Religionspolitik, 1933–1941,* ed. Hans Günter Hockerts et al. Paderborn: Ferdinand Schöningh, 2002.

Dierks, Margarete. *Jakob Wilhelm Hauer, 1881–1962: Leben, Werk, Wirkung, mit einer Personalbibliographie.* Heidelberg: Lambert Schneider, 1986.

Dinter, Arthur. *Das Evangelium unseres Herrn und Heilandes Jesus Christus.* Langensalza: Thüringische Verlagsanstalt, 1923.

Displaced German Scholars: A Guide to Academics in Peril in Nazi Germany during the 1930s. San Bernardino, CA: Borgo Press, 1993.

Dyer, Richard. *White.* New York: Routledge, 1997.

Edenholm, E. Douglas. "Das germanische Erbe in der Schwedischen Froemmigkeit." In Grundmann, ed., *Die völkische Gestalt des Glaubens,* 221–37.

———. "Germanskt Och Kristet." *Religion och Kultur* 12 (1941): 176–87.

Ehrenfort, Gerhard. *Die schlesische Kirche im Kirchenkampf 1932–1945.* Gottingen: Vandenhoeck u. Ruprecht, 1968.

Eifer, Julius Georg. *Jehovah und seine Auserwählten vor dem Volksgericht!* Bremen: Agnes Eifer/Ahnen Verlag, 1936.

———. *Die Rache Jehovahs in Russland.* Bremen: Agnes Eifer/Ahnen Verlag, 1935.

Eisenstein, Jehuda David. *Ozar Vikuhim.* New York, 1928.

Elert, Werner. "Bericht über das Dekanat der theologischen Fakultät Erlangen 1935–43." In *Die Erlanger Theologie,* ed. Karlmann Beyschlag (Erlangen: Martin-Luther Verlag in Zusammenarbeit mit dem Verein für bayerische Kirchengeschichte, 1993), 268–86.

Engelmann, Hans. *Kirche am Abgrund: Adolf Stoecker und seine antijüdische Bewegung,* ed. Peter von der Osten-Sacken. Berlin: Institut Kirche und Israel, 1984.

Erbt, Wilhelm. "Ein nordisches Jesusbild." *Zeitschrift für den Evangelischen Religionsunterricht* 42 (1931).

Ericksen, Robert P. "Hiding the Nazi Past: Denazification and Christian Postwar Reckoning in Germany." In *A Lutheran Vocation: Philip A. Nordquist and the Study of History at Pacific Lutheran University,* ed. Robert P. Ericksen and Michael J. Halvorson (Tacoma, WA: Pacific Lutheran University Press, 2005), 137–56.

———. *Theologians under Hitler: Gerhard Kittel, Paul Althaus, and Emanuel Hirsch.* New Haven: Yale University Press, 1987.

———. "Wilhelm Niemöller and the Historiography of the Kirchenkampf." In *Nationalprotestantische Mentalitäten in Deutschland—1870–1970,* ed. Manfred Gailus and Hartmut Lehmann (Göttingen: Vandenhoek & Ruprecht, 2005), 433–52.

Ericksen, Robert P., and Susannah Heschel, eds. *Betrayal: The German Churches and the Holocaust.* Minneapolis: Augsburg-Fortress Press, 1999.

Ericksen, Robert P., and Susannah Heschel. "Historiography on the Churches and the Holocaust." In *Historiography of the Holocaust,* ed. Dan Stone (London: Palgrave Press, 2004), 296–318.

Euler, Karl Friedrich. *Der Verkündigung vom leidenen Gottesknecht aus Jes 53 in der griechischen Bibel.* Stuttgart-Berlin: W. Kohlhammer Verlag, 1934.

Falcke, Heino. "Kirche im Sozialismus." In Günther Heydemann and Lothar Kettenacker, eds., *Kirchen in der Diktatur* (Göttingen: Vandenhoeck and Ruprecht, 1993), 259–81.

Faulenbach, *Heiner. Ein Weg durch die Kirche: Heinrich Josef Oberheid.* Cologne: Rheinland Verlag, 1992.

Faulhaber, Michael von. *Judaism, Christianity and Germany,* trans. George D. Smith. New York: Macmillan and Co., 1934.

Faust, Anselm. "Professoren für die NSDAP: Zum politischen Verhalten der Hochschullehrer 1932/3." In *Erziehung und Schulung im Dritten Reich,* ed. Manfred Heinemann (Stuttgart: Klett-Cotta, 1980), 31–49.

Fenske, Wolfgang. *Wie Jesus zum "Arier" wurde: Auswirkungen der Entjudaisierung Christi im 19. und zu Beginn des 20. Jahrhunderts.* Darmstadt: Wissenschaftliche Buchgesellschaft, 2005.

Fiebig, Paul. *Der Menschensohn: Jesu Selbstbezeichnung mit besonderer Berücksichtigung des aramäischen Sprachgebrauches für "Mensch."* Tübingen: J.C.B. Mohr, 1901.

Field, Geoffrey G. "Nordic Racism." *Journal of the History of Ideas* 38, no. 3 (1977): 523–40.

———. *Evangelist of Race: The Germanic Vision of Houston Stewart Chamberlain.* New York: Columbia University Press, 1981.

Fischer, Eugen. "Rassenentstehung und älteste Rassengeschichte der Hebräer." *Forschungen zur Judenfrage* 3 (1938): 121–36.

Fischer, Eugen, and Kittel, Gerhard. *Das antike Weltjudentum: Tatsachen, Texte, Bilder.* Hamburg: Hanseatische Verlagsanstalt, 1943.

Fischer, Joachim. *Die Sächsische Landeskirche Im Kirchenkamf 1933–1937.* Göttingen: Vandenhoeck & Ruprecht, 1972.

Forstman, Jack. *Christian Faith in Dark Times: Theological Conflicts in the Shadow of Hitler.* 1st ed. Louisville, KY: Westminster/John Knox Press, 1992.

Fredriksen, Paula. "What You See Is What You Get: Context and Content in Current Research on the Historical Jesus." *Theology Today* 52, no. 1 (1995): 75–97.

Frei, Hans W. *The Eclipse of Biblical Narrative: A Study in Eighteenth and Nineteenth Century Hermeneutics.* New Haven: Yale University Press, 1974.

Frei, Norbert. *Adenauer's Germany and the Nazi Past: The Politics of Amnesty and Integration,* trans. Joel Golb. New York: Columbia University Press, 2002.

Frenssen, Gustav. *Der Glaube der Nordmark.* Stuttgart: G. Truckenmüller, 1936.

———. Gustav. *Hilligenlei.* Berlin: Grote, 1905.

Freudenberg, Adolf. "Bermerkungen zur kirchlichen Lage in Deutschland, Juli 1945." In *Die evangelische Kirche nach dem Zusammenbruch: Berichte ausländischer Beobachter aus dem Jahre 1945,* ed. Clemens Vollnhals (Göttingen: Vandenhoeck und Ruprecht, 1988).

Freyne, Sean. "Galilean Questions to Crossan's Mediterranean Jesus." In *Whose Historical Jesus?,* ed. William E. Arnal and Michel R. Desjardins (Waterloo, Ont.: Wilfrid Laurier University Press, 1997), 63–91.

———. *Galilee, Jesus and the Gospels: Literary Approaches and Historical Investigations.* Philadelphia: Fortress Press, 1988.

———. *Jesus, a Jewish Galilean.* London, New York: T&T Clark International, 2004.

Friedländer, Saul. *Nazi Germany and the Jews*, vol. 1, *The Years of Persecution, 1933–1939*. New York: Harper Collins, 1997; vol. 2, *The Years of Extermination: Nazi Germany and the Jews, 1939–1945*. New York: HarperCollins, 2007.

Friedman, Saul S. *The Oberammergau Passion Play: A Lance against Civilization*. Carbondale and Edwardsville: Southern Illinois University Press, 1984.

Fritsch, Theodor. *Der falsche Gott: Beweismaterial gegen Jahwe*. 9th ed. Leipzig: Hammer, 1911.

Fritz, Stephen. Endkampf: *Soldiers, Civilians, and the Death of the Third Reich*. Lexington: University Press of Kentucky, 2004.

Gailus, Manfred, ed. *Kirchengemeinden im Nationalsozialismus: Sieben Beispiele aus Berlin*. Berlin: Hentrich, 1990.

Gailus, Manfred. *Protestantismus und Nationalsozialismus: Studien zur nationalsozialistischen Durchdringung des protestantischen Sozialmilieus in Berlin*. Cologne, Weimar, Vienna: Böhlau, 2001.

Gailus, Manfred, and Wolfgang Krogel. *Von der babylonischen Gefangenschaft der Kirche im Nationalen: Regionalstudien zu Protestantismus, Nationalsozialismus und Nachkriegsgeschichte 1930 bis 2000*. Berlin: Wichern, 2006.

Gentile, Emilio. "The Theatre of Politics in Fascist Italy." In *Fascism and Theatre: Comparative Studies on the Aesthetics and Politics of Performance in Europe, 1925–1945*, ed. Günter Berghaus (Providence: Berghahn Books, 1996), 72–93.

Gerdmar, Anders. "Ein Germanischer Jesus auf Schwedischem Boden: Schwedisch-Deutche Forschungszusammenarbeit mit rassistischen Vorzeichen 1941–1945." In Deines, Leppin, and Niebuhr, eds., *Walter Grundmann*, 319–48.

Gerhardsson, Birger. *Fridrichsen, Odeberg, Aulen, Nygren: Fyra Teologer*. Lund: Novapress, 1994.

Gerlach, Wolfgang. *Als die Zeugen schwiegen: Bekennende Kirche und die Juden*. Berlin: Institut Kirche und Judentum, 1987; in English, as *And the Witnesses Were Silent: The Confessing Church and the Persecution of the Jews*, trans. Victoria J. Barnett. Lincoln: University of Nebraska Press, 2000.

Giles, Geoffrey J. *Students and National Socialism in Germany*. Princeton, NJ: Princeton University Press, 1985.

Glondys, Bishop Viktor. *Tagebuch: Aufzeichnungen von 1933–1947*, ed. Johann Böhm and Dieter Braeg. Dinklage: AGK Verlag, 1997.

Göhres, Annette, Stephan Linck, and Joachim Liss-Walther. *Als Jesus "arisch" Wurde: Kirchen, Christen, Juden in Nordelbien, 1933–1945: Die Ausstellung in Kiel*. 2nd ed. Bremen: Edition Temmen, 2004.

Goldziher, Ignaz. *Der Mythos bei den Hebräern und seine geschichtliche Entwickelung: Untersuchung zur Mythologie und Religionswissenschaft*. Leipzig: F. A. Brockhaus, 1876.

Golling, Ralf, and Peter von der Osten-Sacken, eds. *Hermann L. Strack und das Institutum Judaicum in Berlin: Mit einem Anhang über das Institut Kirche und Judentum*. Berlin: Institut Kirche und Judentum, 1996.

Gottwald, Herbert, and Matthias Steinbach, eds. *Zwischen Wissenschaft und Politik: Studien zur Jenaer Universität im 20. Jahrhundert*. Jena: Bussert & Stadeler, 2000.

Graetz, Heinrich. *Geschichte der Juden*. Leipzig: O. Leiner, 1863.

Graf, Friedrich Wilhelm. *Profile des Neuzeitlichen Protestantismus*. Gütersloh: G. Mohn, 1990.

———. "Wilhelm Stapel." In *Biographisch-Bibliographisches Kirchenlexicon*, 1165–1200. Nordhausen: Traugott Bautz, 1995.

Gramley, Hedda. *Propheten des deutschen Nationalismus: Theologen, Historiker und Nationalökonomen 1848–1880*. Frankfurt am Main, New York: Campus, 2001.

Gregor, Birgit. "Von jüdischem Einfluß befreit: 'Großer Gott wir loben dich': Ein Deutsch-Christliches Gesangbuch aus dem Jahre 1941." In Seidel, ed., *Thüringer Gratwanderungen*, 124–42.

Greschat, Martin. "Die evangelisch-theologische Fakultät in Gießen in der Zeit des Nationalsozialismus." In *Theologie im Kontext der Geschichte der Alma Mater Ludoviciana*, eds. Bernhard Jendorff, Cornelius Petrus Mayer, and Gerhard Schmalenberg (Giessen: Ferber, 1983).

Grundmann, Walter. *Acht und zwanzig Thesen der sächsischen Volkskirche zum inneren Aufbau der deutschen evangelischen Kirche*. Dresden: Deutsch-Christlicher Verlag, 1934.

———. "Das Angebot der eröffneten Freiheit. Zugleich eine Studie nach der Rechtfertigungslehre. Heinz Schürmann Erfurt zum 60. Geburtstag in Verehrungsvoller Freundschaft." *Catholica* 28 (1974): 304–33.

———. "Antwort an Einen Kritiker." *Sigrune* 4, no. 28 (July 9, 1939).

———. "Antwort Auf F. Büchsel." *Das evangelische Deutschland* 17, no. 4 (1940).

———. "Das apokalyptische Geschichtsbild und das deutsche Geschichtsdenken." In *Germanentum, Christentum und Judentum* (Leipzig: Georg Wigand, 1940), 55–78.

———. "Die Apostel zwischen Jerusalem und Antiochia." *Zeitschrift für neutestamentliche Wissenschaft* 39 (1940): 110–37.

———. "Die Arbeit des ersten Evangelisten am Bilde Jesu." In Grundmann, ed., *Christentum und Judentum*, I: 53–78.

———. "Aufbruch der Nation und christliche Gemeinde." Mitteilungen aus der deutschen christlichen Studentenvereinigung, 1933.

———. *Aufnahme und deutung der Botschaft Jesu im Urchristentum*. Studien zu deutscher Theologie und Frömmigkeit, vol. 3. Weimar: Deutsche Christen, 1941.

———. "Aufwärts Abwärts." In *Reallexikon für Antike und Christentum* (Stuttgart: Hiersemann, 1950–), 954–57.

———. *Der Begriff der Kraft in der Neutestamentlichen Gedankenwelt*, Stuttgart: W. Kohlhammer, 1932.

———. "Die Bergpredigt nach der Lukasfassung." *Studia Evangelica* 1 (1959): 180–89.

———. "Die biblische Geschichte im kirchlichen Unterricht." In *Domine, Dirige Me in Verbo Tuo*, ed. H. von Hintzenstern (Berlin: Evangelische Verlagsanstalt, 1961) 179–96.

———. *Der Brief des Judas und der zweite Brief des Petrus*. Berlin: Evangelische Verlagsanstalt, 1974.

———. "The Decision of the Supreme Court to Put Jesus to Death (John 11:47–57) in Its Context. Tradition and Redaction in the Gospel of John." In Bammel and Moule, eds., *Jesus and the Politics of His Day*, 295–318.

———. *Deutsche Frömmigkeit, ihr Wesen und ihre Erscheinung*. Weimar: Verlag Deutsche Christen, 1941.

———. "Das Doppelgebot Der Liebe." *Zeichen der Zeit* 11 (1957): 449–55.

———. *Die Entjudung des religiösen Lebens als Aufgabe deutscher Theologie und Kirche*. Weimar: Verlag Deutsche Christen, 1939; microform.

———. *Die Entscheidung Jesu. Zur geschichtlichen Bedeutung der Gestalt Jesu von Nazareth*. Berlin: Evangelische Verlagsanstalt, 1972.

———. *Der Erfurter Regler-Altar*, Berlin: Evangelische Verlagsanstalt, 1957.

———. *Das Evangelium nach Lukas*. Theologischer Handkommentar zum Neuen Testament. Berlin: Evangelische Verlagsanstalt, 1961.

———. *Das Evangelium nach Markus*. Theologischer Handkommentar zum Neuen Testament. Berlin: Evangelische Verlagsanstalt, 1959.

———. *Das Evangelium nach Matthäus*. Theologischer Handkommentar zum Neuen Testament. Berlin: Evangelische Verlagsanstalt, 1968.

———. "Die ewige Wahrheit des Evangeliums und seine Zeitgebundenheit." In *Die Bedeutung der Bibel für den Glauben*, ed. von H. E. Eisenhuth (Leipzipg: Georg Wigand, 1941).

———. "Die Frage nach der Gottessohnschaft des Messias im Lichte von Qumran." In *Bibel und Qumran: Festschrift für Hans Bardtke*, eds. H. Bardtke and S. Wagner (Berlin: Evangelische Haupt-Bibelgesellschaft, 1968).

———. "Fragen der Komposition des Lukanischen 'Reiseberichts.'" *Zeitschrift für neutestamentliche Wissenschaft* 50 (1959): 252–70.

———. "Führererlebnis und Priestertum." In *Glaube und Volk* 2 (1933): 147–55.

———. "Der Geist der Sohnschaft. Eine Studie zu Röm 8,15 und Gal 4,6 zu ihrer Stellung in der Paulinischen Theologie und ihren traditionsgeschichtlichen Grundlagen." In *In Disciplina Domini. Thüringer kirchliche Studien I*, ed. H. von Hintzenstern (Berlin: Evangelische Verlagsanstalt, 1963), 171–92.

———. *Die Geschichte Jesu Christi*. Berlin: Evangelische Verlagsanstalt, 1957.

———. "Geschichte und Botschaft des Urchristentums in ihrer religiösen Umwelt." In Leipoldt and Grundmann, eds., *Umwelt des Urchristentums*.

———. "Gesetz, Rechtfertigung und Mystik bei Paulus. Zum Problem der Einheitlichkeit der Paulinischen Verkündigung." *Zeitschrift für neutestamentliche Wissenschaft* (1933): 52–65.

———. *Der Gott Jesu Christi*. Weimar: Verlag Deutschen Christen, 1936.

———. *Gott und Nation. Ein evangelisches Wort zum Wollen des Nationalsozialismus und zu Rosenbergs Sinndeutung*. Stimmen aus der Deutschen Christlichen Studentenbewegung, vol. 81. Berlin: Furche Verlag, 1933.

———. *Die Gotteskindschaft in der Geschichte Jesu und ihre religionsgeschichtlichen Voraussetzungen*. Studien zu deutscher Theologie und Frömmigkeit 1. Weimar: Verlag Deutschen Christen, 1938.

301

————. "Das Heil kommt von den Juden: Eine Schicksalsfrage an die Christen deutscher Nation." *Deutsche Frömmigkeit* 9 (September 1938): 1–8.

————. Im Kampf um Gott, Ein Wort zur Gottlosenbewegung, Leipzig/Chemnitz, 1931.

————. "Der Isenheimer Altar." In *Glaube und Freiheit: Ein Gruss an die Evangelischen Theologen an der Front*, ed. Emanuel Hirsch, Walter Grundmann, et al. (Leipzig: Georg Wigand, 1940), 129–35.

————. *Jesus der Galiläer und das Judentum*. Leipzig: Verlag Georg Wigand, 1940.

————. *Jesus von Nazareth: Bürge zwischen Gott und Mensch*. Göttingen: Musterschmidt, 1975.

————. "Kirche und Staat nach der Zwei-Reiche-Lehre Luthers." In *Im Dienst des Rechts in Kirche und Staat* (Festschrift for Franz Arnold), ed. Willibald M. Plöchl and Inge Gampl (Vienna: Herder, 1963), 38–54.

————. "Der Lehrer der Gerechtigkeit von Qumran und die Frage nach der Glaubensgerechtigkeit in der Theologie des Apostels." *Revue de Qumran* 2 (1960): 237–59. In English, as "The Teacher of Righteousness of Qumran and the Question of Justification by Faith in the Theology of the Apostle Paul." In *Paul and Qumran: Studies in New Testament Exegesis*, ed. Jerome Murphy-O'Connor (Chicago: Priory Press, 1968), 85–114.

————. *Die Losung: Der weitere Weg der Deutschen Christen*. Dresden, [Leipzig]: Deutschchristlicher Verl., [H. G. Wallmann], 1935.

————. "Matthäus XI:22 und die Johanneischen "Der Vater-Der Sohn"-Stellen." *New Testament Studies* 12 (1965–66): 42–49.

————. *Der Meister H.W.: Das Schaffen Hans Wittens*. Klaus G. Beyer, 1976.

————. "Das Messiasproblem." In *Germanentum, Christentum und Judentum*, vol. 2, 379–412.

————. *Theologischen Wörterbuch zum Neuen Testament*, ed. Gerhard Kittel: vol. 1: 10–18, 72–75, 290–95, 299–320, 347–50, 358–59; vol. II: 21–25, 37–39, 49–59, 62–64, 258–64, 286–318, 338–40, 702–4, 768; vol. III: 25–27, 400–405, 470–87, 539–53, 619–22, 898–904; vol. IV: 535–50, 576–78; vol. VII: 615–35, 635–52, 766–98; vol. VIII: 1–27; vol. IX: 482–85, 518–76.

————. "Moses Mendelssohn und der Einbruch des Judentums in das deutsche Geistesleben." *Der Weltkampf*, no. 1 (1944): 9–20.

————. "Die nationale Bewegung unter dem Wort Gottes." *Pastoralblätter für Predigt, Seelsorge und kirchliche Unterweisung* 75 (1932–33): 321–27.

————. "Die nationalsozialistische Bewegung und das Christentum: 10 Thesen." *Mitteilungen aus der deutschen christlichen Studentenvereinigung* 362 (1932): 89f.

————. "Die Neubesinnung der Theologien und der Aufbruch der Nation." *Deutsche Theologie* 1 (1934): 39–54.

————. *Die Passion des Heilandes der deutschen Gegenwart verkündigt: Eine homiletische Studie zur Passionsverkuendigung*. Dresden: Welzel, 1936.

————. "Paulus aus dem Volke Israel. Apostel der Völker." *Novum Testamentum* 5 (1961): 267–91.

———. "Paulus und Luther: Ein Beitrag zum Problem der Formung des Christentums." In *Luther, Kant, Schleiermacher* (Festschrift for Georg Wobbermin), ed. Friedrich Wilhelm Schmidt, et al. (Berlin: Arthur Collignon, 1939): 182–216.

———. "Der Pfingstbericht der Apostelgeschichte in seinem theologischen Sinn." *Studia Evangelica* 2 (1963): 584–94.

———. "Das Problem der neutestamentlichen Christologie." *Theologische Literaturzeitung* 65 (1940): 65–73.

———. "Das Problem des hellenistischen Christentums innerhalb der Jerusalemer Urgemeinde." *Zeitschrift für alttestamentliche Wissenschaft* 38 (1939): 45–73.

———. *Das Reich der Deutschen*. Vol. 52, Schriftenreihe zur Truppenbetreuung, 1944.

———. "Religion und Rasse." *Christenkreuz und Hakenkreuz* 1, no. 4 (1933): 39.

———. *Religion und Rasse: Ein Beitrag zur Frage "Nationaler Aufbruch" und "Lebendiger Christusglaube."* Werdau: Oskar Meister, 1933.

———. *Der Römerbrief des Apostels Paulus und seine Auslegung durch Martin Luther*, Weimar: Böhlau, 1964.

———. *Die Sprache des Altars: Zur Glaubensaussage im deutschen Flügel- und Schreinaltar*. Berlin: Evangelische Verlagsanstalt, 1966.

———. "Stehen und Fallen im qumranischen und neutestamentlichen Schrifttum." In *Qumran-Probleme: Vorträge des Leipziger Symposions über Qumran-Probleme vom 9. bis 14. Oktober 1961*, ed. Hans Bardtke (Berlin: Akademie-Verlag, 1963), 147–66.

———. *Totale Kirche im totalen Staat: Kirche im Dritten Reich*, Dresden: O. Günther, 1934.

———. "Um die Wirklichkeit des Bildes Jesu. Zum Echo auf Mein Buch, "Die Gotteskindschaft Jesu." *Deutsches Christentum* 5, no. 2 (1940).

———. "Unsere Arbeit am Neuen Testament." *Verbandsmitteilungen* 1 (December 1939).

———. *Dem Ursprung neu verbunden*. Berlin: Evangelische Verlagsanstalt, 1965.

———. *Der Weg der deutschen Christen zum deutschen Christentum*, Dresden: Deutsche Christen Verlag, 1934.

———. *Weisheit im Horizont des Reiches Gottes: Erwägungen zur Christusbotschaft und zum Christusverständnis im Lichte der Weisheit in Israel*. Stuttgart/Eisenach: privately printed, 1988.

———. *Wer ist Jesus von Nazareth?* Weimar: Verlag Deutsche Christen, 1940.

———, ed. *Anschaulichkeit als katechetisches Problem. Karl Brinkel in Memoriam*. Berlin: Evangelische Verlagsanstalt, 1966.

———, ed. *Christentum und Judentum: Studien zur Erforschung ihres gegenseitigen Verhältnisses*, vol. 1. Leipzig: G. Wigand, 1940; *Germanentum, Christentum und Judentum: Studien zur Erforschung ihres gegenseitigen Verhältnisses*, vol. 2: Leipzig: Georg Wigand 1942; vol. 3: Nuremberg, Leipzig: Georg Wigand, 1943.

Grundmann, Walter, Wilhelm Büchner, et al., eds. *Deutsche mit Gott: Ein deutsches Glaubensbuch*. Weimar: Verlag Deutsche Christen, 1941.

Grundmann, Walter, and Karl Friedrich Euler. *Das religiöse Gesicht des Judentums: Entstehung und Art*. Leipzig: Verlag Georg Wigand, 1942.

Grundmann, Walter, and Helmut Kramer, eds. *Auf dass ich sein Eigen sei: Glaubenshilfe für die evangelische Familie*. Berlin: Evangelische Verlagsanstalt, 1963.

——, eds. *Du gehörst Gott: Handbuch für den Katechismusunterricht nach Martin Luthers Kleinem Katechismus*. Berlin: Evangelische Verlagsanstalt, 1960.

Grundmann, Walter, Hugo Odeberg, and Wolf Meyer-Erlach, eds. *Die völkische Gestalt des Glaubens*. Leipzig: Georg Wigand, 1943.

Gruner, Wolf. "Die NS-Judenverfolgung und die Kommunen: Zur wechselseitigen Dynamisierung von zentraler und lokaler Politik 1933–1941." *Vierteljahrshefte für Zeitgeschichte* 48 (2000): 75–126.

Grüttner, Michael. *Studenten im Dritten Reich*, Paderborn: Ferdinand Schöningh, 1995.

Günther, Hans F. K. *Frömmigkeit nordischer Artung*. Jena: Eugen Diderichs Verlag, 1934.

——. *Rassenkunde des deutschen Volkes*. Munich: J. F. Lehmann, 1922.

——. *Rassenkunde des jüdischen Volkes*. Munich: Lehmann, 1930.

——. "Wie sah Jesus aus?" *Volk und Rasse* 2 (1932): 118–19.

—— (as Heinrich Ackermann). *Entstellung und Klärung der Botschaft Jesu*. Pähl: Verlag Hohe Warte, 1961.

Hahn, Hugo, *Kämpfer wider Willen: Erinnerungen aus D. Kirchenkampf 1933–1945*, ed. Georg Prater. Metzingen: Brunnquell-Verlag, 1969.

Halbfass, Wilhelm. *India and Europe: An Essay in Understanding*. Albany: SUNY Press, 1988.

Hanche, Elisabeth. "Christliche Frauengedanken über Nationalsozialismus." *Christenkreuz und Hakenkreuz* 7 (July 1936): 14.

Harnack, Adolf von. Das Wesen des Christentums. Leipzig: J. C. Hinrichs, 1900.

——. *Marcion: Das Evangelium vom Fremden Gott*. Leipzig: J. C. Hinrichs, 1924.

——. *The Mission and Expansion of Christianity in the First Three Centuries*, trans. James Moffatt. New York: Harper, 1962.

Hauer, J. Wilhelm. *Ein arischer Christus?* Karlsruhe/Leipzig: Verlag Boltze, 1939.

Haupt, Paul. "The Aryan Ancestry of Jesus." *Open Court* (1908): 193–204.

——. "The Ethnology of Galilee." *Proceedings of the Third International Congress for the History of Religions* (Oxford: Clarendon Press, 1908), I: 302–4.

Hauptmann, Hans. *Jesus der Arier: Ein Heldenleben*. Munich: Deutscher Volksverlag Dr. E. Boepple, 1930.

Haury, Herald. *Von Riesa nach Schloss Elmau: Johannes Müller (1864–1949) als Prophet, Unternehmer und Seelenführer eines völkisch naturfrommen Protestantismus*. Gütersloh: Gütersloh Verlagshaus, 2005.

Hausmann, Frank-Rutger. *Deutsche Geisteswissenschaft im zweiten Weltkrieg: Die Aktion Ritterbusch, 1940–1945*. Dresden: Dresden University Press, 1998.

——. *Auch im Krieg schweigen die Musen nicht: Die deutschen wissenschaftlichen Institute im zweiten Weltkrieg*. Göttingen: Vandenhoeck & Ruprecht, 2001.

Head, Peter M. "The Nazi Quest for an Aryan Jesus." *Journal for the Study of the Historical Jesus* 2 (2004): 55–89.

Hecht, Cornelia. *Deutsche Juden und Antisemitismus in der Weimarer Republik*. Bonn: Dietz, 2003.

Hecht, Jennifer Michael. "Vacher de Lapouge and the Rise of Nazi Science." *Journal of the History of Ideas* 61, no. 2 (2000): 285–304.

Heiber, Helmut. *Universität unterm Hakenkreuz*. Munich, New Providence: K. G. Saur, 1991.

Heiden, Detlev, and Gunther Mai, eds. *Nationalsozialismus in Thüringen*. Weimar: Böhlau, 1995.

Hein, Annette. *"Es ist viel Hitler in Wagner": Rassismus und antisemitische Deutschtumside-ologie in den Bayreuther Blättern (1878–1938)*. Tübingen: M. Niemeyer, 1996.

Heinonen, Reijo E. *Anpassung und Identität: Theologie und Kirchenpolitik der Bremer Deutschen Christen 1933–1945*. Göttingen: Vandenhoeck und Ruprecht, 1978.

Helmreich, William. *The German Churches under Hitler*. Detroit: Wayne State University Press, 1979.

Hempel, Johannes. "Chronik vom Herausgeber." *Zeitschrift für alttestamentliche Wissenschaft,* new series (1942/43): 209–15.

———. *Fort mit dem Alten Testament?* Giessen: A. Töpelmann, 1932.

———. *Luther und das Alte Testament*. Bremen: Hauschild, 1935.

Hengel, Martin, and Ulrich Heckel, eds. *Paulus und das antike Judentum*. Tübingen: J.C.B. Mohr, 1991.

Herbert, Ulrich. "Ideological Legitimization and Political Practice of the Leadership of the National Socialist Secret Police," in *The Third Reich between Vision and Reality: New Perspectives on German History, 1918–1945*, ed. Hans Mommsen (Oxford, NY: Berg, 2001), 95–108.

Herf, Jeffrey. *The Jewish Enemy: Nazi Propaganda during World War II and the Holocaust*. Cambridge, MA: The Belknap Press of Harvard University Press, 2006.

———. "The 'Jewish War': Goebbels and the Antisemitic Campaigns of the Nazi Propaganda Ministry." *Holocaust and Genocide Studies* 19, no. 1 (2005): 51–80.

Hering, Rainer. *Theologische Wissenschaft und "Drittes Reich."* Pfaffenweiler: Centaurus, 1990.

Herntrich, Volkmar. *Völkische Religiosität und Altes Testament, zur Auseinandersetzung der nationalsozialistischen Weltanschauung mit dem Christentum*. Gütersloh: C. Bertelsmann, 1933.

———. *Neuheidentum und Christusglaube*. Gütersloh: C. Bertelsmann, 1935.

Herntrich, Volkmar. "Jesus Christus: Knecht und Herr." *Wort und Tat* 13, no. 2 (1937).

Hertzsch, Klaus-Peter. *Sag meinen Kindern, dass sie Weiterziehn: Erinnerungen*. Stuttgart: Radius, 2002.

Herzog, Dagmar. *Sex after Fascism: Memory and Morality in Twentieth-Century Germany*. Princeton, NJ: Princeton University Press, 2005.

Heschel, Susannah. *Abraham Geiger and the Jewish Jesus*. Chicago: University of Chicago Press, 1998.

———. "Church Protests during the Third Reich: A Report on Two Cases." *Kirchliche Zeitgeschichte* 10, no. 2 (1998): 377–88.

———. "Dejudaizing Jesus: On Nazi 'Judenforschung' and Its Christian Ramifications." In *"Judenforschung": Wissenschaft, Denkstil und Ideologie zwischen Jahrhundertwende und Nationalsozialismus*. Jahrbuch, Simon Dubnow Institut für jüdische Geschichte und Kultur (Leipzig) 5 (2006): 1–22.

———. "Deutsche Theologen für Hitler: Walter Grundmann und das Eisenacher Institut zur Erforschung und Beseitigung des jüdischen Einflusses auf das deutsche kirchliche Leben." *Jahrbuch des Fritz Bauer Instituts* (1999): 147–67.

———. "For 'Volk, Blood, and God': The Theological Faculty at the University of Jena during the Third Reich." In *Nazi Germany and the Humanities*, ed. Wolfgang Bialas and Anson Rabinbach (Oxford: Oneworld Publications, 2006), 365–98.

———. "Nazifying Christian Theology: Walter Grundmann and the Institute for the Study and Eradication of Jewish Influence on German Church Life." *Church History* 63, no. 4 (1994): 587–605.

———. "The Quest for the Aryan Jesus: The Archaeology of Nazi Orientalist Theology." In *Jews, Antiquity, and the Nineteenth Century Imagination*, ed. Hayim Lapin (Bethesda: University Press of Maryland, 2003), 65–84.

———. "Reading Jesus as a Nazi." In *A Shadow of Glory: Reading the New Testament after the Holocaust*, ed. Tod Linafelt (New York: Routledge, 2002), 27–41.

———. "Redemptive Antisemitism: The De-Judaization of the New Testament in the Third Reich." In *In God's Name: Genocide and Religion in the Twentieth Century*, ed. Omer Bartov and Phyllis Mack (New York: Berghahn, 2001), 79–105.

———. "Theologen für Hitler: Walter Grundmann und das "Institut zur Erforschung und Beseitigung des jüdischen Einflusses auf das deutsche kirchliche Leben." In Siegele-Wenschkewitz, ed., *Christlicher Antijudaismus und Antisemitismus*, 125–70.

———. "Theological Bulimia: Christianity and Its Dejudaization." In *After the Passion Is Gone: American Religious Consequences*, ed. Michael Berenbaum and Shawn Landres (Walnut Creek, CA: AltaMira Press, 2004), 177–92.

———. "The Theological Faculty at the University of Jena as 'a Stronghold of National Socialism.'" In *Kämpferische Wissenschaft: Studien zur Universität Jena im Nationalsozialismus*, ed. Jürgen John, Rüdiger Stutz, and Uwe Hoßfeld (Cologne and Weimar: Böhlau Verlag, 2003), 452–70.

———. "Theology as a Vision for Colonialism: From Supercessionism to Dejudaization in German Protestantism." In *Germany's Colonial Pasts: An Anthology in Memory of Susanne Zantop*, ed. Eric Ames, Marcia Klotz, and Lora Wildenthal (Lincoln: University of Nebraska Press, 2005).

———. "When Jesus Was an Aryan: The Protestant Church and Antisemitic Propaganda." In Ericksen and Heschel, eds., *Betrayal: The German Churches and the Holocaust*, 68–89.

Heussi, Karl. "Die Germanisierung des Christentums als historisches Problem." *Zeitschrift für Theologie und Kirche* 15 (1934): 119–44.

———. *Geschichte der theologischen Fakultät zu Jena*. Weimar: H. Böhlaus Nachf., 1954.

———. *Der Ursprung des Mönchtums*. Tübingen: Mohr, 1936.

Hintzenstern, Herbert von. "Abschied von Kirchenrat Dr. theol. Walter Grundmann." *Glaube und Heimat* 37, no. 12 (1976): 9.

———. "Das religiöse Problem im Bayreuther Kreis." In Grundmann, *Christentum und Judentum*, I: 167–92.

Hirsch, Emanuel. *Jesus: Wort und Geschichte Jesu nach den ersten drei Evangelien.* Bremen: Kommende Kirche, 1939.

———. *Das Wesen des Christentums.* Weimar: Deutsche Christen, 1939.

Hirsch, Rudolf, and Rosemarie Schuder. *Der gelbe Fleck: Wurzeln und Wirkungen des Judenhasses in der deutschen Geschichte.* Berlin: Rütten & Loening, 1987.

Hodge, John L. "Domination and the Will in Western Thought and Culture." In *Cultural Bases of Racism and Group Oppression*, ed. Donald K. Struckmann, John L. Hodge, and Lynn Dorland Trost (Berkeley: Two Riders Press, 1975), 165–72.

Hohmann, Joachim S. *Landvolk unterm Hakenkreuz: Agrar- und Rassenpolitik in der Rhön.* Frankfurt am Main: Peter Lang, 1992.

Holz, Karl. "Was Christus Jude? Die Wahrheit gegen Lüge und Unwissenheit." *Der Stürmer* 15 (April 1938): 1.

Horn, Gisela. "Lulu von Strauß und Torney-Diederichs: Ein Beispiel weiblicher Anpassung." In *Entwurf und Wirklichkeit: Frauen in Jena 1900 bis 1933*, ed. Gisela Horn and Birgitt Hellmann (Rudolstadt: Hain, 2001).

Horsley, Richard A. *Galilee: History, Politics, People.* Valley Forge, PA: Trinity Press, 1995.

Hoßfeld, Uwe. *Kämpferische Wissenschaft : Studien zur Universität Jena im Nationalsozialismus.* Cologne: Böhlau, 2003.

Hoßfeld, Uwe, Jürgen John, and Rüdiger Stutz. "Weaving Networks: The University of Jena in the Weimar Republic, the Third Reich, and the Postwar East German State." In *Science and Ideology: A Comparative View*, ed. Mark Walker (London, New York: Routledge, 2003), 186–226.

Howard, Thomas Albert. *Religion and the Rise of Historicism: W.J.L. De Wette, Jacob Burckhardt, and the Theological Origins of Nineteenth-Century Historical Consciousness.* Cambridge: Cambridge University Press, 2000.

Hull, Isabel V. *Absolute Destruction: Military Culture and the Practices of War in Imperial Germany.* Ithaca and London: Cornell University Press, 2005.

Hunger, Heinz. *Geschändete Neutralität: Das English-Französische Verbrechen an Griechenland.* Berlin: Informationsstelle, 1940.

———. "Jüdische Psychoanalyse und deutsche Seelsorge." In Grundmann, ed., *Germanentum, Judentum und Christentum*, II: 307–54.

———. "Wesen und Methode einer rassekundlichen Religionsgeschite." In Grundmann, ed., *Christentum und Judentum*, I: 193–233.

Hutter-Wolandt, Ulrich. *Die evangelische Kirche Schlesiens im Wandel der Zeiten: Studien und Quellen zur Geschichte einer Territorialkirche.* Dortmund: Forschungsstelle Ostmitteleuropa, 1991.

———. "Spagat zwischen Wissenschaft und Anpassung: Die Breslauer evangelische theologische Fakultät unter ihrem Dekan Herbert Preisker von 1936 bis 1945." In Deines, Leppin, and Niebuhr, eds., *Walter Grundmann*, 275–318.

Jacolliot, Louis. *La Bible dans L'inde: Vie de Iezeus Christna.* Paris: Librairie Internationale, 1869.

Jensen, Peter. *Das Gilgamesch-Epos in der Weltliteratur*. Strassburg: K. J. Trübner, 1906.
————. *Hat der Jesus der Evangelien wirklich gelebt? Eine Antwort auf Prof. Dr. Jülicher.* Frankfurt am Main: Neuer Frankfurter Verlag, 1910.

Jeremias, Gret, Heinz-Wolfgang Kuhn, and Hartmut Stegemann. *Tradition und Glaube: Das frühe Christentum in seiner Umwelt. Festgabe für Karl Georg Kuhn zum 65. Geburtstag.* Göttingen: Vandenhoeck & Ruprecht, 1971.

Jeremias, Joachim. *Abba: Studien zur Neutestamentlichen Theologie und Zeitgeschichte.* Göttingen: Vandenhoeck & Ruprecht, 1966.

Jerke, Birgit. "Wie wurde das Neue Testament zu einem sogenannten Volkstestament 'entjudet'?" In Siegele-Wenschkewitz, ed., *Christlicher Antijudaismus und Antisemitismus.*

John, Jürgen. "Die Jenaer Universität im Jahre 1945." In John, et al., eds., *Die Wiedereröffnung der Friedrich-Schiller-Universität Jena 1945.*

John, Jürgen, et al., eds. *Die Wiedereröffnung der Friedrich-Schiller-Universität Jena 1945: Dokumente und Festschrift.* Rudolstadt: Hain Verlag, 1998.

Judt, Tony. *Postwar: A History of Europe since 1945.* New York: Penguin Press, 2005.

Jülicher, Adolf. *Hat der Jesus der Evangelien wirklich gelebt?* Frankfurt am Main: Neuer Frankfurter Verlag, 1910.

Junginger, Horst. *Von der philologischen zur völkischen Religionswissenschaft.* Stuttgart: Franz Steiner Verlag, 1999.

Junginger, Horst. "Das Bild des Juden in der nationalsozialistischen Judenforschung." In *Die kulturelle Seite des Antisemitismus zwischen Aufklärung und Schoah*, ed. Andrea Hoffmann et al. (Tübingen: Vereinigung für Volkskunde, 2006), 171–220.

Junginger, Horst. "Politische Wissenschaft." *Süddeutsche Zeitung*, November 9, 2005.

Jursch, Hanna. "Zum 70. Geburtstag von Karl Heussi." *Theologische Literaturzeitung* 2 (1947): 106.

Kaffanke, Eva-Maria. *Der deutsche Heiland: Christusdarstellungen um 1900 im Kontext der völkischen Bewegung.* Frankfurt am Main, New York: P. Lang, 2001.

Kalthoff, Albert. *Zarathustra-Predigten: Reden über die sittliche Lebensauffassung Friedrich Nietzsches.* Jena: Diederichs Verlag, 1904; reprint, 1908.

Kapferer, Friedrich. *An die Katholiken Deutschlands: Die sieghaften Ideen der Deutschen Christen.* Weimar: Verlag Deutsche Christen, 1939.
————. *Die Bergpredigt als Kampfansage gegen das Judentum*, 1944.

Kater, Michael H. *Studentenschaft und Rechtsradikalismus in Deutschland 1918–1933: Eine sozialgeschichtliche Studie zur Bildungskrise in der Weimarer Republik.* Hamburg: Hoffmann und Campe, 1975.

Keinhorst, Willi. *Wilhelm Stapel. Ein evangelischer Journalist im Nationalsozialismus.* Frankfurt am Main, New York: P. Lang, 1993.

Kellenbach, Katharina von. "God's Love and Women's Love: Prison Chaplains Counsel the Wives of Nazi Perpetrators." *Journal of Feminist Studies in Religion* 20, no. 2 (2005): 7–24.

Kelley, Shawn. *Racializing Jesus: Race, Ideology and the Formation of Modern Biblical Scholarship.* London and New York: Routledge, 2002.

Kershaw, Ian. *Hitler: 1889–1936: Hubris.* New York: Norton, 1999.

Kidd, Colin. *The Forging of Races: Race and Scripture in the Protestant Atlantic World, 1600–2000*. Cambridge: Cambridge University Press, 2006.

King, Karen L. *What Is Gnosticism?* Cambridge, MA: The Belknap Press of Harvard University Press, 2003.

Kittel, Gerhard. *Jesus und die Juden*. Berlin: Furche, 1926.

———. *Jesus und die Rabbinen*. Berlin: Edwin Runge, 1914.

———. *Die Judenfrage*. Stuttgart: W. Kohlhammer, 1933.

———. *Die Probleme des palästischen Spätjudentums und das Urchristentum*. Stuttgart: W. Kohlhammer, 1926.

———. "Die Wurzeln des englischen Erwählungsglaubens." *Historische Zeitschrift* 163 (1941): 43–81.

———, ed. *Theological Dictionary of the New Testament*. 10 vols. Grand Rapids, MI: Eerdmans, 1964–.

Klein, Charlotte. *Theologie und Anti-Judaismus: Eine Studie zur deutschen theologischen Literatur der Gegenwart*. Abhandlungen zum christlich-jüdischen Dialog, vol. 6. Munich: Kaiser, 1975; in English, as *Anti-Judaism in Christian Theology*, trans. Edward Quinn, London: SPCK, 1978.

Klein, Ernst. *Der Tor von Nazareth*. Dortmund: Im Volkschaft Verlag, 1939.

Kleine, Christoph. "Religion im Dienste einer ethnisch-nationalen Identitätskonstruktion." *Marburg Journal of Religion* 7, no. 1 (2002).

Klemm, Hermann. *Ich konnte nicht zuschauer bleiben: Karl Fischers theologische Arbeit für die bekennende Kirche Sachsens*. Berlin: Evangelische Verlagsanstalt, 1985.

Knudsen, Johannes. "One Hundred Years Later: The Grundtvigian Heritage." *Lutheran Quarterly* 25 (1973): 71–77.

Knust, Jennifer Wright. *Abandoned to Lust: Sexual Slander and Ancient Christianity*. New York: Columbia University Press, 2006.

Koelsch, Ruth-Erika. *Pastoralpsychologie als Suchbewegung und Erfüllung in Begegnung und Verantwortung: Hans-Joachim Thilo, Leben und Werk*. Muenster: Lit Verlag, 2001.

Koonz, Claudia. *The Nazi Conscience*. Cambridge, MA: Harvard University Press, 2005.

Kraus, Hans-Joachim. "Die evangelische Kirche." In *Entscheidungsjahr 1932: Zur Judenfrage in der Endphase der Weimarer Republik*, ed. Werner Mosse (Tübingen: J.C.B. Mohr (Paul Siebeck), 1966), 249–70.

Kreutzer, Heike. *Das Reichskirchenministerium im Gefüge der nationalsozialistischen Herrschaft*. Düsseldorf: Droste, 2000.

Krieg, Robert A. *Catholic Theologians in Nazi Germany*. New York: Continuum, 2004.

Kroll, Frank-Lothar. *Utopie als Ideologie: Geschichtsdenken und politisches Handeln im Dritten Reich*. Paderborn: Schöningh, 1998.

Kühl-Freudenstein, Olaf. *Evangelische Religionspädagogik und völkische Ideologie*. Studien zum "Bund für deutsche Kirche" und der "Glaubensbewegung Deutsche Christen." Würzburg: Königshausen & Neumann, 2003.

Kühl-Freudenstein, Olaf, and Claus P. Wagener. "Kirchenkreis Potsdam I." In *Kirchenkampf in Berlin 1932–1945*, ed. Peter Noss, Olaf Kühl-Freudenstein, and Claus P. Wagener (Berlin: Institut Kirche und Judentum, 1999).

Kuhn, Karl Georg. "Ursprung und Wesen der talmudischen Einstellung zum Nich-tjuden." *Forschungen zur Judenfrage* 3 (1938): 199–234.

Kümmel, Werner Georg. "Das Urchristentum." *Theologische Rundschau,* new series 17, no. 2 (1948): 103–42.

Kümmel, Werner Georg, Erich Grässer, Otto Merk, and Adolf Fritz. *Heilsgeschehen und Geschichte.* Marburg: N. G. Elwert, 1965.

Kunz, Johannes. *Die deutsche Schule und das Alte Testament.* Berlin: Bund für deutsche Kirche, 1932.

Kupisch, Karl. *Studenten entdecken die Bibel: Die Geschichte der deutsch-christlichen Studentenvereinigung (DCSV).* Hamburg: Furche Verlag, 1964.

Lächele, Rainer. *Ein Volk, ein Reich, ein Glaube: Die Deutschen Christen in Württemeberg 1925–1960.* Stuttgart: Calwer, 1994.

———. "'Germanisches' Christentum und die Protestanten im deutschen Kaiserreich: Die Kontroverse um Gustav Frenssens Roman 'Hilligenlei.'" *Jahrbuch der Gesellschaft für Niedersächsische Kirchengeschichte* 93 (1995): 27–46.

———. "Germanisiertes Christentum: Der Bestsellerautor Gustav Frenssen." *Evangelische Kommentare* 2 (1997): 107–9.

———. "Germanisierung des Christentums, Heroisierung Christi: Arthur Bonus, Max Bewer, Julius Bode." In Schnurbein and Ulbricht, eds., *Völkische Religion und Krisen der Moderne,* 165–83.

———. "Religionsfreiheit und Vergangenheitsbewältigung: Die Deutschen Christen und Besatzungsmächte nach 1945." *Evangelische Theologie* 51, no. 2 (1991).

Laeuchli, Samuel. *Power and Sexuality: The Emergence of Canon Law at the Synod of Elvira.* Philadelphia: Temple University Press, 1972.

Langerbeck, Hermann. "Review of Carl Schneider, *Geistesgeschichte des antiken Christentums.*" *Gnomon* 28 (1956): 481–501.

Langmuir, Gavin. *History, Religion, and Antisemitism.* Berkeley: University of California Press, 1990.

Large, David C., and William Weber, eds. *Wagnerism in European Culture and Politics.* Ithaca, NY: Cornell University Press, 1985.

Lautenschlager, Gabriele. "Der Kirchenkampf in Thüringen." In Heiden and Mai, *Nationalsozialismus in Thüringen.*

———. "Nationalsozialismus und Religion." *Zeitschrift fuer Religions- und Geisteswissenschaft* 40 (1988).

Lebouton, Ekkehart. *Die evangelische Pfarrgemeinde A. B. Czernowitz zwischen den beiden Weltkriegen (1918–1940).* Vienna: Evangelische Presseverband in Österreich, 1968.

Leffler, Siegfried. *Christus im Dritten Reich der Deutschen: Wesen, Weg und Ziel der Kirchenbewegung "Deutsche Christen."* Weimar: Verlag Deutsche Christen, 1935.

Lehmann, Paul. *Todeskampf der Christentümer und der gegenwärtigen Wiedergeburt des Urchristentums im deutschen Volk.* Stuttgart: Bonz' Erben, 1937.

Leipoldt, Johannes. *Gegenwärtsfragen in der Neutestamentlichen Wissenschaft.* Leipzig: A. Deichert, 1935.

Leipoldt, Johannes. *Jesus der Künder und Kämpfer Gottes*. Breslau: Arbeitsgemeinschaft Deutscher Religionsunterricht, 1937.

———. "Jesus und das Judentum." In Grundmann, ed., *Germanentum, Christentum, und Judentum*, vol. 1, pp. 29–52.

———. *Die männliche Art Jesu*. Leipzig: A. Deichert, 1918.

———. *War Jesus Jude?* Leipzig: A. Deichert, 1923.

Leipoldt, Johannes, and Walter Grundmann, eds. *Umwelt des Urchristentums*. 3 vols. Berlin: Evangelische Verlagsanstalt, 1966–67.

Leipoldt, Johannes, and Siegfried Morenz. *Heilige Schriften: Betrachtungen zur Religionsgeschichte der antiken Mittelmeerwelt*. Leipzig: Otto Harrassowitz, 1953.

Leutheuser, Julius. *Die Deutsche Christusgemeinde: Der Weg zur deutschen Nationalkirche*. 2nd ed. Weimar: Verlag Deutsche Christen, 1935.

———. "Der Weg zum Gottglauben der Deutschen." *Die Nationalkirche: Briefe an Deutsche Christen* 28, no. 29 (1939).

Levine, Amy-Jill. *The Misunderstood Jew: The Church and the Scandal of the Jewish Jesus*. San Francisco: HarperSanFrancisco, 2006.

Levinson, Bernard M., and David Dance. "The Metamorphosis of Law into Gospel: Gerhard von Rad's Attempt to Reclaim the Old Testament for the Church." In *Recht und Ethik im Alten Testament: Beiträge des Symposiums "Das Alte Testament und die Kultur der Moderne" anlässlich des 100. Geburtstags Gerhard von Rads*, ed. Bernard M. Levinson and E. Otto (Münster: LIT, 2004), 83–109.

Levy, Isaac. *La Synagogue et M. Renan: Reponse au livre de la vie de Jesus*. Luneville: Chez Mme. George, libraire-relieur, 1863.

Lewy, Gunter. *The Catholic Church and Nazi Germany*. New York: McGraw-Hill, 1964.

Liesenberg, Carsten. "'Wir täuschen uns nicht über die Schwere der Zeit . . .': Die Verfolgung und Vernichtung der Juden." In Heiden and Mai, *Nationalsozialismus in Thüringen*.

Linck, Stephan. "Epilog: Zur Wirkungs-Bedeutung Friedrich Andersens." In *Friedrich Andersen: Ein deutscher Prediger des Antisemitismus*, ed. Hauke Wattenberg (Flensburg: Gesellschaft für Flensburger Stadtgeschichte, 2004).

———. "'Vor zersetzendem jüdischen Einfluss bewahren': Antisemitismus in der Schleswig-Holsteinischen Landeskirche." In Göhres, Linck, and Liss-Walther, eds., *Als Jesus "arisch" wurde*, 132–46.

Lincoln, Bruce. *Theorizing Myth: Narrative, Ideology, and Scholarship*. Chicago: University of Chicago Press, 1999.

Lindemann, Gerhard. *"Typisch jüdisch": Die Stellung der Evangelisch-lutherischen Landeskirche Hannovers zu Antijudaismus, Judenfeindschaft und Antisemitismus 1919–1949*. Berlin: Duncker & Humblot, 1998.

Locke, H.-D. "Zur 'Grossgermanischen Politike' des Dritten Reiches." *Vierteljahreshefte für Zeitgeschichte* 8 (1960).

Lohmeyer, Ernst. *Galiläa und Jerusalem*. Göttingen: Vandenhoeck & Ruprecht, 1936.

Löwith, Karl. "Nietzsches antichristliche Bergpredigt." *Heidelberger Jahrbücher* 6 (1962): 39–50.

Lubitnetzki, Volker. *Von der Knechtsgestalt des Neuen Testaments: Beobachtungen zu seiner Verwendung und Auslegung in Deutschland vor dem sowie im Kontext des Dritten Reiches.* Munster: LIT, 2000.

Lüdemann, Gerd. *Die Religionsgeschichtliche Schule: Facetten eines theologischen Umbruchs* Frankfurt: Peter Lang, 1996.

Ludendorff, Mathilde Spiess. *Aus der Gotterkenntnis meiner Werke.* Munich: Ludendorff Verlag, 1935.

Lutzhöft, Hans-Jürgen. *Der nordische Gedanke in Deutschland 1920–1940.* Kieler Historische Studien, vol. 14. Stuttgart: E. Klett, 1971.

Mager, Inge. "Göttinger theologische Promotionen 1933–1945." In Siegele-Wenschkewitz and Nicolaisen, eds., *Theologische Fakultäten im Nationalsozialismus,* 347–58.

Marchand, Suzanne. "Philhellenism and the Furor Orientalis." *Modern Intellectual History* 1, no. 3 (2004): 331–58.

Markus, Gustav. "Altbischof Wilhelm Staedel." *Südostdeutsche Vierteljahresblätter* 21, no. 1 (1972): 11.

Masuzawa, Tomoko. *The Invention of World Religions, or, How European Universalism Was Preserved in the Language of Pluralism.* Chicago: University of Chicago Press, 2005.

Maurenbrecher, Max. *Über Friedrich Nietzsche zum deutschen Evangelium.* 1926.

Max Müller, Friedrich. *Biographies of Words and the Home of the Aryas.* London [etc.]: Longmans, 1888.

———. *Chips from a German Workshop.* New York: Charles Scribner's Sons, 1907.

McElligott, Anthony, and Tim Kirk, eds. *Working towards the Führer: Essays in Honour of Sir Ian Kershaw.* Manchester, UK: Manchester University Press, 2003.

McNutt, James. "Adolf Schlatter and the Jews." *German Studies Review* 26, no. 2 (2003): 353–70.

———. "Vessels of Wrath Prepared to Perish: Adolf Schlatter and the Spiritual Extermination of the Jews." *Theology Today* 63 (2006): 176–90.

Mees, Bernard. "Völkische Altnordistik: The Politics of Nordic Studies in the German-Speaking Countries 1926–45." In *Old Norse Myths, Literature, and Society: Proceedings of the Eleventh International Saga Conference (2000),* ed. Geraldine Barnes and Margaret Clunies Ross (Sydney: Centre for Medieval Studies, 2000), 316–26.

Meier, Kurt. *Die Deutschen Christen: Das Bild einer Bewegung im Kirchenkampf des Dritten Reiches.* Göttingen: Vandenhoeck & Ruprecht, 1964.

———. *Der evangelische Kirchenkampf,* 3 vols. Göttingen: Vandenhoeck & Ruprecht, 1976.

———. *Kirche und Judentum: Die Haltung der evangelischen Kirche zur Judenpolitik des Dritten Reiches.* Göttingen: Vandenhoeck & Ruprecht, 1968.

———. *Kreuz und Hakenkreuz: Die evangelische Kirche im Dritten Reich.* Munich: Deutscher Taschenbuch Verlag, 1992.

———. *Die theologischen Fakultäten im Dritten Reich.* Berlin: de Gruyter, 1996.

Meisiek, Cornelius Heinrich. *Evangelisches Theologiestudium im Dritten Reich.* Frankfurt am Main, New York: P. Lang, 1993.

Merk, Otto. "'Und viele waren Neutestamentler': Zur Lage Neutestamentlicher Wissenschaft 1933–1945." *Theologische Literaturzeitung* 130 (2005): 106–20.

———. "Paul Anton De Lagarde und die Theologie in den ersten Jahrzehnten des 20. Jahrhunderts." In Deines, Leppin, and Niebuhr, eds., *Walter Grundmann*.

Meyer, Ben F. "A Caricature of Joachim Jeremias and His Scholarly Work." *Journal of Biblical Literature* 110, no. 3 (1991): 451–62.

Meyer, Rudolf. *Der Prophet aus Galiläa: Studie zum Jesusbild der drei ersten Evangelien.* (Leipzig: Lunkenbein, 1940). Darmstadt: Wissenschaftliche Buchges., 1970.

Meyer-Christian, Wolf. *Die englisch-jüdisch Allianz: Werden and Wirken der kapitalistischen Weltherrschaft.* Berlin, Leipzig: Niebelungen-Verlag, 1940.

Meyer-Erlach, Wolf. *Das deutsche Leid.* Munich: Lehmann, 1923.

———. "Der Einfluss der Juden auf das englische Christentum." In Grundmann, ed., *Christentum und Judentum*, vol. 1, 1–28.

———. *Die Friedrich-Schiller-Universität im Geisteskampf der Jahrhunderte.* Jena: G. Fischer, 1936.

———. *Das neue Deutschland und die Christliche Verkündigung: Die Aufsehen erregende Antrittsvorlesung des Verfassers an der Universität Jena.* Weimar: Verlag Deutsche Christen, 1934.

———. *Ist Gott Engländer?* Freiburg im Breisgau,: Sturmhut-Verlag, 1941.

———. *Juden, Mönche und Luther.* Weimar: Deutsche Christen, 1937.

———. *Kirche oder Sekte.* Weimar: Verlag Deutsche Christen, 1934.

———. *Universität und Volk.* Jena: Fischer, 1935.

———. *Verrat an Luther.* Weimar: Verlag Deutsche Christen, 1936.

Moltmann-Wendel, Elisabeth. *Freiheit, Gleichheit, Schwesterlichkeit: Zur Emanzipation der Frau in Kirche und Gesellschaft.* Munich: Kaiser, 1977.

Mosse, George L. *The Crisis of German Ideology: The Intellectual Origins of the Third Reich.* New York: Howard Fertig, 1964.

Mott, Lewis Freeman. *Ernest Renan.* New York: D. Appleton and Company, 1921.

Moxnes, Halvor. "The Construction of Galilee as a Place for the Historical Jesus." *Biblical Theology Bulletin* 31, nos. 1 and 2 (2001): 26–37, 64–77.

Mulack, Christa. *Am Anfang war die Weisheit.* Munich: Kaiser, 1988.

Muller, Jerry Z. *The Other God That Failed: Hans Freyer and the Deradicalization of German Conservatism.* Princeton, NJ: Princeton University Press, 1987.

Müller, A. *Jesus ein Arier: Ein Beitrag zur völkischen Erziehung.* Leipzig: Max Sängewald, 1904.

Müller, Johannes. *Jesus wie ich ihn sehe.* Elmau: Verlag der Grünen Blätter, 1930.

Müller, Ludwig. *Deutsche Gottesworte: Aus der Bergpredigt verdeutscht.* Weimar: Verlag Deutsche Christen, 1936; in English, as *The Germanisation of the New Testament*, London: Friends of Europe, 1938.

Murawski, Friedrich. *Die Juden bei den Kirchenvätern und Scholastikern: Eine kirchengeschichtliche Skizze als Beitrag zum Kampf gegen den Antisemitismus.* Berlin: C.A. Schwetschke, 1925.

Nanko, Ulrich. "Von 'Deutsch' nach 'Frei' und zurück? Jakob Wilhelm Hauer und die Frühgeschichte der Freien Akademie." In *Das evangelische Württemberg zwischen Weltkrieg und Wiederaufbau*, ed. Rainer Lächele and Jörg Thierfelder. (Stuttgart: Calwer, 1995), 214–33.

Neuer, Werner. *Adolf Schlatter: A Biography of Germany's Premier Biblical Theologian*, trans. Robert W. Yarbrough. Grand Rapids, MI: Baker Books, 1995.

Niedlich, Joachim Kurd. *Das Mythenbuch. Die germanische Mythen- und Märchenwelt als Quelle deutscher Weltanschauung*. Bund für Deutsche Kirche. Leipzig: Dürrsche Buchhandlung, 1921.

———. *Jahwe oder Jesus? Die Quelle unserer Entartung*. Leipzig: Dürrsche Buchhandlung, 1925.

Noakes, Jeremy. "The Ivory Tower under Siege: German Universities in the Third Reich." *Journal of European Studies* 23 (1993), 371–407.

Nonn, Christoph. "Saxon Politics during the First World War: Modernization, National Liberal Style." In *Saxony in German History: Culture, Society, and Politics, 1830–1933*, ed. James Retallack (Ann Arbor: University of Michigan Press, 2000), 309–21.

Odeberg, Hugo. "Ist das Christentum hellenistisch oder jüdisch?" *Zeitschrift für systematische Theologie* 17 (1940): 569–86.

———. "Die Muttersprache Jesu als wissenschaftliche Aufgabe." In Grundmann, ed., *Germanentum, Christentum und Judentum*, vol. 3.

Oepke, Albrecht. "Bevölkerungsproblem Galilaeas." *Theologisches Literaturblatt* 62, no. 26 (Dec. 19, 1941): 201–5 and 63, no. 1 (Jan. 2, 1942): 1–5.

Olender, Maurice. *The Languages of Paradise: Race, Religion, and Philology in the Nineteenth Century*. Cambridge, MA: Harvard University Press, 1992.

Oredsson, Sverker. "Svenska Teologer under Nazitiden." *Svensk Teologisk Kvartalskrift* 73 (1997).

Osten-Sacken, Peter von der. "'Die Grosse Lästerung': Beobachtungen zur Gründung des Eisenacher Instituts und zeitgenössische Dokumente zur kritischen Wertung seiner Arbeit sowie zur Beurteilung Walter Grundmanns." In Osten-Sacken, *Das mißbrauchte Evangelium*, 313–47.

———. "Der nationalsozialistische Lutherforscher Theodor Pauls: Vervollständigung eines fragmentarischen Bildes." In Osten-Sacken, *Das mißbrauchte Evangelium*: 136–66.

Osten-Sacken, Peter von der, ed. *Das mißbrauchte Evangelium: Studien zu Theologie und Praxis der Thüringer Deutschen Christen*. Berlin: Institut Kirche und Judentum, 2002.

Ostmeyer, Irena. *Zwischen Schuld und Sühne: Evangelische Kirche und Juden in SBZ und DDR 1945–1990*. Berlin: Institut Kirche und Judentum, 2002.

Otto, Rudolf. *The Kingdom of God and the Son of Man: A Study in the History of Religion*, trans. Floyd Vivian Filson and Bertram Lee Woolf. Boston: Starr King Press, 1957.

Pältz, Eberhard. "Geschichte als Selbstorientierung in der Zeit. Zum Vermächtnis Karl Heussis (1877–1961)." In *Mosaiksteine: Zweiundzwanzig Beiträge zur Thüringischen Kirchengeschichte* (Berlin: Evangelische Verlagsanstalt, 1977), 19–43.

Pauli, Sabine. "Geschichte Der Theologischen Institute an Der Universität Rostock." *Wissenschaftliche Zeitschrift der Universität Rostock* 17 (1968): 310–65.

Pauls, Theodor. "Die Ursprünglichkeit des Gotteslobes bei Luther." In Grundmann, ed., *Germanentum, Christenum und Judentum*, vol. 3, 137–92.

Pearson, Birger A. "The Gospel According to the Jesus Seminar." *Religion* 25 (1995): 317–38.

———. "James 1–2 Peter, Jude." In *The New Testament and Its Modern Interpreters*, ed. Eldon Jay Epp and George W. MacRae (Philadelphia, Atlanta: Scholars Press, 1989).

Penner, Hans. "You Don't Read a Myth for Information." In *Radical Interpretation in Religion*, ed. Nancy Frankenberry (Cambridge, New York: Cambridge University Press, 2002), 161–70.

Penner, Todd. "Die Judenfrage and the Construction of Ancient Judaism: Toward a Foregrounding of the Backgrounds Approach to Early Christianity." Unpublished manuscript, 2007.

Peter, Antonio. "Landesamt für Rassewesen," in Heiden and Mai, eds., *Nationalsozialismus in Thüringen*, 313–32.

Petersmann, Werner. *Auch die Kirche verrät die Nation?* Hannover: DN Verlag, 1972.

———. *Die Deutschland-Frage in Ganzheits-Schau.* Munich: Bergstadtverlag Wilh. Gottl. Korn, 1965.

———. *Was ist des Deutschen Vaterland?* Munich: Bergstadtverlag Wilh. Gottl. Korn, 1968.

———. *Wider die "Irrlehre" des Weltkirchenrates: Zur Rassengliederung in Südafrika.* Goslar: Hübener, 1975.

Pfau, Dieter. *Christenkreuz und Hakenkreuz: Siegen und das Siegerland am Vorabend des "Dritten Reiches."* 2nd ed. Bielefeld: Verlag für Regionalgeschichte, 2001.

Pictet, Adolphe. *Les Origines Indo-Européennes, ou, les aryas primitifs: Essai de paléontologie linguistique.* 2 vols. Paris [etc.]: J. Cherbuliez, 1859.

Piper, Ernst. *Alfred Rosenberg: Hitlers Chefideologe.* Munich: Blessing, 2005.

———. "Steigmann-Gall, the Holy Reich." *Journal of Contemporary History* 42, no. 1 (2007): 47–57.

Poesche, Theodor. *Die Arier: Ein Beitrag zur historischen Anthropologie.* Jena: Hermann Costenoble, 1878.

Poewe, Karla O. *New Religions and the Nazis.* New York, London: Routledge, 2006.

Pohlmann, Hans. *Der Gottesgedanke Jesu als Gegensatz gegen den israelitisch-judischen Gottesgedanken*, Studien zu deutscher Theologie und Frömmigkeit, vol. 4. Weimar: Deutsche Christen, 1939.

Poliakov, Léon. *The Aryan Myth: A History of Racist and Nationalist Ideas in Europe.* New York: Basic Books, 1974.

Porter, James I. *Nietzsche and the Philology of the Future.* Stanford, CA: Stanford University Press, 2000.

Potter, Pamela Maxine. *Most German of the Arts: Musicology and Society from the Weimar Republic to the End of Hitler's Reich.* New Haven, CT: Yale University Press, 1998.

Preisker, Herbert. "Christentum und Ehe in den ersten drei Jahrhunderten: Eine Studie zur Kulturgeschichte der alten Welt—theologische Habilitationsschrift." Ph.D. dissertation, University of Berlin, 1927.

———. *Das Ethos der Arbeit im Neuen Testament*, ed. Werner Petersmann. Aufbau im Positiven Christentum, vol. 19. Gnadenfrei in Schlesien: Gustav Winter, 1936.

———. *Neutestamentliche Zeitgeschichte*. Berlin: Töpelmann, 1937.

———. "Der Verrat des Judas und das Abendmahl." *Zeitschrift für neutestamentliche Wissenschaft* 41 (1942): 151–55.

Prolingheuer, Hans. *Ausgetan aus dem Land der Lebendigen: Leidens-geschichten unter Kreuz und Hakenkreuz*. Neukirchen Vluyn: Neukirchener Verlag, 1983.

———. "Der Lutherisch Deutsch-Christliche Weg am Beispiel des Eisenacher Entjudungsinstituts." In *Vom protestantischen Antijudaismus und seinen Lügen: Versuche einer Standort- und Gehwegbestimmung des Christlich-Jüdischen Gesprächs*, ed. Christian Staffa (Wittenberg: Evangelische Akademie Sachsen-Anhalt, 1993), 57–92.

———. *Wir Sind in die Irre gegangen: Die Schuld der Kirche unterm Hakenkreuz, nach dem Bekenntnis des "Darmstädter Wortes" von 1947*. Cologne: Pahl-Rugenstein, 1987.

Protz, Albert, ed. *So singen deutsche Christen*. Berlin: Gesellschaft für Zeitungsdienst, 1934.

Puschner, Uwe. "'One People, One God, One Reich.' The Völkische Weltanschauung and Movement." *German Historical Institute London Bulletin* 24, no. 1 (2002): 5–27.

Quell, Gottfried, ed. *Sin*. London: A. and C. Black, 1951.

Quinn, Malcolm. *The Swastika: Constructing the Symbol*. London, New York: Routledge, 1994.

Rabenau, Konrad von. "Als Student bei Gerhard von Rad in Jena 1943–1945." In *Das Alte Testament und die Kultur der Moderne,* ed. Manfred Oeming, Konrad Schmid, and Michael Welker (Münster: Lit, 2004), 7–12.

Rad, Gerhard von. *Das formgeschichtliche Problem des Hexateuchs*, Stuttgart: Kohlhammer, 1938.

———. *Deuteronomium Studien: Forschungen zur Religion und Literatur des Alten und Neuen Testaments*. Göttingen: Vandenhoeck & Ruprecht, 1947.

———. *Erinnerungen aus der Kriegsgefangenschaft: Frühjahr 1945*. Neukirchen: Neukirchener, 1976.

Raisig, Christoph Matthias. *Wege der Erneuerung: Christen und Juden—der Rheinische Synodalbeschluss von 1980*. Potsdam: Verlag für Berlin-Brandenburg, 2002.

Raschzok, Klaus. "Wolf Meyer-Erlach und Hans Asmussen." In *Zwischen Volk und Bekenntnis: Praktische Theologie im Dritten Reich*, ed. Klaus Raschzok. Leipzig: Evangelische Verlagsanstalt, 2000.

Reardon, Bernard M.G. *Liberalism and Tradition: Aspects of Catholic Thought in Nineteenth-Century France*. Cambridge, New York: Cambridge University Press, 1975.

Redeker, Martin."Der britische Cant: Politische Weltanschauung und englische Religiosität." *Kieler Blätter zur Volkskunde* 3 (1940): 257–65.

———. *Friedrich Schleiermacher: Leben und Werk*. Berlin: de Gruyter, 1968.

————. "Theologie und Weltanschauung: Mit besonderer Berücksichtigung des Hegelschülers Marheineke." In Wobbermin, et al., eds., *Luther, Kant, Schleiermacher*, 394–413.

Reed, Jonathan L. "Galileans, 'Israelite Village Communities,' and the Sayings Gospel Q." In *Galilee through the Centuries: Confluence of Cultures*, ed. Eric M. Meyers (Winona Lake, IN: Eisenbrauns, 1999), 87–108.

Reichrath, Hans L. "Die evangelischen Sonntagsblätter der Pfalz und die Judenfrage im Dritten Reich." *Blätter für pfälzische Kirchengeschichte und religiöse Volkskunde* 54 (1987): 51–64.

————. "Die Judenfrage im Lichte der evangelischen Sonntagsblätter der Pfalz im 3. Reich." *Judaica: Beiträge zum Verständnis des jüdischen Schicksals in Vergangenheit und Gegenwart* 3 (1990).

————. *Ludwig Diehl: Kreuz und Hakenkreuz im Leben eines Pfälzischen Pfarrers*. Speyer: Evangelischer Presseverlag Pfalz, 1996.

Remy, Steven P. *The Heidelberg Myth: The Nazification and Denazification of a German University*. Cambridge, MA: Harvard University Press, 2002.

Renan, Ernest. "Des religions de l'antiquité et de leurs derniers historiens." *Revue des deux Mondes* 23, no. 2 (1853): 821–48.

————. *Histoire générale et système comparé des langues sémitiques*, 5th ed. Paris: Imprimerie Impériale, 1855.

————. *The Life of Jesus*, trans. Charles E. Wilbour. New York: Carleton, 1864.

Rendtorff, Trutz. "Das Wissenschaftsverständnis der protestantischen Universitätstheologie im Dritten Reich." In Siegele-Wenschkewitz and Nicolaisen, *Theologische Fakultäten im Nationalsozialismus*, 19–44.

Retallack, James, ed. *Saxony in Germany History: Culture, Society, and Politics, 1830–1933*. Ann Arbor: University of Michigan Press, 2000.

Reumann, Klauspeter, ed. *Kirche und Nationalsozialismus: Beiträge zur Geschichte des Kirchenkampfes in den evangelischen Landeskirchen Schleswig-Holsteins*. Neumünster: K. Wachholtz, 1988.

Rieger, Reinhold. "Die Tübinger evangelische-theologische Fakultät während der Zeit der Weimarer Republik." In *Württembergs Protestantismus in der Weimarer Republik*, ed. Rainer Lächele and Jörg Thierfelder (Stuttgart: Calwer Verlag, 2003), 174–86.

Rinnen, Anja. *Kirchenmann und Nationalsozialist: Siegfried Lefflers ideelle Verschmelzung von Kirche und Drittem Reich*. Weinheim: Deutscher Studien Verlag, 1995.

Rissmann, Michael. *Hitlers Gott: Vorsehungsglaube und Sendungsbewusstsein des deutschen Diktators*. Zurich: Pendo, 2001.

Robakidse, Grigol. *Adolf Hitler: Von einem fremden Dichter gesehen*. Jena: Eugen Diederichs Verlag, 1939, 1943.

————. *Mussolini: Visionen auf Capri*. Jena: Eugen Diederichs Verlag, 1942.

Rodrigue, Aron. "Totems, Taboos, and Jews: Salomon Reinach and the Politics of Scholarship in Fin-de-Siècle France." *Jewish Social Studies* 10, no. 2 (2004): 1–19.

Rosen, Alan. "'Familiarly Known as Kittel': The Moral Politics of the Theological Dictionary of the New Testament." In *Tainted Greatness*, ed. Nancy A. Harrowitz. (Philadelphia: Temple University Press, 1994), 37–50.

Rosenberg, Alfred. *Der Mythus des 20. Jahrhunderts: Eine Wertung der seelisch-geistigen Gestaltenkämpfe unserer Zeit.* Munich: Hoheneichen, 1930.

Roth, Josef. "Die Katholische Kirche und die Judenfrage." *Forschungen zur Judenfrage* 4 (1940): 163–76.

Rubenstein, Richard L. *After Auschwitz: Radical Theology and Contemporary Judaism.* Indianapolis: Bobbs-Merrill, 1966.

Ruoff, Manuel. *Landesbischof Franz Tügel.* Hamburg: Krämer, 2000.

Rupnow, Dirk. "Antijüdische Wissenschaft im Dritten Reich": Wege, Probleme und Perspektiven der Forschung." *Jahrbuch des Simon-Dubnow-Instituts* 5 (2006): 539–98.

———. "'Judenforschung" im 'Dritten Reich': Wissenschaft zwischen Ideologie, Propaganda und Politik." In *Historische West- und Ostforschung in Zentraleuropa zwischen dem ersten und dem zweiten Weltkrieg: Verflechtung und Vergleich*, ed. Matthias Middell and Ulrike Sommer (Leipzig: Akademische Verlagsanstalt, 2004), 107–32.

Saller, Karl. *Die Rassenlehre des Nationalsozialismus in Wissenschaft und Propaganda.* Darmstadt: Progress-Verlag, 1961.

Sanders, E. P. "Defending the Indefensible." *Journal of Biblical Literature* 110, no. 3 (1991): 463–77.

———. "Jesus and the Kingdom: The Restoration of Israel and the New People of God." In *Jesus, the Gospels, and the Church: Essays in Honor of William R. Farmer*, ed. E. P. Sanders (Macon, GA: Mercer University Press, 1987), 225–39.

———. *Paul and Palestinian Judaism.* Philadelphia: Fortress Press, 1977.

Schairer, Immanuel Berthold. *Volk, Blut, Gott: Ein Gruss des Evangeliums an die deutsche Freiheitsbewegung.* Berlin, Martin Warneck Verlag, 1933.

Scheiner, Andreas. *Das Dogma der evangelischen Landeskirche A.B. in Rumänien.* Sibiu-Hermannstadt: Sibiu-Hermannstadt: Honterus, 1942.

Schemann, Ludwig. *Gobineaus Rassenwerk.* Stuttgart: F. Frommann, 1910.

Schenk, Wolfgang. "Der Jenaer Jesus." In Osten-Sacken, ed., *Das mißbrauchte Evangelium*, 167–279.

Schieder, Rolf. *Religion im Radio: Protestantische Rundfunkarbeit in der Weimarer Republik und im Dritten Reich.* Stuttgart: W. Kohlhammer, 1995.

Schlatter, Adolf. *The Church in the New Testament Period*, trans. Paul P. Levertoff. London: SPCK, 1955.

———. *Die Geschichte der ersten Christenheit.* Gütersloh: Bertelsmann, 1926.

———. *Geschichte Israels von Alexander dem Grossen bis Hadrian.* Stuttgart: Calwer Vereinsbuchhandlung, 1901.

———. *Gesunde Lehre: Reden und Aufsätze* Essen: Freizeiten Verlag, 1929.

———. *History of the Christ*, trans. Andreas J. Köstenberger. Grand Rapids, MI: Baker Books, 1997.

———. *Der neue deutsche Art in der Kirche.* Bethel bei Bielefeld: Verlagshandlung der Anstalt Bethel, 1933.

————. *Wir Christen und die Juden*. Essen: Velbert, 1930.

————. *Wird der Jude über uns Siegen? Ein Wort für die Weihnachtszeit*. Essen: Freizeiten Verlag, 1935.

Schmidt, Siegfried. *Alma Mater Jenensis: Geschichte der Universitat Jena*. Weimar: Harmann Bohlaus Nachfolger, 1983.

Schmidt-Clausing, Fritz. *Geschichte des Hansa-Viertels*. Berlin: Gemeindekirchenrat d. Kaiser-Friedrich-Gedächtnis-Gemeinde, 1954.

Schmökel, Hartmut. *Altes Testament und heutiges Judentum*, trans. Paul Siebeck. Tubingen: J.C.B. Mohr, 1936.

Schneider, Carl. *Einführung in die neutestamentliche Zeitgeschichte*. Leipzig: Deichert, 1934.

————. *Das Frühchristentum als antisemitische Bewegung*. Bremen: Verlag Kommende Kirche, 1940.

————. *Geistesgeschichte des antiken Christentums*. Munich: Beck, 1954.

————. *Paulusfragen*. Aufbau im Positiven Christentum, vol. 10. Bonn: Gebet Scheut, 1937.

Schnurbein, Stefanie von. *Religion als Kulturkritik: Neugermanisches Heidentum im 20. Jahrhundert*. Skandinavistische Arbeiten, vol. 13. Heidelberg: Winter, 1992.

Schnurbein, Stefanie von, and Justus H. Ulbricht, eds. *Völkische Religiosität und Krisen der Moderne: Entwürfe "arteigener" Glaubenssysteme seit der Jahrhundertwende*. Würzburg: Königshausen & Neumann, 2001.

Schopenhauer, Arthur. *Parerga and Paralipomena: Short Philosophical Essays*, trans. E.F.J. Payne, vol. 2. New York: Oxford University Press, 2000.

Schreiner, Helmut. *Nationalsozialismus und Protestantismus*, vol. 1. Berlin: Verlag des Evangelischen Bundes, 1931.

Schröder, Leopold von. *Arische Religion*. 2 vols. Leipzig: H. Haessel, 1914–16.

————. *Lebenserinnerungen*, ed. Felix Carl von Schröder. Leipzig: H. Haessel, 1921.

Schröder, Leopold von, ed. *Reden und Aufsätze vornehmlich über Indiens Literatur und Kultur*. Leipzig: H. Haessel, 1905.

Schüfer, Tobias. "Die Theologische Fakultät der Friedrich-Schiller-Universität Jena in den Jahren 1933–1945: Einige Forschungserträge." Unpublished manuscript.

————. "Die Theologische Fakultät Jena und die Landeskirche im Nationalsozialismus." In *Thüringer Gratwanderungen: Beiträge zur fünfundsiebzigjährigen Geschichte der evangelischen Landeskirche Thüringens*, ed. Thomas A. Seidel (Leipzig: Evangelische Verlagsanstalt, 1998).

Schwaner, Wilhelm, ed. *Germanen-Bibel: Aus heiligen Schriften germanischer Völker*. Stuttgart: Deutsche Verlags Anstalt, 1904.

Schwarz, Karl W. "'Grenzburg' und 'Bollwerk': Ein Bericht über die Wiener Evangelisch-Theologische Fakultät in den Jahren 1938 bis 1945." *Evangelischer Bund in Österreich* 125 (1991).

————. "'Eine Fakultät für den Südosten': Die Evangelisch-Theologische Fakultät in Wien und der 'Außendeutsche Protestantismus.'" *Südostdeutsches Archiv* 36/37 (1993/94): 84–120.

Seidel, J. Juergen. "Neubeginn" in der Kirche? Die evangelischen Landes- und Provinzi-
alkirchen in Der SBZ/DDR im gesellschaftspolitischen Kontext der Nachkriegszeit (1945–
1953). Göttingen: Vandenhöck & Ruprecht, 1989.

Seidel, Thomas A. "Die 'Entnazifizierungs-Akte Grundmanns': Anmerkungen zur Kar-
riere eines vormals führenden DC-Theologen." In Deines, Leppin, and Niebuhr,
eds., Walter Grundmann, 349–70.

———. ". . . In Sturm und Gericht der Gegenwart: Kirchliche Neuordnung in Thüringen 1945–1951." In Seidel, ed., Thüringer Gratwanderungen, 166–88.

———. Im Übergang der Diktaturen: Eine Untersuchung zur kirchlichen Neuordnung in
Thüringen 1945–1951, Konfession und Gesellschaft. Stuttgart: W. Kohlhammer, 2003.

———, ed. Gottlose Jahre? Rückblicke auf die Kirche im Sozialismus der DDR. Leipzig:
Evangelische Verlagsanstalt, 2002.

———, ed. Thüringer Gratwanderungen: Beiträge zur fünfundsiebzigjährigen Geschichte
der evangelischen Landeskirche Thüringens. Leipzig: Evangelische Verlagsanstalt,
1998.

Seier, Hellmut. "Die Hochschullehrerschaft im Dritten Reich." In Deutsche Hochschullehrer als Elite, 1815–1945: Büdinger Forschungen zur Sozialgeschichte 1983, ed. Klaus
Schwabe (Boppard am Rhein: H. Boldt, 1988), 247–95.

Seims, Gisela. "Pastor Friedrich Andersen, Bund für Deutsche Kirche: Ein Wegbereiter
des Nationalsozialismus in der Stadt Flensburg." In Kirche und Nationalsozialismus:
Beiträge zur Geschichte des Kirchenkampfes in den evangelischen Landeskirchen Schleswig-
Holsteins, ed. Klauspeter Reumann (Neumünster: K. Wachholtz, 1988).

Sellin, Ernst. Das Alte Testament und die Evangelische Kirche der Gegenwart. Leipzig:
A. Deichert, 1921.

Seydel, Rudolf. Die Buddha-Legende und das Leben Jesu nach den Evangelien. Leipzig:
O. Schulze, 1884.

———. Das Evangeliums Jesu in seine Verhältnissen zur Buddha-Sage und Buddha-Lehre
mit fortlaufender Rücksicht auf andere Religionskreise untersucht. Leipzig, 1882.

Shapiro, James S. Oberammergau: The Troubling Story of the World's Most Famous Passion
Play. New York: Pantheon Books, 2000.

Siegele-Wenschkewitz, Leonore. "Ablösung des Christentums vom Judentum? Die
Jesus-Interpretation des Leipziger Neutestamentler Johannes Leipoldt im zeitge-
schichtlichen Kontext." In Theologische Wissenschaft im Dritten Reich, ed. Georg Denzler and Leonore Siegele-Wenschkewitz (Frankfurt am Main: Haag und Herchen,
2000), 114–35.

———. "Adolf Schlatters Sicht des Judentums im politischen Kontext." In Siegele-
Wenschkewitz, ed., Christlicher Antijudaismus und Antisemitismus, 261–92.

———. Neutestamentliche Wissenschaft vor der Judenfrage: Gerhard Kittels theologische
Arbeit im Wandel deutscher Geschichte. Munich: Kaiser, 1980.

———. "Politische Versuche einer Ordnung der Deutschen Evangelischen Kirche
durch den Reichskirchenminister 1937 bis 1939." In Zur Geschichte des Kirchem-
kampfes: Gesammelte Aufsätze, ed. Heinz Brunotte and Ernst Wolf (Göttingen: Vandenhoeck & Ruprecht, 1971).

————, ed. *Christlicher Antijudaismus und Antisemitismus: Theologische und kirchliche Programme Deutscher Christen*. Frankfurt am Main: Haag und Herchen, 1994.

Siegele-Wenschkewitz, Leonore, and Carsten Nicolaisen, eds., *Theologische Fakultäten im Nationalsozialismus*. Göttingen: Vandenhoeck und Ruprecht, 1993.

Sievers, Kai-Detlev. "Völkische Märcheninterpretationen: Zu Joachim Kurd Niedlichs Mythen- und Märchendeutungen." In *Homo Narrans: Studien zur populären Erzählkultur—Festschrift für Siegfried Neumann zum 65. Geburtstag*, ed. Siegfried Armin Neumann and Christoph Schmitt (Münster, New York: Waxmann Verlag, 1999) 91–110.

Simon-Nahum, Perrine. *La Cité investie: La "science du Judaïsme " français et la République* (Paris: Cerf, 1991).

Skarsten, Trygve R. "Rise and Fall of Grundtvigianism in Norway." *Lutheran Quarterly* 17 (1965): 122–42.

Slotty, Martin. *Kann die deutsche Christenheit das Alte Testament preisgeben?* Breslau: Verlag des Lutherischen Buechervereins, 1936.

Smend, Rudolf. *Deutsche Alttestamentler in drei Jahrhunderten*. Göttingen: Vandenhoeck & Ruprecht, 1989.

————. "Fünfzig Jahre International Organization for the Study of the Old Testament und Vetus Testamentum." *Vetus Testamentum* 15–16 (1965–66).

Sneen, Donald J. "The Hermeneutics of N.F.S.G." *Interpretation* 26 (1972): 42–61.

Soden, Hans von. "Die synoptische Frage und der geschichtliche Jesus." Essen: Lichtweg-Verlag, 1941.

————. "Walter Grundmann, Jesus der Galiläer und das Judentum." *Deutsches Pfarrerblatt* 46, no. 13/14 (1942): 49–50.

Spanuth, Heinrich. *Das Leben Jesu auf Grund der synoptischen Evangelien für den Religionsunterricht deutsch und evangelisch geschaut*. 9th ed. Osterwieck: A. W. Zickfeldt, 1937.

Spicer, Kevin P. *Hitler's Priests: Catholic Clergy and National Socialism*. DeKalb: Northern Illinois University Press, 2008.

————. *Resisting the Third Reich: The Catholic Clergy in Hitler's Berlin*. DeKalb: Northern Illinois University Press, 2004.

Spotts, Frederick. *The Churches and Politics in Germany*. Middletown, CT: Wesleyan University Press, 1973.

Staerk, Willy. *Das religiöse Leben der westeuropaeischen Judenheit: Vornehmlich Deutschlands und seine Wertung vom christlichen Gottesgedanken aus*. Berlin: Furche-Verlag, 1926.

Stapel, Wilhelm. *Antisemitismus und Antigermanismus: Über das seelische Problem der Symbiose des deutschen und des jüdischen Volkes*. Hamburg: Hanseatische Verlagsanstalt, 1928.

————. *Der christliche Staatsmann: Eine Theologie des Nationalismus*. Hamburg: Hanseatische Verlagsanstalt, 1932.

————. *Die Kirche Christi und der Staat Hitlers*. Hamburg: Hanseatische Verlagsanstalt, 1933.

————. *Volk: Untersuchungen über Volkheit und Volkstum*, 4th ed. Hamburg: Hanseatische Verlagsanstalt, 1942.

————. "Wilhelm Raabes Meinung über Juden und Christen." In Grundmann, ed., *Christentum und Judentum,* vol. 1, 107–32.

Stauffer, Ethelbert. *Die Botschaft Jesu, Damals und Heute.* Bern, Munich: Francke Verlag, 1959.

————. *Jesus: Gestalt und Geschichte.* Bern, Munich: Francke Verlag, 1957.

————. "Jesus, Geschichte und Verkündigung." *Aufstieg und Niedergang der römischen Welt II* 25, no. 1 (1982): 3–130.

————. *Theologisches Lehramt in Kirche und Reich.* Bonn: Bonner Universität Buchdruck, 1935.

Steffens, Henrich. *The Story of My Career as Student and Professor,* trans. William L. Gage. Philadelphia: J. B. Lippincott and Co., 1874.

Stegmann, Erich. *Der Kirchenkampf in der Thüringer Evangelischen Kirche, 1933–1945: Ein Kapitel Thüringer Kirchengeschichte,* Berlin: Evangelische Verlagsanstalt, 1984.

Steigmann-Gall, Richard. *The Holy Reich: Nazi Conceptions of Christianity, 1919–1945.* Cambridge, New York: Cambridge University Press, 2003.

————. "Was National Socialism a Political Religion or a Religious Politics?" In *Religion und Nation: Nation und Religion. Beiträge zu einer unbewältigten Geschichte,* ed. Michael Geyer and Hartmut Lehmann (Göttingen: Wallstein Verlag, 2003), 386–408.

Stein, Harry. "Funktionswander des Konzentrationslager Buchenwald." In *Die nationalsozialistischen Lager: Entwicklung und Struktur,* ed. Karin Orth, Ulrich Herbert, and Christoph Dieckmann (Göttingen: Wallstein, 1998), 167–92.

Steinmetzer, Franz X. *Jesus und Wir Arier.* Prague: E. Bayands Nachf. in Krummau, 1924.

Steinweis, Alan E. *Studying the Jew: Scholarly Antisemitism in Nazi Germany.* Cambridge, MA: Harvard University Press, 2006.

Stern, Fritz Richard. *The Politics of Cultural Despair; a Study in the Rise of the Germanic Ideology.* Berkeley: University of California Press, 1961.

Stieglitz, Ann. "The Reproduction of Agony: Toward a Reception-History of Grünewald's Isenheim Altar after the First World War." *Oxford Art Journal* 12, no. 2 (1989): 87–103.

Stoler, Ann. "Racial Histories and Their Regimes of Truth." *Political Power and Social Theory* 11 (1997).

Strack, Hermann L., and Paul Billerbeck, *Kommentar zum Neuen Testament aus Talmud und Midrasch,* 4 vols. Munich: C.H. Beck, 1922–28.

Stutz, Rüdiger. "Im Schatten von Zeiss: Die NSDAP in Jena." In Heiden and Mai, eds., *Nationalsozialismus in Thüringen,* 119–42.

————. "Wissenschaft als 'Dienst an Volk und Vaterland': Die Rektoren der Universität Jena und das 'Dritten Reich'." In Gottwald and Steinbach, Zwischen Wissenschaft und Politik.

Sulzbach, Abraham. *Renan und der Judaismus.* Frankfurt am Main: J. Kauffmann, 1867.

Szejnmann, Claus-Christian. *Nazism in Central Germany: The Brownshirts in "Red" Saxony.* New York: Berghahn Books, 1999.

Szobar, Patricia. "Telling Sexual Stories in the Nazi Courts of Law: Race Defilement in Germany, 1933 to 1945." *History of Sexuality* 11, nos. 1–2 (2002): 131–63.

Tal, Uriel. *Christians and Jews in Germany: Religion, Politics and Ideology in the Second Reich, 1870–1914*, trans. Noah Jonathan Jacobs. Ithaca, NY: Cornell University Press, 1975.

———. *Religious and Anti-Religious Roots of Modern Antisemitism*, Leo Baeck Memorial Lecture, no. 14. New York: Leo Baeck Institute, 1971; reprinted in Tal, ed., *Religion, Politics and Ideology in the Third Reich*, 171–90.

———, ed. *Religion, Politics and Ideology in the Third Reich: Selected Essays*. London and New York: Routledge, 2004.

Tanner, Eugene S. *The Nazi Christ*. Tulsa, OK: printed privately, 1942.

Thalmann, Rita R. "Die Schwäche des Kulturprotestantismus bei der Bekämpfung des Antisemitismus." In *Protestantismus und Antisemitismus in der Weimarer Republik*, ed. Kurt Nowak and Gerard Raulet (Frankfurt am Main, New York: Campus, 1994).

Thierfelder, Jörg, and Eberhard Röhm, eds. *Evangelische Kirche zwischen Kreuz und Hakenkreuz: Bilder und Texte einer Ausstellung*. Stuttgart: Calwer, 1981.

Thilo, Hans-Joachim. *Unter den Narben tut es noch weh: Gratwanderung einer Generation*. Göttingen: Vandenhoeck & Ruprecht, 1996.

Thompson, Dorothy. "Goodbye to Germany." *Harper's Bazaar*, December 1934, 43–51.

Tiefel, Hans. "The German Lutheran Church and the Rise of National Socialism." *Church History* (1972): 326–36.

Tilgner, Wolfgang. *Volksnomostheologie und Schöpfungsglaube: Ein Beitrag zur Geschichte des Kirchenkampfes*. Göttingen: Vandenhoeck und Ruprecht, 1966.

Todorov, Tzvetan. *On Human Diversity: Nationalism, Racism, and Exoticism in French Thought*, trans. Catherine Porter. Cambridge: Harvard University Press, 1993.

Trautman, Thomas R. *Aryans and British India*. Berkeley: University of California Press, 1997.

Tügel, Franz, *Mein Weg, 1888–1946: Erinnerungen eines Hamburger Bischofs*, ed. Carsten Nicolaisen. Hamburg: Friedrich Wittig, 1972.

Tyson, Joseph B. *Luke, Judaism, and the Scholars: Critical Approaches to Luke-Acts*. Columbia: University of South Carolina Press, 1999.

Vaart-Smit, H. W. van der. *De Duitsche Kerkstrijd*. Amsterdam: Uitgeversmaatschappij Holland, 1935.

———. *Kamptoestanden 1944/45 bis 1948*. Keizersbroon, Haarlem, Leuven: Pauw, 1976.

Vollnhals, Clemens. *Entnazifizierung und Selbstreinigung im Urteil der evangelischen Kirche: Dokumente und Reflexionen, 1945–1949*. Studienbücher zur kirchlichen Zeitgeschichte, vol. 8. Munich: Kaiser, 1989.

———. *Die evangelische Kirche nach dem Zusammenbruch: Berichte ausländischer Beobachter aus dem Jahre 1945*. Göttingen: Vandenhoeck und Ruprecht, 1988.

———. *Evangelische Kirche und Entnazifizierung, 1945–1949: Die Last der Nationalsozialistischen Vergangenheit*. Munich: R. Oldenbourg, 1989.

Volney, Constantin-François. *Les Ruines, ou Méditation sur les révolutions des empires*. Paris: Desenne, 1792.

Vos, J. S. "Antijudaismus/Antisemitismus im theologischen Wörterbuch zum Neuen Testament." *Nederlands Theologisch Tijdschrift* 35 (1984): 89–110.

Wagener, Claus P. "Gott sprach: Es werde Volk, und es ward Volk!" In Osten-Sacken, ed., *Das mißbrauchte Evangelium*, 35–69.

Wagenführer, Max-Adolf. Die Bedeutung Christi für Welt und Kirche: Studien zum Kolosser- und Epheserbrief. Leipzig: Otto Wigand, 1941.

Walter, Franz. "Von der roten zur braunen Hochburg: Wahlanalytische Überlegungen zur NSDAP in den beiden thüringischen Industrielandschaften." In *Thüringen auf dem Weg ins "Dritte Reich,"* ed. Detlev Heiden and Gunther Mai (Erfurt: Landeszentrale für politische Bildung Thüringen, 1997), 119–45.

Wassermann, Henry. *False Start: Jewish Studies at German Universities During the Weimar Republic.* Amherst, NY: Humanity Books, 2003.

Weber, Cornelia. *Altes Testament und völkische Frage: Der biblische Volksbegriff in der Alttestamentlichen Wissenschaft der nationalsozialistischen Zeit.* Tübingen: J.C.B. Mohr, 2000.

Webster, Ronald D. "Dr. Georg Biundo: German Pastor, Ardent Nationalist, Sometime Antisemite." *Kirchliche Zeitgeschichte* 13, no. 1 (2000): 92–111.

Weiler, Gerda. *Ich verwerfe im Lande die Kriege.* Munich: Frauenoffensive, 1984.

Weiling, Christoph. *Die "Christlich-Deutsche Bewegung": Eine Studie zum konservativen Protestantismus in der Weimarer Republik.* Göttingen: Vandenhoeck und Ruprecht, 1998.

Weinreich, Max. *Hitler's Professors: The Part of Scholarship in Germany's Crimes against the Jewish People.* New Haven: Yale University Press, 1999.

Weitenhagen, Holger. *Evangelisch und Deutsch: Heinz Dungs und die Pressepolitik der Deutschen Christen.* Cologne: Rheinland-Verlag, 2001.

Weitzman, Steven. "Forced Circumcision and the Shifting Role of Gentiles in Hasmonean Ideology." *Harvard Theological Review* 91, no. 1 (1999): 37–59.

Werdermann, Hermann. "Die Gefahr des Judaisierens in der religiösen Erziehung und ihre Überwindung." In Grundmann, ed., *Germanentum, Christenum und Judentum,* vol. 3, 217–48.

Werner, Meike G. *Moderne in der Provinz: Kulturelle Experimente im fin-de-siècle Jena.* Göttingen: Wallstein, 2003.

Wilken, Karl-Erich. *Der Stein des Pilatus: Erinnerungen an Besuche im Heiligen Land.* Lahr-Dinglingen, Baden: St.-Johannis-Druckerei Schweickhardt, 1966.

——. *Denen, die Gott lieben: Erzählungen aus dem Leben.* 4th ed. Dinglingen, Baden: St.-Johannis-Druckerei Schweickhardt, 1989.

Williamson, George S. *The Longing for Myth in Germany: Religion and Aesthetic Culture from Romanticism to Nietzsche.* Chicago: University of Chicago Press, 2004.

Windisch, Ernst. *Buddhas Geburt und die Lehre von der Seelenwanderung.* Leipzig: B. G. Teubner, 1908.

Winston, David. "The Iranian Component in the Bible, Apocrypha, and Qumran: A Review of the Evidence." *History of Religions* 5 (1966): 183–216.

Wobbermin, Georg, et al., eds. *Luther, Kant, Schleiermacher in ihrer Bedeutung für den Protestantismus : Forschungen und Abhandlungen. Georg Wobbermin zum 70. Geburtstag (27. Oktober 1939)*. Berlin: Collignon, 1939.

Wolf, Ernst. "Volk, Nation, Vaterland im protestantischen Denken von 1933 bis zur Gegenwart." In *Volk, Nation, Vaterland: Der deutsche Protestantismus und der Nationalismus*, ed. Horst Zillessen (Gütersloh: Verlagshaus G. Mohn, 1970).

Wolgast, Eike. "Nationalsozialistische Hochschulpolitik und die evangelisch-theologischen Fakultäten." In Siegele-Wenschkewitz and Nicolaisen, eds., *Theologische Fakultäten im Nationalsozialismus*, 45–80.

Wolter, Franz. *Wie sah Christus aus?* Munich: Hugo Schmidt, 1930.

Wrede, Wilhelm. *Das Messiasgeheimnis in den Evangelien: Zugleich ein Beitrag zum Verständnis des Markusevangeliums*. Göttingen: Vandenhoeck & Ruprecht, 1901.

Wright, J.R.C. "Above Parties": *The Political Attitudes of the German Protestant Church Leadership, 1918–1933*. Oxford: Oxford University Press, 1974.

Wright, Terence R. "The Letter and the Spirit: Deconstructing Renan's *Life of Jesus* and the Assumptions of Modernity." *Religion and Literature* 26:2 (Summer, 1994), 55–71.

Wüst, Walter. *Indogermanisches Bekenntnis*. Berlin: Ahnenerbe-Stiftung Verlag, 1942.

Young, Robert J. C. *Colonial Desire: Hybridity in Theory, Culture and Race*. London and New York: Routledge, 1995.

Younger, K. Lawson. "The Deportation of the Israelites." *Journal of Biblical Literature* 117 (1998): 201–27.

Zabel, James A. *Nazism and the Pastors: A Study of the Ideas of Three Deutsche Christen Groups*. Missoula, MT: Scholars Press for the American Academy of Religion, 1976.

Zahn, Günther. "Thüringer Blick-Punkte." In *Thüringer Gratwanderungen: Beiträge zur fünfundsiebzigjährigen Geschichte der evangelischen Landeskirche Thüringens*, ed. Thomas A. Seidel. Leipzig: Evangelische Verlagsanstalt, 1998.

Zimmermann, Susanne. *Die medizinische Fakultät der Universität Jena während der Zeit des Nationalsozialismus*. Berlin: Verlag für Wissenschaft und Bildung, 2000.

Zimmern, Heinrich. *Zum Streit um die "Christusmythe": Das babylonische Material in seinen Hauptpunkten dargestellt*. Berlin: Reuther & Reichard, 1910.

Zurhellen-Pfleiderer, Else. *Frau Ludendorffs Anklage gegen Jesus Christus*. Görlitz: Hutten-Verlag, 1933.

Illustration Permissions

Wolf Meyer-Erlach with a swastika lapel pin during the Third Reich, Landeskirchen Archive of Thuringia

Gerhard von Rad, photograph by Frank Döbert

Heinrich Weinel, University of Jena Archive

Heinz Eisenhuth during the Third Reich, University of Jena Archive Bestand D, Nr. 603

Karl Heussi during the Third Reich, University of Jena Archive Dozentenkartei

Wolf Meyer-Erlach, 1935, University of Jena Archive

University of Jena theological faculty during the Third Reich, University of Jena Archive

Chapter Six

Walter Grundmann, Church Archive of Thuringia, Eisenach

Heinz Eisenhuth, Church Archive of Thuringia, Eisenach

Conclusion

Poster of the Passion Play at Oberammergau, Germany, 1934. U.S. Holocaust Memorial Museum 09909

Broken iron cross by Christoph Seidel. Reproduced with permission of Pastor Wolfgang Gerlach, Bonhoefferhaus, Essen, Germany

Index

Page numbers in italics refer to illustrations. Citations to scriptural works are listed separately following this index.

Scriptural Citations Index

Scriptural text references are given in italics.

9 780691 148052